Get the eBook FREE!

(PDF, ePub, Kindle, and liveBook all included)

We believe that once you buy a book from us, you should be able to read it in any format we have available. To get electronic versions of this book at no additional cost to you, purchase and then register this book at the Manning website.

Go to https://www.manning.com/freebook and follow the instructions to complete your pBook registration.

That's it!
Thanks from Manning!

Acing the System Design Interview

ZHIYONG TAN

MANNING
SHELTER ISLAND

Manning Publications Co.
20 Baldwin Road
PO Box 761
Shelter Island, NY 11964

Development editor:	Katie Sposato Johnson
Technical editor:	Mohit Kumar
Senior technical development editor:	Al Scherer
Review editor:	Adriana Sabo
Production editor:	Aleksandar Dragosavljević
Copy editor:	Katie Petito
Technical proofreader:	Victor Duran
Typesetter:	Tamara Švelić Sabljić
Cover designer:	Marija Tudor

ISBN: 9781633439108
Printed in the United States of America

To Mom and Dad.

contents

PART 2.. 145

11 Autocomplete/typeahead 245

12 *Design Flickr   266*

13 *Design a Content Distribution Network (CDN)   287*

14 Design a text messaging app 308

A   *Monoliths vs. microservices*   395

foreword

Over the course of the last 20 years, I have focused on building teams of distributed systems engineers at some of the largest tech companies in the industry (Google, Twitter, and Uber). In my experience, the fundamental pattern of building high-functioning teams at these companies is the ability to identify engineering talent that can demonstrate their mastery of system design through the interview process. *Acing the System Design Interview* is an invaluable guide that equips aspiring software engineers and seasoned professionals alike with the knowledge and skills required to excel in one of the most critical aspects of technical interviews. In an industry where the ability to design scalable and reliable systems is paramount, this book is a treasure trove of insights, strategies, and practical tips that will undoubtedly help readers navigate the intricacies of the system design interview process.

As the demand for robust and scalable systems continues to soar, companies are increasingly prioritizing system design expertise in their hiring process. An effective system design interview not only assesses a candidate's technical prowess but also evaluates their ability to think critically, make informed decisions, and solve complex problems. Zhiyong's perspective as an experienced software engineer and his deep understanding of the system design interview landscape make him the perfect guide for anyone seeking to master this crucial skill set.

In this book, Zhiyong presents a comprehensive roadmap that takes readers through each step of the system design interview process. After an overview of the fundamental principles and concepts, he then delves into various design aspects, including scalability, reliability, performance, and data management. With clarity and precision, he breaks down each topic, providing concise explanations and real-world examples that illustrate their practical application. He is able to demystify the system design interview process by drawing on his own experiences and interviews with experts in the field. He offers valuable insights into the mindset of interviewers, the types of questions commonly asked, and the key factors interviewers consider when evaluating a candidate's performance. Through these tips, he not only helps readers understand what to expect during an interview but also equips them with the confidence and tools necessary to excel in this high-stakes environment.

By combining the theory chapters of part 1 with the practical application chapters of part 2, Zhiyong ensures that readers not only grasp the theoretical foundations but also cultivate the ability to apply that knowledge to real-world scenarios. Moreover, this book goes beyond technical know-how and emphasizes the importance of effective communication in the system design interview process. Zhiyong explores strategies for effectively articulating ideas, presenting solutions, and collaborating with interviewers. This holistic approach recognizes that successful system design is not solely dependent on technical brilliance but also on the ability to convey ideas and work collaboratively with others.

Whether you are preparing for a job interview or seeking to enhance your system design expertise, this book is an essential companion that will empower you to tackle even the most complex system design challenges with confidence and finesse.

So, dive into the pages ahead, embrace the knowledge and insights, and embark on a journey to master the art of building scalable and reliable systems. You will undoubtedly position yourself as an invaluable asset to any organization and pave the way for a successful career as a software engineer.

Start your path to acing the system design interview!

—ANTHONY ASTA
DIRECTOR OF ENGINEERING AT LINKEDIN
(EX-ENGINEERING MANAGEMENT AT GOOGLE, TWITTER, AND UBER)

Software development is a world of continuous *everything*. Continuous improvement, continuous delivery, continuous monitoring, and continuous re-evaluation of user needs and capacity expectations are the hallmarks of any significant software system. If you want to succeed as a software engineer, you must have a passion for continuous learning and personal growth. With passion, software engineers can literally change how our society connects with each other, how we share knowledge, and how we manage our lifestyles.

Software trends are always evolving, from the trendiest programming language or framework to programmable cloud-native infrastructure. If you stick with this industry for decades, you'll see these transitions several times over, just like I have. However, one immutable constant remains through it all: understanding the systematic reasoning of how a software system manages work, organizes its data, and interacts with humans is critical to being an effective software engineer or technology leader.

As a software engineer and then IBM Distinguished Engineer, I've seen firsthand how design tradeoffs can make or break the successful outcomes of a software system. Whether you're a new engineer seeking your first role or a seasoned technology veteran looking for a new challenge in a new company, this book can help you refine your approach to reasoning by explaining the tradeoffs inherent with any design choices.

Acing the System Design Interview brings together and organizes the many dimensions of system design that you need to consider for any software system. Zhiyong Tan has brilliantly organized a crash course in the fundamentals of system design tradeoffs and presents many real-world case studies that you can use to reinforce your readiness for even the most challenging of system design interviews.

Part 1 of the book begins with an informative survey of critical aspects of system design. Starting with non-functional requirements, you'll learn about many of the common dimensions that you must keep in mind while considering system design tradeoffs. Following an elaboration on , you will walk through how to organize the application programming interface (API) specification to explain how your system design addresses the use cases of the interview problem statement. Behind the API, you'll learn several industry best practices for organizing the system data model using industry-standard datastores and patterns for managing distributed transactions. And beyond addressing the prima facie use cases, you'll learn about key aspects of system operation, including modern approaches to observability and log management.

In part 2, ride along for 11 distinct system design problems, from text messaging to Airbnb. In each interview problem, you can pick up new skills on how to tease out the right questions to organize the non-functional system requirements, followed by what tradeoffs to invest in further discussion. System design is a skill set often rooted in an experience that lends itself well to learning from prior art and examples based on others' experiences. If you internalize the many lessons and wisdom from the examples presented in this book, you'll be well prepared for even the most challenging system design interview problems.

I'm excited to see the contribution that Zhiyong Tan has made to the industry with the following work. Whether you are approaching the material after a recent graduation or after many years of already working in the industry, I hope you'll find new opportunities for personal growth as I did when absorbing the experiences represented in *Acing the System Design Interview*.

—MICHAEL D. ELDER
DISTINGUISHED ENGINEER & SENIOR DIRECTOR, PAYPAL
FORMER IBM DISTINGUISHED ENGINEER AND IBM MASTER INVENTOR, IBM

It is Wednesday at 4 p.m. As you leave your last video interview for your dream company, you are filled with a familiar mix of feelings: exhaustion, frustration, and déjà vu. You already know that in one to two days you will receive the email that you have seen so many times in your years as an engineer. "Thank you for your interest in the senior software engineer role at XXX. While your experience and skill set are impressive, after much consideration, we regret to inform you that we will not be proceeding with your candidacy."

It was the system design interview again. You had been asked to design a photo-sharing app, and you made a brilliant design that is scalable, resilient, and maintainable. It used the latest frameworks and employed software development lifecycle best practices. But you could see that the interviewer was unimpressed. They had that faraway look in their eyes and the bored, calm, polite tone that told you they believed they spent their time with you on this interview to be professional and to deliver "a great candidate experience."

This is your seventh interview attempt at this company in four years, and you have also interviewed repeatedly at other companies you really want to join. It is your dream to join this company, which has a userbase of billions and develops some of the most impressive developer frameworks and programming languages that dominate the industry. You know that the people you will meet and what you will learn at this company will serve you well in your career and be a great investment of your time.

Meanwhile, you have been promoted multiple times at the companies you have worked at, and you're now a senior software engineer, making it even harder when you don't pass the interviews for the equivalent job at your dream companies. You have been a tech lead of multiple systems, led and mentored teams of junior engineers, and authored and discussed system designs with senior and staff engineers, making tangible and valuable contributions to multiple system designs. Before each interview at a dream company, you read through all the engineering blog posts and watched all their engineering talks published in the last three years. You have also read every highly rated book on microservices, data-intensive applications, cloud-native patterns, and domain-driven design. Why can't you just nail those system design interviews?

Has it just been bad luck all these attempts? The supply versus demand of candidates versus jobs at those companies? The statistical unlikelihood of being selected? Is it a lottery? Do you simply have to keep trying every six months until you get lucky? Do you need to light incense and make more generous offerings to the interview/performance review/promotion gods (formerly known as the exam gods back in school)?

Taking a deep breath and closing your eyes to reflect, you realize that there is so much you can improve in those 45 minutes that you had to discuss your system design. (Even though each interview is one hour, between introductions and Q&A, you essentially have only 45 minutes to design a complex system that typically evolves over years.) Chatting with your fellow engineer friends confirms your hypothesis. You did not thoroughly clarify the system requirements. You assumed that what was needed was a minimum viable product for a backend that serves mobile apps in storing and sharing photos, and you started jotting down sample API specifications. The interviewer had to interrupt you to clarify that it should be scalable to a billion users. You drew a system design diagram that included a CDN, but you didn't discuss the tradeoffs and alternatives of your design choices. You were not proactive in suggesting other possibilities beyond the narrow scope that the interviewer gave you at the beginning of the interview, such as analytics to determine the most popular photos or personalization to recommend photos to share with a user. You didn't ask the right questions, and you didn't mention important concepts like logging, monitoring, and alerting.

You realize that even with your engineering experience and your hard work in studying and reading to keep up with industry best practices and developments, the breath of system design is vast, and you lack much formal knowledge and understanding of many system design components that you'll never directly touch, like load balancers or certain NoSQL databases, so you cannot create a system design diagram of the level of completeness that the interviewer expects, and you cannot fluently zoom in and out when discussing various levels of the system. Until you learn to do so, you cannot meet the hiring bar, and you cannot truly understand a complex system or ascend to a more senior engineering leadership or mentorship role.

acknowledgments

I thank my wife Emma for her consistent encouragement in my various endeavors, diving into various difficult and time-consuming projects at work, writing various apps, and writing this book. I thank my daughter Ada, my inspiration to endure the frustration and tedium of coding and writing.

I thank my brother Zhilong, who gave me much valuable feedback on my drafts and is himself an expert in system design and video encoding protocols at Meta. I thank my big sister Shumin for always being supportive and pushing me to achieve more.

Thank you, Mom and Dad, for your sacrifices that made it all possible.

I wish to thank the staff at Manning for all their help, beginning with my book proposal reviewers Andreas von Linden, Amuthan Ganeshan, Marc Roulleau, Dean Tsaltas, and Vincent Liard. Amuthan provided detailed feedback and asked good questions about the proposed topics. Katie Sposato Johnson was my guide for the 1.5-year process of reviewing and revising the manuscript. She proofread each chapter, and her feedback considerably improved the book's presentation and clarity. My technical editor, Mohit Chilkoti, provided many good suggestions to improve clarity and pointed out errors. My review editor Adriana Sabo and her team organized the panel reviews, which gathered invaluable feedback that I used to substantially improve this book. To all the reviewers: Abdul Karim Memon, Ajit Malleri, Alessandro Buggin, Alessandro Campeis, Andres Sacco, Anto Aravinth, Ashwini Gupta, Clifford Thurber, Curtis Washington, Dipkumar Patel, Fasih Khatib, Ganesh Swaminathan, Haim Raman, Haresh Lala, Javid Asgarov, Jens Christian B. Madsen, Jeremy Chen, Jon Riddle, Jonathan Reeves, Kamesh Ganesan, Kiran Anantha, Laud Bentil, Lora Vardarova, Matt Ferderer, Max Sadrieh, Mike B., Muneeb Shaikh, Najeeb Arif, Narendran Solai Sridharan, Nolan To, Nouran Mahmoud, Patrick Wanjau, Peiti Li, Péter Szabó, Pierre-Michel Ansel, Pradeep

Chellappan, Rahul Modpur, Rajesh Mohanan, Sadhana Ganapathiraju, Samson Hailu, Samuel Bosch, Sanjeev Kilarapu, Simeon Leyzerzon, Sravanthi Reddy, Vincent Ngo, Zoheb Ainapore, Zorodzayi Mukuya, your suggestions helped make this a better book.

I'd like to thank Marc Roulleau, Andres von Linden, Amuthan Ganesan, Rob Conery, and Scott Hanselman for their support and their recommendations for additional resources.

I wish to thank the tough northerners (not softie southerners) Andrew Waldron and Ian Hough. Andy pushed me to fill in many useful gritty details across all the chapters and guided me on how to properly format the figures to fit the pages. He helped me discover how much more capable I am than I previously thought. Aira Dučić and Matko Hrvatin helped much with marketing, and Dragana Butigan-Berberović and Ivan Martinović did a great job on formatting. Stjepan Jureković and Nikola Dimitrijević guided me through my promo video.

about this book

This book is about web services. A candidate should discuss the system's requirements and then design a system of reasonable complexity and cost that fulfills those requirements.

Besides coding interviews, system design interviews are conducted for most software engineering, software architecture, and engineering manager interviews.

The ability to design and review large-scale systems is regarded as more important with increasing engineering seniority. Correspondingly, system design interviews are given more weight in interviews for senior positions. Preparing for them, both as an interviewer and candidate, is a good investment of time for a career in tech.

The open-ended nature of system design interviews makes it a challenge to prepare for and know how or what to discuss during an interview. Moreover, there are few dedicated books on this topic. This is because system design is an art and a science. It is not about perfection. It is about making tradeoffs and compromises to design the system we can achieve with the given resources and time that most closely suits current and possible future requirements. With this book, the reader can build a knowledge foundation or identify and fill gaps in their knowledge.

A system design interview is also about verbal communication skills, quick thinking, asking good questions, and handling performance anxiety. This book emphasizes that one must effectively and concisely express one's system design expertise within a less-than-1-hour interview and drive the interview in the desired direction by asking the interviewer the right questions. Reading this book, along with practicing system design discussions with other engineers, will allow you to develop the knowledge and fluency required to pass system design interviews and participate well in designing systems in the organization you join. It can also be a resource for interviewers who conduct system design interviews.

Who should read this book

This book is for software engineers, software architects, and engineering managers looking to advance their careers.

This is not an introductory software engineering book. This book is best used after one has acquired a minimal level of industry experience—perhaps a student doing a first internship may read the documentation websites and other introductory materials of unfamiliar tools and discuss them together with other unfamiliar concepts in this book with engineers at her workplace. This book discusses how to approach system design interviews and does not duplicate introductory material that we can easily find online or in other books. At least intermediate proficiency in coding and SQL are assumed.

How this book is organized: A roadmap

This book has 17 chapters across two parts and four brief appendixes.

Part 1 is presented like a typical textbook, with chapters that cover various topics discussed in a system design interview.

Part 2 consists of discussions of sample interview questions that reference the concepts covered in part 1. Each chapter was chosen to use some or most of the concepts covered in part 1. This book focuses on general web services, and we exclude highly specialized and complex topics like payments, video streaming, location services, or database development. Moreover, in my opinion, asking a candidate to spend 10 minutes to discuss database linearizability or consistency topics like coordination services, quorum, or gossip protocols does not reveal any expertise other than having read enough to discuss the said topic for 10 minutes. An interview for a specialized role that requires expertise on a highly specialized topic should be the focus of the entire interview and deserves its own dedicated books. In this book, wherever such topics are referenced, we refer to other books or resources that are dedicated to these said topics.

liveBook discussion forum

Purchase of *Acing the System Design Interview* includes free access to liveBook, Manning's online reading platform. Using liveBook's exclusive discussion features, you can attach comments to the book globally or to specific sections or paragraphs. It's a snap to make notes for yourself, ask and answer technical questions, and receive help from the author and other users. To access the forum, go to https://livebook.manning .com/book/acing-the-system-design-interview/discussion. You can also learn more about Manning's forums and the rules of conduct at https://livebook.manning.com/ discussion.

Manning's commitment to our readers is to provide a venue where a meaningful dialogue between individual readers and between readers and the author can take place. It is not a commitment to any specific amount of participation on the part of the author, whose contribution to the forum remains voluntary (and unpaid). We suggest you try asking the author some challenging questions lest his interest stray! The forum and the archives of previous discussions will be accessible from the publisher's website as long as the book is in print.

Other online resources

- https://github.com/donnemartin/system-design-primer
- https://bigmachine.io/products/mission-interview/
- http://geeksforgeeks.com
- http://algoexpert.io
- https://www.learnbay.io/
- http://leetcode.com
- https://bigmachine.io/products/mission-interview/

about the author

ZHIYONG TAN is a manager at PayPal. Previously, he was a senior full-stack engineer at Uber, a software engineer at Teradata, and a data engineer at various startups. Over the years, he has been on both sides of the table in numerous system design interviews. Zhiyong has also received prized job offers from prominent companies such as Amazon, Apple, and ByteDance/TikTok.

ABOUT THE TECHNICAL EDITOR

Mohit Chilkoti is a Platform Architect at Chargebee. He is an AWS-certified Solutions Architect and has designed an Alternative Investment Trading Platform for Morgan Stanley and a Retail Platform for Tekion Corp.

about the cover illustration

The figure on the cover of *Acing the System Design Interview* is "Femme Tatar Tobolsk," or "A Tatar woman from the Tobolsk region," taken from a collection by Jacques Grasset de Saint-Sauveur, published in 1784. The illustration is finely drawn and colored by hand.

In those days, it was easy to identify where people lived and what their trade or station in life was just by their dress. Manning celebrates the inventiveness and initiative of the computer business with book covers based on the rich diversity of regional culture centuries ago, brought back to life by pictures from collections such as this one.

Part 1

This part of the book discusses common topics in system design interviews. It sets the stage for part 2, where we discuss sample system design interview questions.

We begin in chapter 1 by walking through a sample system and introducing many system design concepts along the way without explaining them in detail, then deep dive into these concepts in subsequent chapters.

In chapter 2, we discuss one's experience in a typical system design interview. We'll learn to clarify the requirements of the question and what aspects of the system to optimize at the expense of others. Then we discuss other common topics, including storing and searching data, operational concerns like monitoring and alerting, and edge cases and new constraints.

In chapter 3, we dive into non-functional requirements, which are usually not explicitly requested by the customer or interviewer and must be clarified prior to designing a system.

A large system may serve hundreds of millions of users and receive billions of data read and write requests every day. We discuss in chapter 4 how we can scale our databases to handle such traffic.

The system may be divided into services, and we may need to write related data to these multiple services, which we discuss in chapter 5.

Many systems require certain common functionalities. In chapter 6, we discuss how we can centralize such cross-cutting functionalities into services that can serve many other systems.

A walkthrough of
system design concepts

This chapter covers

- Learning the importance of the system design interview
- Scaling a service
- Using cloud hosting vs. bare metal

A system design interview is a discussion between the candidate and the interviewer about designing a software system that is typically provided over a network. The interviewer begins the interview with a short and vague request to the candidate to design a particular software system. Depending on the particular system, the user base may be non-technical or technical.

System design interviews are conducted for most software engineering, software architecture, and engineering manager job interviews. (In this book, we collectively refer to software engineers, architects, and managers as simply *engineers*.) Other components of the interview process include coding and behavioral/cultural interviews.

1.1   *A discussion about tradeoffs*

The following factors attest to the importance of system design interviews and preparing well for them as a candidate and an interviewer.

Run in performance as a candidate in the system design interviews is used to estimate your breadth and depth of system design expertise and your ability to communicate and discuss system designs with other engineers. This is a critical factor in determining the level of seniority at which you will be hired into the company. The ability to design and review large-scale systems is regarded as more important with increasing engineering seniority. Correspondingly, system design interviews are given more weight in interviews for senior positions. Preparing for them, both as an interviewer and candidate, is a good investment of time for a career in tech.

The tech industry is unique in that it is common for engineers to change companies every few years, unlike other industries where an employee may stay at their company for many years or their whole career. This means that a typical engineer will go through system design interviews many times in their career. Engineers employed at a highly desirable company will go through even more system design interviews as an interviewer. As an interview candidate, you have less than one hour to make the best possible impression, and the other candidates who are your competition are among the smartest and most motivated people in the world.

System design is an art, not a science. It is not about perfection. We make tradeoffs and compromises to design the system we can achieve with the given resources and time that most closely suits current and possible future requirements. All the discussions of various systems in this book involve estimates and assumptions and are not academically rigorous, exhaustive, or scientific. We may refer to software design patterns and architectural patterns, but we will not formally describe these principles. Readers should refer to other resources for more details.

A system design interview is not about the right answer. It is about one's ability to discuss multiple possible approaches and weigh their tradeoffs in satisfying the requirements. Knowledge of the various types of requirements and common systems discussed in part 1 will help us design our system, evaluate various possible approaches, and discuss tradeoffs.

1.2   *Should you read this book?*

The open-ended nature of system design interviews makes it a challenge to prepare for and know how or what to discuss during an interview. An engineer or student who searches for online learning materials on system design interviews will find a vast quantity of content that varies in quality and diversity of the topics covered. This is confusing and hinders learning. Moreover, until recently, there were few dedicated books on this topic, though a trickle of such books is beginning to be published. I believe this is because a high-quality book dedicated to the topic of system design interviews is, quoting the celebrated 19th-century French poet and novelist Victor Hugo, "an idea whose time has come." Multiple people will get this same idea at around the same time, and this affirms its relevance.

This is not an introductory software engineering book. This book is best used after one has acquired a minimal level of industry experience. Perhaps if you are a student in your first internship, you can read the documentation websites and other introductory materials of unfamiliar tools and discuss them together with other unfamiliar concepts in this book with engineers at your workplace. This book discusses how to approach system design interviews and minimizes duplication of introductory material that we can easily find online or in other books. At least intermediate proficiency in coding and SQL is assumed.

This book offers a structured and organized approach to start preparing for system design interviews or to fill gaps in knowledge and understanding from studying the large amount of fragmented material. Equally valuably, it teaches how to demonstrate one's engineering maturity and communication skills during a system design interview, such as clearly and concisely articulating one's ideas, knowledge, and questions to the interviewer within the brief ~50 minutes.

A system design interview, like any other interview, is also about communication skills, quick thinking, asking good questions, and performance anxiety. One may forget to mention points that the interviewer is expecting. Whether this interview format is flawed can be endlessly debated. From personal experience, with seniority one spends an increasing amount of time in meetings, and essential abilities include quick thinking, being able to ask good questions, steering the discussion to the most critical and relevant topics, and communicating one's thoughts succinctly. This book emphasizes that one must effectively and concisely express one's system design expertise within the <1 hour interview and drive the interview in the desired direction by asking the interviewer the right questions. Reading this book, along with practicing system design discussions with other engineers, will allow you to develop the knowledge and fluency required to pass system design interviews and participate well in designing systems in the company you join. It can also be a resource for interviewers who conduct system design interviews.

One may excel in written over verbal communication and forget to mention important points during the ~50-minute interview. System design interviews are biased in favor of engineers with good verbal communication and against engineers less proficient in verbal communication, even though the latter may have considerable system design expertise and have made valuable system design contributions in the organizations where they worked. This book prepares engineers for these and other challenges of system design interviews, shows how to approach them in an organized way, and coaches how not to be intimidated.

If you are a software engineer looking to broaden your knowledge of system design concepts, improve your ability to discuss a system, or are simply looking for a collection of system design concepts and sample system design discussions, read on.

1.3   *Overview of this book*

This book is divided into two parts. Part 1 is presented like a typical textbook, with chapters that cover the various topics discussed in a system design interview. Part 2 consists of discussions of sample interview questions that reference the concepts covered in part 1 and also discusses antipatterns and common misconceptions and mistakes. In those discussions, we also state the obvious that one is not expected to possess all knowledge of all domains. Rather, one should be able to reason that certain approaches will help satisfy requirements better, with certain tradeoffs. For example, we don't need to calculate file size reduction or CPU and memory resources required for Gzip compression on a file, but we should be able to state that compressing a file before sending it will reduce network traffic but consume more CPU and memory resources on both the sender and recipient.

An aim of this book is to bring together a bunch of relevant materials and organize them into a single book so you can build a knowledge foundation or identify gaps in your knowledge, from which you can study other materials.

The rest of this chapter is a prelude to a sample system design that mentions some of the concepts that will be covered in part 1. Based on this context, we will discuss many of the concepts in dedicated chapters.

1.4 Prelude: A brief discussion of scaling the various services of a system

We begin this book with a brief description of a typical initial setup of an app and a general approach to adding scalability into our app's services as needed. Along the way, we introduce numerous terms and concepts and many types of services required by a tech company, which we discuss in greater detail in the rest of the book.

> **DEFINITION**   The *scalability* of a service is the ability to easily and cost-effectively vary resources allocated to it to serve changes in load. This applies to both increasing or decreasing user numbers and/or requests to the system. This is discussed more in chapter 3.

1.4.1 The beginning: A small initial deployment of our app

Riding the rising wave of interest in artisan bagels, we have just built an awesome consumer-facing app named Beigel that allows users to read and create posts about nearby bagel cafes.

Initially, Beigel consists primarily of the following components:

- Our consumer apps. They are essentially the same app, one for each of the three common platforms:
  - A browser app. This is a ReactJS browser consumer app that makes requests to a JavaScript runtime service. To reduce the size of the JavaScript bundle that users need to download, we compress it with Brotli. Gzip is an older and more popular choice, but Brotli produces smaller compressed files.
  - An iOS app, which is downloaded on a consumer's iOS device.
  - An Android app, which is also downloaded on a consumer's Android device.
- A stateless backend service that serves the consumer apps. It can be a Go or Java service.
- A SQL database contained in a single cloud host.

We have two main services: the frontend service and the backend service. Figure 1.1 illustrates these components. As shown, the consumer apps are client-side components, while services and database are server-side components.

> **NOTE**   Refer to sections 6.5.1 and 6.5.2 for a discussion on why we need a frontend service between the browser and the backend service.

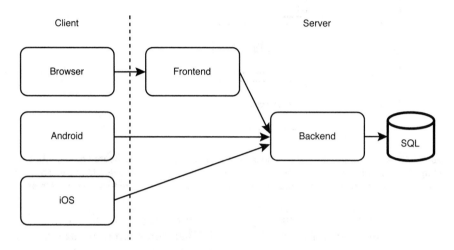

Figure 1.1   Initial system design of our app. For a more thorough discussion on the rationale for having three client applications and two server applications (excluding the SQL application/database), refer to chapter 6.

When we first launch a service, it may only have a small number of users and thus a low request rate. A single host may be sufficient to handle the low request rate. We will set up our DNS to direct all requests to this host.

Initially, we can host the two services within the same data center, each on a single cloud host. (We compare cloud vs. bare metal in the next section.) We configure our DNS to direct all requests from our browser app to our Node.js host and from our Node.js host and two mobile apps to our backend host.

1.4.2   Scaling with GeoDNS

Months later, Beigel has gained hundreds of thousands of daily active users in Asia, Europe, and North America. During periods of peak traffic, our backend service receives thousands of requests per second, and our monitoring system is starting to report status code 504 responses due to timeouts. We must scale up our system.

We have observed the rise in traffic and prepared for this situation. Our service is stateless as per standard best practices, so we can provision multiple identical backend hosts and place each host in a different data center in a different part of the world. Referring to figure 1.2, when a client makes a request to our backend via its domain beigel.com, we use GeoDNS to direct the client to the data center closest to it.

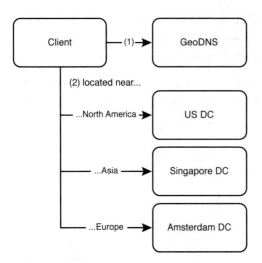

Figure 1.2 We may provision our service in multiple geographically distributed data centers. Depending on the client's location (inferred from its IP address), a client obtains the IP address of a host of the closest data center, to which it sends its requests. The client may cache this host IP address.

If our service serves users from a specific country or geographical region in general, we will typically host our service in a nearby data center to minimize latency. If your service serves a large geographically distributed userbase, we can host it on multiple data centers and use GeoDNS to return to a user the IP address of our service hosted in the closest data center. This is done by assigning multiple A records to our domain for various locations and a default IP address for other locations. (An *A record* is a DNS configuration that maps a domain to an IP address.)

When a client makes a request to the server, the GeoDNS obtains the client's location from their IP address and assigns the client the corresponding host IP address. In the unlikely but possible event that the data center is inaccessible, GeoDNS can return an IP address of the service on another data center. This IP address can be cached at various levels, including the user's Internet Service Provider (ISP), OS, and browser.

1.4.3   *Adding a caching service*

Referring to figure 1.3, we next set up a Redis cache service to serve cached requests from our consumer apps. We select certain backend endpoints with heavy traffic to serve from the cache. That bought us some time as our user base and request load continued to grow. Now, further steps are needed to scale up.

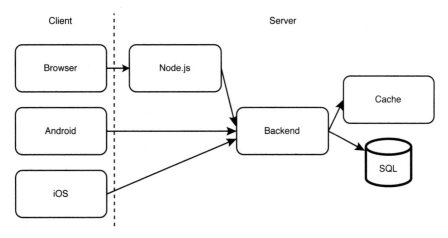

Figure 1.3 Adding a cache to our service. Certain backend endpoints with heavy traffic can be cached. The backend will request data from the database on a cache miss or for SQL databases/tables that were not cached.

1.4.4 Content distribution network

Our browser apps had been hosting static content/files that are displayed the same to any user and unaffected by user input, such as JavaScript, CSS libraries, and some images and videos. We had placed these files within our app's source code repository, and our users were downloading them from our Node.js service together with the rest of the app. Referring to figure 1.4, we decided to use a third-party content distribution network (CDN) to host the static content. We selected and provisioned sufficient capacity from a CDN to host our files, uploaded our files onto our CDN instance, rewrote our code to fetch the files from the URLs of the CDN, and removed the files from our source code repository.

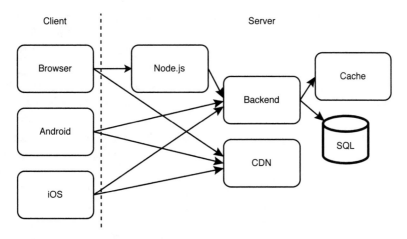

Figure 1.4 Adding a CDN to our service. Clients can obtain CDN addresses from the backend, or certain CDN addresses can be hardcoded in the clients or Node.js service.

Referring to figure 1.5, a CDN stores copies of the static files in various data centers across the world, so a user can download these files from the data center that can provide them the lowest latency, which is usually the geographically closest one, though other data centers may be faster if the closest one is serving heavy traffic or suffering a partial outage.

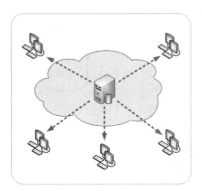 

Figure 1.5   The left illustration shows all clients downloading from the same host. The right illustration shows clients downloading from various hosts of a CDN. (Copyright cc-by-sa https://creativecommons .org/licenses/by-sa/3.0/. Image by Kanoha from https://upload.wikimedia.org/wikipedia/ commons/f/f9/NCDN_-_CDN.png.)

Using a CDN improved latency, throughput, reliability, and cost. (We discuss all these concepts in chapter 3.) Using a CDN, unit costs decrease with demand because maintenance, integration overhead, and customer support are spread over a larger load.

Popular CDNs include CloudFlare, Rackspace, and AWS CloudFront.

1.4.5   *A brief discussion of horizontal scalability and cluster management, continuous integration, and continuous deployment*

Our frontend and backend services are idempotent (we discuss some benefits of idempotency and its benefits in sections 4.6.1, 6.1.2, and 7.7), thus they are horizontally scalable, so we can provision more hosts to support our larger request load without rewriting any source code and deploy the frontend or backend service to those hosts as needed.

Each of our services has multiple engineers working on its source code. Our engineers submit new commits every day. We change software development and release practices to support this larger team and faster development, hiring two DevOps engineers in the process to develop the infrastructure to manage a large cluster. As scaling requirements of a service can change quickly, we want to be able to easily resize its cluster. We need to be able to easily deploy our services and required configurations to new hosts. We also want to easily build and deploy code changes to all the hosts in our service's cluster. We can take advantage of our large userbase for experimentation by deploying different code or configurations to various hosts. This section is a brief discussion of cluster management for horizontal scalability and experimentation.

CI/CD AND INFRASTRUCTURE AS CODE

To allow new features to be released quickly while minimizing the risk of releasing bugs, we adopt continuous integration and continuous deployment with Jenkins and unit testing and integration testing tools. (A detailed discussion of CI/CD is outside the scope of this book.) We use Docker to containerize our services, Kubernetes (or Docker Swarm) to manage our host cluster including scaling and providing load balancing, and Ansible or Terraform for configuration management of our various services running on our various clusters.

> **NOTE** Mesos is widely considered obsolete. Kubernetes is the clear winner. A couple of relevant articles are https://thenewstack.io/apache-mesos-narrowly -avoids-a-move-to-the-attic-for-now/ and https://www.datacenterknowledge.com/ business/after-kubernetes-victory-its-former-rivals-change-tack.

Terraform allows an infrastructure engineer to create a single configuration compatible with multiple cloud providers. A configuration is authored in Terraform's domain-specific language (DSL) and communicates with cloud APIs to provision infrastructure. In practice, a Terraform configuration may contain some vendor-specific code, which we should minimize. The overall consequence is less vendor lock-in.

This approach is also known as *Infrastructure as Code*. Infrastructure as Code is the process of managing and provisioning computer data centers through machine-readable definition files, rather than physical hardware configuration or interactive configuration tools (Wittig, Andreas; Wittig, Michael [2016]. *Amazon Web Services in Action*. Manning Publications. p. 93. ISBN 978-1-61729-288-0).

GRADUAL ROLLOUTS AND ROLLBACKS

In this section, we briefly discuss gradual rollouts and rollbacks, so we can contrast them with experimentation in the next section.

When we deploy a build to production, we may do so gradually. We may deploy the build to a certain percentage of hosts, monitor it and then increase the percentage, repeating this process until 100% of production hosts are running this build. For example, we may deploy to 1%, 5%, 10%, 25%, 50%, 75%, and then finally 100%. We may manually or automatically roll back deployments if we detect any problems, such as:

- Bugs that slipped through testing.
- Crashes.
- Increased latency or timeouts.
- Memory leaks.
- Increased resource consumption like CPU, memory, or storage utilization.
- Increased user churn. We may also need to consider user churn in gradual outs—that is, that new users are signing on and using the app, and certain users may stop using the app. We can gradually expose an increasing percentage of users to a new build and study its effect on churn. User churn may occur due to the mentioned factors or unexpected problems such as many users disliking the changes.

For example, a new build may increase latency beyond an acceptable level. We can use a combination of caching and dynamic routing to handle this. Our service may specify a one-second latency. When a client makes a request that is routed to a new build, and a timeout occurs, our client may read from its cache, or it may repeat its request and be routed to a host with an older build. We should log the requests and responses so we can troubleshoot the timeouts.

We can configure our CD pipeline to divide our production cluster into several groups, and our CD tool will determine the appropriate number of hosts in each group and assign hosts to groups. Reassignments and redeployments may occur if we resize our cluster.

EXPERIMENTATION

As we make UX changes in developing new features (or removing features) and aesthetic designs in our application, we may wish to gradually roll them out to an increasing percentage of users, rather than to all users at once. The purpose of experimentation is to determine the effect of UX changes on user behavior, in contrast to gradual rollouts, which are about the effect of new deployments on application performance and user churn. Common experimentation approaches are A/B and multivariate testing, such as multi-armed bandit. These topics are outside the scope of this book. For more information on A/B testing, refer to https://www.optimizely.com/optimization-glossary/ab-testing/. For multivariate testing, see *Experimentation for Engineers* by David Sweet (Manning Publications, 2023) or https://www.optimizely.com/optimization-glossary/multi-armed-bandit/ for an introduction to multi-armed bandit.)

Experimentation is also done to deliver personalized user experiences.

Another difference between experimentation vs. gradual rollouts and rollbacks is that in experimentation, the percentage of hosts running various builds is often tuned by an experimentation or feature toggle tool that is designed for that purpose, while in gradual rollouts and rollbacks, the CD tool is used to manually or automatically roll back hosts to previous builds if problems are detected.

CD and experimentation allow short feedback cycles to new deployments and features.

In web and backend applications, each user experience (UX) is usually packaged in a different build. A certain percentage of hosts will contain a different build. Mobile apps are usually different. Many user experiences are coded into the same build, but each individual user will only be exposed to a subset of these user experiences. The main reasons for this are:

- Mobile application deployments must be made through the app store. It may take many hours to deploy a new version to user devices. There is no way to quickly roll back a deployment.
- Compared to Wi-Fi, mobile data is slower, less reliable, and more expensive. Slow speed and unreliability mean we need to have much content served offline,

already in the app. Mobile data plans in many countries are still expensive and may come with data caps and overage charges. We should avoid exposing users to these charges, or they may use the app less or uninstall it altogether. To conduct experimentation while minimizing data usage from downloading components and media, we simply include all these components and media in the app and expose the desired subset to each individual user.

- A mobile app may also include many features that some users will never use because it is not applicable to them. For example, section 15.1 discusses various methods of payment in an app. There are possibly thousands of payment solutions in the world. The app needs to contain all the code and SDKs for every payment solution, so it can present each user with the small subset of payment solutions they may have.

A consequence of all this is that a mobile app can be over 100MB in size. The techniques to address this are outside the scope of this book. We need to achieve a balance and consider tradeoffs. For example, YouTube's mobile app installation obviously cannot include many YouTube videos.

1.4.6   *Functional partitioning and centralization of cross-cutting concerns*

Functional partitioning is about separating various functions into different services or hosts. Many services have common concerns that can be extracted into shared services. Chapter 6 discusses the motivation, benefits, and tradeoffs.

SHARED SERVICES

Our company is expanding rapidly. Our daily active user count has grown to millions. We expand our engineering team to five iOS engineers, five Android engineers, 10 frontend engineers, 100 backend engineers, and we create a data science team.

Our expanded engineering team can work on many services beyond the apps directly used by consumers, such as services for our expanding customer support and operations departments. We add features within the consumer apps for consumers to contact customer support and for operations to create and launch variations of our products.

Many of our apps contain search bars. We create a shared search service with Elasticsearch.

In addition to horizontal scaling, we use functional partitioning to spread out data processing and requests across a large number of geographically distributed hosts by partitioning based on functionality and geography. We already did functional partitioning of our cache, Node.js service, backend service, and database service into separate hosts, and we do functional partitioning for other services as well, placing each service on its own cluster of geographically distributed hosts. Figure 1.6 shows the shared services that we add to Beigel.

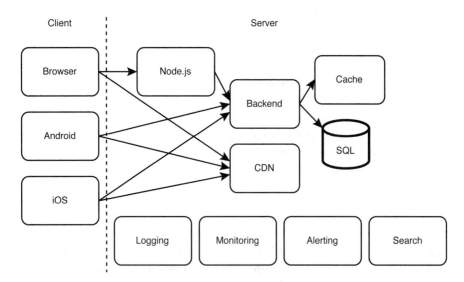

Figure 1.6   Functional partitioning. Adding shared services.

We added a logging service, consisting of a log-based message broker. We can use the Elastic Stack (Elasticsearch, Logstash, Kibana, Beats). We also use a distributed tracing system, such as Zipkin or Jaeger or distributed logging, to trace a request as it traverses through our numerous services. Our services attach span IDs to each request so they can be assembled as traces and analyzed. Section 2.5 discusses logging, monitoring, and alerting.

We also added monitoring and alerting services. We build internal browser apps for our customer support employees to better assist customers. These apps process the consumer app logs generated by the customer and present them with good UI so our customer support employees can more easily understand the customer's problem.

API gateway and service mesh are two ways to centralize cross-cutting concerns. Other ways are the decorator pattern and aspect-oriented programming, which are outside the scope of this book.

API GATEWAY

By this time, app users make up less than half of our API requests. Most requests originate from other companies, which offer services such as recommending useful products and services to our users based on their in-app activities. We develop an API gateway layer to expose some of our APIs to external developers.

An API gateway is a reverse proxy that routes client requests to the appropriate backend services. It provides the common functionality to many services, so individual services do not duplicate them:

- Authorization and authentication, and other access control and security policies
- Logging, monitoring, and alerting at the request level

- Rate limiting
- Billing
- Analytics

Our initial architecture involving an API gateway and its services is illustrated in figure 1.7. A request to a service goes through a centralized API gateway. The API gateway carries out all the functionality described previously, does a DNS lookup, and then forwards the request to a host of the relevant service. The API gateway makes requests to services such as DNS, identity and access control and management, rate-limiting configuration service, etc. We also log all configuration changes done through the API gateway.

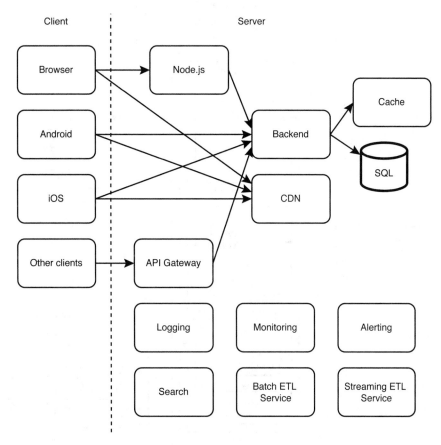

Figure 1.7 Initial architecture with our API gateway and services. Requests to services go through the API gateway

However, this architecture has the following drawbacks. The API gateway adds latency and requires a large cluster of hosts. The API gateway host and a service's host that serves a particular request may be in different data centers. A system design that tries to route requests through API gateway hosts and service hosts will be an awkward and complex design.

A solution is to use a service mesh, also called the sidecar pattern. We discuss service mesh further in chapter 6. Figure 1.8 illustrates our service mesh. We can use a service mesh framework such as Istio. Each host of each service can run a sidecar along the main service. We use Kubernetes pods to accomplish this. Each pod can contain its service (in one container) as well as its sidecar (in another container). We provide an admin interface to configure policies, and these configurations can be distributed to all sidecars.

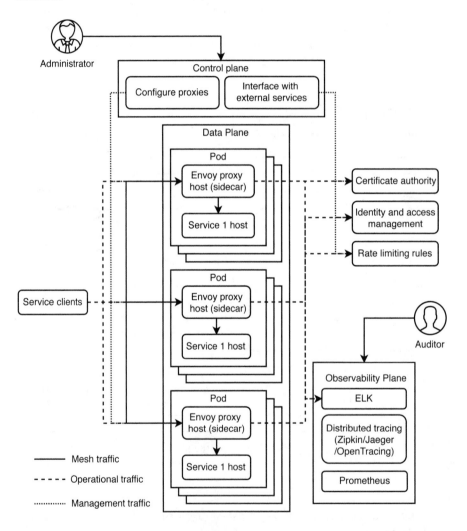

Figure 1.8   Illustration of a service mesh. Prometheus makes requests to each proxy host to pull/ scrape metrics, but this is not illustrated in the diagram because the many arrows will make it too cluttered and confusing. Figure adapted from https://livebook.manning.com/book/cloud-native/ chapter-10/146.

With this architecture, all service requests and responses are routed through the sidecar. The service and sidecar are on the same host (i.e., same machine) so they can address each other over localhost, and there is no network latency. However, the sidecar does consume system resources.

SIDECARLESS SERVICE MESH—THE CUTTING EDGE

The service mesh required our system to nearly double the number of containers. For systems that involve communication between internal services (aka ingress or east-west), we can reduce this complexity by placing the sidecar proxy logic into client hosts that make requests to service hosts. In the design of sidecarless service mesh, client hosts receive configurations from the control plane. Client hosts must support the control plane API, so they must also include the appropriate network communication libraries.

A limitation of sidecarless service mesh is that there must be a client who is in the same language as the service.

The development of sidecarless service mesh platforms is in its early stages. Google Cloud Platform (GCP) Traffic Director is an implementation that was released in April 2019 (https://cloud.google.com/blog/products/networking/traffic-director -global-traffic-management-for-open-service-mesh).

COMMAND QUERY RESPONSIBILITY SEGREGATION (CQRS)

Command Query Responsibility Segregation (CQRS) is a microservices pattern where command/write operations and query/read operations are functionally partitioned onto separate services. Message brokers and ETL jobs are examples of CQRS. Any design where data is written to one table and then transformed and inserted into another table is an example of CQRS. CQRS introduces complexity but has lower latency and better scalability and is easier to maintain and use. The write and read services can be scaled separately.

You will see many examples of CQRS in this book, though they will not be called out. Chapter 15 has one such example, where an Airbnb host writes to the Listing Service, but guests read from the Booking Service. (Though the Booking Service also provides write endpoints for guests to request bookings, which is unrelated to a host updating their listings.)

You can easily find more detailed definition of CQRS in other sources.

1.4.7 *Batch and streaming extract, transform, and load (ETL)*

Some of our systems have unpredictable traffic spikes, and certain data processing requests do not have to be synchronous (i.e., process immediately and return response):

- Some requests that involve large queries to our databases (such as queries that process gigabytes of data).
- It may make more sense to periodically preprocess certain data ahead of requests rather than process it only when a request is made. For example, our app's home

page may display the top 10 most frequently learned words across all users in the last hour or in the seven days. This information should be processed ahead of time once an hour or once a day. Moreover, the result of this processing can be reused for all users, rather than repeating the processing for each user.

- Another possible example is that it may be acceptable for users to be shown data that is outdated by some hours or days. For example, users do not need to see the most updated statistics of the number of users who have viewed their shared content. It is acceptable to show them statistics that are out-of-date by a few hours.

- Writes (e.g., INSERT, UPDATE, DELETE database requests) that do not have to be executed immediately. For example, writes to the logging service do not have to be immediately written to the hard disk drives of logging service hosts. These write requests can be placed in a queue and executed later.

In the case of certain systems like logging, which receive large request volumes from many other systems, if we do not use an asynchronous approach like ETL, the logging system cluster will have to have thousands of hosts to process all these requests synchronously.

We can use a combination of event streaming systems like Kafka (or Kinesis if we use AWS) and batch ETL tools such as Airflow for such batch jobs.

If we wish to continuously process data, rather than periodically running batch jobs, we can use streaming tools such as Flink. For example, if a user inputs some data into our app, and we want to use it to send certain recommendations or notifications to them within seconds or minutes, we can create a Flink pipeline that processes recent user inputs. A logging system is usually streaming because it expects a non-stop stream of requests. If the requests are less frequent, a batch pipeline will be sufficient.

1.4.8   *Other common services*

As our company grows and our userbase expands, we develop more products, and our products should become increasingly customizable and personalized to serve this large, growing, and diverse userbase. We will require numerous other services to satisfy the new requirements that come with this growth and to take advantage of it. They include the following:

- Customer/external user credentials management for external user authentication and authorization.

- Various storage services, including database services. The specific requirements of each system mean that there are certain optimal ways that the data it uses should be persisted, processed, and served. We will need to develop and maintain various shared storage services that use different technologies and techniques.

- Asynchronous processing. Our large userbase requires more hosts and may create unpredictable traffic spikes to our services. To handle traffic spikes, we need asynchronous processing to efficiently utilize our hardware and reduce unnecessary hardware expenditure.

- Notebooks service for analytics and machine learning, including experimentation, model creation, and deployment. We can use our large customer base for experimentation to discover user preferences, personalize user experiences, attract more users, and discover other ways to increase our revenue.

- Internal search and subproblems (e.g., autocomplete/typeahead service). Many of our web or mobile applications can have search bars for users to search for their desired data.

- Privacy compliance services and teams. Our expanding user numbers and large amount of customer data will attract malicious external and internal actors, who will attempt to steal data. A privacy breach on our large userbase will affect numerous people and organizations. We must invest in safeguarding user privacy.

- Fraud detection. The increasing revenue of our company will make it a tempting target for criminals and fraudsters, so effective fraud detection systems are a must.

1.4.9 *Cloud vs. bare metal*

We can manage our own hosts and data centers or outsource this to cloud vendors. This section is a comparative analysis of both approaches.

GENERAL CONSIDERATIONS

At the beginning of this section, we decided to use cloud services (renting hosts from providers such as Amazon's AWS, DigitalOcean, or Microsoft Azure) instead of bare metal (owning and managing our own physical machines).

Cloud providers provide many services we will require, including CI/CD, logging, monitoring, alerting, and simplified setup and management of various database types including caches, SQL, and NoSQL.

If we chose bare metal from the beginning, we would have set up and maintained any of these services that we require. This may take away attention and time from feature development, which may prove costly to our company.

We must also consider the cost of engineering labor vs. cloud tools. Engineers are very expensive resources, and besides being monetarily costly, good engineers tend to prefer challenging work. Bore them with menial tasks such as small-scale setups of common services, and they may move to another company and be difficult to replace in a competitive hiring market.

Cloud tools are often cheaper than hiring engineers to set up and maintain your bare-metal infrastructure. We most likely do not possess the economies of scale and their accompanying unit cost efficiencies or the specialized expertise of dedicated cloud providers. If our company is successful, it may reach a growth stage where we have the economies of scale to consider bare metal.

Using cloud services instead of bare metal has other benefits including the following.

SIMPLICITY OF SETUP

On a cloud provider's browser app, we can easily choose a package most suited for our purposes. On bare metal, we would need steps such as installing server software like Apache or setting up network connections and port forwarding.

COST ADVANTAGES

Cloud has no initial upfront cost of purchasing physical machines/servers. A cloud vendor allows us to pay for incremental use and may offer bulk discounts. Scaling up or down in response to unpredictably changing requirements is easy and fast. If we choose bare metal, we may end up in a situation where we have too few or too many physical machines. Also, some cloud providers offer "auto-scaling" services, which automatically resize our cluster to suit the present load.

That being said, cloud is not always cheaper than bare metal. Dropbox (https:// www.geekwire.com/2018/dropbox-saved-almost-75-million-two-years-building-tech -infrastructure/) and Uber (https://www.datacenterknowledge.com/uber/want-build -data-centers-uber-follow-simple-recipe) are two examples of companies that host on their own data centers because their requirements meant it was the more cost-efficient choice.

CLOUD SERVICES MAY PROVIDE BETTER SUPPORT AND QUALITY

Anecdotal evidence suggests that cloud services generally provide superior performance, user experience, and support and have fewer and less serious outages. A possible reason is that cloud services must be competitive in the market to attract and retain customers, compared to bare metal, which an organization's users have little choice but to use. Many organizations tend to value and pay more attention to customers than internal users or employees, possibly because customer revenue is directly measurable, while the benefit of providing high-quality services and support to internal users may be more difficult to quantify. The corollary is that the losses to revenue and morale from poor-quality internal services are also difficult to quantify. Cloud services may also have economies of scale that bare metal lacks because the efforts of the cloud service's team are spread across a larger user base.

External-facing documentation may be better than internal-facing documentation. It may be better written, updated more often, and placed on a well-organized website that is easy to search. There may be more resources allocated, so videos and step-by-step tutorials may be provided.

External services may provide higher-quality input validation than internal services. Considering a simple example, if a certain UI field or API endpoint field requires the user to input an email address, the service should validate that the user's input is actually a valid email address. A company may pay more attention to external users who complain about the poor quality of input validation because they may stop using and paying for the company's product. Similar feedback from internal users who have little choice may be ignored.

When an error occurs, a high-quality service should return instructive error messages that guide the user on how to remedy the error, preferably without the time-consuming process of having to contact support personnel or the service's developers. External services may provide better error messages as well as allocate more resources and incentives to provide high-quality support.

If a customer sends a message, they may receive a reply within minutes or hours, while it may take hours or days to respond to an employee's questions. Sometimes a question to an internal helpdesk channel is not responded to at all. The response to an employee may be to direct them to poorly written documentation.

An organization's internal services can only be as good as external services if the organization provides adequate resources and incentives. Because better user experience and support improve users' morale and productivity, an organization may consider setting up metrics to measure how well internal users are served. One way to avoid these complications is to use cloud services. These considerations can be generalized to external vs. internal services.

Last, it is the responsibility of individual developers to hold themselves to high standards but not to make assumptions about the quality of others' work. However, the persistent poor quality of internal dependencies can hurt organizational productivity and morale.

UPGRADES

Both the hardware and software technologies used in an organization's bare metal infrastructure will age and be difficult to upgrade. This is obvious for finance companies that use mainframes. It is extremely costly, difficult, and risky to switch from mainframes to commodity servers, so such companies continue to buy new mainframes, which are far more expensive than their equivalent processing power in commodity servers. Organizations that use commodity servers also need the expertise and effort to constantly upgrade their hardware and software. For example, even upgrading the version of MySQL used in a large organization takes considerable time and effort. Many organizations prefer to outsource such maintenance to cloud providers.

SOME DISADVANTAGES

One disadvantage of cloud providers is vendor lock-in. Should we decide to transfer some or all components of our app to another cloud vendor, this process may not be straightforward. We may need considerable engineering effort to transfer data and services from one cloud provider to another and pay for duplicate services during this transition.

There are many possible reasons we will want to migrate out of a vendor. Today, the vendor may be a well-managed company that fulfills a demanding SLA at a competitive price, but there is no guarantee this will always be true. The quality of a company's service may degrade in the future, and it may fail to fulfill its SLA. The price may become uncompetitive, as bare metal or other cloud vendors become cheaper in the future. Or the vendor may be found to be lacking in security or other desirable characteristics.

Another disadvantage is the lack of ownership over the privacy and security of our data and services. We may not trust the cloud provider to safeguard our data or ensure the security of our services. With bare metal, we can personally verify privacy and security.

For these reasons, many companies adopt a multi-cloud strategy, using multiple cloud vendors instead of a single one, so these companies can migrate away from any particular vendor at short notice should the need suddenly arise.

1.4.10 *Serverless: Function as a Service (FaaS)*

If a certain endpoint or function is infrequently used or does not have strict latency requirements, it may be cheaper to implement it as a function on a Function as a Service (FaaS) platform, such as AWS Lambda or Azure Functions. Running a function only when needed means that there does not need to be hosts continuously waiting for requests to this function.

OpenFaaS and Knative are open-source FaaS solutions that we can use to support FaaS on our own cluster or as a layer on AWS Lambda to improve the portability of our functions between cloud platforms. As of this book's writing, there is no integration between open-source FaaS solutions and other vendor-managed FaaS such as Azure Functions.

Lambda functions have a timeout of 15 minutes. FaaS is intended to process requests that can complete within this time.

In a typical configuration, an API gateway service receives incoming requests and triggers the corresponding FaaS functions. The API gateway is necessary because there needs to be a continuously running service that waits for requests.

Another benefit of FaaS is that service developers need not manage deployments and scaling and can concentrate on coding their business logic.

Note that a single run of a FaaS function requires steps such as starting a Docker container, starting the appropriate language runtime (Java, Python, Node.js, etc.) and running the function, and terminating the runtime and Docker container. This is commonly referred to as *cold start*. Frameworks that take minutes to start, such as certain Java frameworks, may be unsuitable for FaaS. This spurred the development of JDKs with fast startups and low memory footprints such as GraalVM (https://www.graalvm .org/).

Why is this overhead required? Why can't all functions be packaged into a single package and run across all host instances, similar to a monolith? The reasons are the disadvantages of monoliths (refer to appendix A).

Why not have a frequently-used function deployed to certain hosts for a certain amount of time, (i.e., with an expiry)? Such a system is similar to auto-scaling microservices and can be considered when using frameworks that take a long time to start.

The portability of FaaS is controversial. At first glance, an organization that has done much work in a proprietary FaaS like AWS Lambda can become locked in; migrating to another solution becomes difficult, time-consuming, and expensive. Open-source FaaS platforms are not a complete solution, because one must provision and maintain one's own hosts, which defeats the scalability purpose of FaaS. This problem becomes especially significant at scale, when FaaS may become much more expensive than bare metal.

However, a function in FaaS can be written in two layers: an inner layer/function that contains the main logic of the function, wrapped by an outer layer/function that contains vendor-specific configurations. To switch vendors for any function, one only needs to change the outer function.

Spring Cloud Function (https://spring.io/projects/spring-cloud-function) is an emerging FaaS framework that is a generalization of this concept. It is supported by AWS Lambda, Azure Functions, Google Cloud Functions, Alibaba Function Compute, and may be supported by other FaaS vendors in the future.

1.4.11 *Conclusion: Scaling backend services*

In the rest of part 1, we discuss concepts and techniques to scale a backend service. A frontend/UI service is usually a Node.js service, and all it does is serve the same browser app written in a JavaScript framework like ReactJS or Vue.js to any user, so it can be scaled simply by adjusting the cluster size and using GeoDNS. A backend service is dynamic and can return a different response to each request. Its scalability techniques are more varied and complex. We discussed functional partitioning in the previous example and will occasionally touch on it as needed.

Summary

- System design interview preparation is critical to your career and also benefits your company.
- The system design interview is a discussion between engineers about designing a software system that is typically provided over a network.
- GeoDNS, caching, and CDN are basic techniques for scaling our service.
- CI/CD tools and practices allow feature releases to be faster with fewer bugs. They also allow us to divide our users into groups and expose each group to a different version of our app for experimentation purposes.
- Infrastructure as Code tools like Terraform are useful automation tools for cluster management, scaling, and feature experimentation.
- Functional partitioning and centralization of cross-cutting concerns are key elements of system design.
- ETL jobs can be used to spread out the processing of traffic spikes over a longer time period, which reduces our required cluster size.
- Cloud hosting has many advantages. Cost is often but not always an advantage. There are also possible disadvantages such as vendor lock-in and potential privacy and security risks.
- Serverless is an alternative approach to services. In exchange for the cost advantage of not having to keep hosts constantly running, it imposes limited functionality.

A typical system design interview flow

2

In this chapter, we will discuss a few principles of system design interviews that must be followed during your 1 hour system design interview. When you complete this book, refer to this list again. Keep these principles in mind during your interviews:

1 Clarify functional and non-functional requirements (refer to chapter 3), such as QPS (queries per second) and P99 latency. Ask whether the interviewer desires wants to start the discussion from a simple system and then scale up and design more features or start with immediately designing a scalable system.

2 Everything is a tradeoff. There is almost never any characteristic of a system that is entirely positive and without tradeoffs. Any new addition to a system to

improve scalability, consistency, or latency also increases complexity and cost and requires security, logging, monitoring, and alerting.

3 Drive the interview. Keep the interviewer's interest strong. Discuss what they want. Keep suggesting topics of discussion to them.

4 Be mindful of time. As just stated, there is too much to discuss in 1 hour.

5 Discuss logging, monitoring, alerting, and auditing.

6 Discuss testing and maintainability including debuggability, complexity, security, and privacy.

7 Consider and discuss graceful degradation and failure in the overall system and every component, including silent and disguised failures. Errors can be silent. Never trust anything. Don't trust external or internal systems. Don't trust your own system.

8 Draw system diagrams, flowcharts, and sequence diagrams. Use them as visual aids for your discussions.

9 The system can always be improved. There is always more to discuss.

A discussion of any system design interview question can last for many hours. You will need to focus on certain aspects by suggesting to the interviewer various directions of discussion and asking which direction to go. You have less than 1 hour to communicate or hint the at full extent of your knowledge. You must possess the ability to consider and evaluate relevant details and to smoothly zoom up and down to discuss high-level architecture and relationships and low-level implementation details of every component. If you forget or neglect to mention something, the interviewer will assume you don't know it. One should practice discussing system design questions with fellow engineers to improve oneself in this art. Prestigious companies interview many polished candidates, and every candidate who passes is well-drilled and speaks the language of system design fluently.

The question discussions in this section are examples of the approaches you can take to discuss various topics in a system design interview. Many of these topics are common, so you will see some repetition between the discussions. Pay attention to the use of common industry terms and how many of the sentences uttered within the time-limited discussion are filled with useful information.

The following list is a rough guide. A system design discussion is dynamic, and we should not expect it to progress in the order of this list:

1 Clarify the requirements. Discuss tradeoffs.

2 Draft the API specification.

3 Design the data model. Discuss possible analytics.

4 Discuss failure design, graceful degradation, monitoring, and alerting. Other topics include bottlenecks, load balancing, removing single points of failure, high availability, disaster recovery, and caching.

5 Discuss complexity and tradeoffs, maintenance and decommissioning processes, and costs.

2.1   *Clarify requirements and discuss tradeoffs*

Clarifying the requirements of the question is the first checkbox to tick off during an interview. Chapter 3 describes the details and importance of discussing functional and non-functional requirements.

We end this chapter with a general guide to discussing requirements in an interview. We will go through this exercise in each question of part 2. We emphasize that you keep in mind that your particular interview may be a unique situation, and you should deviate from this guide as required by your situation.

Discuss functional requirements within 10 minutes because that is already ≥20% of the interview time. Nonetheless, attention to detail is critical. Do not write down the functional requirements one at a time and discuss them. You may miss certain requirements. Rather, quickly brainstorm and scribble down a list of functional requirements and then discuss them. We can tell the interviewer that we want to ensure we have captured all crucial requirements, but we also wish to be mindful of time.

We can begin by spending 30 seconds or 1 minute discussing the overall purpose of the system and how it fits into the big-picture business requirements. We can briefly mention endpoints common to nearly all systems, like health endpoints, signup, and login. Anything more than a brief discussion is unlikely to be within the scope of the interview. We then discuss the details of some common functional requirements:

1. Consider user categories/roles:

   a. Who will use this system and how? Discuss and scribble down user stories. Consider various combinations of user categories, such as manual versus programmatic or consumer versus enterprise. For example, a manual/consumer combination involves requests from our consumers via our mobile or browser apps. A programmatic/enterprise combination involves requests from other services or companies.

   b. Technical or nontechnical? Design platforms or services for developers or non-developers. Technical examples include a database service like key-value store, libraries for purposes like consistent hashing, or analytics services. Non-technical questions are typically in the form of "Design this well-known consumer app." In such questions, discuss all categories of users, not just the non-technical consumers of the app.

   c. List the user roles (e.g., buyer, seller, poster, viewer, developer, manager).

   d. Pay attention to numbers. Every functional and non-functional requirement must have a number. Fetch news items? How many news items? How much time? How many milliseconds/seconds/hours/days?

   e. Any communication between users or between users and operations staff?

   f. Ask about i18n and L10n support, national or regional languages, postal address, price, etc. Ask whether multiple currency support is required.

2 Based on the user categories, clarify the scalability requirements. Estimate the number of daily active users and then estimate the daily or hourly request rate. For example, if a search service has 1 billion daily users, each submitting 10 search requests, there are 10 billion daily requests or 420 million hourly requests.

3 Which data should be accessible to which users? Discuss the authentication and authorization roles and mechanisms. Discuss the contents of the response body of the API endpoint. Next, discuss how often is data retrieved—real-time, monthly reports, or another frequency?

4 Search. What are possible use cases that involve search?

5 Analytics is a typical requirement. Discuss possible machine learning requirements, including support for experimentation such as A/B testing or multi-armed bandit. Refer to https://www.optimizely.com/optimization-glossary/ab-testing/ and https://www.optimizely.com/optimization-glossary/multi-armed-bandit/ for introductions to these topics.

6 Scribble down pseudocode function signatures (e.g., `fetchPosts(userId)`) to fetch posts by a certain user and match them to the user stories. Discuss with the interviewer which requirements are needed and which are out of scope.

Always ask, "Are there other user requirements?" and brainstorm these possibilities. Do not allow the interviewer to do the thinking for you. Do not give the interviewer the impression that you want them to do the thinking for you or want them to tell you all the requirements.

Requirements are subtle, and one often misses details even if they think they have clarified them. One reason software development follows agile practices is that requirements are difficult or impossible to communicate. New requirements or restrictions are constantly discovered through the development process. With experience, one learns the clarifying questions to ask.

Display your awareness that a system can be expanded to serve other functional requirements in the future and brainstorm such possibilities.

The interviewer should not expect you to possess all domain knowledge, so you may not think of certain requirements that require specific domain knowledge. What you do need is demonstrate your critical thinking, attention to detail, humility, and willingness to learn.

Next, discuss non-functional requirements. Refer to chapter 3 for a detailed discussion of non-functional requirements. We may need to design our system to serve the entire world population and assume that our product has complete global market dominance. Clarify with your interviewer whether we should design immediately for scalability. If not, they may be more interested in how we consider complicated functional requirements. This includes the data models we design. After we discuss requirements, we can proceed to discuss our system design.

2.2   Draft the API specification

Based on the functional requirements, determine the data that the system's users expect to receive from and send to the system. We will generally spend less than five minutes scrabbling down a draft of the GET, POST, PUT, and DELETE endpoints, including path and query parameters. It is generally inadvisable to linger on drafting the endpoints. Inform the interviewer that there is much more to discuss within our 50 minutes, so we will not use much time here.

You should have already clarified the functional requirements before scribbling these endpoints; you are past the appropriate section of the interview to clarify functional requirements and should not do so here unless you missed anything.

Next, propose an API specification and describe how it satisfies the functional requirements, then briefly discuss it and identify any functional requirements that you may have missed.

2.2.1   Common API endpoints

These are common endpoints of most systems. You can quickly go over these endpoints and clarify that they are out of scope. It is very unlikely that you will need to discuss them in detail, but it never hurts to display that you are detail-oriented while also seeing the big picture.

HEALTH

GET /health is a test endpoint. A 4xx or 5xx response indicates the system has production problems. It may just do a simple database query, or it may return health information such as disk space, statuses of various other endpoints, and application logic checks.

SIGNUP AND LOGIN (AUTHENTICATION)

An app user will typically need to sign up (POST /signup) and log in (POST /login) prior to submitting content to the app. OpenID Connect is a common authentication protocol, discussed in appendix B.

USER AND CONTENT MANAGEMENT

We may need endpoints to get, modify, and delete user details. Many consumer apps provide channels for users to flag/report inappropriate content, such as content that is illegal or violates community guidelines.

2.3   Connections and processing between users and data

In section 2.1, we discussed the types of users and data and which data should be accessible to which users. In section 2.2, we designed API endpoints for users to CRUD (create, read, update, and delete) data. We can now draw diagrams to represent the connections between user and data and to illustrate various system components and the data processing that occurs between them.

Phase 1:

- Draw a box to represent each type of user.
- Draw a box to represent each system that serves the functional requirements.
- Draw the connections between users and systems.

Phase 2:

- Break up request processing and storage.
- Create different designs based on the non-functional requirements, such as real-time versus eventual consistency.
- Consider shared services.

Phase 3:

- Break up the systems into components, which will usually be libraries or services.
- Draw the connections.
- Consider logging, monitoring, and alerting.
- Consider security.

Phase 4:

- Include a summary of our system design.
- Provide any new additional requirements.
- Analyze fault-tolerance. What can go wrong with each component? Network delays, inconsistency, no linearizability. What can we do to prevent and/or mitigate each situation and improve the fault-tolerance of this component and the overall system?

Refer to appendix C for an overview of the *C4 model*, which is a system architecture diagram technique to decompose a system into various levels of abstraction.

2.4 Design the data model

We should discuss whether we are designing the data model from scratch or using existing databases. Sharing databases between services is commonly regarded as an antipattern, so if we are using existing databases, we should build more API endpoints designed for programmatic customers, as well as batch and/or streaming ETL pipelines from and to those other databases as required.

The following are common problems that may occur with shared databases:

- Queries from various services on the same tables may compete for resources. Certain queries, such as UPDATE on many rows, or transactions that contain other long-running queries may lock a table for an extended period of time.

- Schema migrations are more complex. A schema migration that benefits one service may break the DAO code of other services. This means that although an engineer may work only on that service, they need to keep up to date with the low-level details of the business logic and perhaps even the source code of other services that they do not work on, which may be an unproductive use of both their time and the time of other engineers who made those changes and need to communicate it to them and others. More time will be spent in writing and reading documentation and presentation slides and in meetings. Various teams may take time to agree on proposed schema migrations, which may be an unproductive use of engineering time. Other teams may not be able to agree on schema migrations or may compromise on certain changes, which will introduce technical debt and decrease overall productivity.
- The various services that share the same set of databases are restricted to using those specific database technologies (.g., MySQL, HDFS, Cassandra, Kafka, etc.), regardless of how well-suited those technologies are to each service's use cases. Services cannot pick the database technology that best suits their requirements.

This means that in either case we will need to design a new schema for our service. We can use the request and response bodies of the API endpoints we discussed in the previous section as starting points to design our schema, closely mapping each body to a table's schema and probably combining the bodies of read (GET) and write (POST and PUT) requests of the same paths to the same table.

2.4.1 *Example of the disadvantages of multiple services sharing databases*

If we were designing an ecommerce system, we may want a service that can retrieve business metric data, such as the total number of orders in the last seven days. Our teams found that without a source of truth for business metric definitions, different teams were computing metrics differently. For example, should the total number of orders include canceled or refunded orders? What time zone should be used for the cutoff time of "seven days ago"? Does "last seven days" include the present day? The communication overhead between multiple teams to clarify metric definitions was costly and error-prone.

Although computing business metrics uses order data from the Orders service, we decide to form a new team to create a dedicated Metrics service, since metric definitions can be modified independently of order data.

The Metrics service will depend on the Orders service for order data. A request for a metric will be processed as follows:

1 Retrieve the metric.
2 Retrieve the related data from the Orders service.
3 Compute the metric.
4 Return the metric's value.

If both services share the same database, the computation of a metric makes SQL queries on Orders service's tables. Schema migrations become more complex. For example, the Orders team decides that users of the Order table have been making too many large queries on it. After some analysis, the team determined that queries on recent orders are more important and require higher latency than queries on older orders. The team proposes that the Order table should contain only orders from the last year, and older orders will be moved to an Archive table. The Order table can be allocated a larger number of followers/read replicas than the Archive table.

The Metrics team must understand this proposed change and change metric computation to occur on both tables. The Metrics team may object to this proposed change, so the change may not go ahead, and the organizational productivity gain from faster queries on recent order data cannot be achieved.

If the Orders team wishes to move the Order table to Cassandra to use its low write latency while the Metrics service continues using SQL because of its simplicity and because it has a low write rate, the services can no longer share the same database.

2.4.2 *A possible technique to prevent concurrent user update conflicts*

There are many situations where a client application allows multiple users to edit a shared configuration. If an edit to this shared configuration is nontrivial for a user (if a user needs to spend more than a few seconds to enter some information before submitting their edit), it may be a frustrating UX if multiple users simultaneously edit this configuration, and then overwrite each other's changes when they save them. Source control management prevents this for source code, but most other situations involve non-technical users, and we obviously cannot expect them to learn git.

For example, a hotel room booking service may require users to spend some time to enter their check-in and check-out dates and their contact and payment information and then submit their booking request. We should ensure that multiple users do not overbook the room.

Another example may be configuring the contents of a push notification. For example, our company may provide a browser app for employees to configure push notifications sent to our Beigel app (refer to chapter 1). A particular push notification configuration may be owned by a team. We should ensure that multiple team members do not edit the push notification simultaneously and then overwrite each other's changes.

There are many ways of preventing concurrent updates. We present one possible way in this section.

To prevent such situations, we can lock a configuration when it is being edited. Our service may contain an SQL table to store these configurations. We can add a timestamp column to the relevant SQL table that we can name "unix_locked" and string columns "edit_username" and "edit_email." (This schema design is not normalized, but it is usually ok in practice. Ask your interviewer whether they insist on a normalized schema.) We can then expose a PUT endpoint that our UI can use to notify our backend when a user clicks on an edit icon or button to start editing the query string. Referring to figure 2.1, here are a series of steps that may occur when two users decide to edit a push notification at approximately the same time. One user can lock a configuration for a certain period (e.g., 10 minutes), and another user finds that it is locked:

1   Alice and Bob are both viewing the push notification configuration on our Notifications browser app. Alice decides to update the title from "Celebrate National Bagel Day!" to "20% off on National Bagel Day!" She clicks on the Edit button. The following steps occur:

    a   The click event sends a PUT request, which sends her username and email to the backend. The backend's load balancer assigns this request to a host.

    b   Alice's backend host makes two SQL queries, one at a time. First, it determines the current unix_locked time:

```
SELECT unix_locked FROM table_name WHERE config_id = {config_id}.
```

    c   The backend checks whether the "edit_start" timestamp is less than 12 minutes ago. (This includes a 2 minute buffer in case the countdown timer in step 2 started late, and also because hosts' clocks cannot be perfectly synchronized.) If so, it updates the row to indicate to lock the configuration. The UPDATE query sets "edit_start" to the backend's current UNIX time and overwrites the "edit_username" and "edit_email" with Alice's username and email. We need the "unix_locked" filter just in case another user has changed it in the meantime. The UPDATE query returns a Boolean to indicate whether it ran successfully:

```
UPDATE table_name SET unix_locked = {new_time}, edit_username = {username},
    edit_email = {email} WHERE config_id = {config_id} AND unix_locked =
    {unix_locked}
```

    d   If the UPDATE query was successful, the backend returns 200 success to the UI with a response body like {"can_edit": "true"}.

2   The UI opens a page where Alice can make this edit and displays a 10-minute countdown timer. She erases the old title and starts to type the new title.

3   In between the SQL queries of steps 1b and 1c, Bob decides to edit the configuration too:

    a   He clicks on the Edit button, triggering a PUT request, which is assigned to a different host.

    b   The first SQL query returns the same unix_locked time as in step 1b.

    c   The second SQL query is sent just after the query in step 1c. SQL DML queries are sent to the same host (see section 4.3.2). This means this query cannot run until the query in step 1c completes. When the query runs, the unix_time value had changed, so the row is not updated, and the SQL service returns false to the backend. The backend returns a 200 success to the UI with a response body like {"can_edit": "false", "edit_start": "1655836315", "edit_username": "Alice", "edit_email": "alice@beigel.com"}.

     d The UI computes the number of minutes Alice has left and displays a banner notification that states, "Alice (alice@beigel.com) is making an edit. Try again in 8 minutes."

4 Alice finishes her edits and clicks on the Save button. This triggers a PUT request to the backend, which saves her edited values and erases "unix_locked", "edit_start", "edit_username", and "edit_email".

5 Bob clicks on the Edit button again, and now he can make edits. If Bob had clicked the Edit button at least 12 minutes after the "edit_start" value, he can also make edits. If Alice had not saved her changes before her countdown expires, the UI will display a notification to inform her that she cannot save her changes anymore.

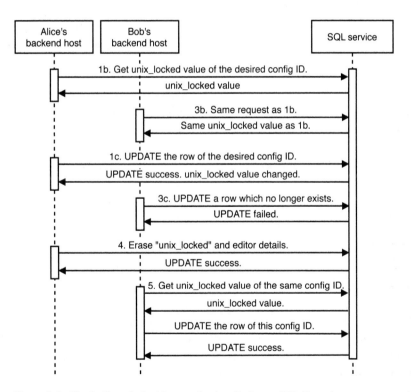

Figure 2.1   Illustration of a locking mechanism that uses SQL. Here, two users request to update the same SQL row that corresponds to the same configuration ID. Alice's host first gets the unix_locked timestamp value of the desired configuration ID, then sends an UPDATE query to update that row, so Alice has locked that specific configuration ID. Right after her host sent that query in step 1c, Bob's host sends an UPDATE query, too, but Alice's host had changed the unix_locked value, so Bob's UPDATE query cannot run successfully, and Bob cannot lock that configuration ID.

What if Bob visits the push notification configuration page after Alice starts editing the configuration? A possible UI optimization at this point is to disable the Edit button and display the banner notification, so Bob knows he cannot make edits because Alice is doing so. To implement this optimization, we can add the three fields to the GET response for the push notification configuration, and the UI should process those fields and render the Edit button as "enabled" or "disabled."

Refer to https://vladmihalcea.com/jpa-entity-version-property-hibernate/ for an overview of version tracking with Jakarta Persistence API and Hibernate.

2.5   Logging, monitoring, and alerting

There are many books on logging, monitoring, and alerting. In this section, we will discuss key concepts that one must mention in an interview and dive into specific concepts that one may be expected to discuss. Never forget to mention monitoring to the interviewer.

2.5.1   The importance of monitoring

Monitoring is critical for every system to provide visibility into the customer's experience. We need to identify bugs, degradations, unexpected events, and other weaknesses in our system's ability to satisfy current and possible future functional and non-functional requirements.

Web services may fail at any time. We may categorize these failures by urgency and how quickly they need attention. High-urgency failures must be attended to immediately. Low-urgency failures may wait until we complete higher-priority tasks. Our requirements and discretion determine the multiple levels of urgency that we define.

If our service is a dependency of other services, every time those services experience degradations, their teams may identify our service as a potential source of those degradations, so we need a logging and monitoring setup that will allow us to easily investigate possible degradations and answer their questions.

2.5.2   Observability

This leads us to the concept of observability. The observability of our system is a measure of how well-instrumented it is and how easily we can find out what's going on inside it (John Arundel & Justin Domingus, *Cloud Native DevOps with Kubernetes*, p. 272, O'Reilly Media Inc, 2019.). Without logging, metrics, and tracing, our system is opaque. We will not easily know how well a code change meant to decrease P99 of a particular endpoint by 10% works in production. If P99 decreased by much less than 10% or much more than 10%, we should be able to derive relevant insights from our instrumentation on why our predictions fell short.

Refer to Google's SRE book (https://sre.google/sre-book/monitoring-distributed -systems/#xref_monitoring_golden-signals) for a detailed discussion of the four golden signals of monitoring: latency, traffic, errors, and saturation.

1   *Latency*—We can set up alerts for latency that exceeds our service-level agreement (SLA), such as more than 1 second. Our SLA may be for any individual request more than 1 second, or alerts that trigger for a P99 over a sliding window (e.g., 5 seconds, 10 seconds, 1 minute, 5 minutes).

2   *Traffic*—Measured in HTTP requests per second. We can set up alerts for various endpoints that trigger if there is too much traffic. We can set appropriate numbers based on the load limit determined in our load testing.

3   *Errors*—Set up high-urgency alerts for 4xx or 5xx response codes that must be immediately addressed. Trigger low-urgency (or high urgency, depending on your requirements) alerts on failed audits.

4   *Saturation*—Depending on whether our system's constraint is CPU, memory, or I/O, we can set utilization targets that should not be exceeded. We can set up alerts that trigger if utilization targets are reached. Another example is storage utilization. We can set up an alert that triggers if storage (due to file or database usage) may run out within hours or days.

The three instruments of monitoring and alerting are metrics, dashboards, and alerts. A *metric* is a variable we measure, like error count, latency, or processing time. A *dashboard* provides a summary view of a service's core metrics. An *alert* is a notification sent to service owners in a reaction to some problem happening in the service. Metrics, dashboards, and alerts are populated by processing log data. We may provide a common browser UI to create and manage them more easily.

OS metrics like CPU utilization, memory utilization, disk utilization, and network I/O can be included in our dashboard and used to tune the hardware allocation for our service as appropriate or detect memory leaks.

On a backend application, our backend framework may log each request by default or provide simple annotations on the request methods to turn on logging. We can put logging statements in our application code. We can also manually log the values of certain variables within our code to help us understand how the customer's request was processed.

Scholl et al. (Boris Scholl, Trent Swanson & Peter Jausovec. *Cloud Native: Using Containers, Functions, and Data to build Next-Generation Applications.* O'Reilly, 2019. p. 145.) states the following general considerations in logging:

- Log entries should be structured to be easy to parse by tools and automation.
- Each entry should contain a unique identifier to trace requests across services and share between users and developers.
- Log entries should be small, easy to read, and useful.
- Timestamps should use the same time zone and time format. A log that contains entries with different time zones and time formats is difficult to read or parse.
- Categorize log entries. Start with debug, info, and error.
- Do not log private or sensitive information like passwords or connection strings. A common term to refer to such information is Personally Identifiable Information (PII).

Logs that are common to most services include the following. Many request-level logging tools have default configurations to log these details:

- Host logging:
  - CPU and memory utilization on the hosts
  - Network I/O
- Request-level logging captures the details of every request:
  - Latency
  - Who and when made the request
  - Function name and line number
  - Request path and query parameters, headers, and body
  - Return status code and body (including possible error messages)

In a particular system, we may be particularly interested in certain user experiences, such as errors. We can place log statements within our application and set up customized metrics, dashboards, and alerts that focus on these user experiences. For example, to focus on 5xx errors due to application bugs, we can create metrics, dashboards and alerts that process certain details like request parameters and return status codes and error messages, if any.

We should also log events to monitor how well our system satisfies our unique functional and non-functional requirements. For example, if we build a cache, we want to log cache faults, hits, and misses. Metrics should include the counts of faults, hits, and misses.

In enterprise systems, we may wish to give users some access to monitoring or even build monitoring tools specifically for users for example, customers can create dashboards to track the state of their requests and filter and aggregate metrics and alerts by categories such as URL paths.

We should also discuss how to address possible silent failures. These may be due to bugs in our application code or dependencies such as libraries and other services that allow the response code to be 2xx when it should be 4xx or 5xx or may indicate your service requires logging and monitoring improvements.

Besides logging, monitoring, and alerting on individual requests, we may also create batch and streaming audit jobs to validate our system's data. This is akin to monitoring our system's data integrity. We can create alerts that trigger if the results of the job indicate failed validations. Such a system is discussed in chapter 10.

2.5.3   *Responding to alerts*

A team that develops and maintains a service may typically consist of a few engineers. This team may set up an on-call schedule for the service's high-urgency alerts. An on-call engineer may not be intimately familiar with the cause of a particular alert, so we should prepare a runbook that contains a list of the alerts, possible causes, and procedures to find and fix the cause.

As we prepare the runbook, if we find that certain runbook instructions consist of a series of commands that can easily be copied and pasted to solve the problem (e.g., restarting a host), these steps should be automated in the application, along with logging that these steps were run (Mike Julian, *Practical Monitoring,* chapter 3, O'Reilly Media Inc, 2017). Failure to implement automated failure recovery when possible is runbook abuse. If certain runbook instructions consist of running commands to view particuar metrics, we should display these metrics on our dashboard.

A company may have a Site Reliability Engineering (SRE) team, which consists of engineers who develop tools and processes to ensure high reliability of critical services and are often on-call for these critical services. If our service obtains SRE coverage, a build of our service may have to satisfy the SRE team's criteria before it can be deployed. This criteria typically consists of high unit test coverage, a functional test suite that passes SRE review, and a well-written runbook that has good coverage and description of possible problems and has been vetted by the SRE team.

After the outage is resolved, we should author a postmortem that identifies what went wrong, why, and how the team will ensure it does not recur. Postmortems should be blameless, or employees may attempt to downplay or hide problems instead of addressing them.

Based on identifying patterns in the actions that are taken to resolve the problem, we can identify ways to automate the mitigation of these problems, introducing self-healing characteristics to the system.

2.5.4 *Application-level logging tools*

The open-source ELK (Elasticsearch, Logstash, Beats, Kibana) suite and the paid-service Splunk are common application-level logging tools. Logstash is used to collect and manage logs. Elasticsearch is a search engine, useful for storage, indexing, and searching through logs. Kibana is for visualization and dashboarding of logs, using Elasticsearch as a data source and for users to search logs. Beats was added in 2015 as a light data shipper that ships data to Elasticsearch or Logstash in real time.

In this book, whenever we state that we are logging any event, it is understood that we log the event to a common ELK service used for logging by other services in our organization.

There are numerous monitoring tools, which may be proprietary or FOSS (Free and open-source software). We will briefly discuss a few of these tools, but an exhaustive list, detailed discussion, and comparison are outside the scope of this book.

These tools differ in characteristics such as

- Features. Various tools may offer all or a subset of logging, monitoring, alerting, and dashboarding.
- Support for various operating systems and other types of equipment besides servers, such as load balancers, switches, modems, routers, or network cards, etc.
- Resource consumption.

- Popularity, which is proportionate to the ease of finding engineers familiar with the system.
- Developer support, such as the frequency of updates.

They also differ in subjective characteristics like

- Learning curve.
- Difficulty of manual configuration and the likelihood of a new user to make mistakes.
- Ease of integration with other software and services.
- Number and severity of bugs.
- UX. Some of the tools have browser or desktop UI clients, and various users may prefer the UX of one UI over another.

FOSS monitoring tools include the following:

- *Prometheus + Grafana*—Prometheus for monitoring, Grafana for visualization and dashboarding.
- *Sensu*—A monitoring system that uses Redis to store data. We can configure Sensu to send alerts to a third-party alerting service.
- *Nagios*—A monitoring and alerting system.
- *Zabbix*—A monitoring system that includes a monitoring dashboard tool.

Proprietary tools include Splunk, Datadog, and New Relic.

A *time series database* (TSDB) is a system that is optimized for storing and serving time series, such as the continuous writes that happen with logging time series data. Examples include the following. Most queries may be made on recent data, so old data will be less valuable, and we can save storage by configuring down sampling on TSDB. This rolls up old data by computing averages over defined intervals. Only these averages are saved, and the original data is deleted, so less storage is used. The data retention period and resolution depend on our requirements and budget.

To further reduce the cost of storing old data, we can compress it or use a cheap storage medium like tape or optical disks. Refer to https://www.zdnet.com/article/could -the-tech-beneath-amazons-glacier-revolutionise-data-storage/ or https://arstechnica .com/information-technology/2015/11/to-go-green-facebook-puts-petabytes-of-cat -pics-on-ice-and-likes-windfarming/ for examples of custom setups such as hard disk storage servers that slow down or stop when not in use:

- *Graphite*—Commonly used to log OS metrics (though it can monitor other setups like websites and applications), which are visualized with the Grafana web application.
- *Prometheus*—Also typically visualized with Grafana.
- *OpenTSDB*—A distributed, scalable TSDB that uses HBase.
- *InfluxDB*—An open-source TSDB written in Go.

Prometheus is an open-source monitoring system built around a time series database. Prometheus pulls from target HTTP endpoints to request metrics, and a Pushgateway pushes alerts to Alertmanager, which we can configure to push to various channels such as email and PagerDuty. We can use Prometheus query language (PromQL) to explore metrics and draw graphs.

Nagios is a proprietary legacy IT infrastructure monitoring tool that focuses on server, network, and application monitoring. It has hundreds of third-party plugins, web interfaces, and advanced visualization dashboarding tools.

2.5.5 *Streaming and batch audit of data quality*

Data quality is an informal term that refers to ensuring that data represents the real-world construct to which it refers and can be used for its intended purposes. For example, if a particular table that is updated by an ETL job is missing some rows that were produced by that job, the data quality is poor.

Database tables can be continuously and/or periodically audited to detect data quality problems. We can implement such auditing by defining streaming and batch ETL jobs to validate recently added and modified data.

This is particularly useful to detect silent errors, which are errors that were undetected by earlier validation checks, such as validation checks that occur during processing of a service request.

We can extend this concept to a hypothetical shared service for database batch auditing, discussed in chapter 10.

2.5.6 *Anomaly detection to detect data anomalies*

Anomaly detection is a machine learning concept to detect unusual datapoints. A full description of machine-learning concepts is outside the scope of this book. This section briefly describes anomaly detection to detect unusual datapoints. This is useful both to ensure data quality and for deriving analytical insights, as an unusual rise or fall of a particular metric can indicate problems with data processing or changing market conditions.

In its most basic form, anomaly detection consists of feeding a continuous stream of data into an anomaly detection algorithm. After it processes a defined number of datapoints, referred to in machine learning as the training set, the anomaly detection algorithm develops a statistical model. The model's purpose is to accept a datapoint and assign a probability that the datapoint is anomalous. We can validate that this model works by using it on a set of datapoints called the validation set, where each datapoint has been manually labeled as normal or anomalous. Finally, we can quantify accuracy characteristics of the model by testing it on another manually-labeled set, called the test set.

Many parameters are manually tunable, such as which machine-learning models are used, the number of datapoints in each of the three sets, and the model's parameters to adjust characteristics, such as precision vs. recall. Machine-learning concepts such as precision and recall are outside the scope of this book.

In practice, this approach to detecting data anomalies is complex and costly to implement, maintain, and use. It is reserved for critical datasets.

2.5.7   Silent errors and auditing

Silent errors may occur due to bugs where an endpoint may return status code 200 even though errors occurred. We can write batch ETL jobs to audit recent changes to our databases and raise alerts on failed audits. Further details are provided in chapter 10.

2.5.8   Further reading on observability

- Michael Hausenblas, *Cloud Observability in Action*, Manning Publications, 2023. A guide to applying observability practices to cloud-based serverless and Kubernetes environments.
- https://www.manning.com/liveproject/configure-observability. A hands-on course in implementing a service template's observability-related features.
- Mike Julian, *Practical Monitoring*, O'Reilly Media Inc, 2017. A dedicated book on observability best practices, incident response, and antipatterns.
- Boris Scholl, Trent Swanson, and Peter Jausovec. *Cloud Native: Using Containers, Functions, and Data to build Next-Generation Applications.* O'Reilly, 2019. Emphasizes that observability is integral to cloud-native applications.
- John Arundel and Justin Domingus, *Cloud Native DevOps with Kubernetes,* chapters 15 and 16, O'Reilly Media Inc, 2019. These chapters discuss observability, monitoring, and metrics in cloud-native applications.

2.6   Search bar

Search is a common feature of many applications. Most frontend applications provide users with search bars to rapidly find their desired data. The data can be indexed in an Elasticsearch cluster.

2.6.1   Introduction

A search bar is a common UI component in many apps. It can be just a single search bar or may contain other frontend components for filtering. Figure 2.2 is an example of a search bar.

Figure 2.2   Google search bar with drop-down menus for filtering results. Image from Google.

Common techniques of implementing search are:

1 Search on a SQL database with the LIKE operator and pattern matching. A query may resemble something like SELECT <column> FROM <table> WHERE Lower(<column>) LIKE "%Lower(<search_term>)%".

2 Use a library such as match-sorter (https://github.com/kentcdodds/match-sorter), which is a JavaScript library that accepts search terms and does matching and sorting on the records. Such a solution needs to be separately implemented on each client application. This is a suitable and technically simple solution for up to a few GB of text data (i.e., up to millions of records). A web application usually downloads its data from a backend, and this data is unlikely to be more than a few megabytes, or the application will not be scalable to millions of users. A mobile application may store data locally, so it is theoretically possible to have GBs of data, but data synchronization between millions of phones may be impractical.

3 Use a search engine such as Elasticsearch. This solution is scalable and can handle PBs of data.

The first technique has numerous limitations and should only be used as a quick temporary implementation that will soon be either discarded or changed to a proper search engine. Disadvantages include:

- Difficult to customize the search query.
- No sophisticated features like boosting, weight, fuzzy search, or text preprocessing such as stemming or tokenization.

This discussion assumes that individual records are small; that is, they are text records, not video records. For video records, the indexing and search operations are not directly on the video data, but on accompanying text metadata. The implementation of indexing and search in search engines is outside the scope of this book.

We will reference these techniques in the question discussions in part 2, paying much more attention to using Elasticsearch.

2.6.2 *Search bar implementation with Elasticsearch*

An organization can have a shared Elasticsearch cluster to serve the search requirements of many of its services. In this section, we first describe a basic Elasticsearch full-text search query, then the basic steps for adding Elasticsearch to your service given an existing Elasticsearch cluster. We will not discuss Elasticsearch cluster setup in this book or describe Elasticsearch concepts and terminology in detail. We will use our Beigel app (from chapter 1) for our examples.

To provide basic full-text search with fuzzy matching, we can attach our search bar to a GET endpoint that forwards the query to our Elasticsearch service. An Elasticsearch query is done against an Elasticsearch index (akin to a database in a relational database). If the GET query returns a 2xx response with a list of search results, the frontend loads a results page that displays the list.

For example, if our Beigel app provides a search bar, and a user searches for the term "sesame," the Elasticsearch request may resemble either of the following.

The search term may be contained in a query parameter, which allows exact matches only:

```
GET /beigel-index/_search?q=sesame
```

We can also use a JSON request body, which allows us to use the full Elasticsearch DSL, which is outside the scope of this book:

```
GET /beigel-index/_search
{
  "query": {z6
    "match": {
      "query": "sesame",
      "fuzziness": "AUTO"
    }
  }
}
```

`"fuzziness": "AUTO"` is to allow fuzzy (approximate) matching, which has many use cases, such as if the search term or search results contain misspellings.

The results are returned as a JSON array of hits sorted by decreasing relevance, such as the following example. Our backend can pass the results back to the frontend, which can parse and present them to the user.

2.6.3   *Elasticsearch index and ingestion*

Creating an Elasticsearch index consists of ingesting the documents that should be searched when the user submits a search query from a search bar, followed by the indexing operation.

We can keep the index updated with periodic or event-triggered indexing or delete requests using the Bulk API.

To change the index's mapping, one way is to create a new index and drop the old one. Another way is to use Elasticsearch's reindexing operation, but this is expensive because the internal Lucene commit operation occurs synchronously after every write request (https://www.elastic.co/guide/en/elasticsearch/reference/current/index-modules -translog.html#index-modules-translog).

Creating an Elasticsearch index requires all data that you wish to search to be stored in the Elasticsearch document store, which increases our overall storage requirements. There are various optimizations that involve sending only a subset of data to be indexed.

Table 2.1 is an approximate mapping between SQL and Elasticsearch terminology.

Table 2.1   Approximate mapping between SQL and Elasticsearch terminology. There are differences between the mapped terms, and this table should not be taken at face value. This mapping is meant for an Elasticsearch beginner with SQL experience to use as a starting point for further learning.

SQL	Elasticsearch
Database	Index
Partition	Shard
Table	Type (deprecated without replacement)
Column	Field
Row	Document
Schema	Mapping
Index	Everything is indexed

2.6.4   Using Elasticsearch in place of SQL

Elasticsearch can be used like SQL. Elasticsearch has the concept of query context vs. filter context (https://www.elastic.co/guide/en/elasticsearch/reference/current/query-filter-context.html). From the documentation, in a filter context, a query clause answers the question, "Does this document match this query clause?" The answer is a simple yes or no; no scores are calculated. In a query context, a query clause answers the question, "How well does this document match this query clause?". The query clause determines whether the document matches and calculates a relevance score. Essentially, query context is analogous to SQL queries, while filter context is analogous to search.

Using Elasticsearch in place of SQL will allow both searching and querying, eliminate duplicate storage requirements, and eliminate the maintenance overhead of the SQL database. I have seen services that use only Elasticsearch for data storage.

However, Elasticsearch is often used to complement relational databases instead of replacing them. It is a schemaless database and does not have the concept of normalization or relations between tables such as primary key and foreign key. Unlike SQL, Elasticsearch also does not offer Command Query Responsibility Segregation (refer to section 1.4.6) or ACID.

Moreover, the Elasticsearch Query Language (EQL) is a JSON-based language, and it is verbose and presents a learning curve. SQL is familiar to non-developers, such as data analysts, and non-technical personnel. Non-technical users can easily learn basic SQL within a day.

Elasticsearch SQL was introduced in June 2018 in the release of Elasticsearch 6.3.0 (https://www.elastic.co/blog/an-introduction-to-elasticsearch-sql-with-practical-examples-part-1 and https://www.elastic.co/what-is/elasticsearch-sql). It supports all common filter and aggregation operations (https://www.elastic.co/guide/en/elasticsearch/reference/current/sql-functions.html). This is a promising development. SQL's dominance is well-established, but in the coming years, it is possible that more services will use Elasticsearch for all their data storage as well as search.

2.6.5   *Implementing search in our services*

Mentioning search during the user stories and functional requirements discussion of the interview demonstrates customer focus. Unless the question is to design a search engine, it is unlikely that we will describe implementing search beyond creating Elasticsearch indexes, ingesting and indexing, making search queries, and processing results. Most of the question discussions of part 2 discuss search in this manner.

2.6.6   *Further reading on search*

Here are more resources on Elasticsearch and indexing:

- https://www.elastic.co/guide/en/elasticsearch/reference/current/index.html. The official Elasticsearch guide.
- Madhusudhan Konda, *Elasticsearch in Action (Second Edition)*, Manning Publications, 2023. A hands-on guide to developing fully functional search engines with Elasticsearch and Kibana.
- https://www.manning.com/livevideo/elasticsearch-7-and-elastic-stack. A course on Elasticsearch 7 and Elastic Stack.
- https://www.manning.com/liveproject/centralized-logging-in-the-cloud-with -elasticsearch-and-kibana. A hands-on course on logging in the cloud with Elasticsearch and Kibana.
- https://stackoverflow.com/questions/33858542/how-to-really-reindex-data -in-elasticsearch. This is a good alternative to the official Elasticsearch guide regarding how to update an Elasticsearch index.
- https://developers.soundcloud.com/blog/how-to-reindex-1-billion-documents -in-1-hour-at-soundcloud. A case study of a large reindexing operation.

2.7   *Other discussions*

When we reach a point in our discussion where our system design satisfies our requirements, we can discuss other topics. This section briefly discusses a few possible topics of further discussion.

2.7.1   *Maintaining and extending the application*

We've discussed the requirements at the beginning of the interview and have established a system design for them. We can continue to improve our design to better serve our requirements.

We can also expand the discussion to other possible requirements. Anyone who works in the tech industry knows that application development is never complete. There are always new and competing requirements. Users submit feedback they want developed or changed. We monitor the traffic and request contents of our API endpoints to make scaling and development decisions. There is constant discussion on what features to develop, maintain, deprecate, and decommission. We can discuss these topics:

- Maintenance may already be discussed during the interview. Which system components rely on technology (such as software packages), and which are developed fastest and require the most maintenance work? How will we handle upgrades that introduce breaking changes in any component?

- Features we may need to develop in the future and the system design.

- Features that may not be needed in the future and how to gracefully deprecate and decommission them. What is an adequate level of user support to provide during this process and how to best provide it?

2.7.2 Supporting other types of users

We can extend the service to support other types of users. If we focused on either consumer or enterprise, manual or programmatic, we may discuss extending the system to support the other user categories. We can discuss extending the current services, building new services, and the tradeoffs of both approaches.

2.7.3 Alternative architectural decisions

During the earlier part of the interview, we should have discussed alternative architectural decisions. We can revisit them in greater detail.

2.7.4 Usability and feedback

Usability is a measure of how well our users can use our system to effectively and efficiently achieve the desired goals. It is an assessment of how easy our user interface is to use. We can define usability metrics, log the required data, and implement a batch ETL job to periodically compute these metrics and update a dashboard that displays them. Usability metrics can be defined based on how we intend our users to use our system.

For example, if we made a search engine, we want our users to find their desired result quickly. One possible metric can be the average index of the result list that a user clicks on. We want the results to be ordered in decreasing relevance, and we assume that a low average chosen index indicates that a user found their desired result close to the top of the list.

Another example metric is the amount of help users need from our support department when they use our application. It is ideal for our application to be self-service; that is, a user can perform their desired tasks entirely within the application without having to ask for help. If our application has a help desk, this can be measured by the number of help desk tickets created per day or week. A high number of help desk tickets indicates that our application is not self-service.

Usability can also be measured with user surveys. A common usability survey metric is *Net Promoter Score (NPS)*. NPS is defined as the percentage of customers rating their likelihood to recommend our application to a friend or colleague as 9 or 10 minus the percentage rating this at 6 or below on a scale of 0 to 1,083.

We can create UI components within our application for users to submit feedback. For example, our web UI may have an HTML link or form for users to email feedback and comments. If we do not wish to use email, because of reasons such as possible spam, we can create an API endpoint to submit feedback and attach our form submission to it.

Good logging will aid the reproducibility of bugs by helping us match the user's feedback with her logged activities.

2.7.5   *Edge cases and new constraints*

Near the end of the interview, the interviewer may introduce edge cases and new constraints, limited only to the imagination. They may consist of new functional requirements or pushing certain non-functional requirements to the extreme. You may have anticipated some of these edge cases during requirements planning. We can discuss if we can make tradeoffs to fulfill them or redesign our architecture to support our current requirements as well as these new requirements. Here are some examples.

- New functional requirements: We designed a sales service that supports credit card payments. What if our payment system needs to be customizable to support different credit card payment requirements in each country? What if we also need to support other payment types like store credit? What if we need to support coupon codes?
- We designed a text search service. How may we extend it to images, audio, and video?
- We designed a hotel room booking service. What if the user needs to change rooms? We'll need to find an available room for them, perhaps in another hotel.
- What if we decide to add social networking features to our news feed recommendation service?

Scalability and performance:

- What if a user has one million followers or one million recipients of their messages? Can we accept a long P99 message delivery time? Or do we need to design for better performance?
- What if we need to perform an accurate audit of our sales data for the last 10 years?

Latency and throughput:

- What if our P99 message delivery time needs to be within 500 ms?
- If we designed a video streaming service that does not accommodate live streaming, how may we modify the design to support live streaming? How may we support simultaneously streaming of a million high-resolution videos across 10 billion devices?

Availability and fault-tolerance:

- We designed a cache that didn't require high availability since all our data is also in the database. What if we want high availability, at least for certain data?
- What if our sales service was used for high-frequency trading? How may we increase its availability?
- How may each component in your system fail? How may we prevent or mitigate these failures?

Cost:

- We may have made expensive design decisions to support low latency and high performance. What may we trade for lower costs?
- How may we gracefully decommission our service if required?
- Did we consider portability? How may we move our application to the cloud (or off the cloud)? What are the tradeoffs in making our application portable? (Higher costs and complexity.) Consider MinIO (https://min.io/) for portable object storage.

Every question in part 2 of this book ends with a list of topics for further discussion.

2.7.6 *Cloud-native concepts*

We may discuss addressing the non-functional requirements via cloud-native concepts like microservices, service mesh and sidecar for shared services (Istio), containerization (Docker), orchestration (Kubernetes), automation (Skaffold, Jenkins), and infrastructure as code (Terraform, Helm). A detailed discussion of these topics is outside the scope of this book. Interested readers can easily find dedicated books or online materials.

2.8 *Post-interview reflection and assessment*

You will improve your interview performance as you go through more interviews. To help you learn as much as possible from each interview, you should write a post-interview reflection as soon as possible after each interview. Then you will have the best possible written record of your interview, and you can write your honest critical assessment of your interview performance.

2.8.1 *Write your reflection as soon as possible after the interview*

To help with this process, at the end of an interview, politely ask for permission to take photos of your diagrams, but do not persist if permission is denied. Carry a pen and a paper notebook with you in your bag. If you cannot take photos, use the earliest possible opportunity to redraw your diagrams from memory into your notebook. Next, scribble down as much detail you can recall.

You should write your reflection as soon as possible after the interview, when you can still remember many details. You may be tired after your interview, but it is counterproductive to relax and possibly forget information valuable to improving your future interview performance. Immediately go home or back to your hotel room and write your reflection, so you may write it in a comfortable and distraction-free environment.

Your reflection may have the following outline:

1   Header:
   a   The company and group the interview was for.
   b   The interview's date.
   c   Your interviewer's name and job title.
   d   The question that the interviewer asked.
   e   Were diagrams from your photos or redrawn from memory?
2   Divide the interview into approximate 10-minute sections. Place your diagrams within the sections when you started drawing them. Your photos may contain multiple diagrams, so you may need to split your photos into their separate diagrams.
3   Fill in the sections with as much detail of the interview as you can recall.
   a   What you said.
   b   What you drew.
   c   What the interviewer said.
4   Write your personal assessment and reflections. Your assessments may be imprecise, so you should aim to improve them with practice.
   a   Try to find the interviewer's resume or LinkedIn profile.
   b   Put yourself in the interviewer's shoes. Why do you think the interviewer chose that system design question? What did you think the interviewer expected?
   c   The interviewer's expressions and body language. Did the interviewer seem satisfied or unsatisfied with your statements and your drawings? Which were they? Did the interviewer interrupt or was eager to discuss any statements you made? What statements were they?
5   In the coming days, if you happen to recall more details, append them to these as separate sections, so you do not accidentally introduce inaccuracies into your original reflection.

While you are writing your reflection, ask yourself questions such as the following:

- What questions did the interviewer ask you about your design?
- Did the interviewer question your statements by asking , for example, "Are you sure?"
- What did the interviewer not tell you? Do you believe this was done on purpose to see if you would mention it, or might the interviewer have lacked this knowledge?

When you have finished your reflection and recollections, take a well-deserved break.

2.8.2 *Writing your assessment*

Writing your assessment serves to help you learn as much as possible about your areas of proficiency and deficiency that you demonstrated at the interview. Begin writing your assessment within a few days of the interview.

Before you start researching the question that you were asked, first write down any additional thoughts on the following. The purpose is for you to be aware of the current limit of your knowledge and how polished you are at a system design interview.

2.8.3 *Details you didn't mention*

It is impossible to comprehensively discuss a system within 50 minutes. You choose which details to mention within that time. Based on your current knowledge (i.e., before you begin your research), what other details do you think you could have added? Why didn't you mention them during the interview?

Did you consciously choose not to discuss them? Why? Did you think those details were irrelevant or too low level, or were there other reasons you decided to use the interview time to discuss other details?

Was it due to insufficient time? How could you have managed the interview time better, so you had time to discuss it?

Were you unfamiliar with the material? Now you are clearly aware of this shortcoming. Study the material so you can describe it better.

Were you tired? Was it due to lack of sleep? Should you have rested more the day before instead of cramming too much? Was it from the interviews before this one? Should you have requested a short break before the interview? Perhaps the aroma of a cup of coffee on the interview table will improve your alertness.

Were you nervous? Were you intimidated by the interviewer or other aspects of the situation? Look up the numerous online resources on how to keep calm.

Were you burdened by the weight of expectations of yourself or others? Remember to keep things in perspective. There are numerous good companies. Or you may be lucky and enter a company that isn't prestigious but has excellent business performance in the future so your experience and equity become valuable. You know that you are humble and determined to keep learning every day, and no matter what, this will be one of many experiences that you are determined to learn as much from as possible to improve your performance in the many interviews to come.

Which details were probably incorrect? This indicates concepts that you are unfamiliar with. Do your research and learn these concepts better?

Now, you should find resources on the question that was asked. You may search in books and online resources such as the following:

- Google
- Websites such as http://highscalability.com/
- YouTube videos

As emphasized throughout this book, there are many possible approaches to a system design question. The materials you find will share similarities and also have numerous differences from each other. Compare your reflection to the materials that you found. Examine how each of those resources did the following compared to you:

- Clarifying the question. Did you ask intelligent questions? What points did you miss?

- Diagrams. Did the materials contain understandable flow charts? Compare the high-level architecture diagrams and low-level component design diagrams with your own.

- How well does their high-level architecture address the requirements? What tradeoffs were made? Do you think the tradeoffs were too costly? What technologies were chosen and why?

- Communication proficiency.
  - How much of the material did you understand the first time you read or watched it?
  - What did you not understand? Was it due to your lack of knowledge, or was the presentation unclear? What can be changed so that you will understand it the first time? Answering these questions improves your ability to clearly and concisely communicate complex and intricate ideas.

You can always add more material to your assessment at any time in the future. Even months after the interview, you may have new insights into all manner of topics, ranging from areas of improvement to alternative approaches you could have suggested, and you can add these insights to your assessment then. Extract as much value as possible from your interview experiences.

You can and should discuss the question with others, but never disclose the company where you were asked this question. Respect the privacy of your interviewers and the integrity of the interview process. We are all ethically and professionally obliged to maintain a level playing field so companies can hire on merit, and we can work and learn from other competent engineers. Industry productivity and compensation will benefit from all of us doing our part.

2.8.4   *Interview feedback*

Ask for interview feedback. You may not receive much feedback if the company has a policy of not providing specific feedback, but it never hurts to ask.

The company may request feedback by email or over the phone. You should provide interview feedback if asked. Remind yourself that even though there will be no effect on the hiring decision, you can help the interviewers as a fellow engineer.

2.9   *Interviewing the company*

In this book, we have been focused on how to handle a system design interview as the candidate. This section discusses some questions that you, as the candidate, may wish to ask to decide whether this company is where you wish to invest the next few years of your finite life.

The interview process goes both ways. The company wants to understand your experience, expertise, and suitability to fill the role with the best candidate it can find. You will spend at least a few years of your life at this company, so you must work with the best people and development practices and philosophy that you can find, which will allow you to develop your engineering skills as much as possible.

Here are some ideas to estimate how you can develop your engineering skills.

Before the interview, read the company's engineering blog to understand more about the following. If there are too many articles, read the top 10 most popular ones and those most relevant to your position. For each article about a tool, understand the following:

1 What is this tool?

2 Who uses it?

3 What does it do? How does it do these things? How does it do certain things similarly or differently from other similar tools? What can it do that other tools cannot? How does it do these things? What can't it do that other tools can?

Consider writing down at least two questions about each article. Before your interview, look through your questions and plan which ones to ask during the interview.

Some points to understand about the company include the following:

- The company's technology stack in general.
- The data tools and infrastructure the company uses.
- Which tools were bought, and which were developed? How are these decisions made?
- Which tools are open source?
- What other open-source contributions has the company made?
- The history and development of various engineering projects.
- The quantity and breakdown of engineering resources the projects consumed—the VP and director overseeing the project, and the composition, seniority, expertise, and experience of the engineering managers, project managers, and engineers (frontend, backend, data engineers and scientists, mobile, security, etc.).
- The status of the tools. How well did the tools anticipate and address their users' requirements? What are the best experiences and pain points with the company's

tools, as reflected in frequent feedback? Which ones were abandoned, and why? How do these tools stack up to competitors and to the state of the art?

- What has the company or the relevant teams within the company done to address these points?

- What are the experiences of engineers with the company's CI/CD tools? How often do engineers run into problems with CI/CD? Are there incidents where CI builds succeed but CD deployments fail? How much time do they spend to troubleshoot these problems? How many messages were sent to the relevant help desk channels in the last month, divided by the number of engineers?

- What projects are planned, and what needs do they fulfill? What is the engineering department's strategic vision?

- What were the organizational-wide migrations in the last two years? Examples of migrations:

  - Shift services from bare metal to a cloud vendor or between cloud vendors.

  - Stop using certain tools (e.g., a database like Cassandra, a particular monitoring solution).

- Have there been sudden U-turns—for example, migrating from bare metal to Google Cloud Platform followed by migrating to AWS just a year later? How much were these U-turns motivated by unpredictable versus overlooked or political factors?

- Have there been any security breaches in the history of the company, how serious were they, and what is the risk of future breaches? This is a sensitive question, and companies will only reveal what is legally required.

- The overall level of the company's engineering competence.

- The management track record, both in the current and previous roles.

Be especially critical of your prospective manager's technical background. As an engineer or engineering manager, never accept a non-technical engineering manager, especially a charismatic one. An engineering manager who cannot critically evaluate engineering work, cannot make good decisions on sweeping changes in engineering processes or lead the execution of such changes (e.g., cloud-native processes like moving from manual deployments to continuous deployment), and may prioritize fast feature development at the cost of technical debt that they cannot recognize. Such a manager has typically been in the same company (or an acquired company) for many years, has established a political foothold that enabled them to get their position, and is unable to get a similar position in other companies that have competent engineering organizations. Large companies that breed the growth of such managers have or are about to be disrupted by emerging startups. Working at such companies may be more lucrative in the short term than alternatives currently available to you, but they may set back your long-term growth as an engineer by years. They may also be financially worse for you because companies that you rejected for short-term financial gain end up performing better in the market, with higher growth in the valuation of your equity. Proceed at your own peril.

Overall, what can I learn and cannot learn from this company in the next four years? When you have your offers, you can go over the information you have collected and make a thoughtful decision.

https://blog.pragmaticengineer.com/reverse-interviewing/ is an article on interviewing your prospective manager and team.

Summary

- Everything is a tradeoff. Low latency and high availability increase cost and complexity. Every improvement in certain aspects is a regression in others.
- Be mindful of time. Clarify the important points of the discussion and focus on them.
- Start the discussion by clarifying the system's requirements and discuss possible tradeoffs in the system's capabilities to optimize for the requirements.
- The next step is to draft the API specification to satisfy the functional requirements.
- Draw the connections between users and data. What data do users read and write to the system, and how is data modified as it moves between system components?
- Discuss other concerns like logging, monitoring, alerting, search, and others that come up in the discussion.
- After the interview, write your self-assessment to evaluate your performance and learn your areas of strength and weakness. It is a useful future reference to track your improvement.
- Know what you want to achieve in the next few years and interview the company to determine if it is where you wish to invest your career.
- Logging, monitoring, and alerting are critical to alert us to unexpected events quickly and provide useful information to resolve them.
- Use the four golden signals and three instruments to quantify your service's observability.
- Log entries should be easy to parse, small, useful, categorized, have standardized time formats, and contain no private information.
- Follow the best practices of responding to alerts, such as runbooks that are useful and easy to follow, and continuously refine your runbook and approach based on the common patterns you identify.

3
Non-functional
requirements

This chapter covers

- Discussing non-functional requirements at the start of the interview
- Using techniques and technologies to fulfill non-functional requirements
- Optimizing for non-functional requirements

A system has functional and non-functional requirements. Functional requirements describe the inputs and outputs of the system. You can represent them as a rough API specification and endpoints.

Non-functional requirements refer to requirements other than the system inputs and outputs. Typical non-functional requirements include the following, to be discussed in detail later in this chapter.

- *Scalability*—The ability of a system to adjust its hardware resource usage easily and with little fuss to cost-efficiently support its load.
- *Availability*—The percentage of time a system can accept requests and return the desired response.

- *Performance/latency/P99 and throughput*—Performance or latency is the time taken for a user's request to the system to return a response. The maximum request rate that a system can process is its bandwidth. Throughput is the current request rate being processed by the system. However, it is common (though incorrect) to use the term "throughput" in place of "bandwidth." Throughput/bandwidth is the inverse of latency. A system with low latency has high throughput.
- *Fault-tolerance*—The ability of a system to continue operating if some of its components fail and the prevention of permanent harm (such as data loss) should downtime occur.
- *Security*—Prevention of unauthorized access to systems.
- *Privacy*—Access control to Personally Identifiable Information (PII), which can be used to uniquely identify a person.
- *Accuracy*—A system's data may not need to be perfectly accurate, and accuracy tradeoffs to improve costs or complexity are often a relevant discussion.
- *Consistency*—Whether data in all nodes/machines match.
- *Cost*—We can lower costs by making tradeoffs against other non-functional properties of the system.
- *Complexity, maintainability, debuggability, and testability*—These are related concepts that determine how difficult it is to build a system and then maintain it after it is built.

A customer, whether technical or non-technical, may not explicitly request non-functional requirements and may assume that the system will satisfy them. This means that the customer's stated requirements will almost always be incomplete, incorrect, and sometimes excessive. Without clarification, there will be misunderstandings on the requirements. We may not obtain certain requirements and therefore inadequately satisfy them, or we may assume certain requirements, which are actually not required and provide an excessive solution.

A beginner is more likely to fail to clarify non-functional requirements, but a lack of clarification can occur for both functional and non-functional requirements. We must begin any systems design discussion with discussion and clarification of both the functional and non-functional requirements.

Non-functional requirements are commonly traded off against each other. In any system design interview, we must discuss how various design decisions can be made for various tradeoffs.

It is tricky to separately discuss non-functional requirements and techniques to address them because certain techniques have tradeoff gains on multiple non-functional requirements for losses on others. In the rest of this chapter, we briefly discuss each non-functional requirement and some techniques to fulfill it, followed by a detailed discussion of each technique.

3.1 *Scalability*

Scalability is the ability of a system to adjust its hardware resource usage easily and with little fuss to cost-efficiently support its load.

The process of expanding to support a larger load or number of users is called *scaling*. Scaling requires increases in CPU processing power, RAM, storage capacity, and network bandwidth. Scaling can refer to vertical scaling or horizontal scaling.

Vertical scaling is conceptually straightforward and can be easily achieved just by spending more money. It means upgrading to a more powerful and expensive host, one with a faster processor, more RAM, a bigger hard disk drive, a solid-state drive instead of a spinning hard disk for lower latency, or a network card with higher bandwidth. There are three main disadvantages of vertical scaling.

First, we will reach a point where monetary cost increases faster than the upgraded hardware's performance. For example, a custom mainframe that has multiple processors will cost more than the same number of separate commodity machines that have one processor each.

Second, vertical scaling has technological limits. Regardless of budget, current technological limitations will impose a maximum amount of processing power, RAM, or storage capacity that is technologically possible on a single host.

Third, vertical scaling may require downtime. We must stop our host, change its hardware and then start it again. To avoid downtime, we need to provision another host, start our service on it, and then direct requests to the new host. Moreover, this is only possible if the service's state is stored on a different machine from the old or new host. As we discuss later in this book, directing requests to specific hosts or storing a service's state in a different host are techniques to achieve many non-functional requirements, such as scalability, availability, and fault-tolerance.

Because vertical scaling is conceptually trivial, in this book unless otherwise stated, our use of terms like "scalable" and "scaling" refer to horizontally scalable and horizontal scaling.

Horizontal scaling refers to spreading out the processing and storage requirements across multiple hosts. "True" scalability can only be achieved by horizontal scaling. Horizontal scaling is almost always discussed in a system design interview.

Based on these questions, we determine the customer's scalability requirements.

- How much data comes to the system and is retrieved from the system?
- How many read queries per second?
- How much data per request?
- How many video views per second?
- How big are sudden traffic spikes?

3.1.1 Stateless and stateful services

HTTP is a stateless protocol, so a backend service that uses it is easy to scale horizontally. Chapter 4 describes horizontal scaling of database reads. A stateless HTTP backend combined with horizontally scalable database read operations is a good starting point to discuss a scalable system design.

Writes to shared storage are the most difficult to scale. We discuss techniques, including replication, compression, aggregation, denormalization, and Metadata Service later in this book.

Refer to section 6.7 for a discussion of various common communication architectures, including the tradeoffs between stateful and stateless.

3.1.2 Basic load balancer concepts

Every horizontally scaled service uses a load balancer, which may be one of the following:

- A hardware load balancer, a specialized physical device that distributes traffic across multiple hosts. Hardware load balancers are known for being expensive and can cost anywhere from a few thousand to a few hundred thousand dollars.
- A shared load balancer service, also referred to as LBaaS (load balancing as a service).
- A server with load balancing software installed. HAProxy and NGINX are the most common.

This section discusses basic concepts of load balancers that we can use in an interview.

In the system diagrams in this book, I draw rectangles to represent various services or other components and arrows between them to represent requests. It is usually understood that requests to a service go through a load balancer and are routed to a service's hosts. We usually do not illustrate the load balancers themselves.

We can tell the interviewer that we need not include a load balancer component in our system diagrams, as it is implied, and drawing it and discussing it on our system diagrams is a distraction from the other components and services that compose our service.

LEVEL 4 VS. LEVEL 7

We should be able to distinguish between level 4 and level 7 load balancers and discuss which one is more suitable for any particular service. A level 4 load balancer operates at the transport layer (TCP). It makes routing decisions based on address information extracted from the first few packets in the TCP stream and does not inspect the contents of other packets; it can only forward the packets. A level 7 load balancer operates at the application layer (HTTP), so it has these capabilities:

- *Load balancing/routing decisions*—Based on a packet's contents.
- *Authentication*—It can return 401 if a specified authentication header is absent.

- *TLS termination*—Security requirements for traffic within a data center may be lower than traffic over the internet, so performing TLS termination (HTTPS → HTTP) means there is no encryption/decryption overhead between data center hosts. If our application requires traffic within our data center to be encrypted (i.e., encryption in transit), we will not do TLS termination.

STICKY SESSIONS

A sticky session refers to a load balancer sending requests from a particular client to a particular host for a duration set by the load balancer or the application. Sticky sessions are used for stateful services. For example, an ecommerce website, social media website, or banking website may use sticky sessions to maintain user session data like login information or profile preferences, so a user doesn't have to reauthenticate or reenter preferences as they navigate the site. An ecommerce website may use sticky sessions for a user's shopping cart.

A sticky session can be implemented using duration-based or application-controlled cookies. In a duration-based session, the load balancer issues a cookie to a client that defines a duration. Each time the load balancer receives a request, it checks the cookie. In an application-controlled session, the application generates the cookie. The load balancer still issues its own cookie on top of this application-issued cookie, but the load balancer's cookie follows the application cookie's lifetime. This approach ensures clients are not routed to another host after the load balancer's cookie expires, but it is more complex to implement because it requires additional integration between the application and the load balancer.

SESSION REPLICATION

In *session replication,* writes to a host are copied to several other hosts in the cluster that are assigned to the same session, so reads can be routed to any host with that session. This improves availability.

These hosts may form a backup ring. For example, if there are three hosts in a session, when host A receives a write, it writes to host B, which in turn writes to host C. Another way is for the load balancer to make write requests to all the hosts assigned to a session.

LOAD BALANCING VS. REVERSE PROXY

You may come across the term "reverse proxy" in other system design interview preparation materials. We will briefly compare load balancing and reverse proxy.

Load balancing is for scalability, while reverse proxy is a technique to manage client–server communication. A reverse proxy sits in front of a cluster of servers and acts as a gateway between clients and servers by intercepting and forwarding incoming requests to the appropriate server based on request URI or other criteria. A reverse proxy may also provide performance features, such as caching and compression, and security features, such as SSL termination. Load balancers can also provide SSL termination, but their main purpose is scalability.

Refer to https://www.nginx.com/resources/glossary/reverse-proxy-vs-load-balancer/ for a good discussion on load balancing versus reverse proxy.

FURTHER READING

- https://www.cloudflare.com/learning/performance/types-of-load-balancing -algorithms/ is a good brief description of various load balancing algorithms.
- https://rancher.com/load-balancing-in-kubernetes is a good introduction to load balancing in Kubernetes.
- https://kubernetes.io/docs/concepts/services-networking/service/#loadbalancer and https://kubernetes.io/docs/tasks/access-application-cluster/create-external -load-balancer/ describe how to attach an external cloud service load balancer to a Kubernetes service.

3.2 Availability

Availability is the percentage of time a system can accept requests and return the desired response. Common benchmarks for availability are shown in table 3.1.

Table 3.1 Common benchmarks for availability

Availability %	Downtime per year	Downtime per month	Downtime per week	Downtime per day
99.9 (three 9s)	8.77 hours	43.8 minutes	10.1 minutes	1.44 minutes
99.99 (four 9s)	52.6 minutes	4.38 minutes	1.01 minutes	8.64 seconds
99.999 (five 9s)	5.26 minutes	26.3 seconds	6.05 seconds	864 milliseconds

Refer to https://netflixtechblog.com/active-active-for-multi-regional-resiliency -c47719f6685b for a detailed discussion on Netflix's multi-region active-active deployment for high availability. In this book, we discuss similar techniques for high availability, such as replication within and across data centers in different continents. We also discuss monitoring and alerting.

High availability is required in most services, and other non-functional requirements may be traded off to allow high availability without unnecessary complexity.

When discussing the non-functional requirements of a system, first establish whether high availability is required. Do not assume that strong consistency and low latency are required. Refer to the CAP theorem and discuss if we can trade them off for higher availability. As far as possible, suggest using asynchronous communication techniques that accomplish this, such as event sourcing and saga, discussed in chapters 4 and 5.

Services where requests do not need to be immediately processed and responses immediately returned are unlikely to require strong consistency and low latency, such as requests made programmatically between services. Examples include logging to long-term storage or sending a request in Airbnb to book a room for some days from now.

Use synchronous communication protocols when an immediate response is absolutely necessary, typically for requests made directly by people using your app.

Nonetheless, do not assume that requests made by people need immediate responses with the requested data. Consider whether the immediate response can be an acknowledgment and whether the requested data can be returned minutes or hours later. For example, if a user requests to submit their income tax payment, this payment need not happen immediately. The service can queue the request internally and immediately respond to the user that the request will be processed in minutes or hours. The payment can later be processed by a streaming job or a periodic batch job, and then the user can be notified of the result (such as whether the payment succeeded or failed) through channels such as email, text, or app notifications.

An example of a situation where high availability may not be required is in a caching service. Because caching may be used to reduce the latency and network traffic of a request and is not needed to fulfill the request, we may decide to trade off availability for lower latency in the caching service's system design. Another example is rate limiting, discussed in chapter 8.

Availability can also be measured with incident metrics. https://www.atlassian.com/incident-management/kpis/common-metrics describes various incident metrics like MTTR (Mean Time to Recovery) and MTBF (Mean Time Between Failures). These metrics usually have dashboards and alerts.

3.3 Fault-tolerance

Fault-tolerance is the ability of a system to continue operating if some of its components fail and the prevention of permanent harm (such as data loss) should downtime occur. This allows graceful degradation, so our system can maintain some functionality when parts of it fail, rather than a complete catastrophic failure. This buys engineers time to fix the failed sections and restore the system to working order. We may also implement self-healing mechanisms that automatically provision replacement components and attach them to our system, so our system can recover without manual intervention and without any noticeable effect on end users.

Availability and fault-tolerance are often discussed together. While availability is a measure of uptime/downtime, fault-tolerance is not a measure but rather a system characteristic.

A closely related concept is failure design, which is about smooth error handling. Consider how we will handle errors in third-party APIs that are outside our control as well as silent/undetected errors. Techniques for fault-tolerance include the following.

3.3.1 Replication and redundancy

Replication is discussed in chapter 4.

One replication technique is to have multiple (such as three) redundant instances/copies of a component, so up to two can be simultaneously down without affecting uptime. As discussed in chapter 4, update operations are usually assigned a particular host, so update performance is affected only if the other hosts are on different data centers geographically further away from the requester, but reads are often done on all replicas, so read performance decreases when components are down.

One instance is designated as the source of truth (often called the leader), while the other two components are designated as replicas (or followers). There are various possible arrangements of the replicas. One replica is on a different server rack within the same data center, and another replica is in a different data center. Another arrangement is to have all three instances on different data centers, which maximizes fault-tolerance with the tradeoff of lower performance.

An example is the Hadoop Distributed File System (HDFS), which has a configurable property called "replication factor" to set the number of copies of any block. The default value is three. Replication also helps to increase availability.

3.3.2 Forward error correction and error correction code

Forward error correction (FEC) is a technique to prevent errors in data transmission over noise or unreliable communication channels by encoding the message in a redundant way, such as by using an *error correction code* (ECC).

FEC is a protocol-level rather than a system-level concept. We can express our awareness of FEC and ECC during system design interviews, but it is unlikely that we will need to explain it in detail, so we do not discuss them further in this book.

3.3.3 Circuit breaker

The circuit breaker is a mechanism that stops a client from repeatedly attempting an operation that is likely to fail. With respect to downstream services, a circuit breaker calculates the number of requests that failed within a recent interval. If an error threshold is exceeded, the client stops calling downstream services. Sometime later, the client attempts a limited number of requests. If they are successful, the client assumes that the failure is resolved and resumes sending requests without restrictions.

> **DEFINITION** If a service B depends on a service A, A is the upstream service and B is the downstream service.

A circuit breaker saves resources from being spent to make requests that are likely to fail. It also prevents clients from adding additional burden to an already overburdened system.

However, a circuit breaker makes the system more difficult to test. For example, say we have a load test that is making incorrect requests but is still properly testing our system's limits. This test will now activate the circuit breaker, and a load that may have previously overwhelmed the downstream services and will now pass. A similar load by our customers will cause an outage. It is also difficult to estimate the appropriate error threshold and timers.

A circuit breaker can be implemented on the server side. An example is Resilience4j (https://github.com/resilience4j/resilience4j). It was inspired by Hystrix (https://github.com/Netflix/Hystrix), which was developed at Netflix and transitioned to maintenance mode in 2017 (https://github.com/Netflix/Hystrix/issues/1876#issuecomment-440065505). Netflix's focus has shifted toward more adaptive implementations that react to an application's real-time performance rather than pre-configured settings, such as adaptive concurrency limits (https://netflixtechblog.medium.com/performance-under-load-3e6fa9a60581).

3.3.4   *Exponential backoff and retry*

Exponential backoff and retry is similar to a circuit breaker. When a client receives an error response, it will wait before reattempting the request and exponentially increase the wait duration between retries. The client also adjusts the wait period by a small random negative or positive amount, a technique called "jitter." This prevents multiple clients from submitting retries at exactly the same time, causing a "retry storm" that may overwhelm the downstream service. Similar to a circuit breaker, when a client receives a success response, it assumes that the failure is resolved and resumes sending requests without restrictions.

3.3.5   *Caching responses of other services*

Our service may depend on external services for certain data. How should we handle the case where an external service is unavailable? It is generally preferable to have graceful degradation instead of crashing or returning an error. We can use a default or empty response in place of the return value. If using stale data is better than no data, we can cache the external service's responses whenever we make successful requests and use these responses when the external service is unavailable.

3.3.6   *Checkpointing*

A machine may perform certain data aggregation operations on many data points by systematically fetching a subset of them, performing the aggregation on them, then writing the result to a specified location, repeating this process until all data points are processed or infinitely, such as in the case of a streaming pipeline. Should this machine fail during data aggregation, the replacement machine should know from which data points to resume the aggregation. This can be done by writing a checkpoint after each subset of data points are processed and the result is successfully written. The replacement machine can resume processing at the checkpoint.

Checkpointing is commonly applied to ETL pipelines that use message brokers such as Kafka. A machine can fetch several events from a Kafka topic, process the events, and then write the result, followed by writing a checkpoint. Should this machine fail, its replacement can resume at the most recent checkpoint.

Kafka offers offset storages at the partition level in Kafka (https://kafka.apache .org/22/javadoc/org/apache/kafka/clients/consumer/KafkaConsumer.html). Flink consumes data from Kafka topics and periodically checkpoints using Flink's distributed checkpointing mechanism (https://ci.apache.org/projects/flink/flink-docs-master/ docs/dev/datastream/fault-tolerance/checkpointing/).

3.3.7   *Dead letter queue*

If a write request to a third-party API fails, we can queue the request in a dead letter queue and try the requests again later.

Are dead letter queues stored locally or on a separate service? We can trade off complexity and reliability:

- The simplest option is that if it is acceptable to miss requests, just drop failed requests.

- Implement the dead letter queue locally with a try-catch block. Requests will be lost if the host fails.

- A more complex and reliable option is to use an event-streaming platform like Kafka.

In an interview, you should discuss multiple approaches and their tradeoffs. Don't just state one approach.

3.3.8 Logging and periodic auditing

One method to handle silent errors is to log our write requests and perform periodic auditing. An auditing job can process the logs and verify that the data on the service we write to matches the expected values. This is discussed further in chapter 10.

3.3.9 Bulkhead

The bulkhead pattern is a fault-tolerance mechanism where a system is divided into isolated pools, so a fault in one pool will not affect the entire system.

For example, the various endpoints of a service can each have their own thread pool, and not share a thread pool, so if an endpoint's thread pool is exhausted, this will not affect the ability of other endpoints to serve requests (To learn more about this, see *Microservices for the Enterprise: Designing, Developing, and Deploying* by Indrasiri and Siriwardena (Apress, 2019).

Another example of bulkhead is discussed in *Release It!: Design and Deploy Production-Ready Software, Second Edition* by Michael T. Nygard's (Pragmatic Bookshelf, 2018). A certain request may cause a host to crash due to a bug. Each time this request is repeated, it will crash another host. Dividing the service into bulkheads (i.e., dividing the hosts into pools) prevents this request from crashing all the hosts and causing a total outage. This request should be investigated, so the service must have logging and monitoring. Monitoring will detect the offending request, and engineers can use the logs to troubleshoot the crash and determine its cause.

Or a requestor may have a high request rate to a service and prevent the latter from serving other requestors. The bulkhead pattern allocates certain hosts to a particular requestor, preventing the latter from consuming all the service's capacity. (Rate limiting discussed in chapter 8 is another way to prevent this situation.)

A service's hosts can be divided into pools, and each pool is allocated requestors. This is also a technique to prioritize certain requestors by allocating more resources to them.

In figure 3.1, a service serves two other services. Unavailability of the service's hosts will prevent it from serving any requestor.

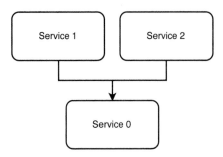

Figure 3.1   All requests to service 0 are load-balanced across its hosts. The unavailability of service 0's hosts will prevent it from serving any requestor.

In figure 3.2, a service's hosts are divided into pools, which are allocated to requestors. The unavailability of the hosts of one pool will not affect other requestors. An obvious tradeoff of this approach is that the pools cannot support each other if there are traffic spikes from certain requestors. This is a deliberate decision that we made to allocate a certain number of hosts to a particular requestor. We can either manually or automatically scale the pools as required.

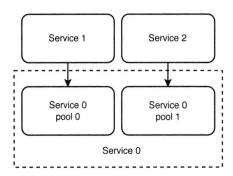

Figure 3.2   Service 0 is divided into two pools, each allocated to a requestor. The unavailability of one pool will not affect the other.

Refer to Michael Nygard's book *Release It!: Design and Deploy Production-Ready Software,* Second Edition (Pragmatic Bookshelf, 2018), for other examples of the bulkhead pattern.

We will not mention bulkhead in the system design discussions of part 2, but it is generally applicable for most systems, and you can discuss it during an interview.

3.3.10   *Fallback pattern*

The fallback pattern consists of detecting a problem and then executing an alternative code path, such as cached responses or alternative services that are similar to the service the client is trying to get information from. For example, if a client requests our backend for a list of nearby bagel cafes, it can cache the response to be used in the future if our backend service is experiencing an outage. This cached response may not be up to date, but it is better than returning an error message to the user. An alternative is for the client to make a request to a third-party maps API like Bing or Google Maps, which may not have the customized content that our backend provides. When we design a fallback, we should consider its reliability and that the fallback itself may fail.

NOTE   Refer to https://aws.amazon.com/builders-library/avoiding-fallback-in
-distributed-systems/ for more information on fallback strategies, why Amazon
almost never uses the fallback pattern, and alternatives to the fallback pattern
that Amazon uses.

3.4   *Performance/latency and throughput*

Performance or latency is the time taken for a user's request to the system to return a
response. This includes the network latency of the request to leave the client and travel
to the service, the time the service takes to process the request and create the response,
and the network latency of the response to leave the service and travel to the client. A
typical request on a consumer-facing app (e.g., viewing a restaurant's menu on a food
delivery app or submitting a payment on an ecommerce app) has a desired latency
of tens of milliseconds to several seconds. High-frequency trading applications may
demand latency of several milliseconds.

Strictly speaking, latency refers to the travel time of a packet from its source to its
destination. However, the term "latency" has become commonly used to have the same
meaning as "performance," and both terms are often used interchangeably. We still use
the term latency if we need to discuss packet travel time.

The term latency can also be used to describe the request-response time between
components within the system, rather than the user's request-response time. For example, if a backend host makes a request to a logging or storage system to store data, the
system's latency is the time required to log/store the data and return a response to the
backend host.

The system's functional requirements may mean that a response may not actually
need to contain the information requested by the user but may simply be an acknowledgment along with a promise that after a specified duration, the requested information will be sent to the user or will be available for the user to obtain by making another
request. Such a tradeoff may simplify the system's design, so we must always clarify
requirements and discuss how soon information is required after a user's request.

Typical design decisions to achieve low latency include the following. We can deploy
the service in a data center geographically close to its users, so packets between users
and our service do not need to travel far. If our users are geographically dispersed, we
may deploy our service in multiple data centers that are chosen to minimize geographical distance to clusters of users. If hosts across data centers need to share data, our service must be horizontally scalable.

Occasionally, there may be other factors that contribute more to latency than the
physical distance between users and data centers, such as traffic or network bandwidth,
or the backend system processing (the actual business logic and the persistence layer).
We can use test requests between users and various data centers to determine the data
center with the lowest latency for users in a particular location.

Other techniques include using a CDN, caching, decreasing the data size with RPC
instead of REST, designing your own protocol with a framework like Netty to use TCP
and UDP instead of HTTP, and using batch and streaming techniques.

In examining latency and throughput, we discuss the characteristics of the data and how it gets in and out of the system, and then we can suggest strategies. Can we count views several hours after they happened? This will allow batch or streaming approaches. What is the response time? If small, data must already be aggregated, and aggregation should be done during writes, with minimal or no aggregation during reads.

3.5   *Consistency*

Consistency has different meanings in ACID and CAP (from the CAP theorem). ACID consistency focuses on data relationships like foreign keys and uniqueness. As stated in Martin Kleppmann's *Designing Data-Intensive Applications* (O'Reilly, 2017), CAP consistency is actually linearizability, defined as all nodes containing the same data at a moment in time, and changes in data must be linear; that is, nodes must start serving the changes at the same time.

Eventually, consistent databases trade off consistency for improvements in availability, scalability, and latency. An ACID database, including RDBMS databases, cannot accept writes when it experiences a network partition because it cannot maintain ACID consistency if writes occur during a network partition. Summarized in table 3.2, MongoDB, HBase, and Redis trade off availability for linearizability, while CouchDB, Cassandra, Dynamo, Hadoop, and Riak trade off linearizability for availability.

Table 3.2   Databases that favor availability vs. linearizability

Favor linearizability	Favor availability
HBase	Cassandra
MongoDB	CouchDB
Redis	Dynamo
	Hadoop
	Riak

During the discussion, we should emphasize the distinction between ACID and CAP consistency, and the tradeoffs between linearizability vs. eventual consistency. In this book, we will discuss various techniques for linearizability and eventual consistency, including the following:

- Full mesh
- Quorum

Techniques for eventual consistency that involve writing to a single location, which propagates this write to the other relevant locations:

- Event sourcing (section 5.2), a technique to handle traffic spikes.
- Coordination service.
- Distributed cache.

Techniques for eventual consistency that trade off consistency and accuracy for lower cost:

- Gossip protocol.
- Random leader selection.

Disadvantages of linearizability include the following:

- Lower availability, since most or all nodes must be sure of consensus before they can serve requests. This becomes more difficult with a larger number of nodes.
- More complex and expensive.

3.5.1 *Full mesh*

Figure 3.3 illustrates an example of full mesh. Every host in the cluster has the address of every other host and broadcasts messages to all of them.

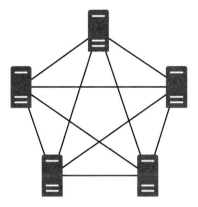

Figure 3.3 Illustration of full mesh. Every host is connected to every other host and broadcasts messages to all of them.

How do hosts discover each other? When a new host is added, how is its address sent to other hosts? Solutions for host discovery include:

- Maintain the list of addresses in a configuration file. Each time the list changes, deploy this file across all hosts/nodes.
- Use a third-party service that listens for heartbeats from every host. A host is kept registered as long as the service receives heartbeats. All hosts use this service to obtain the full list of addresses.

Full mesh is easier to implement than other techniques, but it is not scalable. The number of messages grows quadratically with the number of hosts. Full mesh works well for small clusters but cannot support big clusters. In quorum, only a majority of hosts need to have the same data for the system to be considered consistent. BitTorrent is an example of a protocol that uses full mesh for decentralized p2p file sharing. During an interview, we can briefly mention full mesh and compare it with scalable approaches.

3.5.2   *Coordination service*

Figure 3.4 illustrates a coordination service, a third-party component that chooses a leader node or set of leader nodes. Having a leader decreases the number of messages. All other nodes send their messages to the leader, and the leader may do some necessary processing and send back the final result. Each node only needs to communicate with its leader or set of leaders, and each leader manages a number of nodes.

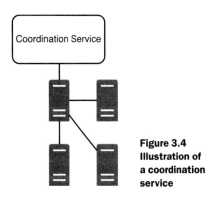

**Figure 3.4
Illustration of
a coordination
service**

Example algorithms are Paxos, Raft, and Zab. Another example is single leader multiple follower in SQL (section 4.3.2), a technique to allow scalable reads. ZooKeeper (https://zookeeper.apache.org/) is a distributed coordination service. ZooKeeper has the following advantages over a config file stored on a single host. (Most of these advantages are discussed at https://stackoverflow.com/q/36312640/1045085.) We can implement these features on a distributed filesystem or distributed database, but ZooKeeper already provides them:

- Access control (https://zookeeper.apache.org/doc/r3.1.2/zookeeperProgrammers .html#sc_ZooKeeperAccessControl).
- Storing data in memory for high performance.
- Scalability, with horizontal scaling by adding hosts to the ZooKeeper Ensemble (https://zookeeper.apache.org/doc/r3.1.2/zookeeperAdmin.html#sc_zkMulit ServerSetup).
- Guaranteed eventual consistency within a specified time bound or strong consistency with higher cost (https://zookeeper.apache.org/doc/current/zookeeper Internals.html#sc_consistency). ZooKeeper trades off availability for consistency; it is a CP system in the CAP theorem.
- Clients can read data in the order it is written.

Complexity is the main disadvantage of a coordination service. A coordination service is a sophisticated component that has to be highly reliable and ensure one and only one leader is elected. (The situation where two nodes both believe they are the leader is called "split brain." Refer to Martin Kleppmann, *Designing Data-Intensive Applications,* O'Reilly, 2017, p. 158.)

3.5.3   *Distributed cache*

We can use a distributed cache like Redis or Memcached. Referring to figure 3.5, our service's nodes can make periodic requests to the origin to fetch new data, then make requests to the distributed cache (e.g., an in-memory store like Redis) to update its data. This solution is simple, has low latency, and the distributed cache cluster can be scaled independently of our service. However, this solution has more requests than every other solution here except the full mesh.

Figure 3.5   Illustration of using a distributed cache to broadcast messages. The nodes can make requests to an in-memory store like Redis to update data, or it can make periodic requests to fetch new data.

NOTE   Redis is an in-memory cache, not a typically distributed one by definition. It is used as a distributed cache for practical intents and purposes. Refer to https://redis.io/docs/about/ and https://stacoverflow.com/questions/18376665/redis-distributed-or-not.

Both a sender and receiver host can validate that a message contains its required fields. This is often done by both sides because the additional cost is trivial while reducing the possibility of errors on either side, resulting in an invalid message. When a sender host sends an invalid message to a receiver host via an HTTP request, and the receiver host can detect that this message is invalid, it can immediately return a 400 or 422. We can set up high-urgency alerts to trigger on 4xx errors, so we will immediately be alerted of this error and can immediately investigate. However, if we use Redis, invalid data written by a node may stay undetected until it is fetched by another node, so there will be a delay in alerts.

Requests sent directly from one host to another go through schema validation. However, Redis is just a database, so it does not validate schema, and hosts can write arbitrary data to it. This may create security problems. (Refer to https://www.trendmicro.com/en_us/research/20/d/exposed-redis-instances-abused-for-remote-code-execution-cryptocurrency-mining.html and https://www.imperva.com/blog/new-research-shows-75-of-open-redis-servers-infected.) Redis is designed to be accessed by trusted clients inside trusted environments (https://redis.io/topics/security). Redis does not support encryption, which may be a privacy concern. Implementing encryption at rest increases complexity, costs, and reduces performance (https://docs.aws.amazon.com/AmazonElastiCache/latest/red-ug/at-rest-encryption.html).

A coordination service addresses these disadvantages but has higher complexity and cost.

3.5.4 *Gossip protocol*

Gossip protocol is modeled after how epidemics spread. Referring to figure 3.6, each node randomly selects another node periodically or with a random interval and then shares data. This approach trades off consistency for lower cost and complexity.

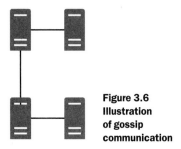

**Figure 3.6
Illustration
of gossip
communication**

Cassandra uses a gossip protocol to maintain consistency across distributed data partitions. DynamoDB uses a gossip protocol called "vector clocks" to maintain consistency across multiple data centers.

3.5.5 *Random Leader Selection*

Referring to figure 3.7, random leader selection uses a simple algorithm to elect a leader. This simple algorithm does not guarantee one and only one leader, so there may be multiple leaders. This is a minor problem because each leader can share data with all other hosts, so all hosts, including all leaders, will have the correct data. The disadvantage is possible duplicate requests and unnecessary network traffic.

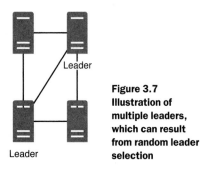

**Figure 3.7
Illustration of
multiple leaders,
which can result
from random leader
selection**

Kafka uses a leader-follower replication model with random leader selection to provide fault-tolerance. YARN uses a random leader selection approach to manage resource allocation across a cluster of hosts.

3.6 *Accuracy*

Accuracy is a relevant non-functional requirement in systems with complex data processing or a high rate of writes. *Accuracy* of data means that the data values are correct and are not approximations. Estimation algorithms trade off accuracy for lower complexity. Examples of estimation algorithms include HyperLogLog for cardinality

(COUNT DISTINCT) estimate in the Presto distributed SQL query engine and count-min sketch for estimating frequencies of events in a stream of data.

A cache is stale if the data in its underlying database has been modified. A cache may have a refresh policy where it will fetch the latest data at a fixed periodic interval. A short refresh policy is more costly. An alternative is for the system to update or delete the associated cache key when data is modified, which increases complexity.

Accuracy is somewhat related to consistency. Systems that are eventually consistent trade off accuracy for improvements in availability, complexity, and cost. When a write is made to an eventually consistent system, results from reads made after this write may not include the effects of the write, which makes them inaccurate. The eventually consistent system is inaccurate until the replicas are updated with the effects of the write operation. However, we use the term "consistency" to discuss such a situation, not "accuracy."

3.7 *Complexity and maintainability*

The first step to minimize complexity is to clarify both functional and non-functional requirements, so we do not design for unnecessary requirements.

As we sketch design diagrams, note which components may be separated into independent systems. Use common services to reduce complexity and improve maintainability. Common services that are generalizable across virtually all services include

- Load balancer service.
- Rate limiting. Refer to chapter 8.
- Authentication and authorization. Refer to appendix B.
- Logging, monitoring, alerting. Refer to section 2.5.
- TLS termination. Refer to other sources for more information.
- Caching. Refer to section 4.8.
- DevOps and CI/CD if applicable. These are outside the scope of this book.

Services that are generalizable for certain organizations, such as those that collect user data for data science, include analytics and machine learning.

Complex systems may require yet more complexity for high availability and high fault-tolerance. If a system has an unavoidable degree of complexity, consider tradeoffs of complexity for lower availability and fault-tolerance.

Discuss possible tradeoffs in other requirements to improve complexity, such as ETL pipelines to delay data processing operations that need not occur in real time.

A common technique to trade off complexity for better latency and performance is to use techniques that minimize the size of messages in network communication. Such techniques include RPC serialization frameworks and Metadata services. (Refer to section 6.3 for a discussion on Metadata service.)

RPC serialization frameworks such as Avro, Thrift, and protobuf can reduce message size at the expense of maintaining schema files. (Refer to section 6.7 for a discussion of REST vs RPC.) We should always suggest using such serialization frameworks in any interview, and we will not mention this point again in the book.

We should also discuss how outages can occur, evaluate the effect of various outages on users and the business, and how to prevent and mitigate outages. Common concepts include replication, failover, and authoring runbooks. Runbooks are discussed in section 2.5.3.

We will discuss complexity in all chapters of part 2.

3.7.1   Continuous deployment (CD)

Continuous deployment (CD) was first mentioned in this book in section 1.4.5. As mentioned in that section, CD allows easy deployments and rollbacks. We have a fast feedback cycle that improves our system's maintainability. If we accidentally deploy a buggy build to production, we can easily roll it back. Fast and easy deployments of incremental upgrades and new features lead to a fast software development lifecycle. This is a major advantage of services over monoliths, as discussed in appendix A.

Other CD techniques include blue/green deployments, also referred to as zero downtime deployments. Refer to sources such as https://spring.io/blog/2016/05/31/zero-downtime-deployment-with-a-database, https://dzone.com/articles/zero-downtime-deployment, and https://craftquest.io/articles/what-are-zero-downtime-atomic-deployments for more information.

Static code analysis tools like SonarQube (https://www.sonarqube.org/) also improve our system's maintainability.

3.8   Cost

In system design discussions, we can suggest trading off other non-functional requirements for lower cost. Examples:

- Higher cost for lower complexity by vertical scaling instead of horizontal scaling.
- Lower availability for improved costs by decreasing the redundancy of a system (such as the number of hosts, or the replication factor in a database).
- Higher latency for improved costs by using a data center in a cheaper location that is further away from users.

Discuss the cost of implementation, cost of monitoring, and cost of each non-functional requirement such as high availability.

Production problems vary in seriousness and how quickly they must be addressed and resolved, so do not implement more monitoring and alerting than required. Costs are higher if engineers need to be alerted to a problem as soon as it occurs, compared to when it is permissible for alerts to be created hours after a problem.

Besides the cost of maintenance in the form of addressing possible production problems, there will also be costs due to the natural atrophy of software over time as libraries and services are deprecated. Identify components that may need future updates. Which dependencies (such as libraries) will prevent other components from being easily updated if these dependencies become unsupported in the future? How may we design our system to more easily replace these dependencies if updates are required?

How likely is it that we will need to change dependencies in the future, particularly third-party dependencies where we have less control? Third-party dependencies may be decommissioned or prove unsatisfactory for our requirements, such as reliability or security problems.

A complete cost discussion should include consideration of the costs to decommission the system if necessary. We may decide to decommission the system for multiple reasons, such as the team deciding to change its focus or the system has too few users to justify its development and maintenance costs. We may decide to provide the existing users with their data, so we will need to extract the data into various text and/or CSV files for our users.

3.9 Security

During an interview, we may need to discuss possible security vulnerabilities in our system and how we will prevent and mitigate security breaches. This includes access both from external parties and internally within our organization. The following topics are commonly discussed with regard to security:

- TLS termination versus keeping data encrypted between services or hosts in a data center (called encryption in transit). TLS termination is usually done to save processing because encryption between hosts in a data center is usually not required. There may be exceptions for sensitive data on which we use encryption in transit.
- Which data can be stored unencrypted, and which should be stored encrypted (called *encryption at rest*). Encryption at rest is conceptually different from storing hashed data.

We should have some understanding of OAuth 2.0 and OpenID Connect, which are described in appendix B.

We may also discuss rate limiting to prevent DDoS attacks. A rate-limiting system can make up its own interview question, and this is discussed in chapter 8. It should be mentioned during the design of almost any external-facing system.

3.10 Privacy

Personally Identifiable Information (PII) is data that can be used to uniquely identify a customer, such as full name, government identifiers, addresses, email addresses, and bank account identifiers. PII must be safeguarded to comply with regulations such as the General Data Protection Regulation (GDPR) and the California Consumer Privacy Act (CCPA). This includes both external and internal access.

Within our system, access control mechanisms should be applied to PII stored in databases and files. We can use mechanisms such as the Lightweight Directory Access Protocol (LDAP). We can encrypt data both in transit (using SSL) and at rest.

Consider using hashing algorithms such as SHA-2 and SHA-3 to mask PII and maintain individual customer privacy in computing aggregate statistics (e.g., mean number of transactions per customer).

If PII is stored on an append-only database or file system like HDFS, a common privacy technique is to assign each customer an encryption key. The encryption keys can be stored in a mutable storage system like SQL. Data associated with a particular customer should be encrypted with their encryption key before it is stored. If a customer's data needs to be deleted, all that must be done is to delete the customer's encryption key, and then all of the customer's data on the append-only storage becomes inaccessible and hence effectively deleted.

We can discuss the complexity, cost, and effects of privacy along many aspects, such as customer service or personalization, including machine learning.

We should also discuss prevention and mitigation strategies for data breaches, such as data retention policies and auditing. The details tend to be specific to each organization, so it is an open-ended discussion.

3.10.1 *External vs. internal services*

If we design an external service, we definitely should design security and privacy mechanisms. What about internal services that only serve other internal services? We may decide to rely on the security mechanisms of our user services against malicious external attackers and assume that internal users will not attempt malicious actions, so security measures are not required for our rate limiter service. We may also decide that we trust our user services not to request data about rate limiter requestors from other user services, so privacy measures are not required.

However, it is likely that we will decide that our company should not trust internal users to properly implement security mechanisms, should not trust that internal users are not malicious, and should not trust internal users to not inadvertently or maliciously violate our customer's privacy. We should adopt an engineering culture of implementing security and privacy mechanisms by default. This is consistent with the internal access controls and privacy policies of all kinds of services and data adopted by most organizations. For example, most organizations have role-based access control for each service's Git repository and CI/CD. Most organizations also have procedures to grant access to employee and customer data only to persons they deem necessary to have access to this data. These access controls and data access are typically limited in scope and duration as much as possible. There is no logical reason to adopt such policies for certain systems and not adopt them for others. We should ensure that our internal service does not expose any sensitive features or data before we decide that it can exclude security and privacy mechanisms. Moreover, every service, external or internal, should log access to sensitive databases.

Another privacy mechanism is to have a well-defined policy for storing user information. Databases that store user information should be behind services that are well-documented and have tight security and strict access control policies. Other services and databases should only store user IDs and no other user data. The user IDs can be changed either periodically or in the event of a security or privacy breach.

Figure 1.8 illustrates a service mesh, including security and privacy mechanisms, illustrated as an external request to an identity and access management service.

3.11 Cloud native

Cloud native is an approach to address non-functional requirements, including scalability, fault-tolerance, and maintainability. The definition of cloud native by the Cloud Native Computing Foundation is as follows (https://github.com/cncf/toc/blob/main/DEFINITION.md). I italicized certain words for emphasis:

> Cloud native technologies empower organizations to build and run scalable applications in modern, dynamic environments such as public, private, and hybrid clouds. *Containers, service meshes, microservices, immutable infrastructure,* and *declarative APIs* exemplify this approach.

> These techniques enable *loosely coupled* systems that are *resilient, manageable,* and *observable.* Combined with *robust automation,* they allow engineers to make high-impact *changes frequently* and *predictably* with minimal toil.

> The Cloud Native Computing Foundation seeks to drive adoption of this paradigm by fostering and sustaining an ecosystem of open source, vendor-neutral projects. We democratize state-of-the-art patterns to make these innovations accessible for everyone.

This is not a book on cloud-native computing, but we utilize cloud-native techniques (containers, service meshes, microservices, serverless functions, immutable infrastructure or Infrastructure as Code, declarative APIs, automation) throughout this book to achieve the benefits (resilient, manageable, observable, allow frequent and predictable changes), and include references to materials on the relevant concepts.

3.12 Further reading

Interested readers can look up the PACELC theorem, which we do not discuss in this book. The PACELC is an extension of the CAP theorem. It states that when a network partition occurs in a distributed system, one must choose between availability and consistency, or else during normal operation, one must choose between latency and consistency.

A useful resource that has content similar to this chapter is *Microservices for the Enterprise: Designing, Developing, and Deploying* (2018, Apress) by Kasun Indrasiri and Prabath Siriwardena.

Summary

- We must discuss both the functional and non-functional requirements of a system. Do not make assumptions about the non-functional requirements. Non-functional characteristics can be traded off against each other to optimize for the non-functional requirements.

- Scalability is the ability to easily adjust the system's hardware resource usage for cost efficiency. This is almost always discussed because it is difficult or impossible to predict the amount of traffic to our system.

- Availability is the percentage of time a system can accept requests and return the desired response. Most, but not all, systems require high availability, so we should clarify whether it is a requirement in our system.

- Fault-tolerance is the ability of a system to continue operating if some components fail and the prevention of permanent harm should downtime occur. This allows our users to continue using some features and buys time for engineers to fix the failed components.

- Performance or latency is the time taken for a user's request to the system to return a response. Users expect interactive applications to load fast and respond quickly to their input.

- Consistency is defined as all nodes containing the same data at a moment in time, and when changes in data occur, all nodes must start serving the changed data at the same time. In certain systems, such as financial systems, multiple users viewing the same data must see the same values, while in other systems such as social media, it may be permissible for different users to view slightly different data at any point in time, as long as the data is eventually the same.

- Eventually, consistent systems trade off accuracy for lower complexity and cost.

- Complexity must be minimized so the system is cheaper and easier to build and maintain. Use common techniques, such as common services, wherever applicable.

- Cost discussions include minimizing complexity, cost of outages, cost of maintenance, cost of switching to other technologies, and cost of decommissioning.

- Security discussions include which data must be secured and which can be unsecured, followed by using concepts such as encryption in transit and encryption at rest.

- Privacy considerations include access control mechanisms and procedures, deletion or obfuscation of user data, and prevention and mitigation of data breaches.

- Cloud native is an approach to system design that employs a collection of techniques to achieve common non-functional requirements.

Scaling databases

This chapter covers

- Understanding various types of storage services
- Replicating databases
- Aggregating events to reduce database writes
- Differentiating normalization vs. denormalization
- Caching frequent queries in memory

In this chapter, we discuss concepts in scaling databases, their tradeoffs, and common databases that utilize these concepts in their implementations. We consider these concepts when choosing databases for various services in our system.

4.1 Brief prelude on storage services

Storage services are stateful services. Compared to stateless services, *stateful services* have mechanisms to ensure consistency and require redundancy to avoid data loss. A stateful service may choose mechanisms like Paxos for strong consistency or eventual-consistency mechanisms. These are complex decisions, and tradeoffs have to be made, which depend on the various requirements like consistency, complexity, security, latency, and performance. This is one reason we keep all services stateless as much as possible and keep state only in stateful services.

NOTE   In strong consistency, all accesses are seen by all parallel processes (or nodes, processors, etc.) in the same order (sequentially). Therefore, only one consistent state can be observed, as opposed to weak consistency, where different parallel processes (or nodes, etc.) can perceive variables in different states.

Another reason is that if we keep state in individual hosts of a web or backend service, we will need to implement sticky sessions, consistently routing the same user to the same host. We will also need to replicate the data in case a host fails and handle failover (such as routing the users to the appropriate new host when their host fails). By pushing all states to a stateful storage service, we can choose the appropriate storage/database technology for our requirements, and take advantage of not having to design, implement, and make mistakes with managing state.

Storage can be broadly classified into the following. We should know how to distinguish between these categories. A complete introduction to various storage types is outside the scope of this book (refer to other materials if required), the following are brief notes required to follow the discussions in this book:

- *Database:*
  - *SQL*—Has relational characteristics such as tables and relationships between tables, including primary keys and foreign keys. SQL must have ACID properties.
  - *NoSQL*—A database that does not have all SQL properties.
  - *Column-oriented*—Organizes data into columns instead of rows for efficient filtering. Examples are Cassandra and HBase.
  - *Key-value*—Data is stored as a collection of key-value pairs. Each key corresponds to a disk location via a hashing algorithm. Read performance is good. Keys must be hashable, so they are primitive types and cannot be pointers to objects. Values don't have this limitation; they can be primitives or pointers. Key-value databases are usually used for caching, employing various techniques like Least Recently Used (LRU). Cache has high performance but does not require high availability (because if the cache is unavailable, the requester can query the original data source). Examples are Memcached and Redis.
- *Document*—Can be interpreted as a key-value database where values have no size limits or much larger limits than key-value databases. Values can be in various formats. Text, JSON, or YAML are common. An example is MongoDB.
- *Graph*—Designed to efficiently store relationships between entities. Examples are Neo4j, RedisGraph, and Amazon Neptune.
- *File storage*—Data stored in files, which can be organized into directories/folders. We can see it as a form of key-value, with path as the key.
- *Block storage*—Stores data in evenly sized chunks with unique identifiers. We are unlikely to use block storage in web applications. Block storage is relevant for designing low-level components of other storage systems (such as databases).

- *Object storage*—Flatter hierarchy than file storage. Objects are usually accessed with simple HTTP APIs. Writing objects is slow, and objects cannot be modified, so object storage is suited for static data. AWS S3 is a cloud example.

4.2 When to use vs. avoid databases

When deciding how to store a service's data, you may discuss using a database vs. other possibilities such as file, block, and object storage. During the interview, remember that even though you may prefer certain approaches and you can state a preference during an interview, you must be able to discuss all relevant factors and consider others' opinions. In this section, we discuss various factors that you may bring up. As always, discuss various approaches and tradeoffs.

The decision to choose between a database or filesystem is usually based on discretion and heuristics. There are few academic studies or rigorous principles. A commonly cited conclusion from an old 2006 Microsoft paper (https://www.microsoft.com/en-us/research/publication/to-blob-or-not-to-blob-large-object-storage-in-a-database-or-a-filesystem) states, "Objects smaller than 256K are best stored in a database while objects larger than 1M are best stored in the filesystem. Between 256K and 1M, the read:write ratio and rate of object overwrite or replacement are important factors." A few other points:

- SQL Server requires special configuration settings to store files larger than 2 GB.
- Database objects are loaded entirely into memory, so it is inefficient to stream a file from a database.
- Replication will be slow if database table rows are large objects because these large blob objects will need to be replicated from the leader node to follower nodes.

4.3 Replication

We scale a database (i.e., implement a distributed database onto multiple hosts, commonly called nodes in database terminology) via replication, partitioning, and sharding. Replication is making copies of data, called replicas, and storing them on different nodes. Partitioning and sharing are both about dividing a data set into subsets. Sharding implies the subsets are distributed across multiple nodes, while partitioning does not. A single host has limitations, so it cannot fulfill our requirements:

- *Fault-tolerance*—Each node can back up its data onto other nodes within and across data centers in case of node or network failure. We can define a failover process for other nodes to take over the roles and partitions/shards of failed nodes.
- *Higher storage capacity*—A single node can be vertically scaled to contain multiple hard drives of the largest available capacity, but this is monetarily expensive, and along the way, the node's throughput may become a problem.

- *Higher throughput*—The database needs to process reads and writes for multiple simultaneous processes and users. Vertical scaling approaches its limits with the fastest network card, a better CPU, and more memory.

- *Lower latency*—We can geographically distribute replicas to be closer to dispersed users. We can increase the number of particular replicas on a data center if there are more reads on that data from that locality.

To scale reads (SELECT operation), we simply increase the number of replicas of that data. Scaling writes is more difficult, and much of this chapter is about handling the difficulties of scaling write operations.

4.3.1   Distributing replicas

A typical design is to have one backup onto a host on the same rack and one backup on a host on a different rack or data center or both. There is much literature on this topic (e.g., https://learn.microsoft.com/en-us/azure/availability-zones/az-overview).

The data may also be sharded, which provides the following benefits. The main tradeoff of sharding is increased complexity from needing to track the shards' locations:

- *Scale storage*—If a database/table is too big to fit into a single node, sharding across nodes allows the database/table to remain a single logical unit.

- *Scale memory*—If a database is stored in memory, it may need to be sharded, since vertical scaling of memory on a single node quickly becomes monetarily expensive.

- *Scale processing*—A sharded database may take advantage of parallel processing.

- *Locality*—A database may be sharded such that the data a particular cluster node needs is likely to be stored locally rather than on another shard on another node.

NOTE   For linearizability, certain partitioned databases like HDFS implement deletion as an append operation (called a logical soft delete). In HDFS, this is called appending a tombstone. This prevents disruptions and inconsistency to read operations that are still running while deletion occurs.

4.3.2   Single-leader replication

In single-leader replication, all write operations occur on a single node, called the leader. Single-leader replication is about scaling reads, not writes. Some SQL distributions such as MySQL and Postgres have configurations for single-leader replication. The SQL service loses its ACID consistency. This is a relevant consideration if we choose to horizontally scale a SQL database to serve a service with high traffic.

Figure 4.1 illustrates single-leader replication with primary-secondary leader failover. All writes (also called Data Manipulation Language or DDL queries in SQL) occur on the primary leader node and are replicated to its followers, including the secondary leader. If the primary leader fails, the failover process promotes the secondary leader to primary. When the failed leader is restored, it becomes the secondary leader.

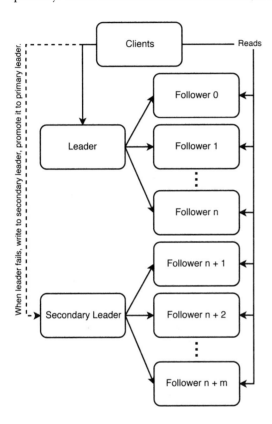

Figure 4.1   Single-leader replication with primary-secondary leader failover. Figure adapted from *Web Scalability for Startup Engineers* by Artur Ejsmont, figure 5.4 (McGraw Hill, 2015).

A single node has a maximum throughput that must be shared by its followers, imposing a maximum number of followers, which in turn limits read scalability. To scale reads further, we can use multi-level replication, shown in figure 4.2. There are multiple levels of followers, like a pyramid. Each level replicates to the one below. Each node replicates to the number of followers that it is capable of handling, with the tradeoff that consistency is further delayed.

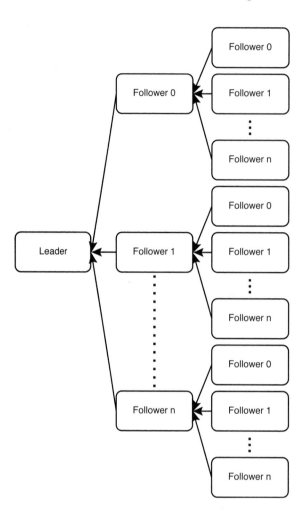

Figure 4.2   Multi-level replication. Each node replicates to its followers, which in turn replicates to their followers. This architecture ensures a node replicates to the number of followers that it is capable of handling, with the tradeoff that consistency is further delayed.

Single-leader replication is the simplest to implement. The main limitation of single-leader replication is that the entire database must fit into a single host. Another limitation is eventual consistency, as write replication to followers takes time.

MySQL binlog-based replication is an example of single-leader replication. Refer to chapter 5 of Ejsmont's book *Web Scalability for Startup Engineers* for a good discussion. Here are some relevant online documents:

- https://dev.to/tutelaris/introduction-to-mysql-replication-97c

- https://dev.mysql.com/doc/refman/8.0/en/binlog-replication-configuration-overview.html
- https://www.digitalocean.com/community/tutorials/how-to-set-up-replication-in-mysql
- https://docs.microsoft.com/en-us/azure/mysql/single-server/how-to-data-in-replication
- https://www.percona.com/blog/2013/01/09/how-does-mysql-replication-really-work/
- https://hevodata.com/learn/mysql-binlog-based-replication/

A HACK TO SCALING SINGLE-LEADER REPLICATION: QUERY LOGIC IN THE APPLICATION LAYER

Manually entered strings increase database size slowly, which you can verify with simple estimates and calculations. If data was programmatically generated or has accumulated for a long period of time, storage size may grow beyond a single node.

If we cannot reduce the database size but we wish to continue using SQL, a possible way is to divide the data between multiple SQL databases. This means that our service has to be configured to connect to more than one SQL database, and we need to rewrite our SQL queries in the application to query from the appropriate database.

If we had to partition a single table into two or more databases, then our application will need to query multiple databases and combine the results. Querying logic is no longer encapsulated in the database and has spilled into the application. The application must store metadata to track which databases contain particular data. This is essentially multi-leader replication with metadata management in the application. The services and databases are more difficult to maintain, particularly if there are multiple services using these databases.

For example, if our bagel cafe recommender Beigel processes billions of searches daily, a single SQL table `fact_searches` that records our searches will grow to TBs within days. We can partition this data across multiple databases, each in its own cluster. We can partition by day and create a new table daily and name the tables in the format `fact_searches_YYYY_MM_DD` (e.g., `fact_searches_2023_01_01` and `fact_searches_2023_01_02`). Any application that queries these tables will need to have this partition logic, which, in this case, is the table-naming convention. In a more complex example, certain customers may make so many transactions that we need tables just for them. If many queries to our search API originate from other food recommender apps, we may create a table for each of them (e.g., `fact_searches_a_2023_01_01`) to store all searches on January 1, 2023, from companies that start with the letter A. We may need another SQL table, `search_orgs`, that stores metadata about companies that make search requests to Beigel.

We may suggest this during a discussion as a possibility, but it is highly unlikely that we will use this design. We should use databases with multi-leader or leaderless replication.

4.3.3 *Multi-leader replication*

Multi-leader and leaderless replication are techniques to scale writes and database storage size. They require handling of race conditions, which are not present in single-leader replication.

In multi-leader replication, as the name suggests, there are multiple nodes designated as leaders and writes can be made on any leader. Each leader must replicate its writes to all other nodes.

CONSISTENCY PROBLEMS AND APPROACHES

This replication introduces consistency and race conditions for operations where sequence is important. For example, if a row is updated in one leader while it is being deleted in another, what should be the outcome? Using timestamps to order operations does not work because the clocks on different nodes cannot be perfectly synchronized. Attempting to use the same clock on different nodes doesn't work because each node will receive the clock's signals at different times, a well-known phenomenon called *clock skew*. So even server clocks that are periodically synchronized with the same source will differ by a few milliseconds or greater. If queries are made to different servers within time intervals smaller than this difference, it is impossible to determine the order in which they were made.

Here we discuss replication problems and scenarios related to consistency that we commonly encounter in a system design interview. These situations may occur with any storage format, including databases and file systems. The book *Designing Data-Intensive Applications* by Martin Kleppmann and its references have more thorough treatments of replication pitfalls.

What is the definition of database consistency? Consistency ensures a database transaction brings the database from one valid state to another, maintaining database invariants; any data written to the database must be valid according to all defined rules, including constraints, cascades, triggers, or any combination thereof.

As discussed elsewhere in this book, consistency has a complex definition. A common informal understanding of consistency is that the data must be the same for every user:

1 The same query on multiple replicas should return the same results, even though the replicas are on different physical servers.
2 Data Manipulation Language (DML) queries (i.e., INSERT, UPDATE, or DELETE) on different physical servers that affect the same rows should be executed in the sequence that they were sent.

We may accept eventual consistency, but any particular user may need to receive data that is a valid state to them. For example, if user A queries for a counter's value, increments a counter by one and then queries again for that counter's value, it will make sense to user A to receive a value incremented by one. Meanwhile, other users who query for the counter may be provided the value before it was incremented. This is called read-after-write consistency.

In general, look for ways to relax the consistency requirements. Find approaches that minimize the amount of data that must be kept consistent for all users.

DML queries on different physical servers that affect the same rows may cause race conditions. Some possible situations:

- DELETE and INSERT the same row on a table with a primary key. If the DELETE executed first, the row should exist. If the INSERT was first, the primary key prevents execution, and DELETE should delete the row.
- Two UPDATE operations on the same cell with different values. Only one should be the eventual state.

What about DML queries sent at the same millisecond to different servers? This is an exceedingly unlikely situation, and there seems to be no common convention for resolving race conditions in such situations. We can suggest various approaches. One approach is to prioritize DELETE over INSERT/UPDATE and randomly break the ties for other INSERT/UPDATE queries. Anyway, a competent interviewer will not waste seconds of the 50-minute interview on discussions that yield no signals like this one.

4.3.4   *Leaderless replication*

In leaderless replication, all nodes are equal. Reads and writes can occur on any node. How are race conditions handled? One method is to introduce the concept of quorum. A quorum is the minimum number of nodes that must be in agreement for consensus. It is easy to reason that if our database has n nodes and reads and writes both have quorums of $n/2 + 1$ nodes, consistency is guaranteed. If we desire consistency, we choose between fast writes and fast reads. If fast writes are required, set a low write quorum and high read quorum, and vice versa for fast reads. Otherwise, only eventual consistency is possible, and UPDATE and DELETE operations cannot be consistent.

Cassandra, Dynamo, Riak, and Voldemort are examples of databases that use leaderless replication. In Cassandra, UPDATE operations suffer from race conditions, while DELETE operations are implemented using tombstones instead of the rows actually being deleted. In HDFS, reads and replication are based on rack locality, and all replicas are equal.

4.3.5   *HDFS replication*

This is a brief refresher section on HDFS, Hadoop, and Hive. Detailed discussions are outside the scope of this book.

HDFS replication does not fit cleanly into any of these three approaches. An HDFS cluster has an active NameNode, a passive (backup) NameNode, and multiple DataNode nodes. The NameNode executes file system namespace operations like opening, closing, and renaming files and directories. It also determines the mapping of blocks to DataNodes. The DataNodes are responsible for serving read and write requests from the file system's clients. The DataNodes also perform block creation, deletion, and replication upon instruction from the NameNode. User data never flows through the

NameNode. HDFS stores a table as one or more files in a directory. Each file is divided into blocks, which are sharded across DataNode nodes. The default block size is 64 MB; this value can be set by admins.

Hadoop is a framework that stores and processes distributed data using the MapReduce programming model. Hive is a data warehouse solution built on top of Hadoop. Hive has the concept of partitioning tables by one or more columns for efficient filter queries. For example, we can create a partitioned Hive table as follows:

```
CREATE TABLE sample_table (user_id STRING, created_date DATE,
    country STRING) PARTITIONED BY (created_date, country);
```

Figure 4.3 illustrates the directory tree of this table. The table's directory has subdirectories for the date values, which in turn have subdirectories for the column values. Queries filtered by created_date and/or country will process only the relevant files, avoiding the waste of a full table scan.

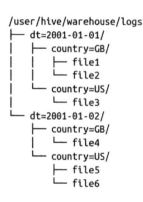

Figure 4.3   An example HDFS directory tree of a table "sample_table" whose columns include date and country, and the table is partitioned by these two columns. The sample_table directory has subdirectories for the date values, which in turn have subdirectories for the column values. (Source: https://stackoverflow.com/questions/44782173/hive-does-hive-support -partitioning-and-bucketing-while-usiing-external-tables.)

HDFS is append-only, and does not support UPDATE or DELETE operations, possibly because of possible replication race conditions from UPDATE and DELETE. INSERT does not have race conditions.

HDFS has name quotas, space quotas, and storage type quotas. Regarding a directory tree:

- A name quota is a hard limit on the number of file and directory names.
- A space quota is a hard limit on the number of bytes in all files.
- A storage type quota is a hard limit on the usage of specific storage types. Discussion of HDFS storage types is outside the scope of this book.

TIP   Novices to Hadoop and HDFS often use the Hadoop INSERT command, which should be avoided. An INSERT query creates a new file with a single row, which will occupy an entire 64 MB block and is wasteful. It also contributes to the number of names, and programmatic INSERT queries will soon exceed the name quota. Refer to https://hadoop.apache.org/docs/current/hadoop-project-dist/hadoop-hdfs/HdfsQuotaAdminGuide.html for more information. One should append directly to the HDFS file, while ensuring that the appended rows have the same fields as the existing rows in the file to prevent data inconsistency and processing errors.

If we are using Spark, which saves data on HDFS, we should use `saveAsTable` or `saveAsTextFile` instead, such as the following example code snippet. Refer to the Spark documentation such as https://spark.apache.org/docs/latest/sql-data-sources-hive-tables.html.

```
val spark = SparkSession.builder().appName("Our app").config("some.config",
    "value").getOrCreate()
val df = spark.sparkContext.textFile({hdfs_file})
df.createOrReplaceTempView({table_name})
spark.sql({spark_sql_query_with_table_name}).saveAsTextFile({hdfs_directory})
```

4.3.6   *Further reading*

Refer to *Designing Data-Intensive Applications* by Martin Kleppmann (O'Reilly, 2017) for more discussion on topics such as

- Consistency techniques like read repair, anti-entropy, and tuples.
- Multi-leader replication consensus algorithm and implementations in CouchDB, MySQL Group replication, and Postgres.
- Failover problems, like split brain.
- Various consensus algorithms to resolve these race conditions. A consensus algorithm is for achieving agreement on a data value.

4.4   *Scaling storage capacity with sharded databases*

If the database size grows to exceed the capacity of a single host, we will need to delete old rows. If we need to retain this old data, we should store it in sharded storage such as HDFS or Cassandra. Sharded storage is horizontally scalable and in theory should support an infinite storage capacity simply by adding more hosts. There are production HDFS clusters with over 100 PB (https://eng.uber.com/uber-big-data-platform/). Cluster capacity of YB is theoretically possible, but the monetary cost of the hardware required to store and perform analytics on such amounts of data will be prohibitively expensive.

> **TIP**   We can use a database with low latency such as Redis to store data used to directly serve consumers.

Another approach is to store the data in the consumer's devices or browser cookies and localStorage. However, this means that any processing of this data must also be done on the frontend and not the backend.

4.4.1   Sharded RDBMS

If we need to use an RDBMS, and the amount of data exceeds what can be stored on a single node, we can use a sharded RDBMS solution like Amazon RDS (https://aws .amazon.com/blogs/database/sharding-with-amazon-relational-database-service/), or implement our own sharded SQL. These solutions impose limitations on SQL operations:

- JOIN queries will be much slower. A JOIN query will involve considerable network traffic between each node and every other node. Consider a JOIN between two tables on a particular column. If both tables are sharded across the nodes, each shard of one table needs to compare the value of this column in every row with the same column in every row of the other table. If the JOIN is being done on the columns that are used as the shard keys, then the JOIN will be much more efficient, since each node will know which other nodes to perform the JOIN on. We may constrain JOIN operations to such columns only.

- Aggregation operations will involve both the database and application. Certain aggregation operations will be easier than others, such as sum or mean. Each node simply needs to sum and/or count the values and then return these aggregated values to the application, which can perform simple arithmetic to obtain the final result. Certain aggregation operations such as median and percentile will be more complicated and slower.

4.5   Aggregating events

Database writes are difficult and expensive to scale, so we should try to reduce the rate of database writes wherever possible in our system's design. Sampling and aggregation are common techniques to reduce database write rate. An added bonus is slower database size growth.

Besides reducing database writes, we can also reduce database reads by techniques such as caching and approximation. Chapter 17 discusses count-min sketch, an algorithm for creating an approximate frequency table for events in a continuous data stream.

Sampling data means to consider only certain data points and ignoring others. There are many possible sampling strategies, including sampling every nth data point or just random sampling. With sampling in writes, we write data at a lower rate than if we write all data points. Sampling is conceptually trivial and is something we can mention during an interview.

Aggregating events is about aggregating/combining multiple events into a single event, so instead of multiple database writes, only a single database write must occur. We can consider aggregation if the exact timestamps of individual events are unimportant.

Aggregation can be implemented using a streaming pipeline. The first stage of the streaming pipeline may receive a high rate of events and require a large cluster with thousands of hosts. Without aggregation, every succeeding stage will also require a large cluster. Aggregation allows each succeeding stage to have fewer hosts. We also use replication and checkpointing in case hosts fail. Referring to chapter 5, we can use a distributed transaction algorithm such as Saga, or quorum writes, to ensure that each event is replicated to a minimum number of replicas.

4.5.1 Single-tier aggregation

Aggregation can be single or multi-tier. Figure 4.4 illustrates an example of single-tier aggregation, for counting numbers of values. In this example, an event can have value A, B, C, etc. These events can be evenly distributed across the hosts by a load balancer. Each host can contain a hash table in memory and aggregate these counts in its hash table. Each host can flush the counts to the database periodically (such as every five minutes) or when it is running out of memory, whichever is sooner.

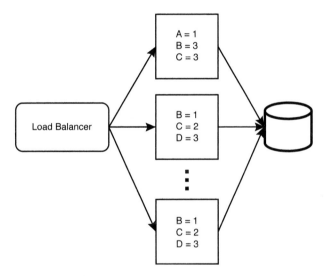

Figure 4.4   An example illustration of single-tier aggregation. A load balancer distributes events across a single layer/tier of hosts, which aggregate them and then writes these aggregated counts to the database. If the individual events were written directly to the database, the write rate will be much higher, and the database will have to be scaled up. Not illustrated here are the host replicas, which are required if high availability and accuracy are necessary.

4.5.2 Multi-tier aggregation

Figure 4.5 illustrates multi-tier aggregation. Each layer of hosts can aggregate events from its ancestors in the previous tier. We can progressively reduce the number of hosts in each layer until there is a desired number of hosts (this number is up to our requirements and available resources) in the final layer, which writes to the database.

The main tradeoffs of aggregation are eventual consistency and increased complexity. Each layer adds some latency to our pipeline and thus our database writes, so database reads may be stale. Implementing replication, logging, monitoring, and alerting also add complexity to this system.

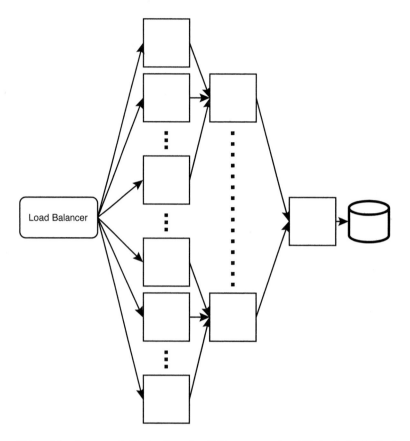

Figure 4.5   An example illustration of multi-tier aggregation. This is similar to the inverse of multi-level replication.

4.5.3   *Partitioning*

This requires a level 7 load balancer. (Refer to section 3.1.2 for a brief description of a level 7 load balancer.) The load balancer can be configured to process incoming events and forward them to certain hosts depending on the events' contents.

Referring to the example in figure 4.6, if the events are simply values from A–Z, the load balancer can be configured to forward events with values of A–I to certain hosts, events with values J–R to certain hosts, and events with values S–Z to certain hosts. The hash tables from the first layer of hosts are aggregated into a second layer of hosts, then into a final hash table host. Finally, this hash table is sent to a max-heap host, which constructs the final max-heap.

We can expect event traffic to follow normal distribution, which means certain partitions will receive disproportionately high traffic. To address this, referring to figure 4.6, we observe that we can allocate a different number of hosts to each partition. Partition A–I has three hosts, J–R has one host, and S–Z has two hosts. We make these partitioning decisions because traffic is uneven across partitions, and certain hosts may receive disproportionately high traffic, (i.e., they become "hot"), more than what they are able to process.

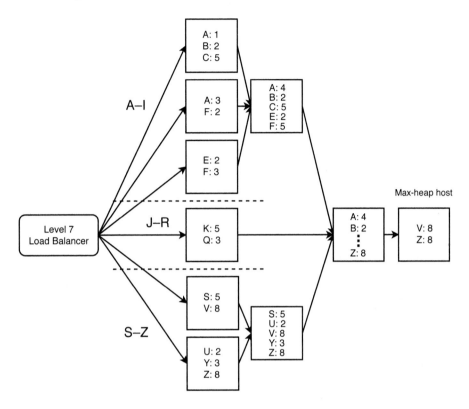

Figure 4.6   An example illustration of multi-tier aggregation with partitioning

We also observe that partition J–R has only one host, so it does not have a second layer. As designers, we can make such decisions based on our situation.

Besides allocating a different number of hosts to each partition, another way to evenly distribute traffic is to adjust the number and width of the partitions. For example, instead of {A-I, J-R, S-Z}, we can create partitions {{A-B, D-F}, {C, G-J}, {K-S}, {T-Z}}. That is, we changed from three to four partitions and put C in the second partition. We can be creative and dynamic in addressing our system's scalability requirements.

4.5.4   Handling a large key space

Figure 4.6 in the previous section illustrates a tiny key space of 26 keys from A–Z. In a practical implementation, the key space will be much larger. We must ensure that the combined key spaces of a particular level do not cause memory overflow in the next level. The hosts in the earlier aggregation levels should limit their key space to less than what their memory can accommodate, so that the hosts in the later aggregation levels have sufficient memory to accommodate all the keys. This may mean that the hosts in earlier aggregation levels will need to flush more frequently.

For example, figure 4.7 illustrates a simple aggregation service with only two levels. There are two hosts in the first level and one host in the second level. The two hosts in the first level should limit their key space to half of what they can actually accommodate, so the host in the second level can accommodate all keys.

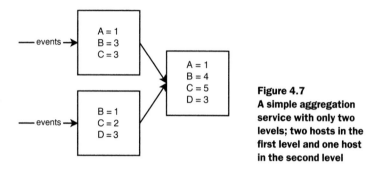

Figure 4.7
A simple aggregation service with only two levels; two hosts in the first level and one host in the second level

We can also provision hosts with less memory for earlier aggregation levels, and hosts with more memory in later levels.

4.5.5   *Replication and fault-tolerance*

So far, we have not discussed replication and fault-tolerance. If a host goes down, it loses all of its aggregated events. Moreover, this is a cascading failure because all its earlier hosts may overflow, and these aggregated events will likewise be lost.

We can use checkpointing and dead letter queues, discussed in sections 3.3.6 and 3.3.7. However, since a large number of hosts may be affected by the outage of a host that is many levels deep, a large amount of processing has to be repeated, which is a waste of resources. This outage may also add considerable latency to the aggregation.

A possible solution is to convert each node into an independent service with a cluster of multiple stateless nodes that make requests to a shared in-memory database like Redis. Figure 4.8 illustrates such a service. The service can have multiple hosts (e.g., three stateless hosts). A shared load balancing service can spread requests across these hosts. Scalability is not a concern here, so each service can have just a few (e.g., three hosts for fault-tolerance).

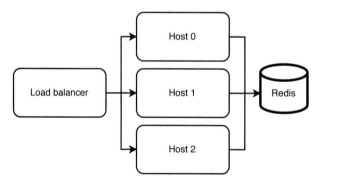

Figure 4.8   We can replace a node with a service, which we refer to as an aggregation unit. This unit has three stateless hosts for fault-tolerance, but we can use more hosts if desired.

At the beginning of this chapter, we discussed that we wanted to avoid database writes, which we seem to contradict here. However, each service has a separate Redis cluster, so there is no competition for writing to the same key. Moreover, these aggregated events are deleted each successful flush, so the database size will not grow uncontrollably.

NOTE We can use Terraform to define this entire aggregation service. Each aggregation unit can be a Kubernetes cluster with three pods, and one host per pod (two hosts if we are using a sidecar service pattern).

4.6   *Batch and streaming ETL*

ETL (Extract, Transform, Load) is a general procedure of copying data from one or more sources into a destination system, which represents the data differently from the source(s) or in a different context than the source(s). Batch refers to processing the data in batches, usually periodically, but it can also be manually triggered. Streaming refers to a continuous flow of data to be processed in real time.

We can think of batch vs. streaming as analogous to polling vs. interrupt. Similar to polling, a batch job always runs at a defined frequency regardless of whether there are new events to process, while a streaming job runs whenever a trigger condition is met, which is usually the publishing of a new event.

An example use case for batch jobs is to generate monthly bills (such as PDF or CSV files) for customers. Such a batch job is especially relevant if the data required for these bills are only available on a certain date each month (e.g., billing statements from our vendors that we need to generate bills for our customers). If all data to generate these periodic files are generated within our organization, we can consider Kappa architecture (refer to chapter 17) and implement a streaming job that processes each piece of data as soon as it is available. The advantages of this approach are that the monthly files are available almost as soon as the month is over, the data processing costs are spread out over the month, and it is easier to debug a function that processes a small piece of data at a time, rather than a batch job that processes GBs of data.

Airflow and Luigi are common batch tools. Kafka and Flink are common streaming tools. Flume and Scribe are specialized streaming tools for logging; they aggregate log data streamed in real time from many servers. Here we briefly introduce some ETL concepts.

An ETL pipeline consists of a Directed Acyclic Graph (DAG) of tasks. In the DAG, a node corresponds to a task, and its ancestors are its dependencies. A job is a single run of an ETL pipeline.

4.6.1   *A simple batch ETL pipeline*

A simple batch ETL pipeline can be implemented using a crontab, two SQL tables, and a script (i.e., a program written in a scripting language) for each job. cron is suitable for small noncritical jobs with no parallelism where a single machine is adequate. The following are the two example SQL tables:

```
CREATE TABLE cron_dag (
  id INT,              -- ID of a job.
  parent_id INT,        -- Parent job. A job can have 0, 1, or multiple
     parents.
  PRIMARY KEY (id),
  FOREIGN KEY (parent_id) REFERENCES cron_dag (id)
);
CREATE TABLE cron_jobs (
  id INT,
  name VARCHAR(255),
  updated_at INT,
  PRIMARY KEY (id)
);
```

The crontab's instructions can be a list of the scripts. In this example, we used Python scripts, though we can use any scripting language. We can place all the scripts in a common directory /cron_dag/dag/, and other Python files/modules in other directories. There are no rules on how to organize the files; this is up to what we believe is the best arrangement:

```
0 * * * * ~/cron_dag/dag/first_node.py
0 * * * * ~/cron_dag/dag/second_node.py
```

Each script can follow the following algorithm. Steps 1 and 2 can be abstracted into reusable modules:

1 Check that the updated_at value of the relevant job is less than its dependent jobs.
2 Trigger monitoring if necessary.
3 Execute the specific job.

The main disadvantages of this setup are:

- It isn't scalable. All jobs run on a single host, which carries all the usual disadvantages of a single host:
  - There's a single point of failure.
  - There may be insufficient computational resources to run all the jobs scheduled at a particular time.
  - The host's storage capacity may be exceeded.
- A job may consist of numerous smaller tasks, like sending a notification to millions of devices. If such a job fails and needs to be retried, we need to avoid repeating the smaller tasks that succeeded (i.e., the individual tasks should be idempotent). This simple design does not provide such idempotency.
- No validation tools to ensure the job IDs are consistent in the Python scripts and SQL tables, so this setup is vulnerable to programming errors.
- No GUI (unless we make one ourselves).

- We have not yet implemented logging, monitoring, or alerting. This is very important and should be our next step. For example, what if a job fails or a host crashes while it is running a job? We need to ensure that scheduled jobs complete successfully.

QUESTION   How can we horizontally scale this simple batch ETL pipeline to improve its scalability and availability?

Dedicated job scheduling systems include Airflow and Luigi. These tools come with web UIs for DAG visualization and GUI user-friendliness. They are also vertically scalable and can be run on clusters to manage large numbers of jobs. In this book, whenever we need a batch ETL service, we use an organizational-level shared Airflow service.

4.6.2   *Messaging terminology*

The section clarifies common terminology for various types of messaging and streaming setups that one tends to encounter in technical discussions or literature.

MESSAGING SYSTEM

A messaging system is a general term for a system that transfers data from one application to another to reduce the complexity of data transmission and sharing in applications, so application developers can focus on data processing.

MESSAGE QUEUE

A message contains a work object of instructions sent from one service to another, waiting in the queue to be processed. Each message is processed only once by a single consumer.

PRODUCER/CONSUMER

Producer/consumer aka publisher/subscriber or pub/sub, is an asynchronous messaging system that decouples services that produce events from services that process events. A producer/consumer system contains one or more message queues.

MESSAGE BROKER

A message broker is a program that translates a message from the formal messaging protocol of the sender to the formal messaging protocol of the receiver. A message broker is a translation layer. Kafka and RabbitMQ are both message brokers. RabbitMQ claims to be "the most widely deployed open-source message broker" (https://www.rabbitmq.com/). AMQP is one of the messaging protocols implemented by RabbitMQ. A description of AMQP is outside the scope of this book. Kafka implements its own custom messaging protocol.

EVENT STREAMING

Event streaming is a general term that refers to a continuous flow of events that are processed in real time. An event contains information about a change of state. Kafka is the most common event streaming platform.

PULL VS. PUSH

Inter-service communication can be done by pull or push. In general, pull is better than push, and this is the general concept behind producer-consumer architectures. In pull, the consumer controls the rate of message consumption and will not be overloaded.

Load testing and stress testing may be done on the consumer during its development, and monitoring its throughput and performance with production traffic and comparing the measurements with the tests allows the team to accurately determine if more engineering resources are needed to improve the tests. The consumer can monitor its throughput and producer queue sizes over time, and the team can scale it as required.

If our production system has a continuously high load, it is unlikely that the queue will be empty for any significant period, and our consumer can keep polling for messages. If we have a situation where we must maintain a large streaming cluster to process unpredictable traffic spikes within a few minutes, we should use this cluster for other lower-priority messages too (i.e., a common Flink, Kafka, or Spark service for the organization).

Another situation where polling or pull from a user is better than push is if the user is firewalled, or if the dependency has frequent changes and will make too many push requests. Pull also will have one less setup step than push. The user is already making requests to the dependency. However, the dependency usually does not make requests to the user.

The flip side (https://engineering.linkedin.com/blog/2019/data-hub) is if our system collects data from many sources using crawlers; development and maintenance of all these crawlers may be too complex and tedious. It may be more scalable for individual data providers to push information to our central repository. Push also allows more timely updates.

One more exception where push is better than pull is in lossy applications like audio and video live-streaming. These applications do not resend data that failed to deliver the first time, and they generally use UDP to push data to their recipients.

4.6.3   *Kafka vs. RabbitMQ*

In practice, most companies have a shared Kafka service, that is used by other services. In the rest of this book, we will use Kafka when we need a messaging or event-streaming service. In an interview, rather than risk the ire of an opinionated interviewer, it is safer to display our knowledge of the details of and differences between Kafka and RabbitMQ and discuss their tradeoffs.

Both can be used to smooth out uneven traffic, preventing our service from being overloaded by traffic spikes, and keeping our service cost-efficient, because we do not need to provision a large number of hosts just to handle periods of high traffic.

Kafka is more complex than RabbitMQ and provides a superset of capabilities over RabbitMQ. In other words, Kafka can always be used in place of RabbitMQ but not vice versa.

If RabbitMQ is sufficient for our system, we can suggest using RabbitMQ, and also state that our organization likely has a Kafka service that we can use so as to avoid the trouble of setup and maintenance (including logging, monitoring and alerting) of another component such as RabbitMQ. Table 4.1 lists differences between Kafka and RabbitMQ.

Table 4.1 Some differences between Kafka and RabbitMQ

Kafka	RabbitMQ
Designed for scalability, reliability, and availability. More complex setup required than RabbitMQ. Requires ZooKeeper to manage the Kafka cluster. This includes configuring IP addresses of every Kafka host in ZooKeeper.	Simple to set up, but not scalable by default. We can implement scalability on our own at the application level by attaching our application to a load balancer and producing to and consuming from the load balancer. But this will take more work to set up than Kafka and being far less mature will almost certainly be inferior in many ways.
A durable message broker because it has replication. We can adjust the replication factor on ZooKeeper and arrange replication to be done on different server racks and data centers.	Not scalable, so not durable by default. Messages are lost if downtime occurs. Has a "lazy queue" feature to persist messages to disk for better durability, but this does not protect against disk failure on the host.
Events on the queue are not removed after consumption, so the same event can be consumed repeatedly. This is for failure tolerance, in case the consumer fails before it finished processing the event and needs to reprocess the event.	Messages on the queue are removed upon dequeuing, as per the definition of "queue" (RabbitMQ 3.9 released on July 26, 2021, has a stream https://www.rabbitmq.com/streams.html feature that allows repeated consumption of each message, so this difference is only present for earlier versions.)
In this regard, it is conceptually inaccurate to use the term "queue" in Kafka. It is actually a list. But the term "Kafka queue" is commonly used.	We may create several queues to allow several consumers per message, one queue per consumer. But this is not the intended use of having multiple queues.
We can configure a retention period in Kafka, which is seven days by default, so an event is deleted after seven days regardless of whether it has been consumed. We can choose to set the retention period to infinite and use Kafka as a database.	Has the concept of AMQP standard per-message queue priority. We can create multiple queues with varying priority. Messages on a queue are not dequeued until higher-priority queues are empty. No concept of fairness or consideration of starvation.
No concept of priority.	

4.6.4   *Lambda architecture*

Lambda architecture is a data-processing architecture for processing big data running batch and streaming pipelines in parallel. In informal terms, it refers to having parallel fast and slow pipelines that update the same destination. The fast pipeline trades off consistency and accuracy for lower latency (i.e., fast updates), and vice versa for the slow pipeline. The fast pipeline employs techniques such as:

- Approximation algorithms (discussed in section 17.7).
- In-memory databases like Redis.
- For faster processing, nodes in the fast pipeline may not replicate the data that they process so there may be some data loss and lower accuracy from node outages.

The slow pipeline usually uses MapReduce databases, such as Hive and Spark with HDFS. We can suggest lambda architecture for systems that involve big data and require consistency and accuracy.

> ### Note on various database solutions
>
> There are numerous database solutions. Common ones include various SQL distributions, Hadoop and HDFS, Kafka, Redis, and Elasticsearch. There are numerous less-common ones, including MongoDB, Neo4j, AWS DynamoDB, and Google's Firebase Realtime Database. In general, knowledge of less common databases, especially proprietary databases, is not expected in a system design interview. Proprietary databases are seldom adopted. If a startup does adopt a proprietary database, it should consider migrating to an open-source database sooner rather than later. The bigger the database, the worse the vendor lock-in as the migration process will be more difficult, error-prone, and expensive.

An alternative to Lambda architecture is Kappa architecture. *Kappa architecture* is a software architecture pattern for processing streaming data, performing both batch and streaming processing with a single technology stack. It uses an append-only immutable log like Kafka to store incoming data, followed by stream processing and storage in a database for users to query. Refer to section 17.9.1 for a detailed comparison between Lambda and Kappa architecture.

4.7   *Denormalization*

If our service's data can fit into a single host, a typical approach is to choose SQL and normalize our schema. The benefits of normalization include the following:

- They are consistent, with no duplicate data, so there will not be tables with inconsistent data.
- Inserts and updates are faster since only one table has to be queried. In a denormalized schema, an insert or update may need to query multiple tables.
- Smaller database size because there is no duplicate data. Smaller tables will have faster read operations.
- Normalized tables tend to have fewer columns, so they will have fewer indexes. Index rebuilds will be faster.
- Queries can JOIN only the tables that are needed.

The disadvantages of normalization include the following:

- JOIN queries are much slower than queries on individual tables. In practice, denormalization is frequently done because of this.

- The fact tables contain codes rather than data, so most queries both for our service and ad hoc analytics will contain JOIN operations. JOIN queries tend to be more verbose than queries on single tables, so they are more difficult to write and maintain.

An approach to faster read operations that is frequently mentioned in interviews is to trade off storage for speed by denormalizing our schema to avoid JOIN queries.

4.8 Caching

For databases that store data on disk, we can cache frequent or recent queries in memory. In an organization, various database technologies can be provided to users as shared database services, such as an SQL service or Spark with HDFS. These services can also utilize caching, such as with a Redis cache.

This section is a brief description of various caching strategies. The benefits of caching include improvements to:

- *Performance:* This is the intended benefit of a cache, and the other benefits below are incidental. A cache uses memory, which is faster and more expensive than a database, which uses disk.

- *Availability:* If the database is unavailable, the service is still available so applications can retrieve data from the cache. This only applies to data that is cached. To save costs, a cache may contain only a subset of data in the database. However, caches are designed for high performance and low latency, not for high availability. A cache's design may trade off availability and other non-functional requirements for high performance. Our database should be highly available, and we must not rely on the cache for our service's availability.

- *Scalability:* By serving frequently requested data, the cache can serve much of the service's load. It is also faster than the database, so requests are served faster which decreases the number of open HTTP connections at any one time, and a smaller backend cluster can serve the same load. However, this is an inadvisable scalability technique if your cache is typically designed to optimize latency and may make tradeoffs against availability to achieve this. For example, one will not replicate a cache across data centers because cross data-center requests are slow and defeat the main purpose of a cache which is to improve latency. So, if a data center experiences an outage (such as from network problems), the cache becomes unavailable, and all the load is transferred to the database, which may be unable to handle it. The backend service should have rate limiting, adjusted to the capacity of the backend and database.

Caching can be done at many levels, including client, API Gateway (Rob Vettor, David Coulter, Genevieve Warren, "Caching in a cloud-native application." Microsoft Docs. May 17, 2020. (https://docs.microsoft.com/en-us/dotnet/architecture/cloud-native/azure-caching), and at each service (*Cloud Native Patterns* by Cornelia Davis, (Manning Publications, 2019). Figure 4.9 illustrates caching at an API Gateway. This cache can scale independently of the services, to serve the traffic volume at any given time.

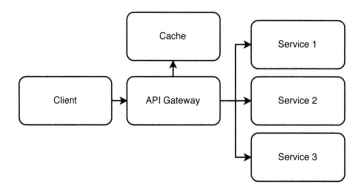

Figure 4.9   Caching at an API gateway. Diagram adapted from Rob Vettor, David Coulter, Genevieve Warren. May 17, 2020. "Caching in a cloud-native application." Microsoft Docs. https://docs.microsoft .com/en-us/dotnet/architecture/cloud-native/azure-caching.

4.8.1   Read strategies

Read strategies are optimized for fast reads.

CACHE-ASIDE (LAZY LOADING)

Cache-aside refers to the cache sitting "aside" the database. Figure 4.10 illustrates cache-aside. In a read request, the application first makes a read request to the cache, which returns the data on a cache hit. On a cache miss, the application makes a read request to the database, then writes the data to the cache so subsequent requests for this data will be cache hits. So, data is loaded only when it is first read, which is called *lazy load*.

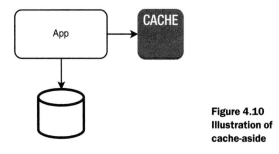

**Figure 4.10
Illustration of
cache-aside**

Cache-aside is best for read-heavy loads. Advantages:

- Cache-aside minimizes the number of read requests and resource consumption. To further reduce the number of requests, the application can store the results of multiple database requests as a single cache value (i.e., a single cache key for the results of multiple database requests).
- Only requested data is written to the cache, so we can easily determine our required cache capacity and adjust it as needed to save costs.
- Simplicity of implementation.

If the cache cluster goes down, all requests will go to the database. We must ensure that the database can handle this load. Disadvantages:

- The cached data may become stale/inconsistent, especially if writes are made directly to the database. To reduce stale data, we can set a TTL or use write-through (refer section below) so every write goes through the cache.
- A request with a cache miss is slower than a request directly to the database, because of the additional read request and additional write request to the cache.

READ-THROUGH

In *read-through, write-through,* or *write-back* caching, the application makes requests to the cache, which may make requests to the database if necessary.

Figure 4.11 illustrates the architecture of read-through, write-through, or write-back caching. In a cache miss on a read-through cache, the cache makes a request to the database and stores the data in the cache (i.e., also lazy load, like cache-aside), then returns the data to the application.

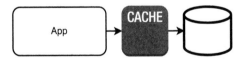

Figure 4.11   In read-through, write-through, or write-back caching, the application makes requests to the cache, which makes requests to the database if necessary. So, this simple architecture diagram can represent all three caching strategies.

Read-through is best for read-heavy loads. As the application does not contact the database, the implementation burden of database requests is shifted from the application to the cache. A tradeoff is that unlike cache-aside, a read-through cache cannot group multiple database requests as a single cache value.

4.8.2   *Write strategies*

Write strategies are optimized to minimize cache staleness, in exchange for higher latency or complexity.

WRITE-THROUGH

Every write goes through the cache, then to the database. Advantages:

- It is consistent. The cache is never stale since cache data is updated with every database write.

Disadvantages:

- Slower writes since every write is done on both the cache and database.
- Cold start problem because a new cache node will have missing data and cache misses. We can use cache-aside to resolve this.
- Most data is never read, so we incur unnecessary cost. We can configure a TTL (time-to-live) to reduce wasted space.
- If our cache is smaller than our database, we must determine the most appropriate cache eviction policy.

WRITE-BACK/WRITE-BEHIND

The application writes data to the cache, but the cache does not immediately write to the database. The cache periodically flushes updated data to the database. Advantages:

- Faster writes on average than write-through. Writes to database are not blocking.

Disadvantages:

- Same disadvantages as write-through, other than slower writes.
- Complexity because our cache must have high availability, so we cannot make tradeoffs against availability to improve performance/latency. The design will be more complex since it must have both high availability and performance.

WRITE-AROUND

In *write-around*, the application only writes to the database. Referring to figure 4.12, write-around is usually combined with cache-aside or read-through. The application updates the cache on a cache miss.

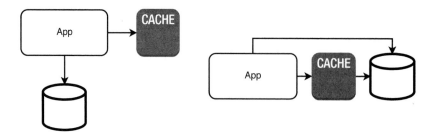

Figure 4.12   Two possible architectures of write-around. (Left) Write-around with cache-aside. (Right) Write-around with read-through.

4.9 Caching as a separate service

Why is caching a separate service? Why not just cache in the memory of a service's hosts?

- Services are designed to be stateless, so each request is randomly assigned to a host. Since each host may cache different data, it is less likely to have cached any particular request that it receives. This is unlike databases, which are stateful and can be partitioned, so each database node is likely to serve requests for the same data.

- Further to the previous point, caching is especially useful when there are uneven request patterns that lead to hot shards. Caching is useless if requests or responses are unique.

- If we cache on hosts, the cache will be wiped out every time our service gets a deployment, which may be multiple times every day.

- We can scale the cache independently of the services that it serves (though this comes with the dangers discussed in the beginning of this chapter). Our caching service can use specific hardware or virtual machines that are optimized for the non-functional requirements of a caching service, which may be different from the services that it serves.

- If many clients simultaneously send the same request that is a cache miss, our database service will execute the same query many times. Caches can deduplicate requests and send a single request to our service. This is called request coalescing, and it reduces the traffic on our service.

Besides caching on our backend service, we should also cache on clients (browser or mobile apps) to avoid the overhead of network requests if possible. We should also consider using a CDN.

4.10 Examples of different kinds of data to cache and how to cache them

We can cache either HTTP responses or database queries. We can cache the body of an HTTP response, and retrieve it using a cache key, which is the HTTP method and URI of the request. Within our application, we can use the cache-aside pattern to cache relational database queries.

Caches can be private or public/shared. Private cache is on a client and is useful for personalized content. Public cache is on a proxy such as a CDN, or on our services.

Information that should not be cached includes the following:

- Private information must never be stored in a cache. An example is bank account details.

- Realtime public information, such as stock prices, or flight arrival times or hotel room availabilities in the near future.

- Do not use private caching for paid or copyrighted content, such as books or videos that require payment.
- Public information that may change can be cached but should be revalidated against the origin server. An example is availability of flight tickets or hotel rooms next month. The server response will be just a response code 304 confirmation that the cached response is fresh, so this response will be much smaller than if there was no caching. This will improve network latency and throughput. We set a `max-age` value that indicates our assessment on how long the cached response remains fresh. However, we may have reason to believe that conditions may change in the future that cause this `max-age` value may become too long, so we may wish to implement logic in our backend that quickly validates that a cached response is still fresh. If we do this, we return `must-revalidate` in our response so clients will revalidate cached responses with our backend before using them.

Public information that will not change for a long time can be cached with a long cache expiry time. Examples include bus or train schedules.

In general, a company can save hardware costs by pushing as much processing and storage as possible onto the clients' devices and use data centers only to back up critical data and for communication between users. For example, WhatsApp stores a user's authentication details and their connections, but does not store their messages (which are the bulk of a user's storage consumption). It provides Google Drive backup, so it pushes message backup costs onto another company. Freed of this cost, WhatsApp can continue to be free to its users, who pay Google for storage if they exceed the free storage tier.

However, we should not assume that the localStorage caching is functioning as intended, so we should always expect cache misses and prepare our service to receive these requests. We cache in every layer (client/browser, load balancer, frontend/API Gateway/sidecar, and in our backend) so *requests pass through as few services as possible.* This allows *lower latency and cost.*

A browser starts rendering a webpage only after it has downloaded and processed all the latter's CSS files, so browser caching of CSS may considerably improve browser app performance.

> **NOTE**   Refer to https://csswizardry.com/2018/11/css-and-network-performance/ for a discussion on optimizing a webpage's performance by allowing the browser to download and process all of a webpage's CSS as quickly as possible.

A disadvantage of caching on the client is that it complicates usage analytics, since the backend will not receive an indication that the client accessed this data. If it is necessary or beneficial to know that the client accessed its cached data, we will need the additional complexity of logging these usage counts in the client and send these logs to our backend.

4.11 Cache invalidation

Cache invalidation is the process where cache entries are replaced or removed. *Cache busting* is cache invalidation specifically for files.

4.11.1 Browser cache invalidation

For browser caches, we typically set a `max-age` for each file. What if a file is replaced by a new version before its cache expiry? We use a technique called *fingerprinting*, which gives these files new identifiers (version numbers, file names or query string hashes). For example, a file named "style.css" can instead be named "style.b3d716.css," and the hash in the file name can be replaced during a new deployment. In another example, an HTML tag `<img src=/assets/image.png />` that contains an image file name can instead be `<img src=/assets/image.png?hash=a3db6e />`; we use a query parameter `hash` to indicate the file version. With fingerprinting, we can also use the `immutable` cache-control option to prevent unnecessary requests to the origin server.

Fingerprinting is important for caching multiple GET requests or files that depend on each other. GET request caching headers cannot express that certain files or responses are interdependent, which may cause old versions of files to be deployed.

For example, we will typically cache CSS and JavaScript but not HTML (unless the webpage is static; many browser apps we build will display different content on each visit). However, all of them may change in a new deployment of our browser app. If we serve new HTML with old CSS or JavaScript, the webpage may be broken. A user may instinctively click the browser reload button, which will resolve the problem as the browser revalidates with the origin server when the user reloads the page. But this is a bad user experience. These problems are difficult to find during testing. Fingerprinting ensures that the HTML contains the correct CSS and JavaScript file names.

We may decide to try to avoid this problem without fingerprinting by caching HTML as well as CSS and JavaScript and setting the same `max-age` for all these files so they will expire simultaneously. However, the browser may make requests for these different files at different times, separated by seconds. If a new deployment happens to be in progress during these requests, the browser may still get a mix of old and new files.

Besides dependent files, an application may also contain dependent GET requests. For example, a user may make a GET request for a list of items (items on sale, hotel rooms, flights to San Francisco, photo thumbnails, etc.), followed by a GET request for details of an item. Caching the first request may cause requests for details of a product that no longer exists. REST architecture best practices dictate that requests are cacheable by default, but depending on these considerations, we should either not cache or set a short expiry time.

4.11.2 Cache invalidation in caching services

We do not have direct access to clients' caches, so this restricts our cache invalidation options to techniques like setting `max-age` or fingerprinting. However, we can directly create, replace, or remove entries in a caching service. There are many online resources on cache replacement policies, and their implementations are outside the scope of this book, so we will only briefly define a few common ones here.

- Random replacement: Replace a random item when the cache is full. It is the simplest strategy.
- Least recently used (LRU): Replace the least recently used item first.
- First in first out (FIFO): Replace the items in the order they were added, regardless of how often they are used/accessed.
- Last in first out (LIFO), also called first in last out (FILO): Replace the items in the reverse order they were added, regardless of how often they are used/accessed.

4.12 Cache warming

Cache warming means to fill a cache with entries ahead of the first requests for these entries, so each first request for an entry can be served from the cache rather than result in a cache miss. Cache warming applies to services like CDNs or our frontend or backend services, not to browser cache.

The advantage of cache warming is that the first request for precached data will have the same low latency as subsequent requests. However, cache warming comes with many disadvantages, including the following:

- Additional complexity and cost of implementing cache warning. A caching service may contain thousands of hosts and warming them can be a complex and costly process. We can reduce the cost by only partially filling the cache, with entries, which will be most frequently requested. Refer to https://netflixtechblog .com/cache-warming-agility-for-a-stateful-service-2d3b1da82642 for a discussion of Netflix's cache warmer system design.
- Additional traffic from querying our service to fill the cache, including on our frontend, backend, and database services. Our service may not be able to take the load of cache warming.
- Assuming we have user base of millions of users, only the first user who accessed that data will receive a slow experience. This may not justify the complexity and cost of cache warming. Frequently accessed data will be cached on its first request, while infrequently accessed data does not justify caching or cache warming.
- The cache expiry time cannot be short, or cache items may expire before they are used, and warming the cache is a waste of time. So, we either need to set a long expiry time, and our cache service is bigger and more expensive than necessary, or we will need to set different expiry times for different entries, introducing additional complexity and possible mistakes.

The P99 for requests made without caching should generally be less than one second. Even if we relax this requirement, it should not exceed 10 seconds. Instead of cache warming, we can ensure that requests served without caching have a reasonable P99.

4.13 Further reading

This chapter uses material from Web Scalability for Startup Engineers by Artur Ejsmont (McGraw Hill, 2015).

4.13.1 Caching references

- Kevin Crawley "Scaling Microservices — Understanding and Implementing Cache," August 22, 2019 (https://dzone.com/articles/scaling-microservices -understanding-and-implementi)
- Rob Vettor, David Coulter, and Genevieve Warren "Caching in a cloud-native application," Microsoft Docs, May 17, 2020 Microsoft Docs. (https://docs.micro-soft.com/en-us/dotnet/architecture/cloud-native/azure-caching)
- *Cloud Native Patterns* by Cornelia Davis (Manning Publications, 2019)
- https://jakearchibald.com/2016/caching-best-practices/
- https://developer.mozilla.org/en-US/docs/Web/HTTP/Headers/Cache-Control
- Tom Barker *Intelligent Caching* (O'Reilly Media, 2017)

Summary

- Designing a stateful service is much more complex and error-prone than a stateless service, so system designs try to keep services stateless, and use shared stateful services.
- Each storage technology falls into a particular category. We should know how to distinguish these categories, which are as follows.
  - Database, which can be SQL or NoSQL. NoSQL can be categorized into column-oriented or key-value.
  - Document.
  - Graph.
  - File storage.
  - Block storage.
  - Object storage.
- Deciding how to store a service's data involves deciding to use a database vs. another storage category.
- There are various replication techniques to scale databases, including single-leader replication, multi-leader replication, leaderless replication, and other techniques such as HDFS replication that do not fit cleanly into these three approaches.
- Sharding is needed if a database exceeds the storage capacity of a single host.

- Database writes are expensive and difficult to scale, so we should minimize database writes wherever possible. Aggregating events helps to reduce the rate of database writes.

- Lambda architecture involves using parallel batch and streaming pipelines to process the same data, and realize the benefits of both approaches while allowing them to compensate for each other's disadvantages.

- Denormalizing is frequently used to optimize read latency and simpler SELECT queries, with tradeoffs like consistency, slower writes, more storage required, and slower index rebuilds.

- Caching frequent queries in memory reduces average query latency.

- Read strategies are for fast reads, trading off cache staleness.

- Cache-aside is best for read-heavy loads, but the cached data may become stale and cache misses are slower than if the cache wasn't present.

- A read-through cache makes requests to the database, removing this burden from the application.

- A write-through cache is never stale, but it is slower.

- A write-back cache periodically flushes updated data to the database. Unlike other cache designs, it must have high availability to prevent possible data loss from outages.

- A write-around cache has slow writes and a higher chance of cache staleness. It is suitable for situations where the cached data is unlikely to change.

- A dedicated caching service can serve our users much better than caching on the memory of our services' hosts.

- Do not cache private data. Cache public data; revalidation and cache expiry time depends on how often and likely the data will change.

- Cache invalidation strategies are different in services versus clients because we have access to the hosts in the former but not the latter.

- Warming a cache allows the first user of the cached data to be served as quickly as subsequent users, but cache warming has many disadvantages.

Distributed transactions

In a system, a unit of work may involve writing data to multiple services. Each write to each service is a separate request/event. Any write may fail; the causes may include bugs or host or network outages. This may cause data inconsistency across the services. For example, if a customer bought a tour package consisting of both an air ticket and a hotel room, the system may need to write to a ticket service, a room reservation service, and a payments service. If any write fails, the system will be in an inconsistent state. Another example is a messaging system that sends messages to recipients and logs to a database that messages have been sent. If a message is successfully sent to a recipient's device, but the write to the database fails, it will appear that the message has not been delivered.

A transaction is a way to group several reads and writes into a logical unit to maintain data consistency across services. They execute atomically, as a single operation, and the entire transaction either succeeds (commit) or fails (abort, rollback). A transaction has ACID properties, though the understanding of ACID concepts differs between databases, so the implementations also differ.

If we can use an event-streaming platform like Kafka to distribute these writes, allowing downstream services to pull instead of push these writes, we should do so. (Refer to section 4.6.2 for a discussion of pull vs. push.) For other situations, we introduce the concept of a *distributed transaction*, which combines these separate write requests as a single distributed (atomic) transaction. We introduce the concept of *consensus*—that is, all the services agree that the write event has occurred (or not occurred). For consistency across the services, consensus should occur despite possible faults during write events. This section describes algorithms for maintaining consistency in distributed transactions:

- The related concepts of event sourcing, Change Data Capture (CDC), and Event Driven Architecture (EDA).
- Checkpointing and dead letter queue were discussed in sections 3.3.6 and 3.3.7.
- Saga.
- Two-phase commit. (This is outside the scope of this book. Refer to appendix D for a brief discussion on two-phase commit.)

Two-phase commit and saga achieve consensus (all commit or all abort), while the other techniques are designed to designate a particular database as a source of truth should inconsistency result from failed writes.

5.1   *Event Driven Architecture (EDA)*

In *Scalability for Startup Engineers* (2015), Artur Ejsmont states, "Event Driven Architecture (EDA) is an architectural style where most interactions between different components are realized by announcing events that have already happened instead of requesting work to be done" (p. 295).

EDA is asynchronous and non-blocking. A request does not need to be processed, which may take considerable time and result in high latency. Rather, it only has to publish an event. If the event is successfully published, the server returns a successful response. The event can be processed afterwards. If necessary, the server can then send the response to the requestor. EDA promotes loose coupling, scalability, and responsiveness (low latency).

The alternative to EDA is that a service makes a request directly to another service. Regardless of whether such a request was blocking or non-blocking, unavailability or slow performance of either service means that the overall system is unavailable. This request also consumes a thread in each service, so there is one less thread available during the time the request takes to process. This effect is especially noticeable if the request takes a long time to process or occurs during traffic spikes. A traffic spike can overwhelm the service and cause 504 timeouts. The requestors will also be affected because each requestor must continue to maintain a thread as long as the request has not completed, so the requestor device has fewer resources for other work.

To prevent traffic spikes from causing outages, we need to use complex auto-scaling solutions or maintain a large cluster of hosts, which incurs more expense. (Rate limiting is another possible solution and is discussed in chapter 8.)

These alternatives are more expensive, complex, error-prone, and less scalable. The strong consistency and low latency that they provide may not actually be needed by users.

A less resource-intensive approach is to publish an event onto an event log. The publisher service does not need to continuously consume a thread to wait for the subscriber service to finish processing an event.

In practice, we may choose not to completely follow the non-blocking philosophy of EDA, such as by performing request validation when a request is made. For example, the server may validate that the request contains all required fields and valid values; a string field may need to be nonempty and not null; it may also have a minimum and maximum length. We may make this choice so that an invalid request can fail quickly, rather than waste resources and time persisting invalid data only to find an error afterwards. Event sourcing and Change Data Capture (CDC) are examples of EDA.

5.2 Event sourcing

Event sourcing is a pattern for storing data or changes to data as events in an append-only log. According to Davis (*Cloud Native Patterns* by Cornelia Davis (Manning Publications, 2019)), the idea of event sourcing is that the event log is the source of truth, and all other databases are projections of the event log. Any write must first be made to the event log. After this write succeeds, one or more event handlers consume this new event and writes it to the other databases.

Event sourcing is not tied to any particular data source. It can capture events from various sources, such as user interactions and external and internal systems. Referring to figure 5.1, event sourcing consists of publishing and persisting fine-grained, state-changing events of an entity as a sequence of events. These events are stored in a log, and subscribers process the log's event to determine the entity's current state. So, the publisher service asynchronously communicates with the subscriber service via the event log.

Figure 5.1   In event sourcing, a publisher publishes a sequence of events to a log that indicates changes to the state of an entity. A subscriber processes the log events in sequence to determine the entity's current state.

This can be implemented in various ways. A publisher can publish an event to an event store or append-only log such as a Kafka topic, write a row to a relational database (SQL), write a document to a document database like MongoDB or Couchbase, or even write to an in-memory database such as Redis or Apache Ignite for low latency.

> **QUESTION**   What if a subscriber host crashes while processing an event? How will the subscriber service know that it must process that event again?

Event sourcing provides a complete audit trail of all events in the system, and the ability to derive insights into the system's past states by replaying events for debugging or analytics. Event sourcing also allows business logic to change by introducing new event types and handlers without affecting existing data.

Event sourcing adds complexity to system design and development because we must manage event stores, replay, versioning, and schema evolution. It increases storage requirements. Event replay becomes more costly and time-consuming as the logs grow.

5.3   *Change Data Capture (CDC)*

Change Data Capture (CDC) is about logging data change events to a change log event stream and providing this event stream through an API.

Figure 5.2 illustrates CDC. A single change or group of changes can be published as a single event to a change log event stream. This event stream has multiple consumers, each corresponding to a service/application/database. Each consumer consumes the event and provides it to its downstream service to be processed.

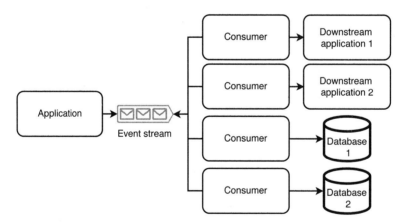

Figure 5.2   Using a change log event stream to synchronize data changes. Besides consumers, serverless functions can also be used to propagate changes to downstream applications or databases.

CDC ensures consistency and lower latency than event sourcing. Each request is processed in near real time, unlike in event sourcing where a request can stay in the log for some time before a subscriber processes it.

The transaction log tailing pattern (Chris Richardson, *Microservices Patterns: With Examples in Java,* pp. 99–100, Manning Publications, 2019) is another system design pattern to prevent possible inconsistency when a process needs to write to a database and produce to Kafka. One of the two writes may fail, causing inconsistency.

Figure 5.3 illustrates the transaction log tailing pattern. In transaction log tailing, a process called the transaction log miner tails a database's transaction log and produces each update as an event.

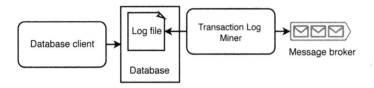

Figure 5.3 Illustration of the transaction log tailing pattern. A service does a write query to a database, which records this query in its log file. The transaction log miner tails the log file and picks up this query, then produces an event to the message broker.

CDC platforms include Debezium (https://debezium.io/), Databus (https://github .com/linkedin/databus), DynamoDB Streams (https://docs.aws.amazon.com/ amazondynamodb/latest/developerguide/Streams.html), and Eventuate CDC Service (https://github.com/eventuate-foundation/eventuate-cdc). They can be used as transaction log miners.

Transaction log miners may generate duplicate events. One way to handle duplicate events is to use the message broker's mechanisms for exactly-once delivery. Another way is for the events to be defined and processed idempotently.

5.4 Comparison of event sourcing and CDC

Event-driven architecture (EDA), event sourcing, and CDC are related concepts used in distributed systems that to propagate data changes to interested consumers and downstream services. They decouple services by using asynchronous communication patterns to communicate these data changes. In some system designs, you might use both event sourcing and CDC together. For example, you can use event sourcing within a service to record data changes as events, while using CDC to propagate those events to other services. They differ in some of their purposes, in their granularity, and in their sources of truth. These differences are discussed in table 5.1.

Table 5.1   Differences between event sourcing and Change Data Capture (CDC)

	Event Sourcing	Change Data Capture (CDC)
Purpose	Record events as the source of truth.	Synchronize data changes by propagating events from a source service to downstream services.
Source of truth	The log, or events published to the log, are the source of truth.	A database in the publisher service. The published events are not the source of truth.
Granularity	Fine-grained events that represent specific actions or changes in state.	Individual database level changes such as new, updated, or deleted rows or documents.

5.5   *Transaction supervisor*

A transaction supervisor is a process that ensures a transaction is successfully completed or is compensated. It can be implemented as a periodic batch job or serverless function. Figure 5.4 shows an example of a transaction supervisor.

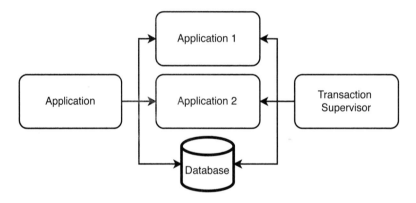

Figure 5.4   Example illustration of a transaction supervisor. An application may write to multiple downstream applications and databases. A transaction supervisor periodically syncs the various destinations in case any writes fail.

A transaction supervisor should generally be first implemented as an interface for manual review of inconsistencies and manual executions of compensating transactions. Automating compensating transactions is generally risky and should be approached with caution. Before automating a compensating transaction, it must first be extensively tested. Also ensure that there are no other distributed transaction mechanisms, or they may interfere with each other, leading to data loss or situations that are difficult to debug.

A compensating transaction must always be logged, regardless of whether it was manually or automatically run.

5.6   *Saga*

A saga is a long-lived transaction that can be written as a sequence of transactions. All transactions must complete successfully, or compensating transactions are run to roll back the executed transactions. A saga is a pattern to help manage failures. A saga itself has no state.

A typical saga implementation involves services communicating via a message broker like Kafka or RabbitMQ. In our discussions in this book that involve saga, we will use Kafka.

An important use case of sagas is to carry out a distributed transaction only if certain services satisfy certain requirements. For example, in booking a tour package, a travel service may make a write request to an airline ticket service, and another write request to a hotel room service. If there are either no available flights or hotel rooms, the entire saga should be rolled back.

The airline ticket service and hotel room service may also need to write to a payments service, which is separate from the airline ticket service and hotel service for possible reasons including the following:

- The payment service should not process any payments until the airline ticket service confirms that the ticket is available, and the hotel room service confirms that the room is available. Otherwise, it may collect money from the user before confirming the entire tour package.
- The airline ticket and hotel room services may belong to other companies, and we cannot pass the user's private payment information to them. Rather, our company needs to handle the user's payment, and our company should make payments to other companies.

If a transaction to the payments service fails, the entire saga should be rolled back in reverse order using compensating transactions on the other two services.

There are two ways to structure the coordination: choreography (parallel) or orchestration (linear). In the rest of this section, we discuss one example of choreography and one example of orchestration, then compare choreography vs. orchestration. Refer to https://microservices.io/patterns/data/saga.html for another example.

5.6.1   *Choreography*

In choreography, the service that begins the saga communicates with two Kafka topics. It produces to one Kafka topic to start the distributed transaction and consumes from another Kafka topic to perform any final logic. Other services in the saga communicate directly with each other via Kafka topics.

Figure 5.5 illustrates a choreography saga to book a tour package. In this chapter, the figures that include Kafka topics illustrate event consumption with the line arrowheads pointing away from the topic. In the other chapters of this book, an event consumption is illustrated with the line arrowhead pointing to the topic. The reason for this difference is that the diagrams in this chapter may be confusing if we follow the same convention as the other chapters. The diagrams in this chapter illustrate multiple services consuming from multiple certain topics and producing to multiple other topics, and it is clearer to display the arrowhead directions in the manner that we chose.

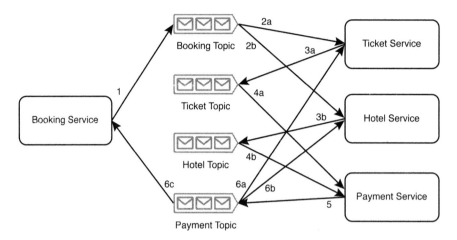

Figure 5.5   A choreography saga to book an airline ticket and a hotel room for a tour package. Two labels with the same number but different letters represent steps that occur in parallel.

The steps of a successful booking are as follows:

1 A user may make a booking request to the booking service. The booking service produces a booking request event to the booking topic.

2 The ticket service and hotel service consume this booking request event. They both confirm that their requests can be fulfilled. Both services may record this event in their respective databases, with the booking ID and a state like "AWAITING_PAYMENT".

3 The ticket service and hotel service each produce a payment request event to the ticket topic and hotel topic, respectively.

4 The payment service consumes these payment request events from the ticket topic and hotel topic. Because these two events are consumed at different times and likely by different hosts, the payment service needs to record the receipt of these events in a database, so the service's hosts will know when all the required events have been received. When all required events are received, the payment service will process the payment.

5 If the payment is successful, the payment service produces a payment success event to the payment topic.

6 The ticket service, hotel service, and booking service consume this event. The ticket service and hotel service both confirm this booking, which may involve changing the state of that booking ID to CONFIRMED, or other processing and business logic as necessary. The booking service may inform the user that the booking is confirmed.

Steps 1–4 are compensable transactions, which can be rolled back by compensating transactions. Step 5 is a pivot transaction. Transactions after the pivot transaction can be retried until they succeed. The step 6 transactions are retriable transactions; this is an example of CDC as discussed in section 5.3. The booking service doesn't need to wait for any responses from the ticket service or the hotel service.

A question that may be asked is how does an external company subscribe to our company's Kafka topics? The answer is that it doesn't. For security reasons, we never allow direct external access to our Kafka service. We have simplified the details of this discussion for clarity. The ticket service and hotel service actually belong to our company. They communicate directly with our Kafka service/topics and make requests to external services. Figure 5.5 did not illustrate these details, so they don't clutter the design diagram.

If the payment service responds with an error that the ticket cannot be reserved (maybe because the requested flight is fully booked or canceled), step 6 will be different. Rather than confirming the booking, the ticket service and hotel service will cancel the booking, and the booking service may return an appropriate error response to the user. Compensating transactions made by error responses from the hotel service or payment service will be similar to the described situation, so we will not discuss them. Other points to note in choreography:

- There are no bidirectional lines; that is, a service does not both produce to and subscribe to the same topic.
- No two services produce to the same topic.
- A service can subscribe to multiple topics. If a service needs to receive multiple events from multiple topics before it can perform an action, it needs to record in a database that it has received certain events, so it can read the database to determine if all the required events have been received.
- The relationship between topics and services can be 1:many or many:1, but not many:many.
- There may be cycles. Notice the cycle in figure 5.5 (hotel topic > payment service > payment topic > hotel service > hotel topic).

In figure 5.5, there are many lines between multiple topics and services. Choreography between a larger number of topics and services can become overly complex, error-prone, and difficult to maintain.

5.6.2 *Orchestration*

In orchestration, the service that begins the saga is the orchestrator. The orchestrator communicates with each service via a Kafka topic. In each step in the saga, the orchestrator must produce to a topic to request this step to begin, and it must consume from another topic to receive the step's result.

An orchestrator is a finite-state machine that reacts to events and issues commands. The orchestrator must only contain the sequence of steps. It must not contain any other business logic, except for the compensation mechanism.

Figure 5.6 illustrates an orchestration saga to book a tour package. The steps in a successful booking process are as shown.

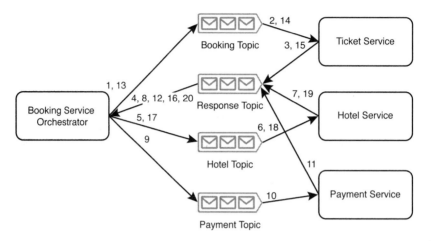

Figure 5.6   An orchestration saga to book an airline ticket and a hotel room for a tour package

1 The orchestrator produces a ticket request event to the booking topic.
2 The ticket service consumes this ticket request event and reserves the airline ticket for the booking ID with the state "AWAITING_PAYMENT".
3 The ticket service produces a "ticket pending payment" event to the response topic.
4 The orchestrator consumes the "ticket pending payment" event.
5 The orchestrator produces a hotel reservation request event to the hotel topic.
6 The hotel service consumes the hotel reservation request event and reserves the hotel room for the booking ID with the state "AWAITING_PAYMENT".
7 The hotel service produces a "room pending payment" event to the response topic.
8 The orchestrator consumes the "room pending payment" event.
9 The orchestrator produces a payment request event to the payment topic.
10 The payment service consumes the payment request event.
11 The payment service processes the payment and then produces a payment confirmation event to the response topic.
12 The orchestrator consumes the payment confirmation event.
13 The orchestrator produces a payment confirmation event to the booking topic.
14 The ticket service consumes the payment confirmation event and changes the state corresponding to that booking to "CONFIRMED".
15 The ticket service produces a ticket confirmation event to the response topic.
16 The orchestrator consumes this ticket confirmation event from response topic.

17 The orchestrator produces a payment confirmation event to the hotel topic.

18 The hotel service consumes this payment confirmation event and changes the state corresponding to that booking to "CONFIRMED".

19 The hotel service produces a hotel room confirmation event to the response topic.

20 The booking service orchestrator consumes the hotel room confirmation event. It can then perform next steps, such as sending a success response to the user, or any further logic internal to the booking service.

Steps 18 and 19 appear unnecessary, as step 18 will not fail; it can keep retrying until it succeeds. Steps 18 and 20 can be done in parallel. However, we carry out these steps linearly to keep the approach consistent.

Steps 1–13 are compensable transactions. Step 14 is the pivot transaction. Steps 15 onward are retriable transactions.

If any of the three services produces an error response to the booking topic, the orchestrator can produce events to the various other services to run compensating transactions.

5.6.3 *Comparison*

Table 5.1 compares choreography vs. orchestration. We should understand their differences and tradeoffs to evaluate which approach to use in a particular system design. The final decision may be partly arbitrary, but by understanding their differences, we also understand what we are trading off by choosing one approach over another.

Table 5.1 Choreography saga vs. orchestration saga

Choreography	Orchestration
Requests to services are made in parallel. This is the observer object-oriented design pattern.	Requests to services are made linearly. This is the controller object-oriented design pattern.
The service that begins the saga communicates with two Kafka topics. It produces one Kafka topic to start the distributed transaction and consumes from another Kafka topic to perform any final logic.	The orchestrator communicates with each service via a Kafka topic. In each step in the saga, the orchestrator must produce to a topic to request this step to begin, and it must consume from another topic to receive the step's result.
The service that begins the saga only has code that produces to the saga's first topic and consumes from the saga's last topic. A developer must read the code of every service involved in the saga to understand its steps.	The orchestrator has code that produces and consumes Kafka topics that correspond to steps in the saga, so reading the orchestrator's code allows one to understand the services and steps in the distributed transaction.
A service may need to subscribe to multiple Kafka topics, such as the Accounting Service in figure 5.5 of Richardson's book. This is because it may produce a certain event only when it has consumed certain other events from multiple services. This means that it must record in a database which events it has already consumed.	Other than the orchestrator, each service only subscribes to one other Kafka topic (from one other service). The relationships between the various services are easier to understand. Unlike choreography, a service never needs to consume multiple events from separate services before it can produce a certain event, so it may be possible to reduce the number of database writes.

Choreography	Orchestration
Less resource-intensive, less chatty, and less network traffic; hence, it has lower latency overall.	Since every step must pass through the orchestrator, the number of events is double that of choreography. The overall effect is that orchestration is more resource-intensive, chattier, and has more network traffic; hence, it has higher latency overall.
Parallel requests also result in lower latency.	Requests are linear, so latency is higher.
Services have a less independent software development lifecycle because developers must understand all services to change any one of them.	Services are more independent. A change to a service only affects the orchestrator and does not affect other services.
No such single point of failure as in orchestration (i.e., no service needs to be highly available except the Kafka service).	If the orchestration service fails, the entire saga cannot execute (i.e., the orchestrator and the Kafka service must be highly available).
Compensating transactions are triggered by the various services involved in the saga.	Compensating transactions are triggered by the orchestrator.

5.7   *Other transaction types*

The following consensus algorithms are typically more useful for achieving consensus for a large number of nodes, typically in distributed databases. We will not discuss them in this book. Refer to *Designing Data-Intensive Applications* by Martin Kleppman for more details.

- Quorum writes
- Paxos and EPaxos
- Raft
- Zab (ZooKeeper atomic broadcast protocol) – Used by Apache ZooKeeper.

5.8   *Further reading*

- *Designing Data-Intensive Applications: The Big Ideas Behind Reliable, Scalable, and Maintainable Systems* by Martin Kleppmann (O'Reilly Media, 2017)
- *Cloud Native: Using Containers, Functions, and Data to Build Next-Generation Applications* by Boris Scholl, Trent Swanson, and Peter Jausovec (O'Reilly Media, 2019)
- *Cloud Native Patterns* by Cornelia Davis (Manning Publications, 2019)
- *Microservices Patterns: With Examples in Java* by Chris Richardson (Manning Publications, 2019). Chapter 3.3.7 discusses the transaction log tailing pattern. Chapter 4 is a detailed chapter on saga.

Summary

- A distributed transaction writes the same data to multiple services, with either eventual consistency or consensus.
- In event sourcing, write events are stored in a log, which is the source of truth and an audit trail that can replay events to reconstruct the system state.
- In Change Data Capture (CDC), an event stream has multiple consumers, each corresponding to a downstream service.
- A saga is a series of transactions that are either all completed successfully or are all rolled back.
- Choreography (parallel) or orchestration (linear) are two ways to coordinate sagas.

Common services for
functional partitioning

Earlier in this book, we discussed functional partitioning as a scalability technique that partitions out specific functions from our backend to run on their own dedicated clusters. This chapter first discusses the API gateway, followed by the sidecar pattern (also called service mesh), which was a recent innovation. Next, we discuss centralization of common data into a metadata service. A common theme of these services is that they contain functionalities common to many backend services, which we can partition from those services into shared common services.

> **NOTE** Istio, a popular service mesh implementation, had its first production release in 2018.

Last, we discuss frameworks that can be used to develop the various components in a system design.

6.1   Common functionalities of various services

A service can have many non-functional requirements, and many services with different functional requirements can share the same non-functional requirements. For example, a service that calculates sales taxes and a service to check hotel room availability may both take advantage of caching to improve performance or only accept requests from registered users.

If engineers implement these functionalities separately for each service, there may be duplication of work or duplicate code. Errors or inefficiencies are more likely because scarce engineering resources are spread out across a larger amount of work.

One possible solution is to place this code into libraries where various services can use them. However, this solution has the disadvantages discussed in section 6.7. Library updates are controlled by users, so the services may continue to run old versions that contain bugs or security problems fixed in newer versions. Each host running the service also runs the libraries, so the different functionalities cannot be independently scaled.

A solution is to centralize these cross-cutting concerns with an *API gateway.* An API gateway is a lightweight web service that consists of stateless machines located across several data centers. It provides common functionalities to our organization's many services for centralization of cross-cutting concerns across various services, even if they are written in different programming languages. It should be kept as simple as possible despite its many responsibilities. Amazon API Gateway (https://aws.amazon.com/api-gateway/) and Kong (https://konghq.com/kong) are examples of cloud-provided API gateways.

The functionalities of an API gateway include the following, which can be grouped into categories.

6.1.1   Security

These functionalities prevent unauthorized access to a service's data:

- *Authentication:* Verifies that a request is from an authorized user.
- *Authorization:* Verifies that a user is allowed to make this request.
- *SSL termination:* Termination is usually not handled by the API gateway itself but by a separate HTTP proxy that runs as a process on the same host. We do termination on the API gateway because termination on a load balancer is expensive. Although the term "SSL termination" is commonly used, the actual protocol is TLS, which is the successor to SSL.
- *Server-side data encryption:* If we need to store data securely on backend hosts or on a database, the API gateway can encrypt data before storage and decrypt data before it is sent to a requestor.

6.1.2   Error-checking

Error-checking prevents invalid or duplicate requests from reaching service hosts, allowing them to process only valid requests:

- *Request validation:* One validation step is to ensure the request is properly formatted. For example, a POST request body should be valid JSON. It ensures that all required parameters are present in the request and their values honor constraints. We can configure these requirements on our service on our API gateway.

- *Request deduplication:* Duplication may occur when a response with success status fails to reach the requestor/client because the requestor/client may reattempt this request. Caching is usually used to store previously seen request IDs to avoid duplication. If our service is idempotent, stateless, or "at least once" delivery, it can handle duplicate requests, and request duplication will not cause errors. However, if our service expects "exactly once" or "at most once" delivery, request duplication may cause errors.

6.1.3   Performance and availability

An API gateway can improve the performance and availability of services by providing caching, rate limiting, and request dispatching.

- *Caching:* The API gateway can cache common requests to the database or other services such as:
  - In our service architecture, the API gateway may make requests to a metadata service (refer to section 6.3). It can cache information on the most actively used entities.
  - Use identity information to save calls to authentication and authorization services.
- *Rate Limiting (also called throttling):* Prevents our service from being overwhelmed by requests. (Refer to chapter 8 for a discussion on a sample rate-limiting service.)
- *Request dispatching:* The API gateway makes remote calls to other services. It creates HTTP clients for these various services and ensures that requests to these services are properly isolated. When one service experiences slowdown, requests to other services are not affected. Common patterns like bulkhead and circuit breaker help implement resource isolation and make services more resilient when remote calls fail.

6.1.4   Logging and analytics

Another common functionality provided by an API gateway is request logging or usage data collection, which is the gathering real-time information for various purposes such as analytics, auditing, billing, and debugging.

6.2 Service mesh/sidecar pattern

Section 1.4.6 briefly discussed using a service mesh to address the disadvantages of an API gateway, repeated here:

- Additional latency in each request, from having to route the request through an additional service.
- A large cluster of hosts, which requires scaling to control costs.

Figure 6.1 is a repeat of figure 1.8, illustrating a service mesh. A slight disadvantage of this design is that a service's host will be unavailable if its sidecar is unavailable, even if the service is up; this is the reason we generally do not run multiple services or containers on a single host.

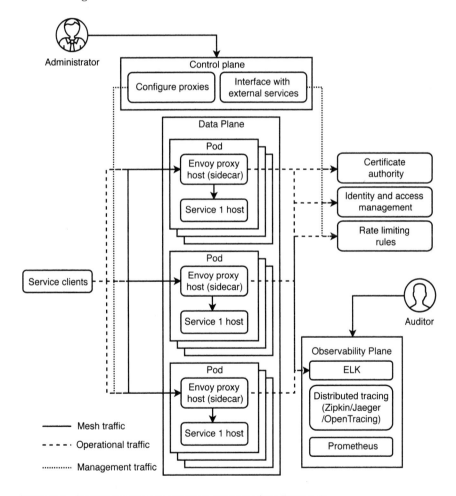

Figure 6.1 Illustration of a service mesh, repeated from figure 1.8

Istio's documentation states that a service mesh consists of a control plane and a data plane (https://istio.io/latest/docs/ops/deployment/architecture/), while Jenn Gile from Nginx also described an observability plane (https://www.nginx.com/blog/how-to-choose-a-service-mesh/). Figure 6.1 contains all three types of planes.

An administrator can use the control plane to manage proxies and interface with external services. For example, the control plane can connect to a certificate authority to obtain a certificate, or to an identity and access control service to manage certain configurations. It can also push the certificate ID or the identify and access control service configurations to the proxy hosts. Interservice and intraservice requests occur between the Envoy (https://www.envoyproxy.io/) proxy hosts, which we refer to as mesh traffic. Sidecar proxy interservice communication can use various protocols including HTTP and gRPC (https://docs.microsoft.com/en-us/dotnet/architecture/cloud-native/service-mesh-communication-infrastructure). The observability plane provides logging, monitoring, alerting, and auditing.

Rate limiting is another example of a common shared service that can be managed by a service mesh. Chapter 8 discusses this in more detail. AWS App Mesh (https://aws.amazon.com/app-mesh) is a cloud-provided service mesh.

NOTE   Refer to section 1.4.6 for a brief discussion on sidecarless service mesh.

6.3   *Metadata service*

A metadata service stores information that is used by multiple components within a system. If these components pass this information between each other, they can pass IDs rather than all the information. A component that receives an ID can request the metadata service for the information that corresponds to that ID. There is less duplicate information in the system, analogous to SQL normalization, so there is better consistency.

One example is ETL pipelines. Consider an ETL pipeline for sending welcome emails for certain products that users have signed up for. The email message may be an HTML file of several MB that contains many words and images, which are different according to product. Referring to figure 6.2, when a producer produces a message to the pipeline queue, instead of including an entire HTML file in the message, the producer can only include the ID of the file. The file can be stored in a metadata service. When a consumer consumes a message, it can request the metadata service for the HTML file that corresponds to that ID. This approach saves the queue from containing large amounts of duplicate data.

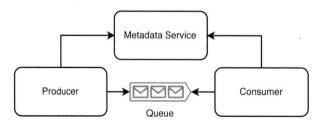

Figure 6.2   **We can use a metadata service to reduce the size of individual messages in a queue, by placing large objects in the metadata service, and enqueuing only IDs in individual messages.**

A tradeoff of using a metadata service is increased complexity and overall latency. Now the producer must write both to the Metadata Service and the queue. In certain designs, we may populate the metadata service in an earlier step, so the producer does not need to write to the metadata service.

If the producer cluster experiences traffic spikes, it will make a high rate of read requests to the metadata service, so the metadata service should be capable of supporting high read volumes.

In summary, a metadata service is for ID lookups. We will use metadata services in many of our sample question discussions in part 2.

Figure 6.3 illustrates the architecture changes from introducing the API gateway and metadata services. Instead of making requests to the backend, clients will make requests to the API gateway, which performs some functions and may send requests to either the metadata service and/or the backend. Figure 1.8 illustrates a service mesh.

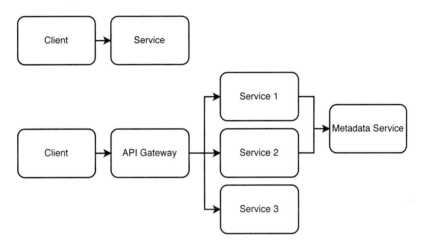

Figure 6.3 Functional partitioning of a service (top) to separate out the API gateway and metadata service (bottom). Before this partitioning, clients query the service directly. With the partitioning, clients query the API gateway, which performs some functions and may route the request to one of the services, which in turn may query the metadata service for certain shared functionalities.

6.4 Service discovery

Service discovery is a microservices concept that might be briefly mentioned during an interview in the context of managing multiple services. Service discovery is done under the hood, and most engineers do not need to understand their details. Most engineers only need to understand that each internal API service is typically assigned a port number via which it is accessed. External API services and most UI services are assigned URLs through which they are accessed. Service discovery may be covered in interviews for teams that develop infrastructure. It is unlikely that the details of service discovery will be discussed for other engineers because it provides little relevant interview signal.

Very briefly, service discovery is a way for clients to identify which service hosts are available. A service registry is a database that keeps track of the available hosts of a service. Refer to sources such as https://docs.aws.amazon.com/whitepapers/latest/ microservices-on-aws/service-discovery.html for details on service registries in Kubernetes and AWS. Refer to https://microservices.io/patterns/client-side-discovery.html and https://microservices.io/patterns/server-side-discovery.html for details on client-side discovery and server-side discovery.

6.5   *Functional partitioning and various frameworks*

In this section, we discuss some of the countless frameworks that can be used to develop the various components in a system design diagram. New frameworks are continuously being developed, and various frameworks fall in and out of favor with the industry. The sheer number of frameworks can be confusing to a beginner. Moreover, certain frameworks can be used for more than one component, making the overall picture even more confusing. This section is a broad discussion of various frameworks, including

- Web
- Mobile, including Android and iOS
- Backend
- PC

The universe of languages and frameworks is far bigger than can be covered in this section, and it is not the aim of this section to discuss them all. The purpose of this section is to provide some awareness of several frameworks and languages. By the end of this section, you should be able to read more easily the documentation of a framework to understand its purposes and where it fits into a system design.

6.5.1   *Basic system design of an app*

Figure 1.1 introduced a basic system design of an app. In almost all cases today, a company that develops a mobile app that makes requests to a backend service will have an iOS app on the iOS app store and an Android app on the Google Play store. It may also develop a browser app that has the same features as the mobile apps or maybe a simple page that directs users to download the mobile apps. There are many variations. For example, a company may also develop a PC app. But attempting to explain every possible combination is counterproductive, and we will not do so.

We will start with discussing the following questions regarding figure 1.1, then expand our discussion to various frameworks and their languages:

- Why is there a separate web server application from the backend and browser app?
- Why does the browser app make requests to this Node.js app, which then makes requests to the backend that is shared with the Android and iOS apps?

6.5.2 *Purposes of a web server app*

The purposes of a web server app include the following:

- When someone using a web browser accesses the URL (e.g., https://google .com/), the browser downloads the browser app from the Node.js app. As stated in section 1.4.1, the browser app should preferably be small so it can be downloaded quickly.
- When the browser makes a specific URL request (e.g., with a specific path like https://google.com/about), Node.js handles the routing of the URL and serves the corresponding page.
- The URL may include certain path and query parameters that require specific backend requests. The Node.js app processes the URL and makes the appropriate backend requests.
- Certain user actions on the browser app, such as filling and submitting forms or clicking on buttons, may require backend requests. A single action may correspond to multiple backend requests, so the Node.js app exposes its own API to the browser app. Referring to figure 6.4, for each user action, the browser app makes an API request to the Node.js app/server, which then makes one or more appropriate backend requests and returns the requested data.

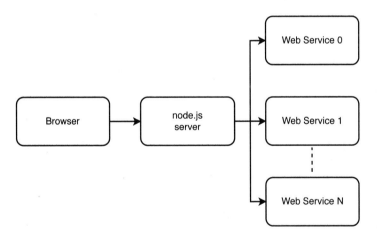

Figure 6.4 A Node.js server can serve a request from a browser by making appropriate requests to one or more web services, aggregate and process their responses, and return the appropriate response to the browser.

Why doesn't a browser make requests directly to the backend? If the backend was a REST app, its API endpoints may not return the exact data required by the browser. The browser may have to make multiple API requests and fetch more data than required. This data transmission occurs over the internet, between a user's device and a data center, which is inefficient. It is more efficient for the Node.js app to make these large requests because the data transmission will likely happen between adjacent hosts in the same data center. The Node.js app can then return the exact data required by the browser.

GraphQL apps allow users to request the exact data required, but securing GraphQL endpoints is more work than a REST app, causing more development time and possible security breaches. Other disadvantages include the following. Refer to section 6.7.4 for more discussion on GraphQL:

- Flexible queries mean that more work is required to optimize performance.
- More code on the client.
- More work needed to define the schema.
- Larger requests.

6.5.3   *Web and mobile frameworks*

This section contains a list of frameworks, classified into the following:

- Web/browser app development
- Mobile app development
- Backend app development
- PC aka desktop app development (i.e., for Windows, Mac, and Linux)

A complete list will be very long, include many frameworks that one will be unlikely to encounter or even read about during their career, and in the author's opinion, will not be useful to the reader. This list only states some of the frameworks that are prominent or used to be prominent.

The flexibility of these spaces makes a complete and objective discussion difficult. Frameworks and languages are developed in countless ways, some of which make sense and others which do not.

BROWSER APP DEVELOPMENT

Browsers accept only HTML, CSS, and JavaScript, so browser apps must be in these languages for backward compatibility. A browser is installed on a user's device, so it must be upgraded by the user themselves, and it is difficult and impractical to persuade or force users to download a browser that accepts another language. It is possible to develop a browser app in vanilla JavaScript (i.e., without any frameworks), but this is impractical for all but the smallest browser apps because frameworks contain many functions that one will otherwise have to reimplement in vanilla JavaScript (e.g., animation or data rendering like sorting tables or drawing charts).

Although browser apps must be in these three languages, a framework can offer other languages. The browser app code written in these languages is transpiled to HTML, CSS, and JavaScript.

The most popular browser app frameworks include React, Vue.js, and Angular. Other frameworks include Meteor, jQuery, Ember.js, and Backbone.js. A common theme of these frameworks is that developers mix the markup and logic in the same files, rather than having separate HTML files for markup and JavaScript files for logic. These frameworks may also contain their own languages for markup and logic. For example, React introduced JSX, which is an HTML-like markup language. A JSX file can include both markup and JavaScript functions and classes. Vue.js has the template tag, which is similar to HTML.

Some of the more prominent web development languages (which are transpiled to JavaScript) include the following:

- TypeScript (https://www.typescriptlang.org/) is a statically typed language. It is a wrapper/superset around JavaScript. Virtually any JavaScript framework can also use TypeScript, with some setup work.
- Elm (https://elm-lang.org/) can be directly transpiled to HTML, CSS, and JavaScript, or it can also be used within other frameworks like React.
- PureScript (https://www.purescript.org/) aims for a similar syntax as Haskell.
- Reason (https://reasonml.github.io/).
- ReScript (https://rescript-lang.org/).
- Clojure (https://clojure.org/) is a general-purpose language. The ClojureScript (https://clojurescript.org/) framework transpiles to Clojure to JavaScript.
- CoffeeScript (https://coffeescript.org/).

These browser app frameworks are for the browser/client side. Here are some server-side frameworks. Any server-side framework can also make requests to databases and be used for backend development. In practice, a company often chooses one framework for server development and another framework for backend development. This is a common point of confusion for beginners trying to distinguish between "server-side frontend" frameworks and "backend" frameworks. There is no strict division between them.

- Express (https://expressjs.com/) is a Node.js (https://nodejs.org/) server framework. Node.js is a JavaScript runtime environment built on Chrome's V8 JavaScript engine. The V8 JavaScript engine was originally built for Chrome, but it can also run on an operating system like Linux or Windows. The purpose of Node.js is for JavaScript code to run on an operating system. Most frontend or full-stack job postings that state Node.js as a requirement are actually referring to Express.
- Deno (https://deno.land/) supports JavaScript and TypeScript. It was created by Ryan Dahl, the original creator of Node.js, to address his regrets about Node.js.
- Goji (https://goji.io/) is a Golang framework.
- Rocket (https://rocket.rs/) is a Rust framework. Refer to https://blog.logrocket .com/the-current-state-of-rust-web-frameworks/ for more examples of Rust web server and backend frameworks.
- Vapor (https://vapor.codes/) is a framework for the Swift language.

- Vert.x (https://vertx.io/) offers development in Java, Groovy, and Kotlin.
- PHP (https://www.php.net/). (There is no universal agreement on whether PHP is a language or a framework. The author's opinion is that there is no practical value in debating this semantic.) A common solution stack is the LAMP (Linux, Apache, MySQL, PHP/Perl/Python) acronym. PHP code can be run on an Apache (https://httpd.apache.org/) server, which in turn runs on a Linux host. PHP was popular before ~2010 (https://www.tiobe.com/tiobe-index/php/), but in the author's experience, PHP code is seldom directly used for new projects. PHP remains prominent for web development via the WordPress platform, which is useful for building simple websites. More sophisticated user interfaces and customizations are more easily done by web developers, using frameworks that require considerable coding, such as React and Vue.js. Meta (formerly known as Facebook) was a prominent PHP user. The Facebook browser app was formerly developed in PHP. In 2014, Facebook introduced the Hack language (https://hacklang.org/) and HipHop Virtual Machine (HHVM) (https://hhvm.com/). Hack is a PHP-like language that does not suffer from the bad security and performance of PHP. It runs on HVVM. Meta is an extensive user of Hack and HHVM.

MOBILE APP DEVELOPMENT

The dominant mobile operating systems are Android and iOS, developed by Google and Apple, respectively. Google and Apple each offer their own Android or iOS app development platform, which are commonly referred to as "native" platforms. The native Android development languages are Kotlin and Java, while the native iOS development languages are Swift and Objective-C.

CROSS-PLATFORM DEVELOPMENT

Cross-platform development frameworks in theory reduce duplicate work by running the same code on multiple platforms. In practice, there may be additional code required to code the app for each platform, which will negate some of this benefit. Such situations occur when the UI (user interface) components provided by operating systems are too different from each other. Frameworks which are cross-platform between Android and iOS include the following:

- React Native is distinct from React. The latter is for web development only. There is also a framework called React Native for Web (https://github.com/necolas/react-native-web), which allows web development using React Native.
- Flutter (https://flutter.dev/) is cross-platform across Android, iOS, web, and PC.
- Ionic (https://ionicframework.com/) is cross-platform across Android, iOS, web, and PC.
- Xamarin (https://dotnet.microsoft.com/en-us/apps/xamarin) is cross-platform across Android, iOS, and Windows.

Electron (https://www.electronjs.org/) is cross-platform between web and PC.

Cordova (https://cordova.apache.org/) is a framework for mobile and PC development using HTML, CSS, and JavaScript. With Cordova, cross-platform development with web development frameworks like Ember.js is possible.

Another technique is to code a *progressive web app* (PWA). A PWA is a browser app or web application that can provide a typical desktop browser experience and also uses certain browser features such as *service workers* and *app manifests* to provide mobile user experiences similar to mobile devices. For example, using service workers, a progressive web app can provide user experiences, such as push notifications, and cache data in the browser to provide offline experiences similar to native mobile apps. A developer can configure an app manifest so the PWA can be installed on a desktop or mobile device. A user can add an icon of the app on their device's home screen, start menu, or desktop and tap on that icon to open the app; this is a similar experience to installing apps from the Android or iOS app stores. Since different devices have different screen dimensions, designers and developers should use a *responsive web design* approach, which is an approach to web design to make the web app render well on various screen dimensions or when the user resizes their browser window. Developers can use approaches like *media queries* (https://developer.mozilla.org/en-US/docs/Web/CSS/Media_Queries/Using_media_queries) or *ResizeObserver* (https://developer.mozilla.org/en-US/docs/Web/API/ResizeObserver) to ensure the app renders well on various browser or screen dimensions.

BACKEND DEVELOPMENT

Here is a list of backend development frameworks. Backend frameworks can be classified into RPC, REST, and GraphQL. Some backend development frameworks are full-stack; that is, they can be used to develop a monolithic browser application that makes database requests. We can also choose to use them for browser app development and make requests to a backend service developed in another framework, but the author has never heard of these frameworks being used this way:

- gRPC (https://grpc.io/) is an RPC framework that can be developed in C#, C++, Dart, Golang, Java, Kotlin, Node, Objective-C, PHP, Python, or Ruby. It may be extended to other languages in the future.

- Thrift (https://thrift.apache.org/) and Protocol Buffers (https://developers.google.com/protocol-buffers) are used to serialize data objects, compressing them to reduce network traffic. An object can be defined in a definition file. We can then generate client and server (backend, not web server) code from a definition file. Clients can use the client code to serialize requests to the backend, which uses the backend code to deserialize the requests, and vice versa for the backend's responses. Definition files also help to maintain backward and forward compatibility by placing limitations on possible changes.

- Dropwizard (https://www.dropwizard.io/) is an example of a Java REST framework. Spring Boot (https://spring.io/projects/spring-boot) can be used to create Java applications, including REST services.
- Flask (https://flask.palletsprojects.com/) and Django (https://www.djangoproject.com/) are two examples of REST frameworks in Python. They can also be used for web server development.

Here are several examples of full-stack frameworks:

- Dart (https://dart.dev) is a language that offers frameworks for any solution. It can be used for full-stack, backend, server, browser, and mobile apps.
- Rails (https://rubyonrails.org/) is a Ruby full-stack framework that can also be used for REST. Ruby on Rails is often used as a single solution, rather than using Ruby with other frameworks or Rails with other languages.
- Yesod (https://www.yesodweb.com/) is a Haskell framework that can also be used just for REST. Browser app development can be done with Yesod using its Shakespearean template languages https://www.yesodweb.com/book/shakespearean-templates, which transpiles to HTML, CSS, and JavaScript.
- Integrated Haskell Platform (https://ihp.digitallyinduced.com/) is another Haskell framework.
- Phoenix (https://www.phoenixframework.org/) is a framework for the Elixir language.
- JavaFX (https://openjfx.io/) is a Java client application platform for desktop, mobile, and embedded systems. It is descended from Java Swing (https://docs.oracle.com/javase/tutorial/uiswing/), for developing GUI for Java programs.
- Beego (https://beego.vip/) and Gin (https://gin-gonic.com/) are Golang frameworks.

6.6   *Library vs. service*

After determining our system's components, we can discuss the pros and cons of implementing each component on the client-side vs. server-side, as a library vs. service. Do not immediately assume that a particular choice is best for any particular component. In most situations, there is no obvious choice between using a library vs. service, so we need to be able to discuss design and implementation details and tradeoffs for both options.

A library may be an independent code bundle, a thin layer that forwards all requests and responses between clients and servers, respectively, or it may contain elements of both. In other words, some of the API logic is implemented within the library while the rest may be implemented by services called by the library. In this chapter, for the purpose of comparing libraries vs. services, the term "library" refers to an independent library.

Table 6.1 summarizes a comparison of libraries vs. services. Most of these points are discussed in detail in the rest of this chapter.

Table 6.1 Summary comparison of libraries vs. services

Library	Service
Users choose which version/build to use and have more choice on upgrading to new versions.	Developers select the build and control when upgrades happen.
A disadvantage is that users may continue to use old versions of libraries that contain bugs or security problems fixed in newer versions.	
Users who wish to always use the latest version of a frequently updated library have to implement programmatic upgrades themselves.	
No communication or data sharing between devices limits applications. If the user is another service, this service is horizontally scaled, and data sharing between hosts is needed, the customer service's hosts must be able to communicate with each other to share data. This communication must be implemented by the user service's developers.	No such limitation. Data synchronization between multiple hosts can be done via requests to each other or to a database. Users need not be concerned about this.
Language-specific.	Technology-agnostic.
Predictable latency.	Less predictable latency due to dependence on network conditions.
Predictable, reproducible behavior.	Network problems are unpredictable and difficult to reproduce, so the behavior may be less predictable and less reproducible.
If we need to scale up the load on the library, the entire application must be scaled up with it. Scaling costs are borne by the user's service.	Independently scalable. Scaling costs are borne by the service.
Users may be able to decompile the code to steal intellectual property.	Code is not exposed to users. (Though APIs can be reverse-engineered. This is outside the scope of this book.)

6.6.1 Language specific vs. technology-agnostic

For ease of use, a library should be in the client's language, so the same library must be reimplemented in each supported language.

Most libraries are optimized to perform a well-defined set of related tasks, so they can be optimally implemented in a single language. However, certain libraries may be partially or completely written in another language because certain languages and frameworks may be better suited for specific purposes. Implementing this logic entirely in the same language may cause inefficiencies during use. Moreover, while developing our library, we may want to utilize libraries written in other languages. There are various utility libraries that one can use to develop a library that contains components in other languages. This is outside the scope of this book. A practical difficulty is that the team or company that develops this library will require engineers fluent in all of these languages.

A service is technology-agnostic because a client can utilize a service regardless of the former or latter's technology stacks. A service can be implemented in the language and frameworks best-suited for its purposes. There is a slight additional overhead for clients, who will need to instantiate and maintain HTTP, RPC, or GraphQL connections to the service.

6.6.2 *Predictability of latency*

A library has no network latency, has guaranteed and predictable response time, and can be easily profiled with tools such as flame graphs.

A service has unpredictable and uncontrollable latency as it depends on numerous factors such as:

- Network latency, which depends on the user's internet connection quality.
- The service's ability to handle its current traffic volume.

6.6.3 *Predictability and reproducibility of behavior*

A service has less predictable and reproducible behavior than a library because its behavior has more dependencies such as:

- A deployment rollout is usually gradual (i.e., the build is deployed to a few service hosts at a time). Requests may be routed by the load balancer to hosts running different builds, resulting in different behavior.
- Users do not have complete control of the service's data, and it may be changed between requests by the service's developers. This is unlike a library, where users have complete control of their machine's file system.
- A service may make requests to other services and be affected by their unpredictable and unreproducible behavior.

Despite these factors, a service is often easier to debug than a library because:

- A service's developers have access to its logs, while a library's developers do not have access to the logs on the users' devices.
- A service's developers control its environment and can set up a uniform environment using tools like virtual machines and Docker for its hosts. A library is run by users on a diversity of environments such as variations in hardware, firmware, and OS (Android vs. iOS). A user may choose to send their crash logs to the developers, but it may still be difficult to debug without access to the user's device and exact environment.

6.6.4 *Scaling considerations for libraries*

A library cannot be independently scaled up since it is contained within the user's application. It does not make sense to discuss scaling up a library on a single user device. If the user's application runs in parallel on multiple devices, the user can scale up the library by scaling the application that uses it. To scale just the library alone, the user can create their own service that is a wrapper around that library and scale that service. But this won't be a library anymore, but simply a service that is owned by the user, so scaling costs are borne by the user.

6.6.5 Other considerations

This section briefly described some anecdotal observations from the author's personal experiences.

Some engineers have psychological hesitations in bundling their code with libraries but are open to connecting to services. They may be concerned that a library will inflate their build size, especially for JavaScript bundles. They are also concerned about the possibility of malicious code in libraries, while this is not a concern for services since the engineers control the data sent to services and have full visibility of the service's responses.

People expect breaking changes to occur in libraries but are less tolerant of breaking changes in services, particularly internal services. Service developers may be forced to adopt clumsy API endpoint naming conventions such as including terms like "/v2," "/v3," etc., in their endpoint names.

Anecdotal evidence suggests that adapter pattern is followed more often when using a library instead of a service.

6.7 Common API paradigms

This section introduces and compares the following common communication paradigms. One should consider the tradeoffs in selecting a paradigm for their service:

- REST (Representational State Transfer)
- RPC (Remote Procedure Call)
- GraphQL
- WebSocket

6.7.1 The Open Systems Interconnection (OSI) model

The *7-layer OSI model* is a conceptual framework/model that characterizes the functions of a networking system without regard to its underlying internal structure and technology. Table 6.2 briefly describes each layer. A convenient way to think of this model is that the protocols of each level are implemented using protocols of the lower level.

Actor, GraphQL, REST, and WebSocket are implemented on top of HTTP. RPC is classified as layer 5 because it handles connections, ports, and sessions directly, rather than relying on a higher-level protocol like HTTP.

Table 6.2   The OSI model

Layer no.	Name	Description	Examples
7	Application	User interface.	FTP, HTTP, Telnet
6	Presentation	Presents data. Encryption occurs here.	UTF, ASCII, JPEG, MPEG, TIFF
5	Session	Distinction between data of separate applications. Maintains connections. Controls ports and sessions.	RPC, SQL, NFX, X Windows
4	Transport	End-to-end connections. Defines reliable or unreliable delivery and flow control.	TCP, UDP
3	Network	Logical addressing.	IP, ICMP
		Defines the physical path the data uses. Routers work at this layer.	
2	Data link	Network format. May correct errors at the physical layer.	Ethernet, wi-fi
1	Physical	Raw bits over physical medium.	Fiber, coax, repeater, modem, network adapter, USB

6.7.2   *REST*

We assume the reader is familiar with the basics of REST as a stateless communication architecture that uses HTTP methods and request/response body most commonly encoded in JSON or XML. In this book, we use REST for APIs and JSON for POST request and response body. We can represent JSON schema with the specification by the JSON Schema organization (https://json-schema.org/), but we don't do so in this book because it is usually too verbose and low-level to discuss JSON schemas in detail in a 50-minute system design interview.

REST is simple to learn, set up, experiment, and debug with (using curl or a REST client). Its other advantages include its hypermedia and caching capabilities, which we discuss below.

HYPERMEDIA

Hypermedia controls (HATEOAS) or hypermedia is about providing a client with information about "next available actions" within a response. This takes the form of a field such as "links" within a response JSON, which contains API endpoints that the client may logically query next.

For example, after an ecommerce app displays an invoice, the next step is for the client to make payment. The response body for an invoice endpoint may contain a link to a payment endpoint, such as this:

```
{
  "data": {
    "type": "invoice",
    "id": "abc123",
  },
```

```
  "links": {
    "pay": "https://api.acme.com/payment/abc123"
  }
}
```

where the response contains an invoice ID, and the next step is to POST a payment for that invoice ID.

There is also the OPTIONS HTTP method, which is for fetching metadata about an endpoint, such as available actions, fields that can be updated, or what data do certain fields expect.

In practice, hypermedia and OPTIONS are difficult for client developers to use, and it makes more sense to provide a client developer with API documentation of each endpoint or function, such as using OpenAPI (https://swagger.io/specification/) for REST or the built-in documentation tools of RPC and GraphQL frameworks.

Refer to https://jsonapi.org/ for conventions on request/response JSON body specification.

Other communication architectures like RPC or GraphQL do not provide hypermedia.

Caching

Developers should declare REST resources as cacheable whenever possible, a practice which carries advantages such as the following:

- Lower latency because some network calls are avoided.
- Higher availability because the resource is available even if the service is not.
- Better scalability, since there is lower load on the server.

Use the `Expires`, `Cache-Control`, `ETag`, and `Last-Modified` HTTP headers for caching.

The `Expires` HTTP header specifies an absolute expiry time for a cached resource. A service can set a time value up to one year ahead of its current clock time. An example header is `Expires: Mon, 11 Dec 2021 18:00 PST`.

The `Cache-Control` header consists of comma-separated directives (instructions) for caching in both requests and responses. An example header is `Cache-Control: max-age=3600`, which means the response is cacheable for 3600 seconds. A POST or PUT request (noun) may include a `Cache-Control` header as a directive to the server to cache this data, but this does not mean that the server will follow this directive, and this directive might not be contained in responses for this data. Refer to https://developer.mozilla.org/en-US/docs/Web/HTTP/Headers/Cache-Control for all cache request and response directives.

An `ETag` value is an opaque string token that is an identifier for a specific version of a resource. (An *opaque token* is a token that has a proprietary format that is only known to the issuer. To validate an opaque token, the recipient of the token needs to call the server that issued the token.) A client can refresh its resource more efficiently by including the `ETag` value in the GET request. The server will only return the resource's value if the latter's `ETag` is different. In other words, the resource's value changed, so it does not unnecessarily return the resource's value if the client already has it.

The `Last-Modified` header contains the date and time the resource was last modified and can be used as a fallback for the `ETag` header if the latter is unavailable. Related headers are `If-Modified-Since` and `If-Unmodified-Since`.

DISADVANTAGES OF REST

A disadvantage is that it has no integrated documentation mechanisms, other than hypermedia or OPTIONS endpoints, which developers can choose not to provide. One must add an OpenAPI documentation framework to a service implemented using a REST framework. Otherwise, clients have no way of knowing the available request endpoints, or their details such as path or query parameters or the request and response body fields. REST also has no standardized versioning procedure; a common convention is to use a path like "/v2," "/v3," etc. for versioning. Another disadvantage of REST is that it does not have a universal specification, which leads to confusion. OData and JSON-API are two popular specifications.

6.7.3   *RPC (Remote Procedure Call)*

RPC is a technique to make a procedure execute in a different address space (i.e., another host), without the programmer having to handle the network details. Popular open-source RPC frameworks include Google's gRPC, Facebook's Thrift, and RPyC in Python.

For an interview, you should be familiar with the following common encoding formats. You should understand how encoding (also called serialization or marshalling) and decoding (also called parsing, deserialization, or unmarshalling) are done.

- CSV, XML, JSON
- Thrift
- Protocol Buffers (protobuf)
- Avro

The main advantages of RPC frameworks like gRPC over REST are:

- RPC is designed for resource optimization, so it is the best communication architecture choice for low-power devices, such as IoT devices like smart home devices. For a large web service, its lower resource consumption compared to REST or GraphQL becomes significant with scale.
- Protobuf is an efficient encoding. JSON is repetitive and verbose, causing requests and responses to be large. Network traffic savings become significant with scale.
- Developers define the schemas of their endpoints in files. Common formats include Avro, Thrift, and protobuf. Clients use these files to create requests and interpret responses. As schema documentation is a required step in developing

the API, client developers will always have good API documentation. These encoding formats also have schema modification rules, which make it clear to developers how to maintain backward and/or forward compatibility in schema modifications.

The main disadvantages of RPC are also from its nature as a binary protocol. It is troublesome for clients to have to update to the latest version of the schema files, especially outside an organization. Also, if an organization wishes to monitor its internal network traffic, it is easier to do so with text protocols like REST than with binary protocols like RPC.

6.7.4   *GraphQL*

GraphQL is a query language that enables *declarative data fetching*, where a client can specify exactly what data it needs from an API. It provides an API data query and manipulation language for pinpoint requests. It also provides an integrated API documentation tool that is essential for navigating this flexibility. The main benefits are:

- The client decides what data they want and its format.
- The server is efficient and delivers exactly what the client requests without under fetching (which necessitates multiple requests) or over-fetching (which inflates response size).

Tradeoffs:

- May be too complex for simple APIs.
- Has a higher learning curve than RPC and REST, including security mechanisms.
- Has a smaller user community than RPC and REST.
- Encodes in JSON only, which carries all the tradeoffs of JSON.
- User analytics may be more complicated because each API user performs slightly different queries. In REST and RPC, we can easily see how many queries were made to each API endpoint, but this is less obvious in GraphQL.
- We should be cautious when using GraphQL for external APIs. It is similar to exposing a database and allowing clients to make SQL queries.

Many of the benefits of GraphQL can be done in REST. A simple API can begin with simple REST HTTP methods (GET, POST, PUT, DELETE) with simple JSON bodies. As its requirements become more complex, it can use more REST capabilities such as OData https://www.odata.org/, or use JSON-API capabilities like https://jsonapi .org/format/#fetching-includes to combine related data from multiple resources into a single request. GraphQL may be more convenient than REST in addressing complex requirements because it provides a standard implementation and documentation of its capabilities. REST, on the other hand, has no universal standard.

6.7.5   *WebSocket*

WebSocket is a communications protocol for full-duplex communication over a persistent TCP connection, unlike HTTP, which creates a new connection for every request and closes it with every response. REST, RPC, GraphQL, and Actor model are design patterns or philosophies, while WebSocket and HTTP are communication protocols. However, it makes sense to compare WebSocket to the rest as API architectural styles because we can choose to implement our API using WebSocket rather than the other four choices.

To create a WebSocket connection, a client sends a WebSocket request to the server. WebSocket uses an HTTP handshake to create an initial connection and requests the server to upgrade to WebSocket from HTTP. Subsequent messages can use WebSocket over this persistent TCP connection.

WebSocket keeps connections open, which increases overhead for all parties. This means that WebSocket is stateful (compared to REST and HTTP, which are stateless). A request must be handled by the host that contains the relevant state/connection, unlike in REST where any host can handle any request. Both the stateful nature of WebSocket and the resource overhead of maintaining connections means that WebSocket is less scalable.

WebSocket allows p2p communication, so no backend is required. It trades off scalability for lower latency and higher performance.

6.7.6   *Comparison*

During an interview, we may need to evaluate the tradeoffs between these architectural styles and the factors to consider in choosing a style and protocol. REST and RPC are the most common. Startups usually use REST for simplicity, while large organizations can benefit from RPC's efficiency and backward and forward compatibility. GraphQL is a relatively new philosophy. WebSocket is useful for bidirectional communication, including p2p communication. Other references include https://apisyouwonthate.com/blog/picking-api-paradigm/ and https://www.baeldung.com/rest-vs-websockets.

Summary

- An API gateway is a web service designed to be stateless and lightweight yet fulfill many cross-cutting concerns across various services, which can be grouped into security, error-checking, performance and availability, and logging.
- A service mesh or sidecar pattern is an alternative pattern. Each host gets its own sidecar, so no service can consume an unfair share.
- To minimize network traffic, we can consider using a metadata service to store data that is processed by multiple components within a system.
- Service discovery is for clients to identify which service hosts are available.

- A browser app can have two or more backend services. One of them is a web server service that intercepts requests and responses from the other backend services.

- A web server service minimizes network traffic between the browser and data center, by performing aggregation and filtering operations with the backend.

- Browser app frameworks are for browser app development. Server-side frameworks are for web service development. Mobile app development can be done with native or cross-platform frameworks.

- There are cross-platform or full-stack frameworks for developing browser apps, mobile apps, and web servers. They carry tradeoffs, which may make them unsuitable for one's particular requirements.

- Backend development frameworks can be classified into RPC, REST, and GraphQL frameworks.

- Some components can be implemented as either libraries or services. Each approach has its tradeoffs.

- Most communication paradigms are implemented on top of HTTP. RPC is a lower-level protocol for efficiency.

- REST is simple to learn and use. We should declare REST resources as cacheable whenever possible.

- REST requires a separate documentation framework like OpenAPI.

- RPC is a binary protocol designed for resource optimization. Its schema modification rules also allow backward- and forward-compatibility.

- GraphQL allows pinpoint requests and has an integrated API documentation tool. However, it is complex and more difficult to secure.

- WebSocket is a stateful communications protocol for full-duplex communication. It has more overhead on both the client and server than other communication paradigms.

Part 2

In part 1, we learned about common topics in system design interviews. We will now go over a series of sample system design interview questions. In each question, we apply the concepts we learned in part 1 as well as introducing concepts relevant to the specific question.

We begin with chapter 7 on how to design a system like Craigslist, a system that is optimized for simplicity.

Chapters 8–10 discuss designs of systems that are themselves common components of many other systems.

Chapter 11 discusses an autocomplete/typeahead service, a typical system that continuously ingests and processes large amounts of data into a few megabytes data structure that users query for a specific purpose.

Chapter 12 discusses an image-sharing service. Sharing and interacting with images and video are basic functionalities in virtually every social application, and a common interview topic. This leads us to the topic of chapter 13, where we discuss a Content Distribution Network (CDN), a system that is commonly used to cost-efficiently serve static content like images and videos to a global audience.

Chapter 14 discusses a text messaging app, a system that delivers messages sent from many users to many other users and should not accidentally deliver duplicate messages.

Chapter 15 discusses a room reservation and marketplace system. Sellers can offer rooms for rent, and renters can reserve and pay for them. Our system must also allow our internal operations staff to conduct arbitration and content moderation.

Chapters 16 and 17 discuss systems that process data feeds. Chapter 16 discusses a news feed system that sorts data for distribution to many interested users, while chapter 17 discusses a data analytics service that aggregates large amounts of data into a dashboard that can be used to make decisions.

Design Craigslist 7

We want to design a web application for classifieds posts. Craigslist is an example of a typical web application that may have more than a billion users. It is partitioned by geography. We can discuss the overall system, which includes browser and mobile apps, a stateless backend, simple storage requirements, and analytics. More use cases and constraints can be added for an open-ended discussion. This chapter is unique in that it is the only one in this book where we discuss a monolith architecture as a possible system design.

7.1   *User stories and requirements*

Let's discuss the user stories for Craigslist. We distinguish two primary user types: viewer and poster.

A poster should be able to create and delete a post and search their posts as they may have many, especially if they were programmatically generated. This post should contain the following information:

- Title.
- Some paragraphs of description.
- Price. Assume a single currency and ignore currency conversions.
- Location.
- Up to 10 photos of 1 MB each.
- Video, though this may be added to a later iteration of our application.

A poster can renew their post every seven days. They will receive an email notification with a click-through to renew their post.

A viewer should be able to

1 View all posts or search in posts within any city made in the last seven days. View a list of results, possibly as an endless scroll.
2 Apply filters on the results.
3 Click an individual post to view its details.
4 Contact the poster, such as by email.
5 Report fraud and misleading posts (e.g., a possible clickbait technique is to state a low price on the post but a higher price in the description).

The non-functional requirements are as follows:

- *Scalable*—Up to 10 million users in a single city.
- *High availability*—99.9% uptime.
- *High performance*—Viewers should be able to view posts within seconds of creation. Search and viewing posts should have 1 second P99.
- *Security*—A poster should log in before creating a post. We can use an authentication library or service. Appendix B discusses OpenID Connect, which is a popular authentication mechanism. We will not discuss this further in the rest of this chapter.

Most of the required storage will be for Craigslist posts. The amount of required storage is low:

- We may show a Craigslist user only the posts in their local area. This means that a data center serving any individual user only needs to store a fraction of all the posts (though it may also back up posts from other data centers).

- Posts are manually (not programmatically) created, so storage growth will be slow.
- We do not handle any programmatically generated data.
- A post may be automatically deleted after one week.

A low storage requirement means that all the data can fit into a single host, so we do not require distributed storage solutions. Let's assume an average post contains 1,000 letters or 1 KB of text. If we assume that a big city has 10 million people and 10% of them are posters creating an average of 10 posts/day (i.e., 10 GB/day), our SQL database can easily store months of posts.

7.2 API

Let's scribble down some API endpoints, separated into managing posts and managing users. (In an interview, we have no time to write down a formal API specification such as in OpenAPI format or GraphQL schema, so we can tell the interviewer that we can use a formal specification to define our API, but in the interest of time we will use rough scribbles during the interview. We will not mention this again in the rest of the book.)

CRUD posts:

- GET and DELETE /post/{id}
- GET /post?search={search_string}. This can be an endpoint to GET all posts. It can have a "search" query parameter to search on posts' content. We may also implement query parameters for pagination, which will be discussed in section 12.7.1.
- POST and PUT /post
- POST /contact
- POST /report
- DELETE /old_posts

User management:

- POST /signup. We do not need to discuss user account management.
- POST /login
- DELETE /user

Other:

- GET /health. Usually automatically generated by the framework. Our implementation can be as simple as making a small GET request and verifying it returns 200, or it can be detailed and include statistics like P99 and availability of various endpoints.

There are various filters, which may vary by the product category. For simplicity, we assume a fixed set of filters. Filters can be implemented both on the frontend and backend:

- *Neighborhood:* enum
- *Minimum price*
- *Maximum price*
- *Item condition:* enum. Values include NEW, EXCELLENT, GOOD, and ACCEPTABLE.

The GET /post endpoint can have a "search" query parameter to search on posts.

7.3   SQL database schema

We can design the following SQL schema for our Craigslist user and post data.

- *User:* id PRIMARY KEY, first_name text, last_name text, signup_ts integer
- *Post:* This table is denormalized, so JOIN queries are not required to get all the details of a post. id PRIMARY KEY, created_at integer, poster_id integer, location_id integer, title text, description text, price integer, condition text, country_code char(2), state text, city text, street_number integer, street_name text, zip_code text, phone_number integer, email text
- *Images:* id PRIMARY KEY, ts integer, post_id integer, image_address text
- *Report:* id PRIMARY KEY, ts integer, post_id integer, user_id integer, abuse_type text, message text
- *Storing images:* We can store images on an object store. AWS S3 and Azure Blob Storage are popular because they are reliable, simple to use and maintain, and cost-efficient.
- *image_address:* The identifier used to retrieve an image from the object store.

When low latency is required, such as when responding to user queries, we usually use SQL or in-memory databases with low latency such as Redis. NoSQL databases that use distributed file systems such as HDFS are for large data-processing jobs.

7.4   Initial high-level architecture

Referring to figure 7.1, we can discuss multiple possibilities for our initial Craigslist design, in order of complexity. We will discuss these two designs in the next two sections.

1 A monolith that uses a user authentication service for authentication and an object store for storing posts.
2 A client frontend service, a backend service, a SQL service, an object store, and a user authentication service.

In all designs, we also include a logging service because logging is almost always a must, so we can effectively debug our system. For simplicity, we can exclude monitoring and alerting. However, most cloud vendors provide logging, monitoring, and alerting tools that are easy to set up, and we should use them.

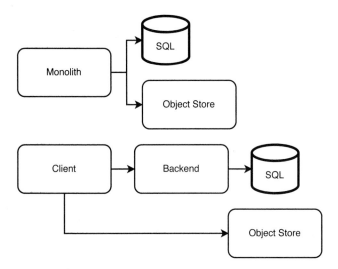

Figure 7.1   Simple initial designs for our high-level architecture. (Top) Our high-level architecture consists of just a monolith and an object store. (Bottom) A conventional high-level architecture with a UI frontend service and a backend service. Image files are stored in an object store, which clients make requests to. The rest of a post is stored in SQL.

7.5   A monolith architecture

Our first suggested design to use a monolith is unintuitive, and the interviewer may even be taken aback. One is unlikely to use monolith architecture for web services in their career. However, we should keep in mind that every design decision is about tradeoffs and not be afraid to suggest such designs and discuss tradeoffs.

We can implement our application as a monolith that contains both the UI and the backend functionality and store entire webpages in our object store. A key design decision is that we can store a post's webpage in its entirety in the object store, including the post's photos. Such a design decision means that we may not use many of the columns of the Post table discussed in section 7.3; we will use this table for the high-level architecture illustrated at the bottom of figure 7.1, which we discuss later in this chapter.

Referring to figure 7.2, the home page is static, except for the location navigation bar (containing a regional location such as "SF bay area" and links to more specific locations such as "sfc," "sby," etc.), and the "nearby cl" section that has a list of other cities. Other sites are static, including the sites on the left navigation bar, such as "craigslist app" and "about craigslist," and the sites on the bottom navigation bar, such as "help," "safety," "privacy," etc., are static.

Figure 7.2   A Craigslist homepage. (Source: https://sfbay.craigslist.org/)

This approach is simple to implement and maintain. Its main tradeoffs are:

1   HTML tags, CSS, and JavaScript are duplicated on every post.

2   If we develop a native mobile app, it cannot share a backend with the browser app. A possible solution is to develop a progressive web app (discussed in section 6.5.3), which is installable on mobile devices and can be used on web browsers on any device.

3   Any analytics on posts will require us to parse the HTML. This is only a minor disadvantage. We can develop and maintain our own utility scripts to fetch post pages and parse the HTML.

A disadvantage of the first tradeoff is that additional storage is required to store the duplicate page components. Another disadvantage is that new features or fields cannot be applied to old posts, though since posts are automatically deleted after one week, this may be acceptable depending on our requirements. We can discuss this with our interviewer as an example of how we should not assume any requirement when designing a system.

We can partially mitigate the second tradeoff by writing the browser app using a responsive design approach and implementing the mobile app as a wrapper around the browser app using WebViews. https://github.com/react-native-webview/react-native -webview is a WebView library for React Native. https://developer.android.com/ reference/android/webkit/WebView is the WebView library for native Android, and https://developer.apple.com/documentation/webkit/wkwebview is the WebView library for native iOS. We can use CSS media queries (https://developer.mozilla.org/ en-US/docs/Learn/CSS/CSS_layout/Responsive_Design#media_queries) to display different page layouts for phone displays, tablet displays, and laptop and desktop displays. This way, we do not need to use UI components from a mobile framework. A comparison of UX between using this approach versus the conventional approach of using the UI components in mobile development frameworks is outside the scope of this book.

For authentication on the backend service and Object Store Service, we can use a third-party user authentication service or maintain our own. Refer to appendix B for a detailed discussion of Simple Login and OpenID Connect authentication mechanisms.

7.6   Using an SQL database and object store

The bottom diagram of figure 7.1 shows a more conventional high-level architecture. We have a UI frontend service that makes requests to a backend service and an object store service. The backend service makes requests to an SQL service.

In this approach, the object store is for image files, while the SQL database stores the rest of a post's data as discussed in section 7.4. We could have simply stored all data in the SQL database, including images, and not had an object store at all. However, this will mean that a client must download image files through the backend host. This is an additional burden on the backend host, increases image download latency, and increases the overall possibility of download failures from sudden network connectivity problems.

If we wish to keep our initial implementation simple, we can consider going without the feature to have images on posts and add the object store when we wish to implement this feature.

That being said, because each post is limited to 10 image files of 1 MB each, and we will not store large image files, we can discuss with the interviewer whether this requirement may change in the future. We can suggest that if we are unlikely to require larger images, we can store the images in SQL. The image table can have a post_id text column and an image blob column. An advantage of this design is its simplicity.

7.7   Migrations are troublesome

While we are on the subject of choosing the appropriate data stores for our non-functional requirements, let's discuss the problem of data migrations before we proceed with discussing other features and requirements.

Another disadvantage of storing image files on SQL is that in the future we will have to migrate to storing them on an object store. Migration from one data store to another is generally troublesome and tedious.

Let's discuss a possible simple migration process, assuming the following:

1 We can treat both data stores as single entities. That is, replication is abstracted away from us, and we do not need to consider how data is distributed across various data centers to optimize for non-functional requirements like latency or availability.

2 Downtime is permissible. We can disable writes to our application during the data migration, so users will not add new data to the old data store while data is being transferred from the old data store to the new data store.

3 We can disconnect/terminate requests in progress when the downtime begins, so users who are making write (POST, PUT, DELETE) requests will receive 500 errors. We can give users advance notification of this downtime via various channels, such as email, browser and mobile push notifications, or a banner notification on the client.

We can write a Python script that runs on a developer's laptop to read records from one store and write it to another store. Referring to figure 7.3, this script will make GET requests to our backend to get the current data records and POST requests to our new object store. Generally, this simple technique is suitable if the data transfer can complete within hours and only needs to be done once. It will take a developer a few hours to write this script, so it may not be worth it for the developer to spend more time improving the script to speed up the data transfer.

We should expect that our migration job may stop suddenly due to bugs or network problems, and we will need to restart the script execution. The write endpoints should be idempotent to prevent duplicate records from being written to our new data store. The script should do checkpointing, so it does not reread and rewrite records that have already been transferred. A simple checkpointing mechanism will suffice; after each write, we can save the object's ID to our local machine's hard disk. If the job fails midway, the job can resume from the checkpoint when we restart it (after fixing bugs if necessary).

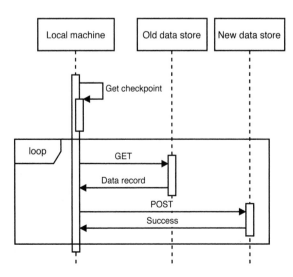

Figure 7.3 Sequence diagram of a simple data migration process. The local machine first finds the checkpoint if there is any, then makes the relevant requests to move each record from the old data store to the new data store.

An alert reader will notice that for this checkpoint mechanism to work, the script needs to read the records in the same order each time it is run. There are many possible ways to achieve this, including the following:

- If we can obtain a complete and sorted list of our records' IDs and store it in our local machine's hard disk, our script can load this list into memory before commencing the data transfer. Our script fetches each record by its ID, writes it to the new data store, and records on our hard disk that this ID has been transferred. Because hard disk writes are slow, we can write/checkpoint these completed IDs in batches. With this batching, a job may fail before a batch of IDs has been checkpointed, so these objects may be reread and rewritten, and our idempotent write endpoints prevent duplicate records.
- If our data objects have any ordinal (indicates position) fields such as timestamps, our script can checkpoint using this field. For example, if we checkpoint by date, our script first transfers the records with the earliest date, checkpoints this date, increments the date, transfers the records with this date, and so on, until the transfer is complete.

This script must read/write the fields of the data objects to the appropriate tables and columns. The more features we add before a data migration, the more complex the migration script will be. More features mean more classes and properties. There will be more database tables and columns, we will need to author a larger number of ORM/ SQL queries, and these query statements will also be more complex and may have JOINs between tables.

If the data transfer is too big to complete with this technique, we will need to run the script within the data center. We can run it separately on each host if the data is distributed across multiple hosts. Using multiple hosts allows the data migration to occur without downtime. If our data store is distributed across many hosts, it is because we have many users, and in these circumstances, downtime is too costly to revenue and reputation.

To decommission the old data store one host at a time, we can follow these steps on each host.

1 Drain the connections on the host. *Connection draining* refers to allowing existing requests to complete while not taking on new requests. Refer to sources like https://cloud.google.com/load-balancing/docs/enabling-connection-draining, https://aws.amazon.com/blogs/aws/elb-connection-draining-remove-instances -from-service-with-care/, and https://docs.aws.amazon.com/elasticloadbalancing/ latest/classic/config-conn-drain.html for more information on connection draining.

2 After the host is drained, run the data transfer script on the host.

3 When the script has finished running, we no longer need this host.

How should we handle write errors? If this migration takes many hours or days to complete, it will be impractical if the transfer job crashes and terminates each time there is an error with reading or writing data. Our script should instead log the errors and continue running. Each time there is an error, log the record that is being read or written, and continue reading and writing the other records. We can examine the errors, fix bugs, if necessary, then rerun the script to transfer these specific records.

A lesson to take away from this is that a data migration is a complex and costly exercise that should be avoided if possible. When deciding which data stores to use for a system, unless we are implementing this system as a proof-of-concept that will handle only a small amount of data (preferably unimportant data that can be lost or discarded without consequences), we should set up the appropriate data stores at the beginning, rather than set them up later then have to do a migration.

7.8   *Writing and reading posts*

Figure 7.4 is a sequence diagram of a poster writing a post, using the architecture in section 7.6. Although we are writing data to more than one service, we will not require distributed transaction techniques for consistency. The following steps occur:

1 The client makes a POST request to the backend with the post, excluding the images. The backend writes the post to the SQL database and returns the post ID to the client.

2 The client can upload the image files one at a time to the object store, or fork threads to make parallel upload requests.

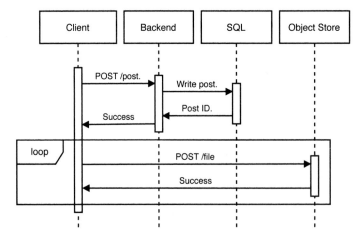

Figure 7.4   Sequence diagram of writing a new post, where the client handles image uploads

In this approach, the backend returns 200 success without knowing if the image files were successfully uploaded to the object store. For the backend to ensure that the entire post is uploaded successfully, it must upload the images to the object store itself.

Figure 7.5 illustrates such an approach. The backend can only return 200 success to the client after all image files are successfully uploaded to the object store, just in case image file uploads are unsuccessful. This may occur due to reasons such as the backend host crashing during the upload process, network connectivity problems, or if the object store is unavailable.

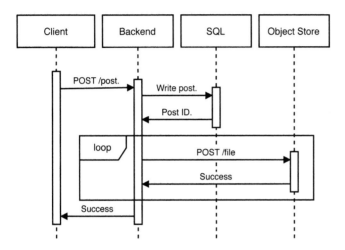

Figure 7.5   Sequence diagram of writing a new post, where the backend handles image uploads

Let's discuss the tradeoffs of either approach. Advantages of excluding the backend from the image uploads include

- *Fewer resources*—We push the burden of uploading images onto the client. If image file uploads went through our backend, our backend must scale up with our object store.
- *Lower overall latency*—The image files do not need to go through an additional host. If we decide to use a CDN to store images, this latency problem will become even worse because clients cannot take advantage of CDN edges close to their locations.

Advantages of including the backend in the image uploads are as follows:

- We will not need to implement and maintain authentication and authorization mechanisms on our object store. Because the object store is not exposed to the outside world, our system has a smaller overall attack surface.
- Viewers are guaranteed to be able to view all images of a post. In the previous approach, if some or all images are not successfully uploaded, viewers will not see them when they view the post. We can discuss with the interviewer if this is an acceptable tradeoff.

One way to capture most of the advantages of both approaches is for clients to write image files to the backend but read image files from the CDN.

QUESTION   What are the tradeoffs of uploading each image file in a separate request vs. uploading all the files in a single request?

Does the client really need to upload each image file in a separate request? This complexity may be unnecessary. The maximum size of a write request will be slightly more than 10 MB, which is small enough to be uploaded in seconds. But this means that retries will also be more expensive. Discuss these tradeoffs with the interviewer.

The sequence diagram of a viewer reading a post is identical to figure 7.4, except that we have GET instead of POST requests. When a viewer reads a post, the backend fetches the post from the SQL database and returns it to the client. Next, the client fetches and displays the post's images from the object store. The image fetch requests can be parallel, so the files are stored on different storage hosts and are replicated, and they can be downloaded in parallel from separate storage hosts.

7.9   *Functional partitioning*

The first step in scaling up can be to employ functional partitioning by geographical region, such as by city. This is commonly referred to as *geolocation routing*, serving traffic based on the location DNS queries originate from the geographic location of our users, for example. We can deploy our application into multiple data centers and route each user to the data center that serves their city, which is also usually the closest data center. So, the SQL cluster in each data center contains only the data of the cities that it serves. We can implement replication of each SQL cluster to two other SQL services in different data centers as described with MySQL's binlog-based replication (refer to section 4.3.2).

Craigslist does this geographical partitioning by assigning a subdomain to each city (e.g., sfbay.craigslist.org, shanghai.craiglist.org, etc). If we go to craigslist.org in our browser, the following steps occur. An example is shown on figure 7.6.

1 Our internet service provider does a DNS lookup for craigslist.org and returns its IP address. (Browsers and OS have DNS caches, so the browser can use its DNS cache or the OS's DNS cache for future DNS lookups, which is faster than sending this DNS lookup request to the ISP.)

2 Our browser makes a request to the IP address of craigslist.org. The server determines our location based on our IP address, which is contained in the address, and returns a 3xx response with the subdomain that corresponds to our location. This returned address can be cached by the browser and other intermediaries along the way, such as the user's OS and ISP.

3 Another DNS lookup is required to obtain the IP address of this subdomain.

4 Our browser makes a request to the IP address of the subdomain. The server returns the webpage and data of that subdomain.

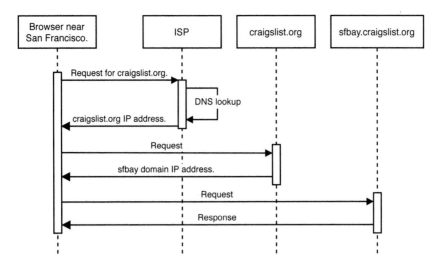

Figure 7.6 Sequence diagram for using GeoDNS to direct user requests to the appropriate IP address

We can use GeoDNS for our Craigslist. Our browser only needs to do a DNS lookup once for craigslist.org, and the IP address returned will be the data center that corresponds to our location. Our browser can then make a request to this data center to get our city's posts. Instead of having a subdomain specified in our browser's address bar, we can state the city in a drop-down menu on our UI. The user can select a city in this drop-down menu to make a request to the appropriate data center and view that city's posts. Our UI can also provide a simple static webpage page that contains all Craigslist cities, where a user can click through to their desired city.

Cloud services such as AWS (https://docs.aws.amazon.com/Route53/latest/ DeveloperGuide/routing-policy-geo.html) provide guides to configuring geolocation routing.

7.10 Caching

Certain posts may become very popular and receive a high rate of read requests, for example, a post that shows an item with a much lower price than its market value. To ensure compliance with our latency SLA (e.g., 1-second P99) and prevent 504 timeout errors, we can cache popular posts.

We can implement an LRU cache using Redis. The key can be a post ID, and the value is the entire HTML page of a post. We may implement an image service in front of the object store, so it can contain its own cache mapping object identifiers to images.

The static nature of posts limits potential cache staleness, though a poster may update their post. If so, the host should refresh the corresponding cache entry.

7.11   *CDN*

Referring to figure 7.7, we can consider using a CDN, although Craigslist has very little static media (i.e., images and video) that are shown to all users. The static contents it does have are CSS and JavaScript files, which are only a few MB in total. We can also use browser caching for the CSS and JavaScript files. (Browser caching was discussed in section 4.10.)

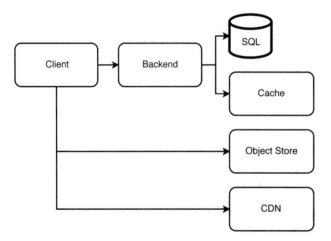

Figure 7.7   Our Craigslist architecture diagram after adding our cache and CDN

7.12   *Scaling reads with a SQL cluster*

It is unlikely that we will need to go beyond functional partitioning and caching. If we do need to scale reads, we can follow the approaches discussed in chapter 3, one of which is SQL replication.

7.13   *Scaling write throughput*

At the beginning of this chapter, we stated that this is a read-heavy application. It is unlikely that we will need to allow programmatic creation of posts. This section is a hypothetical situation where we do allow it and perhaps expose a public API for post creation.

   If there are traffic spikes in inserting and updating to the SQL host, the required throughput may exceed its maximum write throughput. Referring to https://stack-overflow.com/questions/2861944/how-to-do-very-fast-inserts-to-sql-server-2008, certain SQL implementations offer methods for fast INSERT for example, SQL Server's ExecuteNonQuery achieves thousands of INSERTs per second. Another solution is to use batch commits instead of individual *INSERT statements*, so there is no log flush overhead for each INSERT statement.

Use a message broker like Kafka

To handle write traffic spikes, we can use a streaming solution like Kafka, by placing a Kafka service in front of the SQL services.

Figure 7.8 shows a possible design. When a poster submits a new or updated post, the hosts of the Post Writer Service can produce to the Post topic. The service is stateless and horizontally scalable. We can create a new service we name "Post Writer" that continuously consumes from the Post topic and writes to the SQL service. This SQL service can use leader-follower replication, which was discussed in chapter 3.

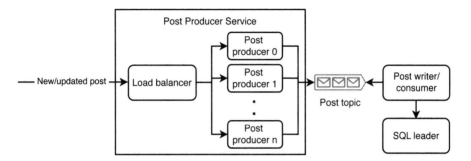

Figure 7.8   Using horizontal scaling and a message broker to handle write traffic spikes

The main tradeoffs of this approach are complexity and eventual consistency. Our organization likely has a Kafka service that we can use, so we don't have to create our own Kafka service, somewhat negating the complexity. Eventual consistency duration increases as writes will take longer to reach the SQL followers.

If the required write throughput exceeds the average write throughput of a single SQL host, we can do further functional partitioning of SQL clusters and have dedicated SQL clusters for categories with heavy write traffic. This solution is not ideal because the application logic for viewing posts will need to read from particular SQL clusters depending on category. Querying logic is no longer encapsulated in the SQL service but present in the application, too. Our SQL service is no longer independent on our backend service, and maintenance of both services becomes more complex.

If we need higher write throughput, we can use a NoSQL database such as Cassandra or Kafka with HDFS.

We may also wish to discuss adding a rate limiter (refer to chapter 8) in front of our backend cluster to prevent DDoS attacks.

7.14   *Email service*

Our backend can send requests to a shared email service for sending email.

To send a renewal reminder to posters when a post is seven days old, this can be implemented as a batch ETL job that queries our SQL database for posts that are seven days old and then requests the email service to send an email for each post.

The notification service for other apps may have requirements such as handling unpredictable traffic spikes, low latency, and notifications should be delivered within a short time. Such a notification service is discussed in the next chapter.

7.15   Search

Referring to section 2.6, we create an Elasticsearch index on the Post table for users to search posts. We can discuss if we wish to allow the user to filter the posts before and after searching, such as by user, price, condition, location, recency of post, etc., and we make the appropriate modifications to our index.

7.16   Removing old posts

Craigslist posts expire after a certain number of days, upon which the post is no longer accessible. This can be implemented with a cron job or Airflow, calling the `DELETE /old_posts` endpoint daily. `DELETE /old_posts` may be its own endpoint separate from `DELETE /post/{id}` because the latter is a single simple database delete operation, while the former contains more complex logic to first compute the appropriate timestamp value then delete posts older than this timestamp value. Both endpoints may also need to delete the appropriate keys from the Redis cache.

This job is simple and non-critical because it is acceptable for posts that were supposed to be deleted to continue to be accessible for days, so a cron job may be sufficient, and Airflow may introduce unneeded complexity. We must be careful not to accidentally delete posts before they are due, so any changes to this feature must be thoroughly tested in staging before a deployment to production. The simplicity of cron over a complex workflow management platform like Airflow improves maintainability, especially if the engineer who developed the feature has moved on and maintenance is being done by a different engineer.

Removing old posts or deletion of old data in general has the following advantages:

- Monetary savings on storage provisioning and maintenance.
- Database operations, such as reads and indexing, are faster.
- Maintenance operations that require copying all data to a new location are faster, less complex, and lower cost, such as adding or migrating to a different database solution.
- Fewer privacy concerns for the organization and limiting the effect of data breaches, though this advantage is not strongly felt since this is public data.

Disadvantages:

- Prevents analytics and useful insights that may be gained from keeping the data.
- Government regulations may make it necessary to keep data for a certain period.
- A tiny probability that the deleted post's URL may be used for a newer post, and a viewer may think they are viewing the old post. The probability of such events is higher if one is using a link-shortening service. However, the probability of this is so low, and it has little user effect, so this risk is acceptable. This risk will be unacceptable if sensitive personal data may be exposed.

If cost is a problem and old data is infrequently accessed, an alternative to data deletion may be compression followed by storing on low-cost archival hardware such as tape, or an online data archival service like AWS Glacier or Azure Archive Storage. When certain old data is required, it can be written onto disk drives prior to data processing operations.

7.17 Monitoring and alerting

Besides what was discussed in section 2.5, we should monitor and send alerts for the following:

- Our database monitoring solution (discussed in chapter 10) should trigger a low-urgency alert if old posts were not removed.
- Anomaly detection for:
  - Number of posts added or removed.
  - High number of searches for a particular term.
  - Number of posts flagged as inappropriate.

7.18 Summary of our architecture discussion so far

Figure 7.9 shows our Craigslist architecture with many of the services we have discussed, namely the client, backend, SQL, cache, notification service, search service, object store, CDN, logging, monitoring, alerting, and batch ETL.

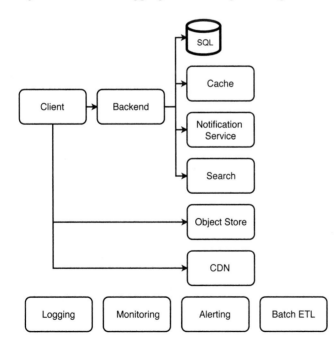

Figure 7.9 Our Craigslist architecture with notification service, search, logging, monitoring, and alerting. Logging, monitoring, and alerting can serve many other components, so on our diagram, they are shown as loose components. We can define jobs on the batch ETL service for purposes such as to periodically remove old posts.

7.19   *Other possible discussion topics*

Our system design fulfills the requirements stated at the beginning of this chapter. The rest of the interview may be on new constraints and requirements.

7.19.1   *Reporting posts*

We have not discussed the functionality for users to report posts because it is straightforward. Such a discussion may include a system design to fulfill such requirements:

- If a certain number of reports are made, the post is taken down, and the poster receives an email notification.
- A poster's account and email may be automatically banned, so the poster cannot log in to Craigslist or create posts. However, they can continue viewing posts without logging in and can continue sending emails to other posters.
- A poster should be able to contact an admin to appeal this decision. We may need to discuss with the interviewer if we need a system to track and record these interactions and decisions.
- If a poster wishes to block emails, they will need to configure their own email account to block the sender's email address. Craigslist does not handle this.

7.19.2   *Graceful degradation*

How can we handle a failure on each component? What are the possible corner cases that may cause failures and how may we handle them?

7.19.3   *Complexity*

Craigslist is designed to be a simple classifieds app that is optimized for simplicity of maintenance by a small engineering team. The feature set is deliberately limited and well-defined, and new features are seldomly introduced. We may want to discuss strategies to achieve this.

MINIMIZE DEPENDENCIES

Any app that contains dependencies to libraries and/or services naturally atrophies over time and requires developers to maintain it just to keep providing its current functionality. Old library versions and occasionally entire libraries are deprecated, and services can be decommissioned, necessitating that developers install a later version or find alternatives. New library versions or service deployments may also break our application. Library updates may also be necessary if bugs or security flaws are found in the currently used libraries. Minimizing our system's feature set minimizes its dependencies, which simplifies debugging, troubleshooting, and maintenance.

This approach requires an appropriate company culture that focuses on providing the minimal useful set of features that do not require extensive customization for each market. For example, possibly the main reason that Craigslist does not provide payments is that the business logic to handle payments can be different in each city.

We must consider different currencies, taxes, payment processors (MasterCard, Visa, PayPal, WePay, etc.), and constant work is required to keep up with changes in these factors. Many big tech companies have engineering cultures that reward program managers and engineers for conceptualizing and building new services; such a culture is unsuitable for us here.

USE CLOUD SERVICES

In figure 7.9, other than the client and backend, every service can be deployed on a cloud service. For example, we can use the following AWS services for each of the services in figure 7.9. Other cloud vendors like Azure or GCP provide similar services:

- *SQL:* RDS (https://aws.amazon.com/rds/)
- *Object Store:* S3 (https://aws.amazon.com/s3/)
- *Cache:* ElastiCache (https://aws.amazon.com/elasticache/)
- *CDN:* CloudFront (https://www.amazonaws.cn/en/cloudfront/)
- *Notification service:* Simple Notification Service (https://aws.amazon.com/sns)
- *Search:* CloudSearch (https://aws.amazon.com/cloudsearch/)
- *Logging, monitoring, and alerting:* CloudWatch (https://aws.amazon.com/cloudwatch/)
- *Batch ETL:* Lambda functions with rate and cron expressions (https://docs.aws.amazon.com/lambda/latest/dg/services-cloudwatchevents-expressions.html)

STORING ENTIRE WEBPAGES AS HTML DOCUMENTS

A webpage usually consists of an HTML template with interspersed JavaScript functions that make backend requests to fill in details. In the case of Craigslist, a post's HTML page template may contain fields such as title, description, price, photo, etc., and each field's value can be filled in with JavaScript.

The simple and small design of Craigslist's post webpage allows the simpler alternative we first discussed in section 7.5, and we can discuss it further here. A post's webpage can be stored as a single HTML document in our database or CDN. This can be as simple as a key-value pair where the key is the post's ID, and the value is the HTML document. This solution trades off some storage space because there will be duplicate HTML in every database entry. Search indexes can be built against this list of post IDs.

This approach also makes it less complex to add or remove fields from new posts. If we decide to add a new required field (e.g., subtitle), we can change the fields without a SQL database migration. We don't need to modify the fields in old posts, which have a retention period and will be automatically deleted. The Post table is simplified, replacing a post's fields with the post's CDN URL. The columns become "id, ts, poster_id, location_id, post_url".

OBSERVABILITY

Any discussion of maintainability must emphasize the importance of observability, discussed in detail in section 2.5. We must invest in logging, monitoring, alerting, automated testing and adopt good SRE practices, including good monitoring dashboards, runbooks, and automation of debugging.

7.19.4 *Item categories/tags*

We can provide item categories/tags, such as "automotive," "real estate," "furniture," etc., and allow posters to place up to a certain number of tags (e.g., three) on a listing. We can create a SQL dimension table for tags. Our Post table can have a column for a comma-separated tag list. An alternative is to have an associative/junction table "post_tag," as shown in figure 7.10.

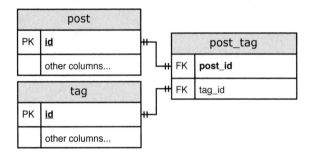

Figure 7.10   Associative/junction table for posts and tags. This schema normalization maintains consistency by avoiding duplicate data. If the data is in a single table, there will be duplicate values across rows.

We can expand this from a flat list to a hierarchical list, so users can apply more precise filters to view posts that are more relevant to their interests. For example, "real estate" may have the following nested subcategories.

- Real estate > Transaction type > Rent
- Real estate > Transaction type > Sale
- Housing type > Apartment
- Housing type > Single-family house
- Housing type > Townhouse

7.19.5 *Analytics and recommendations*

We can create daily batch ETL jobs that query our SQL database and populate dashboards for various metrics:

- Number of items by tag.
- Tags that received the most clicks.
- Tags that got the highest number of viewers contacting posters.
- Tags with the fastest sales, which may be measured by how soon the poster removed the post after posting it.
- Numbers and geographical and time distributions of reported, suspected, and confirmed fraudulent posts.

Craigslist does not offer personalization, and posts are ordered starting from most recent. We may discuss personalization, which includes tracking user activity and recommending posts.

7.19.6 A/B testing

As briefly discussed in section 1.4.5, as we develop new features and aesthetic designs in our application, we may wish to gradually roll them out to an increasing percentage of users, rather than to all users at once.

7.19.7 *Subscriptions and saved searches*

We may provide an API endpoint for viewers to save search terms (with a character limit) and notify them (by email, text message, in-app message, etc.) of any new posts that match their saved searches. A POST request to this endpoint can write a row (timestamp, user_id, search_term) to a SQL table we name "saved_search".

This saved search subscription service can be a complex system in itself, as described in this section.

A user should receive a single daily notification that covers all their saved searches. This notification may consist of a list of search terms and up to 10 corresponding results for each search term. Each result in turn consists of a list of post data for that search term. The data can include a link to the post and some summary information (title, price, first 100 characters of the description) to display in the notification.

For example, if a user has two saved search terms, "san francisco studio apartment" and "systems design interview book," the notification may contain the following. (You certainly do not write down all of this during an interview. You can scribble down some quick snippets and verbally describe what they mean.)

```
[
  {
    "search_term": "san francisco studio apartment",
    "results": [
      {
        "link": "sfbay.craigslist.org/12345",
        "title": "Totally remodeled studio",
        "price": 3000,
        "description_snippet": "Beautiful cozy studio apartment in the
  Mission. Nice views in a beautiful and safe neighborhood. Clo"
      },
      {
        "link": "sfbay.craigslist.org/67890"
        "title": "Large and beautiful studio",
        "price": 3500,
        "description_snippet": "Amenities\nComfortable, open floor plan\nIn
  unit laundry\nLarge closets\nPet friendly\nCeiling fan\nGar"
      },
      ...
    ]
  },
  {
```

```
      "search_term": "systems design interview book",
      "results": [
        ...
      ]
    }
]
```

To send the users new results for their saved searches, we can implement a daily batch ETL job. We can suggest at least two ways to implement this job: a simpler way that allows duplicate requests to the search service and another more complex way that avoids these duplicate requests.

7.19.8 *Allow duplicate requests to the search service*

Elasticsearch caches frequent search requests (https://www.elastic.co/blog/elasticsearch -caching-deep-dive-boosting-query-speed-one-cache-at-a-time), so frequent requests with the same search terms do not waste many resources. Our batch ETL job can process users and their individual saved search terms one at a time. Each process consists of sending a user's search terms as separate requests to the search service, consolidating the results, then sending a request to a notification service (the subject of chapter 9).

7.19.9 *Avoid duplicate requests to the search service*

Our batch ETL job runs the following steps:

1. Deduplicate the search terms, so we only need to run a search on each term once. We can run a SQL query like SELECT DISTINCT LOWER(search_term) FROM saved_search WHERE timestamp >= UNIX_TIMESTAMP(DATEADD(CURDATE(), INTERVAL -1 DAY)) AND timestamp < UNIX_TIMESTAMP(CURDATE()) to deduplicate yesterday's search terms. Our search can be case-insensitive, so we lowercase the search terms as part of deduplication. Since our Craigslist design is partitioned by city, we should not have more than 100M search terms. Assuming an average of 10 characters per search term, there will be 1 GB of data, which easily fits into a single host's memory.

2. For each search term:
   a. Send a request to the (Elasticsearch) search service and get the results.
   b. Query the "saved_search" table for the user IDs associated with this search term.
   c. For each (user ID, search term, results) tuple, send a request to a notification service.

What if the job fails during step 2? How do we avoid resending notifications to users? We can use a distributed transaction mechanism described in chapter 5. Or we can implement logic on the client that checks if a notification has already been displayed (and possibly dismissed) before displaying the notification. This is possible for certain types of clients like a browser or mobile app, but not for email or texting.

If saved searches expire, we can clean up old table rows with a daily batch job that runs a SQL DELETE statement on rows older than the expiry date.

7.19.10 Rate limiting

All requests to our service can pass through a rate limiter to prevent any individual user from sending requests too frequently and thus consuming too many resources. The design of a rate limiter is discussed in chapter 8.

7.19.11 Large number of posts

What if we would like to provide a single URL where all listings are accessible to anyone (regardless of location)? Then the Post table may be too big for a single host, and the Elasticsearch index for posts may also be too big for a single host. However, we should continue to serve a search query from a single host. Any design where a query is processed by multiple hosts and results aggregated in a single host before returning them to the viewer will have high latency and cost. How can we continue to serve search queries from a single host? Possibilities include:

- Impose a post expiry (retention period) of one week and implement a daily batch job to delete expired posts. A short retention period means there is less data to search and cache, reducing the system's costs and complexity.
- Reduce the amount of data stored in a post.
- Do functional partitioning on categories of posts. Perhaps create separate SQL tables for various categories. But the application may need to contain the mappings to the appropriate table. Or this mapping can be stored in a Redis cache, and the application will need to query the Redis cache to determine which table to query.
- We may not consider compression because it is prohibitively expensive to search compressed data.

7.19.12 Local regulations

Each jurisdiction (country, state, county, city, etc.) may have its own regulations that affect Craigslist. Examples include:

- The types of products or services permitted on Craigslist may differ by jurisdiction. How could our system handle this requirement? Section 15.10.1 discusses a possible approach.
- Customer data and privacy regulations may not allow the company to export customer data outside of the country. It may be required to delete customer data on customer demand or share data with governments. These considerations are likely outside the scope of the interview.

We will need to discuss the exact requirements. Is it sufficient to selectively display certain products and services sections on the client applications based on the user's location, or do we also need to prevent users from viewing or posting about banned products and services?

An initial approach to selectively display sections will be to add logic in the clients to display or hide sections based on the country of the user's IP address. Going further, if these regulations are numerous or frequently changing, we may need to create a regulations service that Craigslist admins can use to configure regulations, and the clients will make requests to this service to determine which HTML to show or hide. Because this service will receive heavy read traffic and much lighter write traffic, we can apply CQRS techniques to ensure that writes succeed. For example, we can have separate regulation services for admins and viewers that scale separately and periodic synchronization between them.

If we need to ensure that no forbidden content is posted on our Craigslist, we may need to discuss systems that detect forbidden words or phrases, or perhaps machine learning approaches.

A final thought is that Craigslist does not attempt to customize its listings based on country. A good example was how it removed its Personals section in 2018 in response to new regulations passed in the United States. It did not attempt to keep this section in other countries. We can discuss the tradeoffs of such an approach.

Summary

- We discuss the users and their various required data types (like text, images, or video) to determine the non-functional requirements, which in our Craigslist system are scalability, high availability, and high performance.

- A CDN is a common solution for serving images or video, but don't assume it is always the appropriate solution. Use an object store if these media will be served to a small fraction of users.

- Functional partitioning by GeoDNS is the first step in discussing scaling up.

- Next are caching and CDN, mainly to improve the scalability and latency of serving posts.

- Our Craigslist service is read-heavy. If we use SQL, consider leader-follower replication for scaling reads.

- Consider horizontal scaling of our backend and message brokers to handle write traffic spikes. Such a setup can serve write requests by distributing them across many backend hosts, and buffer them in a message broker. A consumer cluster can consume requests from the message broker and process them accordingly.

- Consider batch or streaming ETL jobs for any functionality that don't require real-time latency. This is slower, but more scalability and lower cost.

- The rest of the interview may be on new constraints and requirements. In this chapter, the new constraints and requirements we mentioned were reporting posts, graceful degradation, decreasing complexity, adding categories/tags of posts, analytics and recommendations, A/B testing, subscriptions and saved searches, rate limiting, serving more posts to each user, and local regulations.

8
Design a
rate-limiting service

This chapter covers

- Using rate limiting
- Discussing a rate-limiting service
- Understanding various rate-limiting algorithms

Rate limiting is a common service that we should almost always mention during a system design interview and is mentioned in most of the example questions in this book. This chapter aims to address situations where 1) the interviewer may ask for more details when we mention rate limiting during an interview, and 2) the question itself is to design a rate-limiting service.

Rate limiting defines the rate at which consumers can make requests to API endpoints. Rate limiting prevents inadvertent or malicious overuse by clients, especially bots. In this chapter, we refer to such clients as "excessive clients".

Examples of inadvertent overuse include the following:

- Our client is another web service that experienced a (legitimate or malicious) traffic spike.
- The developers of that service decided to run a load test on their production environment.

Such inadvertent overuse causes a "noisy neighbor" problem, where a client utilizes too much resource on our service, so our other clients will experience higher latency or higher rate of failed requests.

Malicious attacks include the following. There are other bot attacks that rate limiting does not prevent(see https://www.cloudflare.com/learning/bots/what-is-bot-management/ for more information)

- *Denial-of-service* (DoS) or *distributed denial-of-service (DDoS) attacks*—DoS floods a target with requests, so normal traffic cannot be processed. DoS uses a single machine, while DDoS is the use of multiple machines for the attack. This distinction is unimportant in this chapter, and we refer to them collectively as "DoS".
- *Brute force attack*—A brute force attack is repeated trial and error to find sensitive data, such as cracking passwords, encryption keys, API keys, and SSH login credentials.
- *Web scraping*—Web scraping uses bots to make GET requests to many web pages of a web application to obtain a large amount of data. An example is scraping Amazon product pages for prices and product reviews.

Rate limiting can be implemented as a library or as a separate service called by a frontend, API gateway, or service mesh. In this question, we implement it as a service to gain the advantages of functional partitioning discussed in chapter 6. Figure 8.1 illustrates a rate limiter design that we will discuss in this chapter.

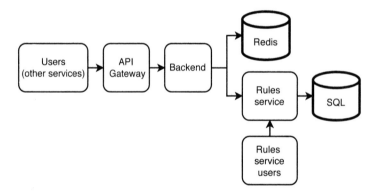

Figure 8.1 Initial high-level architecture of rate limiter. The frontend, backend, and Rules service also log to a shared logging service; this is not shown here. The Redis database is usually implemented as a shared Redis service, rather than our service provisioning its own Redis database. The Rules service users may make API requests to the Rules service via a browser app. We can store the rules in SQL.

8.1   Alternatives to a rate-limiting service and why they are infeasible

Why don't we scale out the service by monitoring the load and adding more hosts when needed, instead of doing rate limiting? We can design our service to be horizontally scalable, so it will be straightforward to add more hosts to serve the additional load. We can consider auto-scaling.

The process of adding new hosts when a traffic spike is detected may be too slow. Adding a new host involves steps that take time, like provisioning the host hardware, downloading the necessary Docker containers, starting up the service on the new host, then updating our load balancer configuration to direct traffic to the new host. This process may be too slow, and our service may already have crashed by the time the new hosts are ready to serve traffic. Even auto-scaling solutions may be too slow.

A load balancer can limit the number of requests sent to each host. Why don't we use our load balancer to ensure that hosts are not overloaded and drop requests when our cluster has no more spare capacity?

We should not serve malicious requests, as we mentioned previously. Rate limiting guards against such requests by detecting their IP addresses and simply dropping them. As discussed later, our rate limiter can usually return 429 Too Many Requests, but if we are sure that certain requests are malicious, we can choose either of these options:

- Drop the request and not return any response and allow the attacker to think that our service is experiencing an outage.
- Shadow ban the user by returning 200 with an empty or misleading response.

Why does rate limiting need to be a separate service? Can each host independently track the request rate from its requestors, and rate limit them?

The reason is that certain requests are more expensive than others. Certain users may make requests that return more data, require more expensive filtering and aggregation, or involve JOIN operations between larger datasets. A host may become slow from processing expensive requests from particular clients.

A level 4 load balancer cannot process a request's contents. We will need a level 7 load balancer for sticky sessions (to route requests from a user to the same host), which introduces cost and complexity. If we do not have other use cases for a level 7 load balancer, it may not be worth it to use level 7 load balancer just for this purpose, and a dedicated and shared rate limiting service may be a better solution. Table 8.1 summarizes our discussion.

Table 8.1 Comparison of rate limiting to its alternatives

Rate limiting	Add new hosts	Use level 7 load balancer
Handles traffic spikes by returning 429 Too Many Requests responses to the users with high request rates.	Adding new hosts may be too slow to respond to traffic spikes. Our service may crash by the time the new hosts are ready to serve traffic.	Not a solution to handle traffic spikes.
Handles DoS attacks by providing misleading responses.	Processes malicious requests, which we should not do.	Not a solution.
Can rate limit users who make expensive requests.	Causes our service to incur the costs of processing expensive requests.	Can reject expensive requests but may be too costly and complex as a standalone solution.

8.2   *When not to do rate limiting*

Rate limiting is not necessarily the appropriate solution for any kind of client overuse. For example, consider a social media service we designed. A user may subscribe to updates associated with a particular hashtag. If a user makes too many subscription requests within a certain period, the social media service may respond to the user, "you have made too many subscription requests within the last few minutes." If we did rate limiting, we will simply drop the user's requests and return 429 (Too Many Requests) or return nothing, and the client decides the response is 500. This will be a poor user experience. If the request is sent by a browser or mobile app, the app can display to the user that they sent too many requests, providing a good user experience.

Another example is services that charge subscription fees for certain request rates (e.g., different subscription fees for 1,000 or 10,000 hourly requests). If a client exceeds its quota for a particular time interval, further requests should not be processed until the next time interval. A shared rate-limiting service is not the appropriate solution to prevent clients from exceeding their subscriptions. As discussed in more detail below, the shared rate-limiting service should be limited to supporting simple use cases, not complex use cases like giving each client a different rate limit.

8.3   *Functional requirements*

Our rate-limiting service is a shared service, and our users are mainly services that are used by parties external to the company and not by internal users such as employees. We refer to such services as "user services." A user should be able to set a maximum request rate over which further requests from the same requestor will be delayed or rejected, with a 429 response. We can assume the interval can be 10 seconds or 60 seconds. We can set a maximum of 10 requests in 10 seconds. Other functional requirements are as follows:

- We assume that each user service must rate limit its requestors across its hosts, but we do not need to rate limit the same users across services. Rate limiting is independent on each user service.

- A user can set multiple rate limits, one per endpoint. We do not need more complicated user-specific configurations, such as allowing different rate limits to particular requestors/users. We want our rate limiter to be a cheap and scalable service that is easy to understand and use.

- Our users should be able to view which users were rate limited and the timestamps these rate limiting events began and ended. We provide an endpoint for this.

- We can discuss with the interviewer whether we should log every request because we will need a large amount of storage to do so, which is expensive. We will assume that this is needed and discuss techniques to save storage to reduce cost.

- We should log the rate-limited requestors for manual follow-up and analytics. This is especially required for suspected attacks.

8.4   *Non-functional requirements*

Rate limiting is a basic functionality required by virtually any service. It must be scalable, have high performance, be as simple as possible, secure, and private. Rate limiting is not essential to a service's availability, so we can trade off high availability and fault-tolerance. Accuracy and consistency are fairly important but not stringent.

8.4.1   Scalability

Our service should be scalable to billions of daily requests that query whether a particular requestor should be rate limited. Requests to change rate limits will only be manually made by internal users in our organization, so we do not need to expose this capability to external users.

How much storage is required? Assume our service has one billion users, and we need to store up 100 requests per user at any moment. Only the user IDs and a queue of 100 timestamps per user need to be recorded; each is 64 bits. Our rate limiter is a shared service, so we will need to associate requests with the service that is being rate limited. A typical big organization has thousands of services. Let's assume up to 100 of them need rate limiting.

We should ask whether our rate limiter actually needs to store data for one billion users. What is the retention period? A rate limiter usually should only need to store data for 10 seconds because it makes a rate limiting decision based on the user's request rate for the last 10 seconds. Moreover, we can discuss with the interviewer whether there will be more than 1–10 million users within a 10-second window. Let's make a conservative worst-case estimate of 10 million users. Our overall storage requirement is 100 * 64 * 101 * 10M = 808 GB. If we use Redis and assign a key to each user, a value's size will be just 64 * 100 = 800 bytes. It may be impractical to delete data immediately after it is older than 10 seconds, so the actual amount of required storage depends on how fast our service can delete old data.

8.4.2   Performance

When another service receives a request from its user (we refer to such requests as *user requests*), it makes a request to our rate limiting service (we refer to such requests as *rate limiter requests*) to determine if the user request should be rate-limited. The rate limiter request is blocking; the other service cannot respond to its user before the rate limiter request is completed. The rate limiter request's response time adds to the user request's response time. So, our service needs very low latency, perhaps a P99 of 100 ms. The decision to rate-limit or not rate-limit the user request must be quick. We don't require low latency for viewing or analytics of logs.

8.4.3   Complexity

Our service will be a shared service, used by many other services in our organization. Its design should be simple to minimize the risk of bugs and outages, aid troubleshooting, allow it to focus on its single functionality as a rate limiter, and minimize costs. Developers of other services should be able to integrate our rate limiting solution as simply and seamlessly as possible.

8.4.4   Security and privacy

Chapter 2 discussed security and privacy expectations for external and internal services. Here, we can discuss some possible security and privacy risks. The security and privacy implementations of our user services may be inadequate to prevent external attackers from accessing our rate limiting service. Our (internal) user services may also attempt to attack our rate limiter, for example, by spoofing requests from another user service to rate limit it. Our user services may also violate privacy by requesting data about rate limiter requestors from other user services.

For these reasons, we will implement security and privacy in our rate limiter's system design.

8.4.5   Availability and fault-tolerance

We may not require high availability or fault-tolerance. If our service has less than three nines availability and is down for an average of a few minutes daily, user services can simply process all requests during that time and not impose rate limiting. Moreover, the cost increases with availability. Providing 99.9% availability is fairly cheap, while 99.99999% may be prohibitively expensive.

As discussed later in this chapter, we can design our service to use a simple highly available cache to cache the IP addresses of excessive clients. If the rate-limiting service identified excessive clients just prior to the outage, this cache can continue to serve rate-limiter requests during the outage, so these excessive clients will continue to be rate limited. It is statistically unlikely that an excessive client will occur during the few minutes the rate limiting service has an outage. If it does occur, we can use other techniques such as firewalls to prevent a service outage, at the cost of a negative user experience during these few minutes.

8.4.6   Accuracy

To prevent poor user experience, we should not erroneously identify excessive clients and rate limit them. In case of doubt, we should not rate limit the user. The rate limit value itself does not need to be precise. For example, if the limit is 10 requests in 10 seconds, it is acceptable to occasionally rate limit a user at 8 or 12 requests in 10 seconds. If we have an SLA that requires us to provide a minimum request rate, we can set a higher rate limit (e.g., 12+ requests in 10 seconds).

8.4.7   Consistency

The previous discussion on accuracy leads us to the related discussion on consistency. We do not need strong consistency for any of our use cases. When a user service updates a rate limit, this new rate limit need not immediately apply to new requests; a few seconds of inconsistency may be acceptable. Eventual consistency is also acceptable for viewing logged events such as which users were rate-limited or performing analytics on these logs. Eventual rather than strong consistency will allow a simpler and cheaper design.

8.5 *Discuss user stories and required service components*

A rate-limiter request contains a required user ID and a user service ID. Since rate limiting is independent on each user service, the ID format can be specific to each user service. The ID format for a user service is defined and maintained by the user service, not by our rate-limiting service. We can use the user service ID to distinguish possible identical user IDs from different user services. Because each user service has a different rate limit, our rate limiter also uses the user service ID to determine the rate limit value to apply.

Our rate limiter will need to store this (user ID, service ID) data for 60 seconds, since it must use this data to compute the user's request rate to determine if it is higher than the rate limit. To minimize the latency of retrieving any user's request rate or any service's rate limit, these data must be stored (or cached) on in-memory storage. Because consistency and latency are not required for logs, we can store logs on an eventually consistent storage like HDFS, which has replication to avoid data loss from possible host failures.

Last, user services can make infrequent requests to our rate-limiting service to create and update rate limits for their endpoints. This request can consist of a user service ID, endpoint ID, and the desired rate limit (e.g., a maximum of 10 requests in 10 seconds).

Putting these requirements together, we need the following:

- A database with fast reads and writes for counts. The schema will be simple; it is unlikely to be much more complex than (user ID, service ID). We can use an in-memory database like Redis.
- A service where rules can be defined and retrieved, which we call the Rules service.
- A service that makes requests to the Rules service and the Redis database, which we can call the Backend service.

The two services are separate because requests to the Rules service for adding or modifying rules should not interfere with requests to the rate limiter that determine if a request should be rate limited.

8.6 *High-level architecture*

Figure 8.2 (repeated from figure 8.1) illustrates our high-level architecture considering these requirements and stories. When a client makes a request to our rate-limiting service, this request initially goes through the frontend or service mesh. If the frontend's security mechanisms allow the request, the request goes to the backend, where the following steps occur:

1. Get the service's rate limit from the Rules service. This can be cached for lower latency and lower request volume to the Rules service.
2. Determine the service's current request rate, including this request.
3. Return a response that indicates if the request should be rate-limited.

Steps 1 and 2 can be done in parallel to reduce overall latency by forking a thread for each step or using threads from a common thread pool.

The frontend and Redis (distributed cache) services in our high-level architecture in figure 8.2 are for horizontal scalability. This is the distributed cache approach discussed in section 3.5.3.

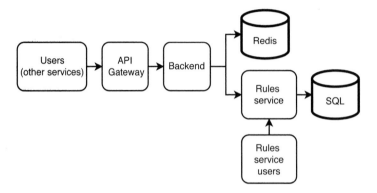

Figure 8.2   Initial high-level architecture of rate limiter. The frontend, backend, and Rules service also log to a shared logging service; this is not shown here. The Redis database is usually implemented as a shared Redis service, rather than our service provisioning its own Redis database. The Rules service users may make API requests to the Rules service via a browser app.

We may notice in figure 8.2 that our Rules service has users from two different services (Backend and Rules service users) with very different request volumes, one of which (Rules service users) does all the writes.

Referring back to the leader-follower replication concepts in sections 3.3.2 and 3.3.3, and illustrated in figure 8.3, the Rules service users can make all their SQL queries, both reads and writes to the leader node. The backend should make its SQL queries, which are only read/SELECT queries, to the follower nodes. This way, the Rules service users have high consistency and experience high performance.

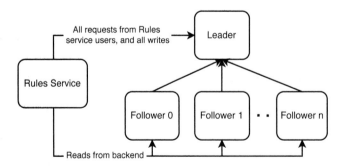

Figure 8.3   The leader host should process all requests from Rules service users, and all write operations. Reads from the backend can be distributed across the follower hosts.

Referring to figure 8.4, as we do not expect rules to change often, we can add a Redis cache to the Rules service to improve its read performance even further. Figure 8.4 displays cache-aside caching, but we can also use other caching strategies from section 3.8. Our Backend service can also cache rules in Redis. As discussed earlier in section 8.4.5, we can also cache the IDs of excessive users. As soon as a user exceeds its rate limit, we can cache its ID along with an expiry time where a user should no longer be rate-limited. Then our backend need not query the Rules service to deny a user's request.

If we are using AWS (Amazon Web Services), we can consider DynamoDB instead of Redis and SQL. DynamoDB can handle millions of requests per second (https:// aws.amazon.com/dynamodb/), and it can be either eventually consistent or strongly consistent (https://docs.aws.amazon.com/whitepapers/latest/comparing-dynamodb -and-hbase-for-nosql/consistency-model.html), but using it subjects us to vendor lock-in.

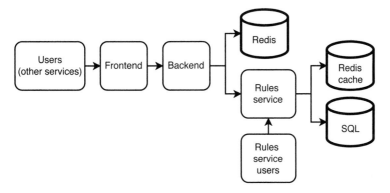

Figure 8.4 Rate limiter with Redis cache on the Rules service. Frequent requests from the backend can be served from this cache instead of the SQL database.

The backend has all our non-functional requirements. It is scalable, has high performance, is not complex, is secure and private, and is eventually consistent. The SQL database with its leader-leader replication is highly available and fault-tolerant, which goes beyond our requirements. We will discuss accuracy in a later section. This design is not scalable for the Rules service users, which is acceptable as discussed in section 8.4.1.

Considering our requirements, our initial architecture may be overengineered, overly complex, and costly. This design is highly accurate and strongly consistent, both of which are not part of our non-functional requirements. Can we trade off some accuracy and consistency for lower cost? Let's first discuss two possible approaches to scaling up our rate limiter:

1 A host can serve any user, by not keeping any state and fetching data from a shared database. This is the stateless approach we have followed for most questions in this book.

2 A host serves a fixed set of users and stores its user's data. This is a stateful approach that we discuss in the next section.

8.7   *Stateful approach/sharding*

Figure 8.5 illustrates the backend of a stateful solution that is closer to our non-functional requirements. When a request arrives, our load balancer routes it to its host. Each host stores the counts of its clients in its memory. The host determines if the user has exceeded their rate limit and returns true or false. If a user makes a request and its host is down, our service will return a 500 error, and the request will not be rate limited.

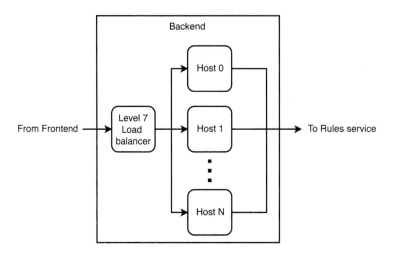

Figure 8.5   Backend architecture of rate limiter that employs a stateful sharded approach. The counts are stored in the hosts' memory, rather than in a distributed cache like Redis.

A stateful approach requires a level 7 load balancer. This may seem to contradict what we discussed in section 8.1 about using a level 7 load balancer, but note that we are now discussing using it in a distributed rate-limiting solution, not just for sticky sessions to allow each host to reject expensive requests and perform its own rate limiting.

A question that immediately arises in such an approach is fault-tolerance, whether we need to safeguard against data loss when a host goes down. If so, this leads to discussions on topics like replication, failover, hot shards, and rebalancing. As briefly discussed in section 3.1, we can use sticky sessions in replication. But in our requirements discussion earlier in the chapter, we discussed that we don't need consistency, high availability, or fault-tolerance. If a host that contains certain users' data goes down, we can simply assign another host to those users and restart the affected users' request rate counts from 0. Instead, the relevant discussion will be on detecting host outages, assigning and provisioning replacement hosts, and rebalancing traffic.

The 500 error should trigger an automated response to provision a new host. Our new host should fetch its list of addresses from the configuration service, which can be a simple manually updated file stored on a distributed object storage solution like AWS S3 (for high availability, this file must be stored on a distributed storage solution and not on a single host), or a complex solution like ZooKeeper. When we develop our rate-limiting service, we should ensure that the host setup process does not exceed a few minutes. We should also have monitoring on the host setup duration and trigger a low-urgency alert if the setup duration exceeds a few minutes.

We should monitor for hot shards and periodically rebalance traffic across our hosts. We can periodically run a batch ETL job that reads the request logs, identifies hosts that receive large numbers of requests, determines an appropriate load balancing configuration, and then writes this configuration to a configuration service. The ETL job can also push the new configuration to the load-balancer service. We write to a configuration service in case any load balancer host goes down. When the host recovers or a new load balancer host is provisioned, it can read the configuration from the configuration service.

Figure 8.6 illustrates our backend architecture with the rebalancing job. This rebalancing prevents a large number of heavy users from being assigned to a particular host, causing it to go down. Since our solution does not have failover mechanisms that distribute the users of a failed host over other hosts, we do not have the risk of a death spiral, where a host fails because of excessive traffic, then its traffic is redistributed over the remaining hosts and increases their traffic, which in turn causes them to fail.

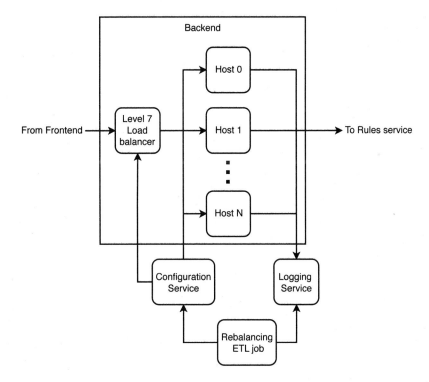

Figure 8.6 Backend architecture with a rebalancing ETL job

A tradeoff of this approach is that it is less resilient to DoS/DDoS attacks. If a user has a very high request rate, such as hundreds of requests per second, its assigned host cannot handle this, and all users assigned to this host cannot be rate limited. We may choose to have an alert for such cases, and we should block requests from this user across all services. Load balancers should drop requests from this IP address—that is, do not send the requests to any backend host, and do not return any response, but do log the request.

Compared to the stateless approach, the stateful approach is more complex and has higher consistency and accuracy, but has lower:

- Cost
- Availability
- Fault-tolerance

Overall, this approach is a poor cousin of a distributed database. We attempted to design our own distributed storage solution, and it will not be as sophisticated or mature as widely used distributed databases. It is optimized for simplicity and low cost and has neither strong consistency nor high availability.

8.8   *Storing all counts in every host*

The stateless backend design discussed in section 8.6 used Redis to store request timestamps. Redis is distributed, and it is scalable and highly available. It also has low latency and will be an accurate solution. However, this design requires us to use a Redis database, which is usually implemented as a shared service. Can we avoid our dependency on an external Redis service, which will expose our rate limiter to possible degradation on that service?

The stateful backend design discussed in section 8.7 avoids this lookup by storing state in the backend, but it requires the load balancer to process every request to determine which host to send it to, and it also requires reshuffling to prevent hot shards. What if we can reduce the storage requirement such that all user request timestamps can fit in memory on a single host?

8.8.1   *High-level architecture*

How can we reduce the storage requirement? We can reduce our 808 GB storage requirement to 8.08 GB ≈ 8 GB by creating a new instance of our rate-limiting service for each of the ~100 services that uses it and use the frontend to route requests by service to the appropriate service. 8 GB can fit into a host's memory. Due to our high request rate, we cannot use a single host for rate limiting. If we use 128 hosts, each host will store only 64 MB. The final number we decide upon will likely be between 1 and 128.

Figure 8.7 is the backend architecture of this approach. When a host receives a request, it does the following in parallel:

- Makes a rate-limiting decision and returns it.
- Asynchronously synchronizes its timestamps with other hosts.

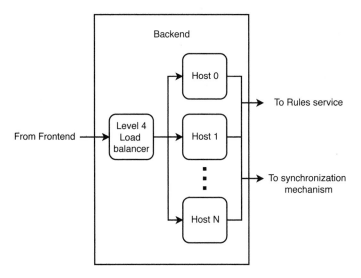

Figure 8.7 **High-level architecture of a rate-limiting service where all user request timestamps can fit into a single backend host, requests are randomly load balanced across hosts, and each host can respond to a user request with a rate limiting decision without first making requests to other services or hosts. Hosts synchronize their timestamps with each other in a separate process.**

Our level 4 load balancer randomly balances requests across hosts, so a user may be directed to different hosts in each rate limiting request. For rate limits to be accurately computed, the rate limits on our hosts need to be kept synchronized. There are multiple possible ways to synchronize the hosts. We discuss them in detail in the next section. Here we'll just say that we will use streaming instead of batch updates because batch updates are too infrequent and cause users to be rate-limited at a much higher request rate than the set request rate.

Compared to the other two designs discussed earlier (the stateless backend design and stateful backend design), this design trades off consistency and accuracy for lower latency and higher performance (it can process a higher request rate). Because a host may not have all the timestamps in memory before making a rate-limiting decision, it may compute a lower request rate than the actual value. It also has these characteristics:

- Use a level 4 load balancer to direct requests to any host like a stateless service (though the frontend).
- A host can make rate limiting decisions with its data in memory.
- Data synchronization can be done in an independent process.

What if a host goes down and its data is lost? Certain users who will be rate limited will be permitted to make more requests before they are rate limited. As discussed earlier, this is acceptable. Refer to pp. 157–158 of Martin Kleppmann's book *Designing Data-Intensive Systems* for a brief discussion on leader failover and possible problems. Table 8.2 summarizes our comparison between the three approaches that we have discussed.

Table 8.2   Comparison of our stateless backend design, stateful backend design, and design that stores counts in every host

Stateless backend design	Stateful backend design	Storing counts in every host
Stores counts in a distributed database.	Stores each user's count in a backend host.	Store every user's counts in every host.
Stateless, so a user can be routed to any host.	Requires a level 7 load balancer to route each user to its assigned host.	Every host has every user's counts, so a user can be routed to any host.
Scalable. We rely on the distributed database to serve both high read and high write traffic.	Scalable. A load balancer is an expensive and vertically scalable component that can handle a high request rate.	Not scalable because each host needs to store the counts of every user. Need to divide users into separate instances of this service and require another component (such as a frontend) to route users to their assigned instances.
Efficient storage consumption. We can configure our desired replication factor in our distributed database.	Lowest storage consumption because there is no backup by default. We can design a storage service with an in-cluster or out-cluster approach, as discussed in section 13.5. Without backup, it is the cheapest approach.	Most expensive approach. High storage consumption. Also, high network traffic from n–n communication between hosts to synchronize counts.
Eventually consistent. A host making a rate limiting decision may do so before synchronization is complete, so this decision may be slightly inaccurate.	Most accurate and consistent since a user always makes requests to the same hosts.	Least accurate and consistent approach because it takes time to synchronize counts between all hosts.
Backend is stateless, so we use the highly available and fault-tolerant properties of the distributed database.	Without backup, any host failure will result in data loss of all the user counts it contains. This is the lowest availability and fault-tolerant of the three designs. However, these factors may be inconsequential because they are not non-functional requirements. If the rate limiter cannot obtain an accurate count, it can simply let the request through.	Hosts are interchangeable, so this is the most highly available and fault-tolerant of the three designs.
Dependent on external database service. Outages of such services may affect our service, and remediating such outages may be outside our control.	Not dependent on external database services. Load balancer needs to process every request to determine which host to send it to. This also requires reshuffling to prevent hot shards.	Not dependent on external database services like Redis. Avoids risk of service outage from outages of such downstream services. Also, it's easier to implement, particularly in big organizations where provisioning or modifying database services may involve considerable bureaucracy.

8.8.2 Synchronizing counts

How can the hosts synchronize their user request counts? In this section, we discuss a few possible algorithms. All the algorithms except all-to-all are feasible for our rate limiter.

Should the synchronization mechanism be pull or push? We can choose push to trade off consistency and accuracy for higher performance, lower resource consumption, and lower complexity. If a host goes down, we can simply disregard its counts and allow users to make more requests before they are rate-limited. With these considerations, we can decide that hosts should asynchronously share their timestamps using UDP instead of TCP.

We should consider that hosts must be able to handle their traffic from these two main kinds of requests:

1 Request to make a rate limiting decision. Such requests are limited by the load balancer and by provisioning a larger cluster of hosts as necessary.

2 Request to update the host's timestamps in memory. Our synchronization mechanism must ensure that a host does not receive a high rate of requests, especially as we increase the number of hosts in our cluster.

ALL-TO-ALL

All-to-all means every node transmits messages to every other node in a group. It is more general than *broadcasting*, which refers to simultaneous transfer of the message to recipients. Referring to figure 3.3 (repeated in figure 8.8), all-to-all requires a *full mesh* topology, where every node in a network is connected to every other node. All-to-all scales quadratically with the number of nodes, so it is not scalable. If we use all-to-all communication with 128 hosts, each all-to-call communication will require 128 * 128 * 64 MB, which is > 1 TB, which is infeasible.

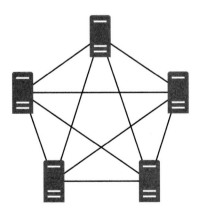

Figure 8.8 A full mesh topology. Every node in a network is connected to every other node. In our rate limiter, every node receives user requests, computes request rate, and approves or denies the request.

GOSSIP PROTOCOL

In *gossip protocol*, referring to figure 3.6 (repeated in figure 8.9), nodes periodically randomly pick other nodes and send them messages. Yahoo's distributed rate limiter uses gossip protocol to synchronize its hosts (https://yahooeng.tumblr.com/post/111288877956/cloud-bouncer-distributed-rate-limiting-at-yahoo). This approach trades off consistency and accuracy for higher performance and lower resource consumption. It is also more complex.

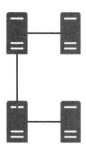

Figure 8.9   Gossip protocol. Each node periodically randomly picks other nodes and sends them messages.

In this section, all-to-all and gossip protocol are the synchronization mechanisms that require all nodes to send messages directly to each other. This means that all nodes must know the IP addresses of the other nodes. Since nodes are continuously added and removed from the cluster, each node will make requests to the configuration service (such as ZooKeeper) to find the other nodes' IP addresses.

In the other synchronization mechanisms, hosts make requests to each other via a particular host or service.

EXTERNAL STORAGE OR COORDINATION SERVICE

Referring to figure 8.10 (almost identical to figure 3.4), these two approaches use external components for hosts to communicate with each other.

Hosts can communicate with each other via a leader host. This host is selected by the cluster's configuration service (such as ZooKeeper). Each host only needs to know the IP address of the leader host, while the leader host needs to periodically update its list of hosts.

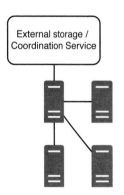

Figure 8.10   Hosts can communicate through an external component, such as an external storage service or coordination service.

RANDOM LEADER SELECTION

We can trade off higher resource consumption for lower complexity by using a simple algorithm to elect a leader. Referring to figure 3.7 (repeated in figure 8.11), this may cause multiple leaders to be elected. As long as each leader communicates with all other hosts, every host will be updated with the all the request timestamps. There will be unnecessary messaging overhead.

Leader

Leader

Figure 8.11 Random leader selection may cause multiple leaders to be elected. This will cause unnecessary messaging overhead but does not present other problems.

8.9 Rate-limiting algorithms

Up to this point, we have assumed that a user's request rate is determined by its request timestamps, but we have not actually discussed possible techniques to compute the request rate. At this point, one of the main questions is how our distributed rate-limiting service determines the requestor's current request rate. Common rate-limiting algorithms include the following:

- Token bucket
- Leaky bucket
- Fixed window counter
- Sliding window log
- Sliding window counter

Before we continue, we note that certain system design interview questions may seem to involve specialized knowledge and expertise that most candidates will not have prior experience with. The interviewer may not expect us to be familiar with rate-limiting algorithms. This is an opportunity for them to assess the candidate's communication skills and learning ability. The interviewer may describe a rate limiting algorithm to us and assess our ability to collaborate with them to design a solution around it that satisfies our requirements.

The interviewer may even make sweeping generalizations or erroneous statements, and assess our ability to critically evaluate them and tactfully, firmly, clearly, and concisely ask intelligent questions and express our technical opinions.

We can consider implementing more than one rate-limiting algorithm in our service and allow each user of this service to choose a rate-limiting algorithm to select the algorithm that most closely suits the user's requirements. In this approach, a user selects the desired algorithm and sets the desired configurations in the Rules service.

For simplicity of discussion, the discussions of the rate limiting algorithms in this section assume that the rate limit is 10 requests in 10 seconds.

8.9.1   *Token bucket*

Referring to figure 8.12, the token bucket algorithm is based on an analogy of a bucket filled with tokens. A bucket has three characteristics:

- A maximum number of tokens.
- The number of currently available tokens.
- A refill rate at which tokens are added to the bucket.

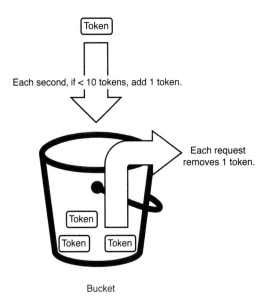

Figure 8.12   A token bucket that enqueues once per second

Each time a request arrives, we remove a token from the bucket. If there are no tokens, the request is rejected or rate limited. The bucket is refilled at a constant rate.

In a straightforward implementation of this algorithm, the following occurs with each user request. A host can store key-value pairs using a hash map. If the host does not have a key for this user ID, the system initializes an entry with a user ID and a token count of 9 (10–1). If the host has a key for this user ID and its value is more than 0, the system decrements its count. If the count is 0, it returns true, i.e., the user should be rate limited. If it returns false, the user should not be rate limited. Our system also needs to increment every value by 1 each second if it is less than 10.

The advantages of token bucket are that it is easy to understand and implement, and it is memory efficient (each user only needs a single integer variable to count tokens).

One obvious consideration with this implementation is that each host will need to increment every key in the hash map. It is feasible to do this on a hash map in a host's memory. If the storage is external to the host, such as on a Redis database, Redis provides the MSET (https://redis.io/commands/mset/) command to update multiple keys, but there may be a limit on the number of keys that can be updated in a single MSET operation (https://stackoverflow.com/questions/49361876/mset-over-400-000 -map-entries-in-redis). (Stack Overflow is not an academically credible source, and the official Redis documentation on MSET does not state an upper limit on the number of keys in a request. However, when designing a system, we must always ask reasonable questions and should not completely trust even official documentation.) Moreover, if each key is 64 bits, a request to update 10 million keys will be 8.08 GB in size, which is much too big.

If we need to divide the update command into multiple requests, each request incurs resource overhead and network latency.

Moreover, there is no mechanism to delete keys (i.e., removing users who have not made recent requests), so the system doesn't know when to remove users to reduce the token refill request rate or to make room in the Redis database for other users who made recent requests. Our system will need a separate storage mechanism to record the last timestamp of a user's request, and a process to delete old keys.

In a distributed implementation like in section 8.8, every host may contain its own token bucket and use this bucket to make rate limiting decisions. Hosts may synchronize their buckets using techniques discussed in section 8.8.2. If a host makes a rate-limiting decision using its bucket before synchronizing this bucket with other hosts, a user may be able to make requests at a higher rate than the set rate limit. For example, if two hosts each receive requests close in time, each one will subtract a token and have nine tokens left, then synchronize with other hosts. Even though there were two requests, all hosts will synchronize to nine tokens.

Cloud Bouncer

Cloud Bouncer, (https://yahooeng.tumblr.com/post/111288877956/cloud-bouncer -distributed-rate-limiting-at-yahoo), which was developed at Yahoo in 2014, is an example of a distributed rate-limiting library that is based on a token bucket.

8.9.2 Leaky bucket

A leaky bucket has a maximum number of tokens, leaks at a fixed rate, and stops leaking when empty. Each time a request arrives, we add a token to the bucket. If the bucket is full, the request is rejected, or rate limited.

Referring to figure 8.13, a common implementation of a leaky bucket is to use a FIFO queue with a fixed size. The queue is dequeued periodically. When a request arrives, a token is enqueued if the queue has spare capacity. Due to the fixed queue size, this implementation is less memory-efficient than a token bucket.

Figure 8.13   A leaky bucket that dequeues once per second

This algorithm has some of the same problems as a token bucket:

- Every second, a host needs to dequeue every queue in every key.
- We need a separate mechanism to delete old keys.
- A queue cannot exceed its capacity, so in a distributed implementation, there may be multiple hosts that simultaneously fill their buckets/queues fully before they synchronize. This means that the user exceeded its rate limit.

Another possible design is to enqueue timestamps instead of tokens. When a request arrives, we first dequeue timestamps until the remaining timestamps in the queue are older than our retention period, then enqueue the request's timestamp if the queue has space. It returns false if the enqueue was successful and true otherwise. This approach avoids the requirement to dequeue from every single queue every second.

QUESTION   Do you notice any possible consistency problems?

An alert reader will immediately notice two possible consistency problems that will introduce inaccuracy into a rate limiting decision:

1 A race condition can occur where a host writes a key-value pair to the leader host, and it is immediately overwritten by another host.
2 Hosts' clocks are not synchronized, and a host may make a rate limiting decision using timestamps written by other hosts with slightly different clocks.

This slight inaccuracy is acceptable. These two problems also apply to all the distributed rate-limiting algorithms discussed in this section that use timestamps, namely fixed window counter and sliding window log, but we will not mention them again.

8.9.3   *Fixed window counter*

Fixed window counters are implemented as key-value pairs. A key can be a combination of a client ID and a timestamp (e.g., user0_1628825241), while the value is the request count. When a client makes a request, its key is incremented if it exists or created if it does not exist. The request is accepted if the count is within the set rate limit and rejected if the count exceeds the set rate limit.

The window intervals are fixed. For example, a window can be between the [0, 60) seconds of each minute. After a window has passed, all keys expire. For example, the key "user0_1628825241" is valid from 3:27:00 AM GMT to 3:27:59 AM GMT because 1628825241 is 3:27:21 AM GMT, which is within the minute of 3:27 AM GMT.

QUESTION   How much can the request rate exceed the set rate limit?

A disadvantage of fixed window counter is that it may allow a request rate of up to twice the set rate limit. For example, referring to figure 8.13, if the rate limit is five requests in one minute, a client can make up to five requests in [8:00:00 AM, 8:01:00 AM) and up to another five requests in [8:01:00 AM, 8:01:30 AM). The client has actually made 10 requests in a one-minute interval, twice the set rate limit of five requests per minute (figure 8.14).

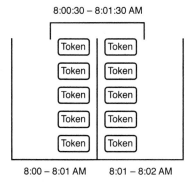

Figure 8.14   The user made five requests in [8:00:30 AM, 8:01:30 AM) and another five in [8:01:00 AM, 8:01:30 AM). Even though it was within the limit of five requests per fixed window, it actually made 10 requests in one minute.

Adapting this approach for our rate limiter, each time a host receives a user request, it takes these steps with its hash map. Refer to figure 8.15 for a sequence diagram of these steps:

1   Determine the appropriate keys to query. For example, if our rate limit had a 10-second expiry, the corresponding keys for user0 at 1628825250 will be ["user0_1628825241", "user0_1628825242", …, "user0_1628825250"].

2   Make requests for these keys. If we are storing key-value pairs in Redis instead of the host's memory, we can use the MGET (https://redis.io/commands/mget/) command to return the value of all specified keys. Although the MGET command is O(N) where N is the number of keys to retrieve, making a single request instead of multiple requests has lower network latency and resource overhead.

3   If no keys are found, create a new key-value pair, such as, for example, (user0_1628825250, 1). If one key is found, increment its value. If more than one key is found (due to race conditions), sum the values of all the returned keys and increment this sum by one. This is the number of requests in the last 10 seconds.

4   In parallel:
   a   Write the new or updated key-value pair to the leader host (or Redis database). If there were multiple keys, delete all keys except the oldest one.
   b   Return true if the count is more than 10 and false otherwise.

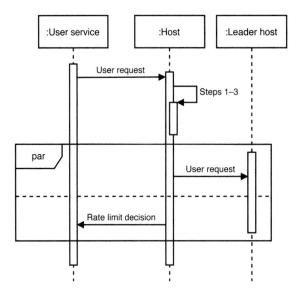

Figure 8.15   Sequence diagram of our fixed window counter approach. This diagram illustrates the approach of using the host's memory to store the request timestamps, instead of Redis. The rate-limiting decision is made immediately on the host, using only data stored in the host's memory. The subsequent steps on the leader host for synchronization are not illustrated.

QUESTION   How may race conditions cause multiple keys to be found in step 5?

Redis keys can be set to expire (https://redis.io/commands/expire/), so we should set the keys to expire after 10 seconds. Otherwise, we will need to implement a separate process to continuously find and delete expired keys. If this process is needed, it is an advantage of the fixed window counter that the key deletion process is independent of the hosts. This independent deletion process can be scaled separately from the host, and it can be developed independently, making it easier to test and debug.

8.9.4   Sliding window log

A sliding window log is implemented as a key-value pair for each client. The key is the client ID, and the value is a sorted list of timestamps. A sliding window log stores a timestamp for each request.

Figure 8.16 is a simple illustration of sliding window log. When a new request comes in, we append its timestamp and check if the first timestamp is expired. If so, perform a binary search to find the last expired timestamp, then remove all timestamps before that. Use a list instead of a queue because a queue does not support binary search. Return true if the list has more than 10 timestamps, and false otherwise.

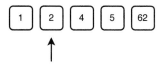

When 62 is appended, do a binary search for 62 − 60 = 2.

Figure 8.16   Simple sliding window log illustration. A timestamp is appended when a new request is made. Next, the last expired timestamp is found using binary search, and then all expired timestamps are removed. The request is allowed if the size of the list does not exceed the limit.

Sliding window log is accurate (except in a distributed implementation, due to the factors discussed in the last paragraph of section 8.9.2) but storing a timestamp value for every request consumes more memory than a token bucket.

The sliding window log algorithm counts requests even after the rate limit is exceeded, so it also allows us to measure the user's request rate.

8.9.5   *Sliding window counter*

Sliding window counter is a further development of fixed window counter and sliding window log. It uses multiple fixed window intervals, and each interval is $1/60^{th}$ the length of the rate limit's time window.

For example, if the rate limit interval is one hour, we use 60 one-minute windows instead of one one-hour window. The current rate is determined by summing the last 60 windows. It may slightly undercount requests. For example, counting requests at 11:00:35 will sum the 60 one-minute windows from the [10:01:00, 10:01:59] window to the [11:00:00, 11:00:59] window, and ignore the [10:00:00, 10:00:59] window. This approach is still more accurate than a fixed window counter.

8.10   *Employing a sidecar pattern*

This brings us to the discussion of applying sidecar pattern to rate limiting policies. Figure 1.8 illustrates our rate limiting service architecture using a sidecar pattern. Like what was discussed in section 1.4.6, an administrator can configure a user service's rate limiting policies in the control plane, which distributes them to the sidecar hosts. With this design where user services contain their rate limiting policies in their sidecar hosts, user service hosts do not need to make requests to our rate-limiting service to look up their rate-limiting policies, saving the network overhead of these requests.

8.11   *Logging, monitoring, and alerting*

Besides the logging, monitoring, and alerting practices discussed in section 2.5, we should configure monitoring and alerting for the following. We can configure monitoring tasks in our shared monitoring service on the logs in our shared logging service, and these tasks should trigger alerts to our shared alerting service to alert developers about these problems:

- Signs of possible malicious activity, such as users, which continue to make requests at a high rate despite being shadow-banned.
- Signs of possible DDoS attempts, such as an unusually high number of users being rate limited in a short interval.

8.12   *Providing functionality in a client library*

Does a user service need to query the rate limiter service for every request? An alternative approach is for the user service to aggregate user requests and then query the rate limiter service in certain circumstances such as when it

- Accumulates a batch of user requests
- Notices a sudden increase in request rate

Generalizing this approach, can rate limiting be implemented as a library instead of a service? Section 6.7 is a general discussion of a library vs. service. If we implement it entirely as a library, we will need to use the approach in section 8.7, where a host can contain all user requests in memory and synchronize the user requests with each other. Hosts must be able to communicate with each other to synchronize their user request timestamps, so the developers of the service using our library must configure a configuration service like ZooKeeper. This may be overly complex and error-prone for most developers, so as an alternative, we can offer a library with features to improve the performance of the rate limiting service, by doing some processing on the client, thereby allowing a lower rate of requests to the service.

This pattern of splitting processing between client and server can generalize to any system, but it may cause tight coupling between the client and server, which is, in general, an antipattern. The development of the server application must continue to support old client versions for a long time. For this reason, a client SDK (software development kit) is usually just a layer on a set of REST or RPC endpoints and does not do any data processing. If we wish to do any data processing in the client, at least one of the following conditions should be true:

- The processing should be simple, so it is easy to continue to support this client library in future versions of the server application.
- The processing is resource-intensive, so the maintenance overhead of doing such processing on the client is a worthy tradeoff for the significant reduction in the monetary cost of running the service.
- There should be a stated support lifecycle that clearly informs users when the client will no longer be supported.

Regarding batching of requests to the rate limiter, we can experiment with batch size to determine the best balance between accuracy and network traffic.

What if the client also measures the request rate and only uses the rate limiting service if the request rate exceeds a set threshold? A problem with this is that since clients do not communicate with each other, a client can only measure the request rate on the specific host it's installed on and cannot measure the request rate of specific users. This means that rate limiting is activated based on the request rate across all users, not on specific users. Users may be accustomed to a particular rate limit and may complain if they are suddenly rate limited at a particular request rate where they were not rate limited before.

An alternative approach is for the client to use anomaly detection to notice a sudden increase in the request rate, then start sending rate-limiting requests to the server.

8.13 *Further reading*

- Smarshchok, Mikhail, 2019. System Design Interview YouTube channel, https:// youtu.be/FU4WlwfS3G0.
- The discussions of fixed window counter, sliding window log, and sliding window counter were adapted from https://www.figma.com/blog/an-alternative -approach-to-rate-limiting/.
- Madden, Neil, 2020. *API Security in Action*. Manning Publications.
- Posta, Christian E. and Maloku, Rinor, 2022. *Istio in Action*. Manning Publications.
- Bruce, Morgan and Pereira, Paulo A., 2018. *Microservices in Action*, chapter 3.5. Manning Publications.

Summary

- Rate limiting prevents service outages and unnecessary costs.
- Alternatives such as adding more hosts or using the load balancer for rate limiting are infeasible. Adding more hosts to handle traffic spikes may be too slow, while using a level 7 load balancer just for rate limiting may add too much cost and complexity.
- Do not use rate limiting if it results in poor user experience or for complex use cases such as subscriptions.
- The non-functional requirements of a rate limiter are scalability, performance, and lower complexity. To optimize for these requirements, we can trade off availability, fault-tolerance, accuracy, and consistency.
- The main input to our rate-limiter service is user ID and service ID, which will be processed according to rules defined by our admin users to return a "yes" or "no" response on rate limiting.
- There are various rate limiting algorithms, each with its own tradeoffs. Token bucket is easy to understand and implement and is memory-efficient, but synchronization and cleanup are tricky. Leaky bucket is easy to understand and implement but is slightly inaccurate. A fixed window log is easy to test and debug, but it is inaccurate and more complicated to implement. A sliding window log is accurate, but it requires more memory. A sliding window counter uses less memory than sliding window log, but it is less accurate than sliding window log.
- We can consider a sidecar pattern for our rate-limiting service.

Design a notification/
alerting service

9

This chapter covers

- Limiting the feature scope and discussion of a service
- Designing a service that delegates to platform-specific channels
- Designing a system for flexible configurations and templates
- Handling other typical concerns of a service

We create functions and classes in our source code to avoid duplication of coding, debugging, and testing, to improve maintainability, and to allow reuse. Likewise, we generalize common functionalities used by multiple services (i.e. centralization of cross-cutting concerns).

Sending user notifications is a common system requirement. In any system design discussion, whenever we discuss sending notifications, we should suggest a common notification service for the organization.

9.1   Functional requirements

Our notification service should be as simple as possible for a wide range of users, which causes considerable complexity in the functional requirements. There are many possible features that a notification service can provide. Given our limited time, we should clearly define some use cases and features for our notification service that will make it useful to our anticipated wide user base. A well-defined feature scope will allow us to discern and optimize for its non-functional requirements. After we design our initial system, we can discuss and design for further possible features.

This question can also be a good exercise in designing an MVP. We can anticipate possible features and design our system to be composed of loosely coupled components to be adaptable to adding new functionality and services and evolve in response to user feedback and changing business requirements.

9.1.1 Not for uptime monitoring

Our notification service will likely be a layer on top of various messaging services (e.g., email, SMS, etc.). A service to send such a message (e.g., an email service) is a complex service in itself. In this question, we will use shared messaging services, but we will not design them. We will design a service for users to send messages via various channels.

Generalizing this approach beyond shared messaging services, we will also use other shared services for functionalities like storage, event streaming, and logging. We will also use the same shared infrastructure (bare metal or cloud infrastructure) that our organization uses to develop other services.

> **QUESTION** Can uptime monitoring be implemented using the same shared infrastructure or services as the other services that it monitors?

Based on this approach, we assume that this service should not be used for uptime monitoring (i.e., trigger alerts on outages of other services). Otherwise, it cannot be built on the same infrastructure or use the same shared services as other services in our organization because outages that affect them will also affect this service, and outage alerts will not be triggered. An uptime monitoring service must run on infrastructure that is independent of the services that it monitors. This is one key reason external uptime monitoring services like PagerDuty are so popular.

All this being said, section 9.14 discusses a possible approach to using this service for uptime monitoring.

9.1.2 Users and data

Our notification service has three types of users:

- Sender: A person or service who CRUDs (create, read, update, and delete) notifications and sends them to recipients.
- Recipient: A user of an app who receives notifications. We also refer to the devices or apps themselves as recipients.
- Admin: A person who has admin access to our notification service. An admin has various capabilities. They can grant permissions to other users to send or receive notifications, and they can also create and manage notification templates (section 9.5). We assume that we as developers of the notification service have admin access, although, in practice, only some developers may have admin access to the production environment.

We have both manual and programmatic senders. Programmatic users can send API requests, especially to send notifications. Manual users may go through a web UI for all their use cases, including sending notifications, as well as administrative features like configuring notifications and viewing sent and pending notifications.

We can limit a notification's size to 1 MB, more than enough for thousands of characters and a thumbnail image. Users should not send video or audio within a notification. Rather, they should include links in the notification to media content or any other big files, and the recipient systems should have features developed separately from our notification service to download and view that content. Hackers may attempt to impersonate the service and send notifications with links to malicious websites. To prevent this, a notification should contain a digital signature. The recipients can verify the signature with the certificate authority. For more information, refer to resources on cryptography.

9.1.3   *Recipient channels*

We should support the ability to send notifications via various channels, including the following. Our notification service needs to be integrated to services that send messages for each of these channels:

- Browser
- Email
- SMS. For simplicity, we do not consider MMS.
- Automated phone calls
- Push notifications on Android, iOS, or browsers.
- Customized notifications within apps, such as, for example, banking or finance apps with stringent privacy and security requirements use internal messaging and notification systems.

9.1.4   *Templates*

A particular messaging system provides a default template with a set of fields that a user populates before sending out the message. For example, an email has a sender email address field, a recipient email addresses field, a subject field, a body field, and a list of attachments; an SMS has a sender phone number field, a recipient phone numbers field, and a body field.

The same notification may be sent to many recipients. For example, an app may send an email or push notification containing a welcome message to any new user who has just signed up. The message can be identical for all users, such as, for example, "Welcome to Beigel. Please enjoy a 20% discount on your first purchase."

The message may also have personalized parameters, such as the user's name and the discount percentage; for example, "Welcome ${first_name}. Please enjoy a ${discount}% discount on your first purchase." Another example is an order confirmation email, text, or push notification that an online marketplace app may wish to send a customer just after they submit an order. The message may have parameters for the customer's name, order confirmation code, list of items (an item can have many parameters), and prices. There may be many parameters in a message.

Our notification service may provide an API to CRUD templates. Each time a user wishes to send a notification, it can either create the entire message itself or select a particular template and fill in the values of that template.

A template feature also reduces traffic to our notification service. This is discussed later in this chapter.

We can provide many features to create and manage templates, and this can be a service in itself (a template service). We will limit our initial discussion to CRUD templates.

9.1.5 *Trigger conditions*

Notifications can be triggered manually or programmatically. We may provide a browser app for users to create a notification, add recipients, and then send it out immediately. Notifications may also be sent out programmatically, and this can be configured either on the browser app or via an API. Programmatic notifications are configured to be triggered on a schedule or by API requests.

9.1.6 *Manage subscribers, sender groups, and recipient groups*

If a user wishes to send a notification to more than one recipient, we may need to provide features to manage recipient groups. A user may address a notification using a recipient group, instead of having to provide a list of recipients every time the former needs to send a notification.

> **WARNING** Recipient groups contain PII (Personally-Identifiable Information), so they are subject to privacy laws such as GDPR and CCPA.

Users should be able to CRUD recipient groups. We may also consider role-based access control (RBAC). For example, a group may have read and write roles. A user requires the group's read role to view its members and other details and then the write role to add or remove members. RBAC for groups is outside the scope of our discussion.

A recipient should be able to opt into notifications and opt out of unwanted notifications; otherwise, they are just spam. We will skip this discussion in this chapter. It may be discussed as a follow-up topic.

9.1.7 *User features*

Here are other features we can provide:

- The service should identify duplicate notification requests from senders and not send duplicate notifications to recipients.
- We should allow a user to view their past notification requests. An important use case is for a user to check if they have already made a particular notification request, so they will not make duplicate notification requests. Although

the notification service can also automatically identify and duplicate notifica-tion requests, we will not completely trust this implementation, since a user may define a duplicate request differently from the notification service.

- A user will store many notification configurations and templates. It should be able to find configurations or templates by various fields, like names or descrip-tions. A user may also be able to save favorite notifications.

- A user should be able to look up the status of notifications. A notification may be scheduled, in progress (similar to emails in an outbox), or failed. If a notifica-tion's delivery is failed, a user should be able to see if a retry is scheduled and the number of times delivery has been retried.

- (Optional) A priority level set by the user. We may process higher-priority noti-fications before lower-priority ones or use a weighted approach to prevent starvation.

9.1.8 Analytics

We can assume analytics is outside the scope of this question, though we can discuss it as we design our notification service.

9.2 Non-functional requirements

We can discuss the following non-functional requirements:

- Scale: Our notification service should be able to send billions of notifications daily. At 1 MB/notification, our notification service will process and send peta-bytes of data daily. There may be thousands of senders and one billion recipients.

- Performance: A notification should be delivered within seconds. To improve the speed of delivering critical notifications, we may consider allowing users to prior-itize certain notifications over others.

- High availability: Five 9s uptime.

- Fault-tolerant: If a recipient is unavailable to receive a notification, it should receive the notification at the next opportunity.

- Security: Only authorized users should be allowed to send notifications.

- Privacy: Recipients should be able to opt out of notifications.

9.3 Initial high-level architecture

We can design our system with the following considerations:

- Users who request creation of notifications do so through a single service with a single interface. Users specify the desired channel(s) and other parameters through this single service/interface.

- However, each channel can be handled by a separate service. Each channel service provides logic specific to its channel. For example, a browser notification channel service can create browser notifications using the web notification API. Refer to documentation like "Using the Notifications API" (https://developer.mozilla .org/en-US/docs/Web/API/Notifications_API/Using_the_Notifications _API) and "Notification" (https://developer.mozilla.org/en-US/docs/Web/ API/notification). Certain browsers like Chrome also provide their own notifications API. Refer to "chrome.notifications" (https://developer.chrome.com/ docs/extensions/reference/notifications/) and "Rich Notifications API" (https://developer.chrome.com/docs/extensions/mv3/richNotifications/) for rich notifications with rich elements like images and progress bars.

- We can centralize common channel service logic in another service, which we can call the "job constructor."

- Notifications via various channels may be handled by external third-party services, illustrated in figure 9.1. Android push notifications are made via Firebase Cloud Messaging (FCM). iOS push notifications are made via Apple Push notification service. We may also employ third-party services for email, SMS/texting, and phone calls. Making requests to third-party services means that we must limit the request rate and handle failed requests.

Figure 9.1   Our Notification Service may make requests to external notification services, so the former must limit the request rate and handle failed requests.

- Sending notifications entirely via synchronous mechanisms is not scalable because the process consumes a thread while it waits for the request and response to be sent over the network. To support thousands of senders and billions of recipients, we should use asynchronous techniques like event streaming.

Based on these considerations, figures 9.2 and 9.3 show our initial high-level architecture. To send a notification, a client makes a request to our notification service. The request is first processed by the frontend service or API gateway and then sent to the backend service. The backend service has a producer cluster, a notification Kafka topic, and a consumer cluster. A producer host simply produces a message on to the notification Kafka topic and returns 200 success. The consumer cluster consumes the messages, generates notification events, and produces them to the relevant channel queues. Each notification event is for a single recipient/destination. This asynchronous event driven approach allows the notification service to handle unpredictable traffic spikes.

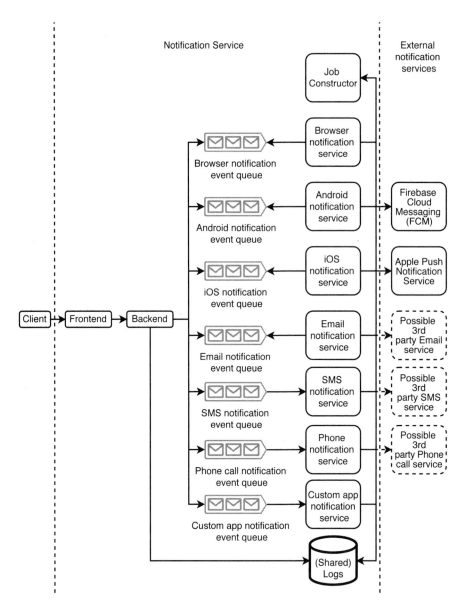

Figure 9.2   High-level architecture of our notification service, illustrating all the possible requests when a client/user sends a notification. We collectively refer to the various Kafka consumers (each of which is a notification service for a specific channel) as channel services. We illustrate that the backend and channel services use a shared logging database, but all the components of our notification service should log to a shared logging service.

On the other side of the queues, we have a separate service for each notification channel. Some of them may depend on external services, such as Android's Firebase Cloud Messaging (FCM) and iOS's Apple Push Notification Service (APNs). The browser notification service may be further broken up into various browser types (e.g., Firefox and Chrome).

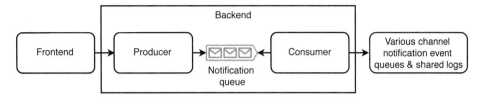

Figure 9.3   Zoom-in of our backend service from figure 9.2. The backend service consists of a producer cluster, a notification Kafka topic, and a consumer cluster. In subsequent illustrations, we will omit the zoom-in diagram of the backend service.

Each notification channel must be implemented as a separate service (we can refer to it as a channel service) because sending notifications on a particular channel requires a particular server application, and each channel has different capabilities, configurations, and protocols. Email notifications use SMTP. To send an email notification via the email notification system, the user provides the sender email address, recipient email addresses, title, body, and attachments. There are also other email types like calendar events. A SMS gateway uses various protocols including HTTP, SMTP, and SMPP. To send an SMS message, the user provides an origin number, a destination number, and a string.

In this discussion, let's use the term "destination" or "address" to refer to a field that that identifies where to send a single notification object, such as a phone number, an email address, a device ID for push notifications, or custom destinations such as user IDs for internal messaging, and so on.

Each channel service should concentrate on its core functionality of sending a notification to a destination. It should process the full notification content and deliver the notification to its destination. But we may need to use third-party APIs to deliver messages by certain channels. For example, unless our organization is a telecommunications company, we will use a telecommunications company's API to deliver phone calls and SMS. For mobile push notifications, we will use Apple Push Notification Service for iOS notifications and Firebase Cloud Messaging for Android notifications. It is only for browser notifications and our custom app notifications that we can deliver messages without using third-party APIs. Wherever we need to use a third-party API, the corresponding channel service should be the only component in our notification service that directly makes requests to that API.

Having no coupling between a channel service and the other services in our notification service makes our system more fault-tolerant and allows the following:

- The channel service can be used by services other than our notification service.
- The channel service can be scaled independently from the other services.
- The services can change their internal implementation details independently of each other and be maintained by separate teams with specialized knowledge. For example, the automated phone call service team should know how to send automated phone calls, and the email service team should know how to send email, but each team need not know about how the other team's service works.
- Customized channel services can be developed, and our notification service can send requests to them. For example, we may wish to implement notifications within our browser or mobile app that are displayed as custom UI components and not as push notifications. The modular design of channel services makes them easier to develop.

We can use authentication (e.g., refer to the discussion of OpenID Connect in the appendix) on the frontend service to ensure that only authorized users, such as service layer hosts, can request channel services to send notifications. The frontend service handles requests to the OAuth2 authorization server.

Why shouldn't users simply use the notification systems of the channels they require? What are the benefits of the development and maintenance overhead of the additional layers?

The notification service can provide a common UI (not shown in figure 13.1) for its clients (i.e., the channel services), so users can manage all their notifications across all channels from a single service and do not need to learn and manage multiple services.

The frontend service provides a common set of operations:

- *Rate limiting*—Prevents 5xx errors from notification clients being overwhelmed by too many requests. Rate limiting can be a separate common service, discussed in chapter 8. We can use stress testing to determine the appropriate limit. The rate limiter can also inform maintainers if the request rate of a particular channel consistently exceeds or is far below the set limit, so we can make an appropriate scaling decision. Auto-scaling is another option we can consider.
- *Privacy*—Organizations may have specific privacy policies that regulate notifications sent to devices or accounts. The service layer can be used to configure and enforce these policies across all clients.
- *Security*—Authentication and authorization for all notifications.

- *Monitoring, analytics, and alerting*—The service can log notification events and compute aggregate statistics such as notification success and failure rates over sliding windows of various widths. Users can monitor these statistics and set alert thresholds on failure rates.
- *Caching*—Requests can be made through a caching service, using one of the caching strategies discussed in chapter 8.

We provision a Kafka topic for each channel. If a notification has multiple channels, we can produce an event for each channel and produce each event to the corresponding topic. We can also have a Kafka topic for each priority level, so if we have five channels and three priority levels, we will have 15 topics.

The approach of using Kafka rather than synchronous request-response follows the cloud native principle of event-driven over synchronous. Benefits include less coupling, independent development of various components in a service, easier troubleshooting (we can replay messages from the past at any point in time), and higher throughput with no blocking calls. This comes with storage costs. If we process one billion messages daily, the storage requirement is 1 PB daily, or ~10 PB, with a one-week retention period.

For a consistent load on the job constructor, each channel service consumer host has its own thread pool. Each thread can consume and process one event at a time.

The backend and each channel service can log their requests for purposes such as troubleshooting and auditing.

9.4   *Object store: Configuring and sending notifications*

The notification service feeds a stream of events into the channel services. Each event corresponds to a single notification task to a single addressee.

QUESTION   What if a notification contains large files or objects? It is inefficient for multiple Kafka events to contain the same large file/object.

In figure 9.3, the backend may produce an entire 1 MB notification to a Kafka topic. However, a notification may contain large files or objects. For example, a phone call notification may contain a large audio file, or an email notification may contain multiple video attachments. Our backend can first POST these large objects in an object store, which will return object IDs. Our backend can then generate a notification event that includes these object IDs instead of the original objects and produce this event to the appropriate Kafka topic. A channel service will consume this event, GET the objects from our object store, assemble the notification, and then deliver it to the recipient. In figure 9.4, we add our metadata service to our high-level architecture.

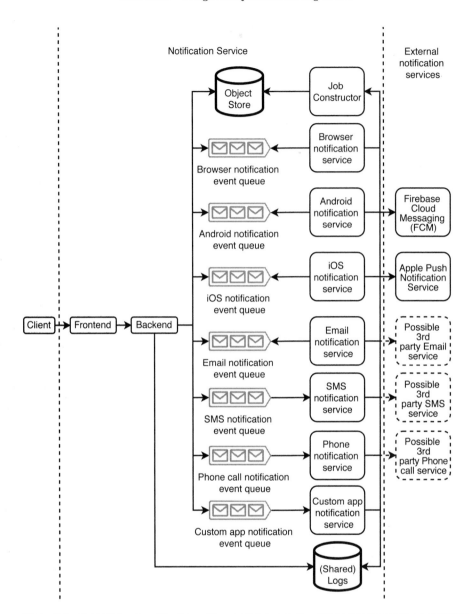

Figure 9.4   Our high-level architecture with a metadata service. Our backend service can POST large objects to the metadata service, so the notification events can be kept small.

If a particular large object is being delivered to multiple recipients, our backend will POST it multiple times to our object store. From the second POST onwards, our object store can return a 304 Not Modified response.

9.5 Notification templates

An addressee group with millions of destinations may cause millions of events to be produced. This may occupy much memory in Kafka. The previous section discussed how we can use a metadata service to reduce the duplicate content in events and thus reduce their sizes.

9.5.1 Notification template service

Many notification events are almost duplicates with a small amount of personalization. For example, figure 9.5 shows a push notification that can be sent to millions of users that contains an image common to all recipients and a string that varies only by the recipient's name. In another example, if we are sending an email, most of the email's contents will be identical to all recipients. The email title and body may only be slightly different for each recipient (such as a different name or a different percentage of discount for each user), while any attachments will likely be identical for all recipients.

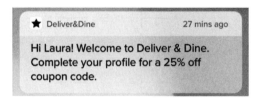

Figure 9.5 Example of a push notification that contains an image common to all recipients and can have a string that only varies by the recipient's name. The common content can be placed in a template such as "Hi ${name}! Welcome to Deliver & Dine." A Kafka queue event can contain a key-value pair of the form ("name" and the recipient's name, destination ID). Image from https://buildfire.com/what-is-a -push-notification/.

In section 9.1.4, we discussed that templates are useful to users for managing such personalization. Templates are also useful to improve our notification service's scalability. We can minimize the sizes of the notification events by placing all the common data into a template. Creation and management of templates can itself be a complex system. We can call it the notification template service, or template service for short. Figure 9.6 illustrates our high-level architecture with our template service. A client only needs to include a template ID in a notification, and a channel service will GET the template from the template service when generating the notification.

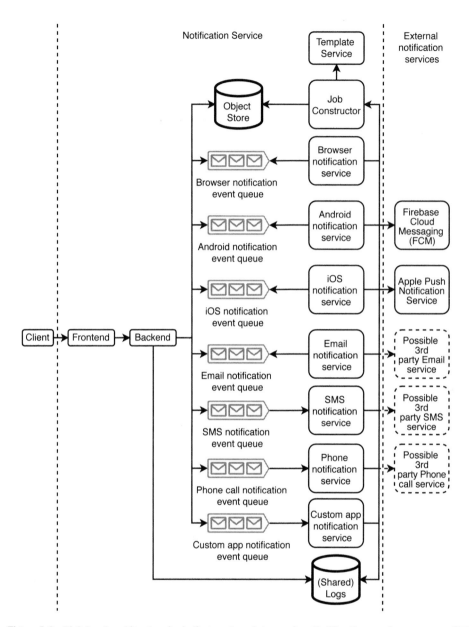

Figure 9.6   High-level architecture including our template service. Notification service users can CRUD templates. The template service should have its own authentication and authorization and RBAC (role-based access control). The job constructor should only have read access. Admins should have admin access so they can create, update, and delete templates or grant roles to other users.

Combining this approach with our metadata service, an event need only contain the notification ID (which can also be used as the notification template key), any personalized data in the form of key-value pairs, and the destination. If the notification has no personalized content (i.e., it is identical for all its destinations), the metadata service contains essentially the entire notification content, and an event will only contain a destination and a notification content ID.

A user can set up a notification template prior to sending notifications. A user can send CRUD requests on notification templates to the service layer, which forwards them to the metadata service to perform the appropriate queries on the metadata database. Depending on our available resources or ease-of-use considerations, we may also choose to allow users not to have to set up a notification template and simply send entire notification events to our service.

9.5.2 Additional features

We may decide that a template requires additional features such as the following. These additional features may be briefly discussed near the end of the interview as follow-up topics. It is unlikely there will be enough time during the interview for an in-depth discussion. A sign of engineering maturity and a good interview signal is the ability to foresee these features, while also demonstrating that one can fluently zoom in and out of the details of any of these systems, and clearly and concisely describe them to the interviewer.

AUTHORING, ACCESS CONTROL, AND CHANGE MANAGEMENT

A user should be able to author templates. The system should store the template's data, including its content and its creation details, such as author ID and created and updated timestamps.

User roles include admin, write, read, and none. These correspond to the access permissions that a user has to a template. Our notification template service may need to be integrated with our organization's user management service, which may use a protocol like LDAP.

We may wish to record templates' change history, including data such as the exact change that was made, the user who made it, and the timestamp. Going further, we may wish to develop a change approval process. Changes made by certain roles may need approval from one or more admins. This may be generalized to a shared approval service that can be used by any application where one or more users propose a write operation, and one or more other users approve or deny the operation.

Extending change management further, a user may need to rollback their previous change or revert to a specific version.

REUSABLE AND EXTENDABLE TEMPLATE CLASSES AND FUNCTIONS

A template may consist of reusable sub-templates, each of which is separately owned and managed. We can refer to them as template classes.

A template's parameters can be variables or functions. Functions are useful for dynamic behavior on the recipient's device.

A variable can have a data type (e.g., integer, varchar(255), etc.). When a client creates a notification from a template, our backend can validate the parameter values. Our notification service can also provide additional constraints/validation rules, such as a minimum or maximum integer value or string length. We can also define validation rules on functions.

A template's parameters may be populated by simple rules (e.g., a recipient name field or a currency symbol field) or by machine-learning models (e.g., each recipient may be offered a different discount). This will require integration with systems that supply data necessary to fill in the dynamic parameters. Content management and personalization are different functions owned by different teams, and the services and their interfaces should be designed to clearly reflect this ownership and division of responsibilities.

SEARCH

Our template service may store many templates and template classes, and some of them may be duplicates or very similar. We may wish to provide a search feature. Section 2.6 discusses how to implement search in a service.

OTHER

There are endless possibilities. For example, how can we manage CSS and JavaScript in templates?

9.6   *Scheduled notifications*

Our notification service can use a shared Airflow service or job scheduler service to provide scheduled notifications. Referring to figure 9.7, our backend service should provide an API endpoint to schedule notifications and can generate and make the appropriate request to the Airflow service to create a scheduled notification.

When the user sets up or modifies a periodic notification, the Airflow job's Python script is automatically generated and merged into the scheduler's code repository. A detailed discussion of an Airflow service is outside the scope of this question. For the purpose of the interview, the interviewer may request that we design our own task scheduling system instead of using an available solution such as Airflow or Luigi. We can use the cron-based solution discussed in section 4.6.1.

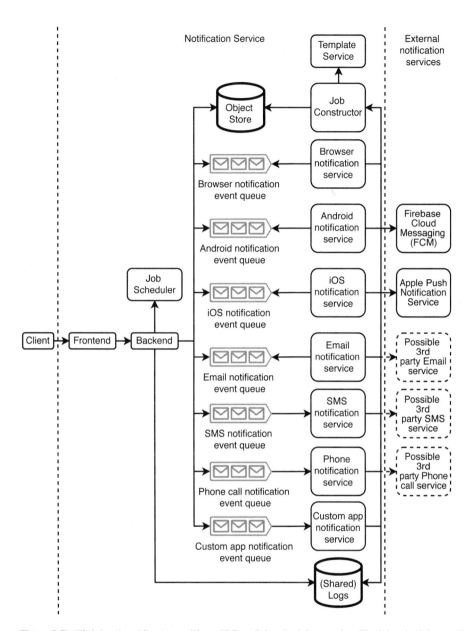

Figure 9.7 High-level architecture with an Airflow/job scheduler service. The job scheduler service is for users to configure periodic notifications. At the scheduled times, the job scheduler service will produce notification events to the backend.

Periodic notifications may compete with ad hoc notifications because both can be limited by the rate limiter. Each time the rate limiter prevents a notification request from immediately proceeding, this should be logged. We should have a dashboard to display the rate of rate limiting events. We also need to add an alert that triggers when there are frequent rate limiting events. Based on this information, we can scale up our cluster sizes, allocate more budget to external notification services, or request or limit certain users from excessive notifications.

9.7   *Notification addressee groups*

A notification may have millions of destinations/addresses. If our users must specify each of these destinations, each user will need to maintain its own list, and there may be much duplicated recipient data among our users. Moreover, passing these millions of destinations to the notification service means heavy network traffic. It is more convenient for users to maintain the list of destinations in our notification service and use that list's ID in making requests to send notifications. Let's refer to such a list as a "notification addressee group." When a user makes a request to deliver a notification, the request may contain either a list of destinations (up to a limit) or a list of Addressee Group IDs.

We can design an address group service to handle notification addressee groups. Other functional requirements of this service may include:

- Access control for various roles like read-only, append-only (can add but cannot delete addresses), and admin (full access). Access control is an important security feature here because an unauthorized user can send notifications to our entire user base of over 1 billion recipients, which can be spam or more malicious activity.

- May also allow addressees to remove themselves from notification groups to prevent spam. These removal events may be logged for analytics.

- The functionalities can be exposed as API endpoints, and all these endpoints are accessed via the service layer.

We may also need a manual review and approval process for notification requests to a large number of recipients. Notifications in testing environments do not require approval, while notifications in the production environment require manual approval. For example, a notification request to one million recipients may require manual approval by an operations staff, 10 million recipients may require a manager's approval, 100 million recipients may require a senior manager's approval, and a notification to the entire user base may require director-level approval. We can design a system for senders to obtain approval in advance of sending notifications. This is outside the scope of this question.

Figure 9.8 illustrates our high-level architecture with an address group service. A user can specify an address group in a notification request. The backend can make GET requests to the address group service to obtain an address group's user IDs. Because there can be over one billion user IDs in a group, a single GET response cannot contain all user IDs, but rather has a maximum number of user IDs. The Address Group Service must provide a `GET /address-group/count/{name}` endpoint that returns the count of addresses in this group, and a `GET /address-group/{name}/start-index/{start-index}/end-index/{end-index}` endpoint so our backend can make GET requests to obtain batches of addresses.

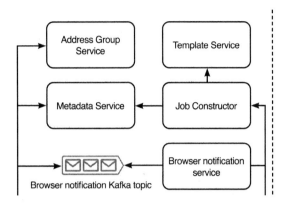

Figure 9.8 Zoom-in of figure 9.6, with the addition of an address group service. An address group contains a list of recipients. The address group service allows a user to send a notification to multiple users by specifying a single address group, instead of having to specify each and every recipient.

We can use a choreography saga (section 5.6.1) to GET these addresses and generate notification events. This can handle traffic surges to our address group service. Figure 9.9 illustrates our backend architecture to perform this task.

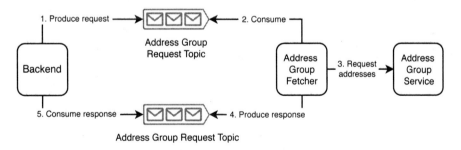

Figure 9.9 Our backend architecture to construct notification events from an address group

Referring to the sequence diagram in figure 9.10, a producer can create an event for such a job. A consumer consumes this event and does the following:

1 Uses GET to obtain a batch of addresses from the address group service
2 Generates a notification event from each address
3 Produces it to the appropriate notification event Kafka topic

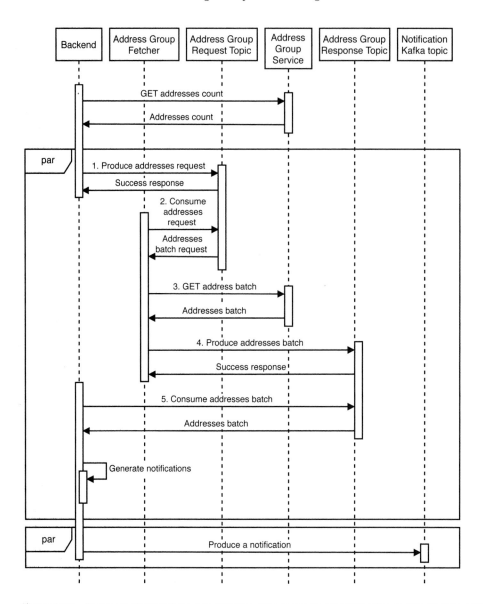

Figure 9.10   Sequence diagram for our backend service to construct notification events from an address group

Should we split the backend service into two services, so that step 5 onward is done by another service? We did not do this because the backend may not need to make requests to the address group service.

TIP   This backend produces to one topic and consumes from another. If you need a program that consumes from one topic and produces to another, consider using Kafka Streams (https://kafka.apache.org/10/documentation/streams/).

QUESTION What if new users are added to a new address group while the address group fetcher is fetching its addresses?

A problem with this that we will immediately discover is that a big address group changes rapidly. New recipients are constantly being added or removed from the group, due to various reasons:

- Someone may change their phone number or email address.
- Our app may gain new users and lose current users during any period.
- In a random population of one billion people, thousands of people are born and die every day.

When is a notification considered delivered to all recipients? If our backend attempts to keep fetching batches of new recipients to create notification events, given a sufficiently big group, this event creation will never end. We should deliver a notification only to recipients who were within an address group at the time the notification was triggered.

A discussion of possible architecture and implementation details of an address group service is outside the scope of this question.

9.8 Unsubscribe requests

Every notification should contain a button, link, or other UI for recipients to unsubscribe from similar notifications. If a recipient requests to be removed from future notifications, the sender should be notified of this request.

We may also add a notification management page in our app for our app users, like figure 9.11. App users can choose the categories of notifications that they wish to receive. Our notification service should provide a list of notification categories, and a notification request should have a category field that is a required field.

Figure 9.11   Notification management in the YouTube Android app. We can define a list of notification categories, so our app users can choose which categories to subscribe to.

QUESTION   Should unsubscribe be implemented on the client or server?

The answer is either to implement it on the server or on both sides. Do not implement it only on the client. If unsubscribe is implemented only on the client, the notification service will continue to send notifications to recipients, and the app on the recipient's device will block the notification. We can implement this approach for our browser and mobile apps, but we cannot implement this on email, phone calls, or SMS. Moreover, it is a waste of resources to generate and send a notification only for it to be blocked by the client. However, we may still wish to implement notification blocking on the client in case the server-side implementation has bugs and continues to send notifications that should have been blocked.

If unsubscribe is implemented on the server, the notification service will block notifications to the recipient. Our backend should provide an API endpoint to subscribe or unsubscribe from notifications, and the button/link should send a request to this API.

One way to implement notification blocking is to modify the Address Group Service API to accept category. The new GET API endpoints can be something like `GET /address-group/count/{name}/category/{category}` and `GET /address-group/{name}/category/{category}/start-index/{start-index}/end-index/{end-index}`. The address group service will return only recipients who accept notifications of that category. Architecture and further implementation details are outside the scope of this question.

9.9   *Handling failed deliveries*

Notification delivery may fail due to reasons unrelated to our notification service:

- The recipient's device was uncontactable. Possible causes may include:
  - Network problems.
  - The recipient's device may be turned off.
  - Third-party delivery services may be unavailable.
  - The app user uninstalled the mobile app or canceled their account. If the app user had canceled their account or uninstalled the mobile app, there should be mechanisms to update our address group service, but the update hasn't yet been applied. Our channel service can simply drop the request and do nothing else. We can assume that the address group service will be updated in the future, and then GET responses from the address group service will no longer include this recipient.
- The recipient has blocked this notification category, and the recipient's device blocked this notification. This notification should not have been delivered, but it was delivered anyway, likely because of bugs. We should configure a low-urgency alert for this case.

Each of the subcases in the first case should be handled differently. Network problems that affect our data center are highly unlikely, and if it does happen, the relevant team should have already broadcasted an alert to all relevant teams (obviously via channels that don't depend on the affected data center). It is unlikely that we will discuss this further in an interview.

If there were network problems that only affected the specific recipient or the recipient's device was turned off, the third-party delivery service will return a response to our channel service with this information. The channel service can add a retry count to the notification event, or it can increment the count if the retry field is already present (i.e., this delivery was already a retry). Next, it produces this notification to a Kafka topic that functions as a dead letter queue. A channel service can consume from the dead letter queue and then retry the delivery request. In figure 9.12, we add dead letter queues to our high-level architecture. If the retry fails three times, the channel service can log this and make a request to the address group service to record that the user is uncontactable. The address group service should provide an appropriate API endpoint for this. The address group service should also stop including this user in future GET requests. The implementation details are outside the scope of this question.

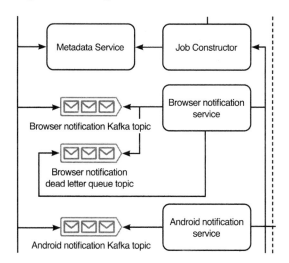

Figure 9.12 Zoom-in of figure 9.6, with the addition of a browser notification dead letter queue. The dead letter queues for the other channel services will be similar. If the browser notification service encounters a 503 Service Unavailable error when delivering a notification, it produces/enqueues this notification event to its dead letter queue. It will retry the delivery later. If delivery fails after three attempts, the browser notification service will log the event (to our shared logging service). We may also choose to also configure a low-urgency alert for such failed deliveries.

If a third-party delivery service is unavailable, the channel service should trigger a high-urgency alert, employ exponential backoff, and retry with the same event. The channel service can increase the interval between retries.

Our notification service should also provide an API endpoint for the recipient app to request missed notifications. When the recipient email, browser, or mobile app is ready to receive notifications, it can make a request to this API endpoint.

9.10 *Client-side considerations regarding duplicate notifications*

Channel services that send notifications directly to recipient devices must allow both push and pull requests. When a notification is created, a channel service should immediately push it to the recipient. However, the recipient client device may be offline or unavailable for some reason. When the device comes back online, it should pull notifications from the notifications service. This is applicable to channels that don't use external notifications services, such as browser or custom app notifications.

How can we avoid duplicate notifications? Earlier we discussed solutions to avoid duplicate notifications for external notification services (i.e., push requests). Avoiding duplicate notifications for pull requests should be implemented on the client side. Our service should not deny requests for the same notifications (perhaps other than rate limiting) because the client may have good reasons to repeat requests. The client should record notifications already shown (and dismissed) by the user, perhaps in browser localStorage or a mobile device's SQLite database. When a client receives notifications in a pull (or perhaps also a push) request, it should look up against the device's storage to determine whether any notification has already been displayed before displaying new notifications to the user.

9.11 *Priority*

Notifications may have different priority levels. Referring to figure 9.13, we can decide how many priority levels we need, such as 2 to 5, and create a separate Kafka topic for each priority level.

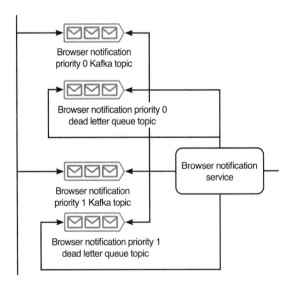

Figure 9.13
Figure 9.12 with
two priority levels

To process higher-priority notifications before lower-priority ones, a consumer host can simply consume from the higher-priority Kafka topics until they are empty, then consume from the lower-priority Kafka topics. For a weighted approach, each time a consumer host is ready to consume an event, it can first use weighted random selection to select a Kafka topic to consume from.

> **QUESTION** Extend the system design to accommodate a different priority configuration for each channel.

9.12 Search

We may provide search for users to search and view existing notification/alerting setups. We can index on notification templates and notification address groups. Referring to section 2.6.1, a frontend search library like match-sorter should be sufficient for this use case.

9.13 Monitoring and alerting

Besides what was discussed in section 2.5, we should monitor and send alerts for the following.

Users should be able to track the state of their notifications. This can be provided via another service that reads from the log service. We can provide a notification service UI for users to create and manage notifications, including templates and tracking notifications' statuses.

We can create monitoring dashboards on various statistics. Besides the success and failure rates already mentioned earlier, other useful statistics are the number of events in the queue and event size percentiles over time, broken down by channel and priority, as well as OS statistics like CPU, memory, and disk storage consumption. High memory consumption and a large number of events in the queue indicate that unnecessary resource consumption, and we may examine the events to determine whether any data can be placed into a metadata service to reduce the events' sizes in the queue.

We can do periodic auditing to detect silent errors. For example, we can arrange with the external notification services we use to compare these two numbers:

- The number of 200 responses received by our notification services that send requests to external notification services.
- The number of valid notifications received by those external notification services.

Anomaly detection can be used to determine an unusual change in the notification rate or message sizes, by various parameters such as sender, receiver, and channel.

9.14 *Availability monitoring and alerting on the notification/alerting service*

We discussed in section 9.1.1 that our notification service should not be used for uptime monitoring because it shares the same infrastructure and services as the services that it monitors. But what if we insist on finding a way for this notification service to be a general shared service for outage alerts? What if it itself fails? How will our alerting service alert users? One solution involves using external devices, such as servers located in various data centers.

We can provide a client daemon that can be installed on these external devices. The service sends periodic heartbeats to these external devices, which are configured to expect these heartbeats. If a device does not receive a heartbeat at the expected time, it can query the service to verify the latter's health. If the system returns a 2xx response, the device assumes there was a temporary network connectivity problem and takes no further action. If the request times out or returns an error, the device can alert its user(s) by automated phone calls, texting, email, push notifications, and/or other channels. This is essentially an independent, specialized, small-scale monitoring and alerting service that serves only one specific purpose and sends alerts to only a few users.

9.15 *Other possible discussion topics*

We can also scale (increase or decrease) the amount of memory of the Kafka cluster if necessary. If the number of events in the queues monotonically increases over time, notifications are not being delivered, and we must either scale up the consumer cluster to process and deliver these notification events or implement rate limiting and inform the relevant users about their excessive use.

We can consider auto-scaling for this shared service. However, auto-scaling solutions are tricky to use in practice. In practice, we can configure auto-scaling to automatically increase cluster sizes of the service's various components up to a limit to avoid outages on unforeseen traffic spikes, while also sending alerts to developers to further increase resource allocation if required. We can manually review the instances where auto-scaling was triggered and refine the auto-scaling configurations accordingly.

A detailed discussion of a notification service can fill an entire book and include many shared services. To focus on the core components of a notification service and keep the discussion to a reasonable length, we glossed over many topics in this chapter. We can discuss these topics during any leftover time in the interview:

- A recipient should be able to opt into notifications and out of unwanted notifications; otherwise, they are just spam. We can discuss this feature.
- How can we address the situation where we need to correct a notification that has already been sent to a large number of users?

- If we discovered this error while the notification is being sent, we may wish to cancel the process and not send the notification to the remaining recipients.

- For devices where the notifications haven't yet been triggered, we can cancel notifications that haven't been triggered.

- For devices where the notifications have already been triggered, we will need to send a follow-up notification to clarify this error.

- Rather than rate-limiting a sender regardless of which channels it uses, design a system that also allows rate limiting on individual channels.

- Possibilities for analytics include:

  - Analysis of notification delivery times of various channels, which can be used to improve performance.

  - Notification response rate and tracking and analytics on user actions and other responses to notifications.

  - Integrating our notification system with an A/B test system.

- APIs and architecture for the additional template service features we discussed in section 9.5.2.

- A scalable and highly available job scheduler service.

- Systems design of the address group service to support the features that we discussed in section 9.7. We can also discuss other features such as:

  - Should we use a batch or streaming approach to process unsubscribe requests?

  - How to manually resubscribe a recipient to notifications.

  - Automatically resubscribe a recipient to notifications if the recipient's device or account makes any other requests to any service in our organization.

- An approval service for obtaining and tracking the relevant approvals to send notifications to a large number of recipients. We can also extend this discussion to system design of mechanisms to prevent abuse or send unwanted notifications.

- Further details on the monitoring and alerts, including examples and elaboration of the exact metrics and alerts to define.

- Further discussion on the client daemon solution.

- Design our various messaging services (e.g., design an email service, SMS service, automated phone call service, etc.).

9.16   *Final notes*

Our solution is scalable. Every component is horizontally scalable. Fault-tolerance is extremely important in this shared service, and we have constantly paid attention to it. Monitoring and availability are robust; there is no single point of failure, and the monitoring and alerting of system availability and health involves independent devices.

Summary

- A service that must serve the same functionality to many different platforms can consist of a single backend that centralizes common processing and directs requests to the appropriate component (or another service) for each platform.
- Use a metadata service and/or object store to reduce the size of messages in a message broker queue.
- Consider how to automate user actions using templates.
- We can use a task scheduling service for periodic notifications.
- One way to deduplicate messages is on the receiver's device.
- Communicate between system components via asynchronous means like sagas.
- We should create monitoring dashboards for analytics and tracking errors.
- Do periodic auditing and anomaly detection to detect possible errors that our other metrics missed.

Design a database
batch auditing service

10

This chapter covers

- Auditing database tables to find invalid data
- Designing a scalable and accurate solution to audit database tables
- Exploring possible features to answer an unusual question

Let's design a shared service for manually defined validations. This is an unusually open-ended system design interview question, even by the usual standards of system design interviews, and the approach discussed in this chapter is just one of many possibilities.

We begin this chapter by introducing the concept of *data quality*. There are many definitions of data quality. In general, data quality can refer to how suitable a dataset is to serve its purpose and may also refer to activities that improve the dataset's suitability for said purpose. There are many dimensions of data quality. We can adopt the dimensions from https://www.heavy.ai/technical-glossary/data-quality:

- *Accuracy*—How close a measurement is to the true value.
- *Completeness*—Data has all the required values for our purpose.
- *Consistency*—Data in different locations has the same values, and the different locations start serving the same data changes at the same time.

- *Validity*—Data is correctly formatted, and values are within an appropriate range.
- *Uniqueness*—No duplicate or overlapping data.
- *Timeliness*—Data is available when it is required.

Two approaches in validating data quality are anomaly detection, which we discussed in section 2.5.6, and manually defined validations. In this chapter, we will discuss only manually defined validations. For example, a certain table may be updated hourly and occasionally have no updates for a few hours, but it may be highly unusual for two updates to be more than 24 hours apart. The validation condition is "latest timestamp is less than 24 hours ago."

Batch auditing with manually defined validations is a common requirement. A transaction supervisor (section 5.5) is one of many possible use cases, though a transaction supervisor does not just check whether data is valid but also returns any data differences between the multiple services/databases that it compares, as well as the operations needed to restore consistency to those services/databases.

10.1 Why is auditing necessary?

The first impression of this question may be that it doesn't make sense. We may argue that other than the case of a transaction supervisor, batch auditing may encourage bad practices.

For example, if we have a situation where data was invalid due to data loss in databases or file systems that are not replicated or backed up, then we should implement replication or backup instead of losing the data. However, replication or backup may take seconds or longer, and the leader host may fail before the data is successfully replicated or backed up.

> **Preventing data loss**
>
> One technique that prevents data loss from occurring due to late replication is quorum consistency (i.e., write to a majority of hosts/nodes in the cluster before returning a success response to the client). In Cassandra, a write is replicated to an in-memory data structure called Memtable across multiple nodes before returning a success response. Writing to memory is also much faster than writing to disk. The Memtable is flushed to disk (called an SSTable) either periodically or when it reaches a certain size (e.g., 4 MB).

If the leader host recovers, the data may be recovered and then replicated to other hosts. However, this will not work in certain databases like MongoDB that, depending on its configuration, can deliberately lose data from a leader host to maintain consistency (Arthur Ejsmont, *Web Scalability for Startup Engineers,* McGraw Hill Education, 2015, pp. 198–199. In a MongoDB database, if the write concern (https://www.mongodb.com/docs/manual/core/replica-set-write-concern/) is set to 1, all nodes must be consistent with the leader node. If a write to the leader node is successful, but the leader node fails before replication occurs, the other nodes use a consensus protocol to select a new leader. If the former leader node recovers, it will roll back any data that is different from the new leader node, including such writes.

We can also argue that data should be validated at the time a service receives it, not after it has already been stored to a database or file. For example, when a service receives invalid data, it should return the appropriate 4xx response and not persist this data. The following 4xx codes are returned for write requests with invalid data. Refer to sources like https://developer.mozilla.org/en-US/docs/Web/HTTP/Status#client_error_responses for more information

- *400 Bad Request*—This is a catch-all response for any request that the server perceives to be invalid.
- *409 Conflict*—The request conflicts with a rule. For example, an upload of a file that is older than the existing one on the server.
- *422 Unprocessable Entity*—The request entity has valid syntax but could not be processed. An example is a POST request with a JSON body containing invalid fields.

One more argument against auditing is that validation should be done in the database and application, rather than an external auditing process. We can consider using database constraints as much as possible because applications change much faster than databases. It is easier to change application code than database schema (do database migrations). At the application level, the application should validate inputs and outputs, and there should be unit tests on the input and output validation functions.

Database constraints

There are arguments that database constraints are harmful (https://dev.to/jonlauridsen/database-constraints-considered-harmful-38), that they are premature optimizations, do not capture all data integrity requirements, and make the system more difficult to test and to adjust to changing requirements. Some companies like GitHub (https://github.com/github/gh-ost/issues/331#issuecomment-266027731) and Alibaba (https://github.com/alibaba/Alibaba-Java-Coding-Guidelines#sql-rules) forbid foreign key constraints.

In practice, there will be bugs and silent errors. Here is an example that the author has personally debugged. A POST endpoint JSON body had a date field that should contain a future date value. POST requests were validated and then written to a SQL table. There was also a daily batch ETL job that processed objects marked with the current date. Whenever a client made a POST request, the backend validated that the client's date value had the correct format and was set up to one week in the future.

However, the SQL table contained a row with a date set five years in the future, and this went undetected for five years until the daily batch ETL job processed it, and the invalid result was detected at the end of a series of ETL pipelines. The engineers who wrote this code had left the company, which made the problem more difficult to debug. The author examined the git history and found that this one-week rule was not implemented until months after the API was first deployed to production and deduced that an invalid POST request had written this offending row. It was impossible to confirm this as there were no logs for the POST request because the log retention period was two weeks. A periodic auditing job on the SQL table would have detected this error, regardless of whether the job was implemented and started running long after the data was written.

Despite our best efforts to stop any invalid data from being persisted, we must assume that this will happen and be prepared for it. Auditing is another layer of validation checks.

A common practical use case for batch auditing is to validate large (e.g., >1 GB) files, especially files from outside our organization over which we have not been able to control how they were generated. It is too slow for a single host to process and validate each row. If we store the data in a MySQL table, we may use LOAD DATA (https://dev.mysql .com/doc/refman/8.0/en/load-data.html), which is much faster than INSERT, then run SELECT statements to audit the data. A SELECT statement will be much faster and also arguably easier than running a script over a file, especially if the SELECT takes advantage of indexes. If we use a distributed file system like HDFS, we can use NoSQL options like Hive or Spark with fast parallel processing.

Moreover, even if invalid values are found, we may decide that dirty data is better than no data and still store them in a database table.

Last, there are certain problems that only batch auditing can find, such as duplicate or missing data. Certain data validation may require previously ingested data; for example, anomaly detection algorithms use previously ingested data to process and spot anomalies in currently ingested data.

10.2 Defining a validation with a conditional statement on a SQL query's result

Terminology clarification: A table has rows and columns. An entry in a particular (row, column) coordinate can be referred to as a cell, element, datapoint, or value. In this chapter, we use these terms interchangeably.

Let's discuss how a manually defined validation can be defined by comparison operators on the results of a SQL query. The result of a SQL query is a 2D array, which we will name "result". We can define a conditional statement on result. Let's go over some examples. All these examples are daily validations, so we validate only yesterday's rows, and our example queries have the WHERE clause "Date(timestamp) > Curdate() - INTERVAL 1 DAY". In each example, we describe a validation, followed by its SQL query and then possible conditional statements.

Manually defined validations can be defined on

- *Individual datapoints of a column*—An example is the "latest timestamp is < 24 hours old" that we discussed previously.

```
SELECT COUNT(*) AS cnt
FROM Transactions
WHERE Date(timestamp) >= Curdate() - INTERVAL 1 DAY
```

Possible true conditional statements are `result[0][0] > 0` and `result['cnt'][0] > 0`.

Let's discuss another example. If a particular coupon code ID expires on a certain date, we can define a periodic validation on our transactions table that raises an alert if this code ID appears after this date. This may indicate that coupon code IDs are being recorded incorrectly.

```
SELECT COUNT(*) AS cnt
FROM Transactions
WHERE code_id = @code_id AND Date(timestamp) > @date
➥AND Date(timestamp) = Curdate() - INTERVAL 1 DAY
```

Possible true conditional statements are `result[0][0] == 0` and: `result['cnt'][0] == 0`.

- *Multiple datapoints of a column*—For example, if an individual app user cannot make more than five purchases per day, we can define a daily validation on our transactions table that raises an alert if there are more than five rows for any user ID since the previous day. This may indicate bugs, that a user was erroneously able to make more than five purchases that day, or that purchases are being incorrectly recorded.

```
SELECT user_id, count(*) AS cnt
FROM Transactions
WHERE Date(timestamp) = Curdate() - INTERVAL 1 DAY
GROUP BY user_id
```

The conditional statement is `result.length <= 5`.

Another possibility:

```
SELECT *
FROM (
  SELECT user_id, count(*) AS cnt
FROM Transactions
  WHERE Date(timestamp) = Curdate() - INTERVAL 1 DAY
  GROUP BY user_id
) AS yesterday_user_counts
WHERE cnt > 5;
```

The conditional statement is `result.length == 0`.

- *Multiple columns in a single row*—For example, the total number of sales that uses a particular coupon code cannot exceed 100 per day.

```
SELECT count(*) AS cnt
FROM Transactions
WHERE Date(timestamp) = Curdate() - INTERVAL 1 DAY
➥AND coupon_code = @coupon_code
```

The conditional statement is `result.length <= 100`.

An alternative query and conditional statement are as follows:

```
SELECT *
FROM (
  SELECT count(*) AS cnt
FROM Transactions
WHERE Date(timestamp) = Curdate() - INTERVAL 1 DAY
➥AND coupon_code = @coupon_code
) AS yesterday_user_counts
WHERE cnt > 100;
```

The conditional statement is `result.length == 0`.

- *Multiple tables*—For example, if we have a fact table sales_na to record sales in North America, that has a country_code column, we can create a dimension table country_codes that has a list of country codes for each geographical region. We can define a periodic validation that checks that all new rows have country_code values of countries within North America:

```
SELECT *
FROM sales_na S JOIN country_codes C ON S.country_code = C.id
WHERE C.region != 'NA';
```

The conditional statement is `result.length == 0`.

- *A conditional statement on multiple queries*—For example, we may wish to raise an alert if the number of sales on a day changes by more than 10% compared to the same day last week. We can run two queries and compare their results as follows. We append the query results to a `result` array, so this `result` array is 3D instead of 2D:

```
SELECT COUNT(*)
FROM sales
WHERE Date(timestamp) = Curdate()

SELECT COUNT(*)
FROM sales
WHERE Date(timestamp) = Curdate() - INTERVAL 7 DAY
```

The conditional statement is `Math.abs(result[0][0][0] - result[1][0][0]) / result[0][0][0] < 0.1`.

There are countless other possibilities for manually defined validations, such as:

- A minimum number of new rows can be written each hour to a table.
- A particular string column cannot contain null values, and string lengths must be between 1 and 255.
- A particular string column must have values that match a particular regex.
- A particular integer column should be nonnegative.

Some of these types of constraints can also be implemented by function annotations in ORM libraries (e.g., `@NotNull` and `@Length(min = 0, max = 255)`) in Hibernate or constraint types in Golang's SQL package. In this case, our auditing service serves as an additional layer of validation. Failed audits indicate silent errors in our service, which we should investigate.

This section's examples were in SQL. We can generalize this concept to define validation queries in other query languages like HiveQL, Trino (formerly called PrestoSQL), or Spark. Though our design focuses on defining queries using database query languages, we can also define validation functions in general purpose programming languages.

10.3 A simple SQL batch auditing service

In this section, we first discuss a simple script for auditing a SQL table. Next, we discuss how we can create a batch auditing job from this script.

10.3.1 An audit script

The simplest form of a batch auditing job is a script that does the following steps:

1 Runs a database query
2 Reads the result into a variable
3 Checks the value of this variable against certain conditions

The example Python script in the following listing runs a MySQL query that checks if the latest timestamp of our transactions table is < 24 hours old and prints the result to console.

Listing 10.1 Python script and MySQL query to check the latest timestamp

```python
import mysql

cnx = mysql.connector.connect(user='admin', password='password',
                              host='127.0.0.1',
                              database='transactions')
cursor = cnx.cursor()

query = """
SELECT COUNT(*) AS cnt
FROM Transactions
WHERE Date(timestamp) >= Curdate() - INTERVAL 1 DAY
"""

cursor.execute(query)
results = cursor.fetchall()
cursor.close()
cnx.close()

# result[0][0] > 0 is the condition.
print(result[0][0] > 0) # result['cnt'][0] > 0 also works.
```

We may need to run several database queries and compare their results. Listing 10.2 is a possible example.

Listing 10.2   An example script that compares the results of several queries

```
import mysql

queries = [
    {
    'database': 'transactions',

    'query': """
            SELECT COUNT(*) AS cnt
            FROM Transactions
            WHERE Date(timestamp) >= Curdate() - INTERVAL 1 DAY
    """,
},
{
    `database': 'transactions`,
    'query': """
            SELECT COUNT(*) AS cnt
            FROM Transactions
            WHERE Date(timestamp) >= Curdate() - INTERVAL 1 DAY
            """
    }
]

results = []
for query in queries:
    cnx = mysql.connector.connect(user='admin', password='password',
                        host='127.0.0.1',
                        database=query['database'])
        cursor = cnx.cursor()
    cursor.execute(query['query'])
    results.append(cursor.fetchall())
cursor.close()
cnx.close()

print(result[0][0][0] > result[1][0][0])
```

10.3.2 An audit service

Next, let's extend this to a batch auditing service. We can generalize the script to allow a user to specify

1 The SQL databases and queries.
2 The condition that will be run on the query result.

Let's implement a Python file template that we can name `validation.py.template`. Listing 10.3 is a possible implementation of this file. This is a simplified implementation. The batch auditing job is divided into two phases:

1 Run the database queries and use their results to determine whether the audit passed or failed.
2 If the audit failed, trigger an alert.

In a practical implementation, the login credentials will be supplied by a secrets management service, and the host is read from a configuration file. These details are outside the scope of this question. The user story for this service can be as follows:

1   The user logs in to the service and creates a new batch auditing job.
2   The user inputs the values for database, queries, and condition.
3   Our service will create a validation.py file from this `validation.py.template` and replace the parameters like `{database}` with the user's input values.
4   Our service creates a new Airflow or cron job that imports validation.py and runs the validation function.

We may notice that these validation.py files are essentially functions. A batch ETL service stores functions rather than objects.

We commented in the `validation.py.template` that we should create an Airflow task for each database query. Our backend should generate such a validation.py file. This will be a good coding interview exercise but is outside the scope of a system design interview.

> **Listing 10.3   A Python file template for an audit service**

```
from datetime import datetime, timedelta
from airflow import DAG
from airflow.operators.bash import BranchPythonOperator
import mysql.connector
import os
import pdpyras

# Example user inputs:
# {name} - ''
# {queries} - ['', '']
# {condition} - result[0][0][0] result[1][0][0]

def _validation():
  results = []
  # Database queries are expensive. An issue with running every query here
  # is that if a query fails, all queries need to be rerun.
  # We can consider instead creating an Airflow task for each query.
  for query in {queries}:
    cnx = mysql.connector.connect(user='admin', password='password',
                          host='127.0.0.1',
                          database=query['database'])
    cursor = cnx.cursor()
    cursor.execute(query['query'])
  results.append(cursor.fetchall())
  cursor.close()
  cnx.close()
  # XCom is an Airflow feature to share data between tasks.
  ti.xcom_push(key='validation_result_{name}', value={condition})

def _alert():
  # Some sample code to trigger a PagerDuty alert if the audit failed.
  # This is just an example and should not be taken as working code.
```

```
   # We may also wish to send this result to our Backend Service.
   # This is discussed later in this chapter.
   result = ti.xcom_pull(key='validation_result_{name}')
   if result:
     routing_key = os.environ['PD_API_KEY']
     session = pdpyras.EventsAPISession(routing_key)
     dedup_key = session.trigger("{name} validation failed", "audit")

with DAG(
    {name},
    default_args={
        'depends_on_past': False,
        'email': ['zhiyong@beigel.com'],
        'email_on_failure': True,
        'email_on_retry': False,
        'retries': 1,
        'retry_delay': timedelta(minutes=5),
    },
    description={description},
    schedule_interval=timedelta(days=1),
    start_date=datetime(2023, 1, 1),
    catchup=False,
    tags=['validation', {name}],
) as dag:
    t1 = BranchPythonOperator(
        task_id='validation',
        python_callable=_validation
    )
    # Alerting is a separate Airflow task, so in case the alert fails,
    # the Airflow job does not rerun the expensive validation function.
    t2 = BranchPythonOperator(
        task_id='alert',
        python_callable=_alert
    )
    t1 >> t2
```

10.4   *Requirements*

Let's design a system where users can define SQL, Hive, or Trino (formerly called Presto) queries for periodic batch audits of their database tables. Functional requirements are as follows:

- CRUD audit jobs. An audit job has the following fields:
  - Interval, such as minute, hour, day, or custom time intervals
  - Owners
  - A validation database query in SQL or related dialects like HQL, Trino, Cassandra, etc.
  - A conditional statement on the SQL query result
- A failed job should trigger an alert
- View logs of past and currently running jobs, including whether there were errors, and the results of their conditional statements. Users should also be able

to view the status and history of any triggered alerts, such as what time they were triggered and whether and, if so, what time they were marked as resolved.

- A job must complete within 6 hours.
- A database query must complete within 15 minutes. Our system should disallow jobs with long-running queries.

Non-functional requirements are as follows:

- *Scale*—We project that there will be less than 10000 jobs (i.e., 10000 database statements). The jobs and their logs are read only through our UI, so traffic is low.
- *Availability*—This is an internal system that no other systems directly depend on. High availability is not required.
- *Security*—Jobs have access control. A job can only be CRUD by its owners.
- *Accuracy*—The audit job result should be accurate as defined by the job's configuration.

10.5 *High-level architecture*

Figure 10.1 is an initial high-level architecture diagram of a hypothetical service for users to define periodic validation checks on their tables. We assume that the batch ETL service is an Airflow service or works similarly to Airflow. It stores the Python files of the batch jobs, runs them at their defined schedules, stores the status and history of these jobs, and returns Boolean values indicating if their audit conditions were true or false. Users will interact with our UI, which makes requests through our backend:

1 Users make requests to a shared batch ETL service to CRUD the batch auditing jobs, including checking on the status and history of these jobs.
2 Our shared batch ETL service is not an alerting service, so it does not have API endpoints to trigger alerts or to view the status and history of any triggered alerts. Users make requests to a shared alerting service via our UI and backend to view this information.

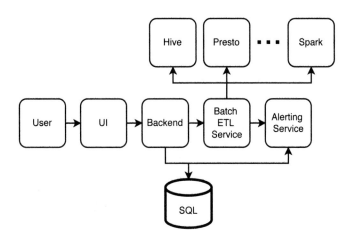

Figure 10.1 Initial high-level architecture of a hypothetical service for users to define periodic validation checks on their data.

When a user submits a request to create a batch auditing job, the following steps occur:

1 Our backend service creates the validation.py file by substituting user's input values into the template. Since this template is just a short string, it can be stored in memory on every backend service host.

2 Our backend service sends a request to the batch ETL service with this file. The batch ETL service creates the batch ETL job and stores this file, then returns a 200 success response to our backend service.

Our batch auditing service is essentially a wrapper over a shared Batch ETL Service.

An audit job's configuration has fields such as the job's owners, a cron expression, the database type (Hive, Trino, Spark, SQL, etc.) and the query to execute. The main SQL table will store the audit jobs' configurations, which we can name `job_config`. We can also create an `owner` table that maps jobs to their owners and has the columns `job_id` and `owner_id`.

Since validation queries can be defined in various SQL-like dialects, our batch ETL service is connected to various shared databases such as SQL, Hive, Trino, Spark, Cassandra, etc. If a job fails or there are any failed audits, the batch ETL service makes requests to a shared alerting service to alert the relevant persons. For security, we can use a shared OpenID Connect service for authentication, which is discussed in appendix B.

10.5.1 *Running a batch auditing job*

An audit job is periodically run with the configured time interval and has two main steps:

1 Run the database query.

2 Run the conditional statement with the database query's result.

Referring to section 4.6.1, a batch ETL job is created as a script (e.g., Python script in an Airflow service). When the user creates an audit job, our backend can generate the corresponding Python script. This generation can utilize a template script that we had predefined and implemented. This template script can contain several sections where the appropriate parameters (interval, database query, and conditional statement) are substituted.

The main scalability challenges are on the batch ETL service and possibly the alerting service, so a scalability discussion is about designing a scalable batch ETL service and scalable alerting service. Refer to chapter 9 for a detailed discussion on an alerting service.

Since the user's audit job is mainly defined as a validation function that runs an SQL statement, we also suggest using a Function as a Service (FaaS) platform and take advantage of its built-in scalability. We can create safeguards against anomalous queries, such as a 15-minute limit on query execution time, or suspend the job if the query result is invalid.

The result of each audit job run can be stored in our SQL database and accessed by users via our UI.

10.5.2 Handling alerts

Should alerts regarding failed audits be triggered by our batch ETL service or by our backend? Our first thought may be that it is our batch ETL service that runs the auditing jobs, so it should trigger such alerts. However, this means that the alerting functionalities used by our batch auditing service are split between two of its components:

- Requests to trigger alerts are made by our batch ETL service.
- Requests to view alert status and history are made from our backend service.

This means that the configuration to connect to our alerting service must be made on both services, which is additional maintenance overhead. A future team maintaining this batch auditing service may have different engineers who are unfamiliar with the code, and if there are problems with alerts, they may initially erroneously believe that interactions with the alerting service are all on one service and may waste time debugging on the wrong service before they find out that the problem was on the other service.

Thus, we may decide that all interactions with our alerting service should be on our backend service. A batch ETL job will only check if the condition is true or false and send this Boolean value to our backend service. If the value is false, our backend service will trigger an alert on our alerting service.

However, this approach may cause a possible bug. If the backend service host handling generating and making alert request crashes or becomes unavailable, the alert may not be sent. Some possible ways to prevent this bug are the following:

- The request from our batch ETL service to our backend service can be blocking, and the backend service returns a 200 only after it has successfully sent the alert request. We can rely on the retry mechanisms of our batch ETL service (such as the retry mechanisms in Airflow) to ensure the alert request is made. However, this approach means that our batch ETL service is essentially still making the alert request, and tightly couples these two services.
- Our batch ETL service can produce to a partitioned Kafka topic, and our backend service hosts can consume from these partitions, and checkpoint on each partition (possibly using SQL). However, this may cause duplicate alerts, as a backend service host may fail after making the alert request but before checkpointing. Our alerting service needs to be able to deduplicate alerts.

Our current architecture does both logging and monitoring. It logs the audit results to SQL. It monitors these audit jobs; if a job fails, our batch auditing service triggers an alert. Only alerting is done by a shared service.

An alternative approach is to log the audit job results both to SQL and a shared logging service. We can use another SQL table for checkpointing every few results.

Referring to the sequence diagram in figure 10.2, each time a host recovers from a failure, it can query this SQL table to obtain the last checkpoint. Writing duplicate logs to SQL is not a problem because we can simply use "INSERT INTO <table> IF NOT EXISTS…" statements. Writing duplicate results to the logging service can be handled in three ways:

1 Assume that the consequences of duplicate logs are trivial, and simply write them to the logging service.
2 The logging service should handle duplicates.
3 Query the logging service to determine whether a result exists before writing to it. This will double our traffic to the logging service.

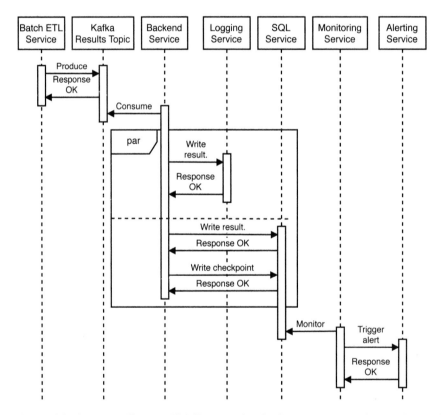

Figure 10.2   Sequence diagram which illustrates logging in parallel to a logging service and SQL service. We can monitor and alert on the SQL service.

Figure 10.3 shows our revised high-level architecture with our shared logging and monitoring services. Logging and alerting are decoupled from the batch ETL service. The developers of the batch ETL service need not be concerned with changes to the alerting service and vice versa, and the batch ETL service need not be configured to make requests to the alerting service.

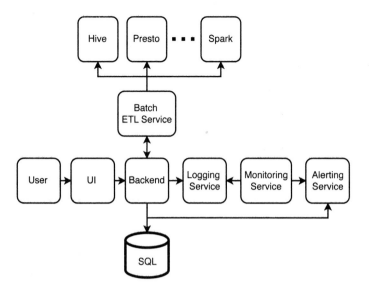

Figure 10.3   High-level architecture using shared services. Every service logs to the shared logging service, but we only illustrate its relationship with the backend and monitoring services.

10.6   *Constraints on database queries*

Database queries are the most expensive and longest-running computations in many services, including this one. For reasons including the following, the batch ETL service should be constrained in the rate and duration of queries it is allowed to run:

- The various database services are shared services. Any user who runs long and expensive queries significantly decreases the service's remaining capacity to serve queries by other users and increases the latency across the board. Queries consume CPU and memory on their hosts. Each connection to a database service also consumes a thread; the process on this thread executes the query and collects and returns the query results. We can allocate a thread pool containing a limited number of threads so there will never be too many concurrent queries.

- Our database services may be provided by third-party cloud providers who bill on usage, and expensive and long-running queries will cost a lot of money.

- The batch ETL service has a schedule of queries to execute. It must ensure that every query can be executed within its period. For example, an hourly query must complete within one hour.

We can implement techniques to parse a user's query definition as they author it in a job configuration, or when they submit the query together with the rest of the job configuration to our backend.

In this section, we discuss constraints we can implement on user queries to fulfill our system's requirements and control costs.

10.6.1   *Limit query execution time*

A simple way to prevent expensive queries is to limit query execution time to 10 minutes when the owner is creating or editing a job configuration and to 15 minutes when the job is running. When a user is authoring or editing a query in a job configuration, our backend should require the user to run the query and validate that it takes less than 10 minutes before allowing the user to save the query string. This will ensure that users are trained to keep their queries within a 10-minute limit. An alternative is to present a nonblocking/asynchronous experience. Allow a user to save a query, execute the query, then alert the user via email or chat of whether their query ran successfully within 10 minutes, so their job configuration is accepted or rejected accordingly. A tradeoff of this UX is that owners may be reluctant to change their query strings, so possible bugs or improvements may not be addressed.

We may wish to prevent multiple users from concurrently editing a query and overwriting each other's updates. Refer to section 2.4.2 for a discussion on preventing this.

If a query's execution exceeds 15 minutes, terminate the query, disable the job until the owner edits and validates the query, and trigger a high-urgency alert to the owners. If a query's execution exceeds 10 minutes, trigger a low-urgency alert to the job configuration's owners to warn them of the consequences that their query may exceed 15 minutes in the future.

10.6.2   *Check the query strings before submission*

Rather than making a user wait for minutes before saving a job configuration or informing the user 10 minutes after they saved a configuration that it was rejected, it will be more convenient to users if our UI can provide immediate feedback to them on their query strings as they are authoring them to prevent them from submitting job configurations with invalid or expensive queries. Such validation may include the following.

Do not allow full table scans. Allow queries to run on only tables that contain partition keys, and queries must contain filters on partition keys. We can also consider going a step further and limiting the number of partition key values within a query. To determine a table's partition keys, our backend will need to run a DESCRIBE query on the relevant database service. Do not allow queries that contain JOINs, which can be extremely expensive.

After a user defines a query, we can display the query execution plan to the user, which will allow the user to tune the query to minimize its execution time. This feature should be accompanied by references to guides on tuning queries in the relevant database query language. Refer to https://www.toptal.com/sql-server/sql-database-tuning-for-developers for a guide on SQL query tuning. For guides to tuning Hive queries, refer to https://cwiki.apache.org/confluence/display/Hive/LanguageManual+Explain or the chapter titled "Performance Considerations" in Dayang Du, *Apache Hive Essentials,* Packt Publishing, 2018.

10.6.3 *Users should be trained early*

Our users who author the queries should be instructed in these constraints early, so they can learn to adapt to these constraints. We should also provide good UX and instructive documentation to guide our users in these constraints. Moreover, these constraints should preferably be defined and set in an early release of our database batch auditing service, rather than added months after the first release. If our users were allowed to submit expensive queries before we impose these constraints, they may resist and argue against these constraints, and it may be difficult or impossible to persuade them to change their queries.

10.7 *Prevent too many simultaneous queries*

We should configure a limit for the number of simultaneous queries that the batch ETL service can execute. Each time a user submits a job configuration, which will contain a query to be run with a particular schedule, the backend can check the number of queries scheduled to be executed simultaneously on the same database and trigger an alert to our service's developers if the number of simultaneous queries approaches the estimated capacity. We can monitor the waiting time of each query before it begins execution and trigger low-urgency alerts if the waiting time exceeds 30 minutes or another benchmark value that we decide on. We can also investigate designing load-testing schemes to estimate the capacity. Our revised high-level architecture is illustrated in figure 10.4.

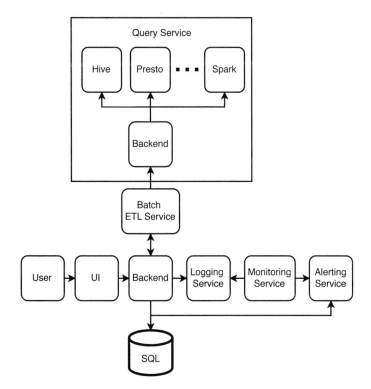

Figure 10.4 Revised high-level architecture with a shared query service through which other services make database requests.

Figure 10.4 contains a new database query service. Since the databases are shared services, cross-cutting concerns such as the configured limit on the number of simultaneous queries should be stored on the database query service, not in our database auditing service.

Another possible optimization is that the batch ETL service can query the alerting service via our backend service before running a database query to check whether there are any unresolved alerts. If so, there is no need to proceed with the audit job.

10.8   *Other users of database schema metadata*

To assist users in authoring queries, our service can automatically derive job configurations from schema metadata. For example, WHERE filters are usually defined on partition columns, so the UI can present query templates that suggest these columns to the user or suggest to the user to author a query that only tests the latest partition. By default, if a new partition passes an audit, our service should not schedule any more audits for that partition. Our users may have reasons to rerun the same audit despite it passing. For example, an audit job may contain bugs and erroneously pass, and the job owner may need to edit the audit job and rerun passing audits. So, our service may allow users to manually rerun an audit or schedule a limited number of audits on that partition.

Tables may have a freshness SLA on how often new roles are appended. This is related to the concept of *data freshness*, about how up-to-date or recent the data is. An audit on a table should not be done before the data is ready, as this is wasteful and will trigger false alerts. Perhaps the database query service can implement a feature to allow table owners to configure freshness SLAs on their tables, or we can develop a database metadata catalog/platform for our organization using a tool like Amundsen (https://www.amundsen.io/), DataHub (https://datahubproject.io/), or Metacat (https://github.com/Netflix/metacat).

Another useful feature of a database metadata platform is to record incidents regarding its tables. A table owner or our service can update the database metadata platform that a particular table is experiencing problems. Our database query service can warn any person or service that queries this table about the failed audits. A user who queries a table may query the table again in the future, so a useful feature in our database metadata platform is to allow users to subscribe to changes in the table's metadata or to be alerted to problems that affect the table.

Our batch ETL service can also monitor changes to database schema and respond accordingly. If a column's name was changed, it should update this column name in audit job configuration query strings that contain it. If a column is deleted, it should disable all related jobs and alert their owners.

10.9   *Auditing a data pipeline*

Figure 10.5 illustrates a data pipeline (such as an Airflow DAG) and its multiple tasks. Each task may write to certain table(s), which are read by the next stage. A job configuration can contain fields for "pipeline name" and "level," which can be added columns in our `job_config` table.

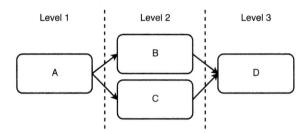

Figure 10.5   A sample data pipeline that has multiple stages. We can create audit jobs for each stage.

When a particular audit job fails, our service should do the following:

- Disable the downstream audits to save resources because it is a meaningless waste to execute audit jobs if their upstream jobs had failed.
- Disable other jobs that contain queries to this table and their downstream jobs, too.
- Trigger high-urgency alerts to the owners of all disabled jobs and to the owners of all downstream jobs.

We should also update our database metadata platform that this table has a problem. Any data pipeline that uses this table should disable all tasks downstream of this table, or bad data from this table may propagate into downstream tables. For example, machine-learning pipelines can use audit results to determine whether they should run, so experiments are not run with bad data. Airflow already allows users to configure *trigger rules* (https://airflow.apache.org/docs/apache-airflow/stable/concepts/dags .html#trigger-rules) so that each task runs only if all its dependencies or at least one dependency successfully finishes execution. Our new batch ETL service feature is an enhancement to Airflow and other workflow management platforms.

All this suggests that our batch ETL service can be generalized into a shared service, so it can provide this feature to batch ETL jobs across our organization.

When the user adds a new level to a pipeline, they also need to update the level values of all downstream tasks. As illustrated in figure 10.6, our backend can assist them by automatically incrementing the level numbers of downstream tasks.

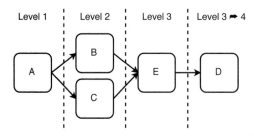

Level 1 ¦ Level 2 ¦ Level 3 ¦ Level 3 � 4

Figure 10.6   When we add a new task "E" in between levels 2 and 3, we can automatically increment the number(s) of the appropriate level(s), so level 3 becomes level 4.

10.10 *Logging, monitoring, and alerting*

Adding to what was discussed in section 2.5, we should monitor and send alerts for the following. The following logs may be useful to users and can be displayed on our UI:

- The current job status (e.g., started, in progress, succeeded, failed) and the time this status was logged.
- Failed batch ETL service database queries. The alert should also contain the reason for the failure, such as query time out or an error in query execution.
- As mentioned earlier, monitor the time taken to execute the database queries and raise alerts if this time exceeds a benchmark value we decide on.
- As mentioned earlier, alert job owners if upstream jobs fail.
- One-second P99 and 4xx and 5xx responses of our backend endpoints.
- One-second P99 and 4xx and 5xx responses on requests to external services.
- High traffic, defined by a request rate higher than our load limit, determined via load testing.
- High CPU, memory, or I/O utilization.
- High storage utilization in our SQL service (if we manage our own SQL service, rather than use a shared service).

4xx responses should trigger high-urgency alerts, while other problems can trigger low-urgency alerts.

10.11 *Other possible types of audits*

Besides the audits/tests discussed so far, we may also discuss other types of tests such as the following.

10.11.1 *Cross data center consistency audits*

It is common for the same data to be stored in multiple data centers. To ensure data consistency across data centers, our database batch auditing service may provide the ability to run sampling tests to compare data across data centers.

10.11.2 *Compare upstream and downstream data*

Referring to section 7.7 on data migrations, a user may need to copy data from one table to another. They can create an audit job to compare the latest partitions in the upstream and downstream tables to ensure data consistency.

10.12 *Other possible discussion topics*

Here are some other possible discussion topics during the interview:

- Design a scalable batch ETL service or a scalable alerting service. We will need a distributed event streaming platform like Kafka for both services.
- Code a function that generates the Airflow Python job from `validation.py .template` and other appropriate templates, with a separate Airflow task for each query, though this is a coding question, not a system design question.
- An audit job alert database table owners of data integrity problems in their tables, but we did not discuss how they can troubleshoot and discover the causes of these problems. How can table owners troubleshoot data integrity problems? Can we enhance our audit service, or what are other possibilities to help them?
- Certain audit jobs may fail on one run and then pass when the owner runs the same query while doing troubleshooting. How may owners troubleshoot such jobs, and what logging or features may our service provide to assist them?
- How may we find and deduplicate identical or similar audit jobs?
- Our database batch auditing service sends large numbers of alerts. A problem with a table may affect multiple audit jobs and trigger multiple alerts to the same user. How may we deduplicate alerts? Which parts of this alert deduplication logic will be implemented in our database batch auditing service, and which parts will be implemented in the shared alerting service?
- Our service can also allow tests to be triggered by certain events and not just run on a schedule. For example, we can track the number of rows changed after each query, sum these numbers, and run a test after a specified number of rows is changed. We can discuss possible events that can trigger tests and their system designs.

10.13 *References*

This chapter was inspired by Uber's Trust data quality platform, though many of the implementation details discussed in this chapter may be considerably different from Trust. A discussion of data quality at Uber can be found at https://eng.uber.com/ operational-excellence-data-quality/, though this article did not mention Trust by name. Refer to the article for an overview of Uber's data quality platform, including a discussion of its constituent services and their interactions between each other and users.

Summary

- During a system design interview, we can discuss auditing as a common approach to maintaining data integrity. This chapter discussed a possible system design for batch auditing.

- We can periodically run database queries to detect data irregularities, which may be due to various problems like unexpected user activity, silent errors, or malicious activity.

- We defined a common solution for detecting data irregularities that encompasses many use cases for these periodic database queries, and we designed a scalable, available, and accurate system.

- We can use task scheduling platforms like Airflow to schedule auditing jobs, rather than defining our own cron jobs, which are less scalable and more error prone.

- We should define the appropriate monitoring and alerting to keep users informed of successful or failed audit jobs. The periodic database auditing service also uses the alerting service, discussed in chapter 9, and OpenID Connect, discussed in appendix B.

- We can provide a query service for users to make ad hoc queries.

Autocomplete/typeahead

This chapter covers

- Comparing autocomplete with search
- Separating data collection and processing from querying
- Processing a continuous data stream
- Dividing a large aggregation pipeline into stages to reduce storage costs
- Employing the byproducts of data processing pipelines for other purposes

We wish to design an autocomplete system. Autocomplete is a useful question to test a candidate's ability to design a distributed system that continuously ingests and processes large amounts of data into a small (few MBs) data structure that users can query for a specific purpose. An autocomplete system obtains its data from strings submitted by up to billions of users and then processes this data into a weighted trie. When a user types in a string, the weighted trie provides them with autocomplete suggestions. We can also add personalization and machine learning elements to our autocomplete system.

11.1 Possible uses of autocomplete

We first discuss and clarify the intended use cases of this system to ensure we determine the appropriate requirements. Possible uses of autocomplete include:

- Complements a search service. While a user enters a search query, the autocomplete service returns a list of autocomplete suggestions with each keystroke. If the user selects a suggestion, the search service accepts it and returns a list of results.
  - General search, such as Google, Bing, Baidu, or Yandex.
  - Search within a specific document collection. Examples include Wikipedia and video-sharing apps.
- A word processor may provide autocomplete suggestions. When a user begins typing a word, they may be provided autocomplete suggestions for common words that begin with the user's currently entered prefix. Using a technique called fuzzy matching, the autocomplete feature can also be a spellcheck feature that suggests words with prefixes that closely match but are not identical to the user's currently entered prefix.
- An integrated development environment (IDE) (for coding) may have an autocomplete feature. The autocomplete feature can record variable names or constant values within the project directory and provide them as autocomplete suggestions whenever the user declares a variable or constant. Exact matches are required (no fuzzy matching).

An autocomplete service for each of these use cases will have different data sources and architecture. A potential pitfall in this interview (or other system design interviews in general) is to jump to conclusions and immediately assume that this autocomplete service is for a search service, which is a mistake you may make because you are most familiar with the autocomplete used in a search engine like Google or Bing.

Even if the interviewer gives you a specific question like "Design a system that provides autocomplete for a general search app like Google," you can spend half a minute discussing other possible uses of autocomplete. Demonstrate that you can think beyond the question and do not make hasty assumptions or jump to conclusions.

11.2 Search vs. autocomplete

We must distinguish between autocomplete and search and not get their requirements mixed up. This way, we will design an autocomplete service rather than a search service. How is autocomplete similar and different from search? Similarities include the following:

- Both services attempt to discern a user's intentions based on their search string and return a list of results sorted by most likely match to their intention.
- To prevent inappropriate content from being returned to users, both services may need to preprocess the possible results.

- Both services may log user inputs and use them to improve their suggestions/ results. For example, both services may log the results that are returned and which the user clicks on. If the user clicks on the first result, it indicates that this result is more relevant to that user.

Autocomplete is conceptually simpler than search. Some high-level differences are described in table 11.1. Unless the interviewer is interested, do not spend more than a minute dwelling on these differences in the interview. The point is to demonstrate critical thinking and your ability to see the big picture.

Table 11.1 Some differences between search and autocomplete

Search	Autocomplete
Results are usually a list of webpage URLs or documents. These documents are preprocessed to generate an index. During a search query, the search string is matched to the index to retrieve relevant documents.	Results are lists of strings, generated based on user search strings.
P99 latency of a few seconds may be acceptable. Higher latency of up to a minute may be acceptable in certain circumstances.	Low latency of ~100 ms P99 desired for good user experience. Users expect suggestions almost immediately after entering each character.
Various result data types are possible, including strings, complex objects, files, or media.	Result data type is just string.
Each result is given a relevance score.	Does not always have a relevance score. For example, an IDE's autocomplete result list may be lexicographically ordered.
Much effort is expended to compute relevance scores as accurately as possible, where accuracy is perceived by the user.	Accuracy requirements (e.g., user clicks on one of the first few suggestions rather than a later one) may not be as strict as search. This is highly dependent on business requirements, and high accuracy may be required in certain use cases.
A search result may return any of the input documents. This means every document must be processed, indexed, and possible to return in a search result. For lower complexity, we may sample the contents of a document, but we must process every single document.	If high accuracy is not required, techniques like sampling and approximation algorithms can be used for lower complexity.
May return hundreds of results.	Typically returns 5–10 results.
A user can click on multiple results, by clicking the "back" button and then clicking another result. This is a feedback mechanism we can draw many possible inferences from.	Different feedback mechanism. If none of the autocomplete suggestions match, the user finishes typing their search string and then submits it.

11.3   *Functional requirements*

We can have the following Q&A with our interviewer to discuss the functional requirements of our autocomplete system.

11.3.1   *Scope of our autocomplete service*

We can first clarify some details of our scope, such as which use cases and languages
should be supported:

- Is this autocomplete meant for a general search service or for other use cases like
  a word processor or IDE?
  - It is for suggesting search strings in a general search service.
- Is this only for English?
  -- Yes.
- How many words must it support?
  - The Webster English dictionary has ~470K words (https://www.merriam
    -webster.com/help/faq-how-many-english-words), while the Oxford English
    dictionary has >171K words (https://www.lexico.com/explore/how-many
    -words-are-there-in-the-english-language). We don't know how many of these
    words are at least 6 characters in length, so let's not make any assumptions.
    We may wish to support popular words that are not in the dictionary, so let's
    support a set of up to 100K words. With an average English word length of 4.7
    (rounded to 5) letters and 1 byte/letter, our storage requirement is only 5 MB.
    Allowing manual (but not programmatic) addition of words and phrases neg-
    ligibly increase our storage requirement.

NOTE   The IBM 350 RAMAC introduced in 1956 was the first computer with
a 5 MB hard drive (https://www.ibm.com/ibm/history/exhibits/650/650_pr2
.html). It weighed over a ton and occupied a footprint of 9 m (30 ft) by 15 m
(50 ft). Programming was done in machine language and wire jumpers on a
plugboard. There were no system design interviews back then.

11.3.2   *Some UX details*

We can clarify some UX (user experience) details of the autocomplete suggestions,
such as whether the autocomplete suggestions should be on sentences or individual words or how many characters a user should enter before seeing autocomplete
suggestions:

- Is the autocomplete on words or sentences?
  - We can initially consider just words and then extend to phrases or sentences if we have time.
- Is there a minimum number of characters that should be entered before suggestions are displayed?
  - 3 characters sound reasonable.
- Is there a minimum length for suggestions? It's not useful for a user to get suggestions for 4 or 5-letter words after typing in 3 characters, since those are just 1 or 2 more letters.
  - Let's consider words with at least 6 letters.
- Should we consider numbers or special characters, or just letters?
  - Just letters. Ignore numbers and special characters.
- How many autocomplete suggestions should be shown at a time, and in what order?
  - Let's display 10 suggestions at a time, ordered by most to least frequent. First, we can provide a suggestions API GET endpoint that accepts a string and returns a list of 10 dictionary words ordered by decreasing priority. Then we can extend it to also accept user ID to return personalized suggestions.

11.3.3 Considering search history

We need to consider if the autocomplete suggestions should be based only on the user's current input or on their search history and other data sources.

- Limiting the suggestions to a set of words implies that we need to process users' submitted search strings. If the output of this processing is an index from which autocomplete suggestions are obtained, does previously processed data need to be reprocessed to include these manually added and removed words/phrases?
  - Such questions are indicative of engineering experience. We discuss with the interviewer that there will be a substantial amount of past data to reprocess. But why will a new word or phrase be manually added? It will be based on analytics of past user search strings. We may consider an ETL pipeline that creates tables easy to query for analytics and insights.
- What is the data source for suggestions? Is it just the previously submitted queries, or are there other data sources, such as user demographics?
  - It's a good thought to consider other data sources. Let's use only the submitted queries. Maybe an extensible design that may admit other data sources in the future will be a good idea.
- Should it display suggestions based on all user data or the current user data (i.e., personalized autocomplete)?
  - Let's start with all user data and then consider personalization.

- What period should be used for suggestions?
  - Let's first consider all time and then maybe consider removing data older than a year. We can use a cutoff date, such as not considering data before January 1 of last year.

11.3.4 Content moderation and fairness

We can also consider other possible features like content moderation and fairness:

- How about a mechanism to allow users to report inappropriate suggestions?
  - That will be useful, but we can ignore it for now.
- Do we need to consider if a small subset of users submitted most of the searches? Should our autocomplete service try to serve the majority of users by processing the same number of searches per user?
  - No, let's consider only the search strings themselves. Do not consider which users made them.

11.4 Non-functional requirements

After discussing the functional requirements, we can have a similar Q&A to discuss the non-functional requirements. This may include a discussion of possible tradeoffs such as availability versus performance:

- It should be scalable so it can be used by a global user base.
- High availability is not needed. This is not a critical feature, so fault-tolerance can be traded off.
- High performance and throughput are necessary. Users must see autocomplete suggestions within half a second.
- Consistency is not required. We can allow our suggestions to be hours out of date; new user searches do not need to immediately update the suggestions.
- For privacy and security, no authorization or authentication is needed to use autocomplete, but user data should be kept private.
- Regarding accuracy, we can reason the following:
  - We may wish to return suggestions based on search frequency, so we can count the frequency of search strings. We can decide that such a count does not need to be accurate, and an approximation is sufficient in our first design pass. We can consider better accuracy if we have time, including defining accuracy metrics.
  - We will not consider misspellings or mixed-language queries. Spellcheck will be useful, but let's ignore it in this question.

- Regarding potentially inappropriate words and phrases, we can limit the suggestions to a set of words, which will prevent inappropriate words, but not phrases. Let's refer to them as "dictionary words," even though they may include words that we added and not from a dictionary. If you like, we can design a mechanism for admins to manually add and remove words and phrases from this set.
- On how up to date the suggestions should be, we can have a loose requirement of 1 day.

11.5 Planning the high-level architecture

We can begin the design thought process of a system design interview by sketching a very high-level initial architecture diagram such as figure 11.1. Users submit search queries, which the ingestion system processes and then stores in the database. Users receive autocomplete suggestions from our database when they are typing their search strings. There may be other intermediate steps before a user receives their autocomplete suggestions, which we label as the query system. This diagram can guide our reasoning process.

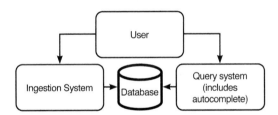

Figure 11.1 A very high-level initial architecture of our autocomplete service. Users submit their strings to the ingestion system, which are saved to the database. Users send requests to the query system for autocomplete suggestions. We haven't discussed where the data processing takes place.

Next, we reason that we can break up the system into the following components:

1 Data ingestion
2 Data processing
3 Query the processed data to obtain autocomplete suggestions.

Data processing is generally more resource-intensive than ingestion. Ingestion only needs to accept and log requests and must handle traffic spikes. So, to scale up, we split the data processing system from the ingestion system. This is an example of the Command Query Responsibility Segregation (CQRS) design pattern discussed in chapter 1.

Another factor to consider is that the ingestion system can actually be the search service's logging service, that can also be the organization's shared logging service.

11.6   *Weighted trie approach and initial high-level architecture*

Figure 11.2 shows our initial high-level architecture of our Autocomplete System. Our Autocomplete System is not a single service but a system where users only query one service (the autocomplete service) and do not directly interact with the rest of the system. The rest of the system serves to collect users' search strings and periodically generate and deliver a weighted trie to our autocomplete service.

The shared logging service is the raw data source from which our autocomplete service derives the autocomplete suggestions that it provides to its users. Search service users send their queries to the search service, which logs them to the logging service. Other services also log to this shared logging service. The autocomplete service may query the logging service for just the search service logs or other services' logs, too, if we find those useful to improve our autocomplete suggestions.

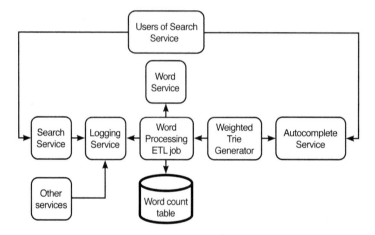

Figure 11.2   Initial high-level architecture of our Autocomplete System. Users of our search service submit their search strings to the search service, and these strings are logged to a shared logging service. The Word Processing ETL job may be a batch or streaming job that reads and processes the logged search strings. The weighted trie generator reads the word counts and generates the weighted trie and then sends it to the autocomplete service, from which users obtain autocomplete suggestions.

The shared logging service should have an API for pulling log messages based on topic and timestamp. We can tell the interviewer that its implementation details, such as which database it uses (MySQL, HDFS, Kafka, Logstash, etc.), are irrelevant to our current discussion, since we are designing the autocomplete service, not our organization's shared logging service. We add that we are prepared to discuss the implementation details of a shared logging service if necessary.

Users retrieve autocomplete suggestions from the autocomplete service's backend. Autocomplete suggestions are generated using a weighted trie, illustrated in figure 11.3. When a user enters a string, the string is matched with the weighted trie. The result list is generated from the children of the matched string, sorted by decreasing weight. For example, a search string "ba" will return the result ["bay", "bat"]. "bay" has a weight of 4 while "bat" has a weight of 2, so "bay" is before "bat."

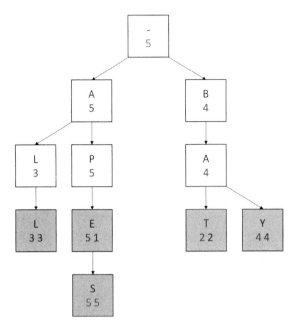

Figure 11.3 A weighted trie of the words "all", "apes," "bat," and "bay." (Source: https://courses .cs.duke.edu/cps100/spring16/autocomplete/trie.html.)

We shall now discuss the detailed implementation of these steps.

11.7 Detailed implementation

The weighted trie generator can be a daily batch ETL pipeline (or a streaming pipeline if real-time updates are required). The pipeline includes the word processing ETL job. In figure 11.2, the word processing ETL job and weighted trie generator are separate pipeline stages because the word processing ETL job can be useful for many other purposes and services, and having separate stages allows them to be implemented, tested, maintained, and scaled independently.

Our word count pipeline may have the following tasks/steps, illustrated as a DAG in figure 11.4:

1 Fetch the relevant logs from the search topic of the logging service (and maybe other topics) and place them in a temporary storage.

2 Split the search strings into words.

3 Filter out inappropriate words.

4 Count the words and write to a word count table. Depending on required accuracy, we can count every word or use an approximation algorithm like count-min sketch (described in section 17.7.1).

5 Filter for appropriate words and record popular unknown words.

6 Generate the weighted trie from the word count table.

7 Send the weighted trie to our backend hosts.

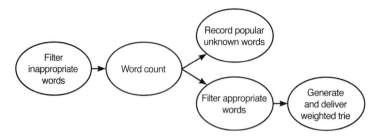

Figure 11.4   DAG of our word count pipeline. Recording popular unknown words and filtering appropriate words can be done independently.

We can consider various database technologies for our raw search log:

- An Elasticsearch index partitioned by day, part of a typical ELK stack, with a default retention period of seven days.
- The logs of each day can be an HDFS file (i.e., partitioned by day). User searches can be produced to a Kafka topic with a retention period of a few days (rather than just one day, in case we need to look at older messages for any reason). At a certain set time each day, the first pipeline stage will consume messages until it reaches a message with a timestamp more recent than the set time (this means it consumes one additional message, but this slight imprecision is fine) or until the topic is empty. The consumer creates a new HDFS directory for the partition corresponding to that date and appends all messages to a single file within that directory. Each message can contain a timestamp, user ID, and the search string. HDFS does not offer any mechanism to configure a retention period, so for those choices, we will need to add a stage to our pipeline to delete old data.
- SQL is infeasible because it requires all the data to fit into a single node.

Let's assume that the logging service is an ELK service. As mentioned in section 4.3.5, HDFS is a common storage system for the MapReduce programming model. We use the MapReduce programming model to parallelize data processing over many nodes. We can use Hive or Spark with HDFS. If using Hive, we can use Hive on Spark (https://spark.apache.org/docs/latest/sql-data-sources-hive-tables.html), so both our Hive or Spark approaches are actually using Spark. Spark can read and write from HDFS into memory and process data in memory, which is much faster than processing on disk. In subsequent sections, we briefly discuss implementations using Elasticsearch, Hive, and Spark. A thorough discussion of code is outside the scope of a system design interview, and a brief discussion suffices.

This is a typical ETL job. In each stage, we read from the database storage of the previous stage, process the data, and write to the database storage to be used by the next stage.

11.7.1 *Each step should be an independent task*

Referring again to the batch ETL DAG in figure 11.4, why is each step an independent stage? When we first develop an MVP, we can implement the weighted trie generation as a single task and simply chain all the functions. This approach is simple, but not maintainable. (Complexity and maintainability seem to be correlated, and a simple system is usually easier to maintain, but here we see an example where there are tradeoffs.)

We can implement thorough unit testing on our individual functions to minimize bugs, implement logging to identify any remaining bugs that we encounter in production, and surround any function that may throw errors with try-catch blocks and log these errors. Nonetheless, we may miss certain problems, and if any error in our weighted trie generation crashes the process, the entire process needs to restart from the beginning. These ETL operations are computationally intensive and may take hours to complete, so such an approach has low performance. We should implement these steps as separate tasks and use a task scheduler system like Airflow, so each task only runs after the previous one successfully completes.

11.7.2 *Fetch relevant logs from Elasticsearch to HDFS*

For Hive, we can use a `CREATE  EXTERNAL  TABLE` command (https://www.elastic .co/guide/en/elasticsearch/hadoop/current/hive.html#_reading_data_from_ elasticsearch) to define a Hive table on our Elasticsearch topic. Next, we can write the logs to HDFS using a Hive command like `INSERT OVERWRITE DIRECTORY '/path/ to/output/dir' SELECT * FROM Log WHERE created_at = date_sub(current_ date, 1);`. (This command assumes we want yesterday's logs.)

For Spark, we can use the SparkContext esRDD method (https://www.elastic .co/guide/en/elasticsearch/hadoop/current/spark.html#spark-read) to connect to our Elasticsearch topic, followed by a Spark filter query (https://spark.apache.org/ docs/latest/api/sql/index.html#filter) to read the data for the appropriate dates, and then write to HDFS using the Spark saveAsTextFile function (https:// spark.apache.org/docs/latest/api/scala/org/apache/spark/api/java/JavaRDD .html#saveAsTextFile(path:String):Unit).

During an interview, even if we don't know that Hive or Spark has Elasticsearch integrations, we can tell our interviewer that such integrations may exist because these are popular mainstream data platforms. If such integrations don't exist, or if our interviewer asks us to, we may briefly discuss how to code a script to read from one platform and write to another. This script should take advantage of each platform's parallel processing capabilities. We may also discuss partitioning strategies. In this step, the input/ logs may be partitioned by service, while the output is partitioned by date. During this stage, we can also trim whitespace from both ends of the search strings.

11.7.3 *Split the search strings into words and other simple operations*

Next, we split the search strings by whitespace with the split function. (We may also need to consider common problems like the users omitting spaces (e.g., "HelloWorld") or using other separators like a period, dash, or comma. In this chapter, we assume that these problems are infrequent, and we can ignore them. We may wish to do analytics on the search logs to find out how common these problems actually are.) We will refer to these split strings as "search words." Refer to https://cwiki.apache.org/confluence/display/Hive/LanguageManual+UDF#LanguageManualUDF-StringFunctions for Hive's split function and https://spark.apache.org/docs/latest/api/sql/index.html#split for Spark's split function. We read from the HDFS file in the previous step and then split the strings.

At this stage, we can also perform various simple operations that are unlikely to change over the lifetime of our system, such as filtering for strings that are at least six characters long and contain only letters (i.e., no numbers or special characters), and lowercasing all strings so we will not have to consider case in further processing. We then write these strings as another HDFS file.

11.7.4 *Filter out inappropriate words*

We will consider these two parts in filtering for appropriate words or filtering out inappropriate words:

1 Managing our lists of appropriate and inappropriate words.
2 Filtering our list of search words against our lists of appropriate and inappropriate words.

WORDS SERVICE

Our words service has API endpoints to return sorted lists of appropriate or inappropriate words. These lists will be at most a few MB and are sorted to allow binary search. Their small size means that any host that fetches the lists can cache them in memory in case the words service is unavailable. Nonetheless, we can still use our typical horizontally scaled architecture for our words service, consisting of stateless UI and backend services, and a replicated SQL service as discussed in section 3.3.2. Figure 11.5 shows our high-level architecture of our words service, which is a simple application to read and write words to a SQL database. The SQL tables for appropriate and inappropriate words may contain a string column for words, and other columns that provide information such as the timestamp when the word was added to the table, the user who added this word, and an optional string column for notes such as why the word was appropriate or inappropriate. Our words service provides a UI for admin users to view the lists of appropriate and inappropriate words and manually add or remove words, all of which are API endpoints. Our backend may also provide endpoints to filter words by category or to search for words.

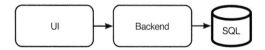

Figure 11.5   High-level architecture of our words service

FILTERING OUT INAPPROPRIATE WORDS

Our word count ETL pipeline requests our words service for the inappropriate words and then writes this list to an HDFS file. We might already have an HDFS file from a previous request. Our words service admins might have deleted certain words since then, so the new list might not have the words that are present in our old HDFS file. HDFS is append-only, so we cannot delete individual words from the HDFS file but instead must delete the old file and write a new file.

With our HDFS file of inappropriate words, we can use the `LOAD DATA` command to register a Hive table on this file and then filter out inappropriate words with a simple query such as the following and then write the output to another HDFS file.

We can determine which search strings are inappropriate words using a distributed analytics engine such as Spark. We can code in PySpark or Scala or use a Spark SQL query to JOIN the users' words with the appropriate words.

In an interview, we should spend less than 30 seconds on an SQL query to scribble down the important logic as follows. We can briefly explain that we want to manage our 50 minutes well, so we do not wish to spend precious minutes to write a perfect SQL query. The interviewer will likely agree that this is outside the scope of a system design interview, that we are not there to display our SQL skills, and allow us to move on. A possible exception is if we are interviewing for a data engineer position:

- Filters, such as WHERE clauses
- JOIN conditions
- Aggregations, such as AVG, COUNT, DISTINCT, MAX, MIN, PERCENTILE, RANK, ROW_NUMBER, etc.

```
SELECT word FROM words WHERE word NOT IN (SELECT word from inappropriate_
words);
```

Since our inappropriate words table is small, we can use a *map join* (mappers in a MapReduce job perform the join. Refer to https://cwiki.apache.org/confluence/display/hive/languagemanual+joins) for faster performance:

```
SELECT /*+ MAPJOIN(i) */ w.word FROM words w LEFT OUTER JOIN inappropriate_
words i ON i.word = w.word WHERE i.word IS NULL;
```

Broadcast hash join in Spark is analogous to map join in Hive. A broadcast hash join occurs between a small variable or table that can fit in memory of each node (in Spark, this is set in the `spark.sql.autoBroadcastJoinThreshold` property, which is 10 MB by default), and a larger table that needs to be divided among the nodes. A broadcast hash join occurs as follows:

1 Create a hash table on the smaller table, where the key is the value to be joined on and the value is the entire row. For example, in our current situation, we are joining on a word string, so a hash table of the inappropriate_words table that has the columns ("word," "created_at," "created_by") may contain entries like

{("apple", ("apple", 1660245908, "brad")), ("banana", ("banana", 1550245908, "grace")), ("orange", ("orange", 1620245107, "angelina")) . . . }.

2 Broadcast/copy this hash table to all nodes performing the join operation.

3 Each node JOINs the smaller table to the node's portion of the larger table.

If both tables cannot fit in memory, a shuffled sort merge join is done, where both datasets are shuffled, the records are sorted by key, and a merge join is done where both sides are iterated and joined based on the join key. This approach assumes that we don't need to keep statistics on inappropriate words. Here are some resources for further reading on Spark joins:

- https://spark.apache.org/docs/3.3.0/sql-performance-tuning.html#join -strategy-hints-for-sql-queries or https://spark.apache.org/docs/3.3.0/rdd -programming-guide.html#broadcast-variables. The official Spark documentation for the various Spark JOIN strategies to improve JOIN performance. It states the various JOIN strategies available but does not discuss their detailed mechanisms. Refer to the resources below for thorough discussions.

- https://spark.apache.org/docs/3.3.0/sql-performance-tuning.html#join -strategy-hints-for-sql-queries

- Damiji, J. et al. A Family of Spark Joins. In *Learning Spark, 2ⁿᵈ Edition.* O'Reilly Media, 2020.

- Chambers, B. and Zaharia, M. Joins. *In Spark: The Definitive Guide: Big Data Processing Made Simple.* O'Reilly Media, 2018.

- https://docs.qubole.com/en/latest/user-guide/engines/hive/hive-mapjoin -options.html

- https://towardsdatascience.com/strategies-of-spark-join-c0e7b4572bcf

11.7.5 *Fuzzy matching and spelling correction*

A final processing step before we count the words is to correct misspellings in users' search words. We can code a function that accepts a string, uses a library with a *fuzzy matching* algorithm to correct possible misspelling, and returns either the original string or fuzzy-matched string. (Fuzzy matching, also called approximate string matching, is the technique of finding strings that match a pattern approximately. An overview of fuzzy matching algorithms is outside the scope of this book.) We can then use Spark to run this function in parallel over our list of words divided into evenly sized sublists and then write the output to HDFS.

This spelling correction step is its own independent task/stage because we have multiple fuzzy matching algorithms and libraries or services to choose from, so we may choose a particular algorithm to optimize for our requirements. Keeping this stage separate allows us to easily switch between a library or service for fuzzy matching, as changes to this pipeline stage will not affect the other stages. If we use a library, we may need to update it to keep up with changing trends and popular new words.

11.7.6 *Count the words*

We are now ready to count the words. This can be a straightforward MapReduce operation, or we can use an algorithm like count-min sketch (refer to section 17.7.1).

The Scala code below implements the MapReduce approach. This code was slightly modified from https://spark.apache.org/examples.html. We map the words in the input HDFS file to (`String, Int`) pairs called `counts`, sort by descending order of counts and then save it as another HDFS file:

```
val textFile = sc.textFile("hdfs://...")
val counts = textFile.map(word => (word, 1)).reduceByKey(_ + _).map(item =>
item.swap).sortByKey(false).map(item => item.swap)
counts.saveAsTextFile("hdfs://...")
```

11.7.7 *Filter for appropriate words*

The word-counting step should significantly reduce the number of words to be filtered. Filtering for appropriate words is very similar to filtering for inappropriate words in section 11.7.4.

We can use a simple Hive command such as `SELECT word FROM counted_words WHERE word IN (SELECT word FROM appropriate_words);` to filter for appropriate words, or a Map Join or broadcast hash join such as `SELECT /*+ MAPJOIN(a) */ c.word FROM counted_words c JOIN appropriate_words a on c.word = a.word;`.

11.7.8 *Managing new popular unknown words*

After counting the words in the previous step, we may find new popular words in the top 100, which were previously unknown to us. In this stage, we write these words to the Words Service, which can write them to a SQL unknown_words table. Similar to section 11.7.4, our words service provides UI features and backend endpoints to allow operations staff to manually choose to add these words to the lists of appropriate or inappropriate words.

As illustrated in our word count batch ETL job DAG in figure 11.4, this step can be done independently and in parallel with the filtering for appropriate words.

11.7.9 *Generate and deliver the weighted trie*

We now have the list of top appropriate words to construct our weighted trie. This list is only a few MB, so the weighted trie can be generated on a single host. The algorithm to construct a weighted trie is outside the scope of a system design interview. It is a possible coding interview question. A partial Scala class definition is as follows, but we code in the language of our backend:

```
class TrieNode(var children: Array[TrieNode], var weight: Int) {
  // Functions for
  // - create and return a Trie node.
  // - insert a node into the Trie.
  // - getting the child with the highest weight.
}
```

We serialize the weighted trie to JSON. The trie is a few MB in size, which may be too large to be downloaded to the client each time the search bar is displayed to the user but is small enough to replicate to all hosts. We can write the trie to a shared object store such as AWS S3 or a document database such as MongoDB or Amazon DocumentDB. Our backend hosts can be configured to query the object store daily and fetch the updated JSON string. The hosts can query at random times, or they can be configured to query at the same time with some jitter to prevent a large number of simultaneous requests from overwhelming the object store.

If a shared object is large (e.g., gigabytes), we should consider placing it in a CDN. Another advantage of this small trie is that a user can download the entire trie when they load our search app, so the trie lookup is client-side rather than server-side. This greatly reduces the number of requests to our backend, which has advantages such as the following:

- If the network is unreliable or slow, a user may sporadically not get suggestions as they enter their search string, which is a poor user experience.
- When the trie is updated, a user that is in the middle of typing in a search string may notice the change. For example, if the strings in the old trie were related in some way, the new trie may not possess these relationships, and the user notices this sudden change. Or if the user does backspace on a few characters, they may notice the suggestions are different from before.

If we have a geographically distributed user base, network latency becomes unacceptable, given our requirement for high performance. We can provision hosts in multiple data centers, though this may be costly and introduce replication lag. A CDN is a cost-effective choice.

Our autocomplete service should provide a PUT endpoint to update its weighted trie, which this stage will use to deliver the generated weighted trie to our autocomplete service.

11.8 Sampling approach

If our autocomplete does not require high accuracy, we should do sampling, so most of the operations to generate the weighted trie can be done within a single host, which has many advantages including the following:

- The trie will be generated much faster.
- As the trie can be generated much faster, it will be easier test code changes before deploying them to the production environment. The overall system will be easier to develop, debug, and maintain.
- Consumes much less hardware resources, including processing, storage, and network.

Sampling can be done at most steps:

1 Sampling the search strings from the logging service. This approach has the lowest accuracy but also the lowest complexity. We may need a large sample to obtain a statistically significant number of words, which are at least six characters long.

2 Sampling words after splitting the search strings to individual words and filtering for words that are at least six characters long. This approach avoids the computational expense of filtering for appropriate words, and we may not need as large a sample as the previous approach.

3 Sampling words after filtering for appropriate words. This approach has the highest accuracy but also the highest complexity.

11.9 Handling storage requirements

Based on our high-level architecture, we can create tables with the following columns, using each table to populate the next:

1 Raw search requests with timestamp, user ID, and search string. This table can be used for many other purposes besides autocomplete (e.g., analytics to discover user interests and trending search terms).

2 After splitting the raw search strings, the individual words can be appended to a table that contains columns for date and word.

3 Determine which search strings are dictionary words and generate a table that contains date (copied from the previous table), user ID, and dictionary word.

4 Aggregate the dictionary words into a table of word counts.

5 Create a weighted trie to provide autocomplete suggestions.

Let's estimate the amount of storage required. We assume one billion users; each user submits 10 searches daily with an average of 20 characters per search. Each day, there may be approximately 1B * 10 * 20 = 200 GB of search strings. We may delete old data once a month, so at any time we have up to 12 months of data, so the search log will need 200 GB * 365 = 73 TB just for the search strings column. If we wish to reduce storage costs, we can consider various ways.

One way is to trade off accuracy, by using approximation and sampling techniques. For example, we may sample and store only ~10% of user searches and generate the trie only on this sample.

Another way is illustrated in figure 11.6. Figure 11.6 illustrates a batch ETL job that aggregates and roll up data at various periods to reduce the amount of data stored. At each stage, we can overwrite the input data with the rolled-up data. At any time, we will have up to one day of raw data, four weeks of data rolled up by week, and 11 months of data rolled up by month. We can further reduce storage requirements by keeping only the top 10% or 20% most frequent strings from each rollup job.

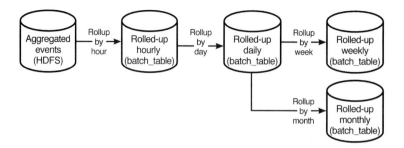

Figure 11.6 Flow diagram of our batch pipeline. We have a rollup job that progressively rolls up by increasing time intervals to reduce the number of rows processed in each stage.

This approach also improves scalability. Without the rollup job, a word count batch ETL job will need to process 73 TB of data, which will take many hours and be monetarily expensive. The rollup job reduces the amount of data processed for the final word count used by the weighted trie generator.

We can set a short retention period on logging service, such as 14–30 days, so its storage requirement will be just 2.8–6 TB. Our daily weighted trie generator batch ETL job can be done on the weekly or monthly rolled up data. Figure 11.7 illustrates our new high-level architecture with the rollup jobs.

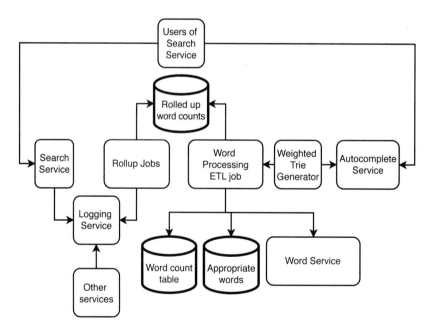

Figure 11.7 High-level architecture of our Autocomplete System with the rollup jobs. By aggregating/rolling up word counts over progressively larger intervals, we can reduce overall storage requirements, and the cluster size of the word processing ETL job.

11.10 Handling phrases instead of single words

In this section, we discuss a couple of considerations for extending our system to handle phrases instead of single words. The trie will become bigger, but we can still limit it to a few MB by keeping only the most popular phrases.

11.10.1 Maximum length of autocomplete suggestions

We can keep to our previous decision that autocomplete suggestions should have a minimum length of five characters. But what should be the maximum length of autocomplete suggestions? A longer maximum length will be most useful to users but comes with cost and performance tradeoffs. Our system will need more hardware resources or take longer to log and process longer strings. The trie may also become too big.

We must decide on the maximum length. This may vary by language and culture. Certain languages like Arabic are more verbose than English. We only consider English in our system, but we should be ready to extend to other languages if this becomes a functional requirement.

One possible solution is to implement a batch ETL pipeline to find the 90th percentile length of our users' search strings and use this as the maximum length. To calculate a median or percentile, we sort the list and then pick the value in the appropriate position. Calculating median or percentile in a distributed system is outside the scope of this book. We may instead simply sample the search strings and compute the 90th percentile.

We may also decide that doing analytics for this decision is overengineering, and we can instead apply simple heuristics. Start with 30 characters and change this number according to user feedback, performance, and cost considerations.

11.10.2 Preventing inappropriate suggestions

We will still need to filter out inappropriate words. We may decide the following:

- If a phrase contains a single inappropriate word, we filter out the entire phrase.
- No longer filter for appropriate words but give autocomplete suggestions for any word or phrase.
- Do not correct misspelled words in phrases. Assume that misspellings are sufficiently uncommon that they will not appear in autocomplete suggestions. We also assume that popular phrases will mostly be spelled correctly, so they will appear in autocomplete suggestions.

The difficult challenge is the need to filter out inappropriate phrases, not just inappropriate words. This is a complex problem to which even Google has not found a complete solution (https://algorithmwatch.org/en/auto-completion-disinformation/), due to the sheer vastness of the problem space. Possible inappropriate autocomplete suggestions include:

- Discrimination or negative stereotypes on religion, gender, and other groups.
- Misinformation, including political misinformation such as conspiracy theories on climate change or vaccination or misinformation driven by business agendas.
- Libel against prominent individuals, or defendants in legal proceedings where no verdict has been reached.

Current solutions use a combination of heuristics and machine learning.

11.11 Logging, monitoring, and alerting

Besides the usual actions in chapter 9, we should log searches that don't return any autocomplete results, which is indicative of bugs in our trie generator.

11.12 Other considerations and further discussion

Here are other possible requirements and discussion points that may come up as the interview progresses:

- There are many common words longer than three letters, such as "then," "continue," "hold," "make," "know," and "take." Some of these words may consistently be in the list of most popular words. It may be a waste of computational resources to keep counting popular words. Can our Autocomplete System keep a list of such words, and use approximation techniques to decide which ones to return when a user enters an input?
- As mentioned earlier, these user logs can be used for many other purposes besides autocomplete. For example, this can be a service that provides trending search terms, with applications to recommender systems.
- Design a distributed logging service.
- Filtering inappropriate search terms. Filtering inappropriate content is a general consideration of most services.
- We can consider other data inputs and processing to create personalized autocomplete.
- We can consider a Lambda architecture. A Lambda architecture contains a fast pipeline, so user queries can quickly propagate to the weighted trie generator, such as in seconds or minutes, so the autocomplete suggestions are updated quickly with a tradeoff in accuracy. A Lambda architecture also contains a slow pipeline for accurate but slower updates.
- Graceful degradation for returning outdated suggestions if upstream components are down.
- A rate limiter in front of our service to prevent DoS attacks.
- A service that is related but distinct from autocomplete is a spelling suggestion service, where a user receives word suggestions if they input a misspelled word. We can design a spelling suggestion service that uses experimentation techniques such as A/B testing or multi-armed bandit to measure the effect of various fuzzy matching functions on user churn.

Summary

- An autocomplete system is an example of a system that continuously ingests and processes large amount of data into a small data structure that users query for a specific purpose.

- Autocomplete has many use cases. An autocomplete service can be a shared service, used by many other services.

- Autocomplete has some overlap with search, but they are clearly for different purposes. Search is for finding documents, while autocomplete is for suggesting what the user intends to input.

- This system involves much data preprocessing, so the preprocessing and querying should be divided into separate components and then they can be independently developed and scaled.

- We can use the search service and logging service as data inputs for our autocomplete service. Our autocomplete service can process the search strings that these services record from users and offer autocomplete suggestions from these strings.

- Use a weighted trie for autocomplete. Lookups are fast and storage requirements are low.

- Break up a large aggregation job into multiple stages to reduce storage and processing costs. The tradeoff is high complexity and maintenance.

- Other considerations include other uses of the processed data, sampling, filtering content, personalization, Lambda architecture, graceful degradation, and rate limiting.

Design Flickr

12

This chapter covers

- Selecting storage services based on non-functional requirements
- Minimizing access to critical services
- Utilizing sagas for asynchronous processes

In this chapter, we design an image sharing service like Flickr. Besides sharing files/images, users can also append metadata to files and other users, such as access control, comments, or favorites.

Sharing and interacting with images and video are basic functionalities in virtually every social application and is a common interview topic. In this chapter, we discuss a distributed system design for image-sharing and interaction among a billion users, including both manual and programmatic users. We will see that there is much more than simply attaching a CDN. We will discuss how to design the system for scalable preprocessing operations that need to be done on uploaded content before they are ready for download.

12.1 User stories and functional requirements

Let's discuss user stories with the interviewer and scribble them down:

- A user can view photos shared by others. We refer to this user as a *viewer*.
- Our app should generate and display thumbnails of 50 px width. A user should view multiple photos in a grid and can select one at a time to view the full-resolution version.
- A user can upload photos. We refer to this user as a *sharer*.
- A sharer can set access control on their photos. A question we may ask is whether access control should be at the level of individual photos or if a sharer may only allow a viewer to view either all the former's photos or none. We choose the latter option for simplicity.
- A photo has predefined metadata fields, which have values provided by the sharer. Example fields are location or tags.
- An example of dynamic metadata is the list of viewers who have read access to the file. This metadata is dynamic because it can be changed.
- Users can comment on photos. A sharer can toggle commenting on and off. A user can be notified of new comments.
- A user can favorite a photo.
- A user can search on photo titles and descriptions.
- Photos can be programmatically downloaded. In this discussion, "view a photo" and "download a photo" are synonymous. We do not discuss the minor detail of whether users can download photos onto device storage.
- We briefly discuss personalization.

These are some points that we will not discuss:

- A user can filter photos by photo metadata. This requirement can be satisfied by a simple SQL path parameter, so we will not discuss it.
- Photo metadata that is recorded by the client, such as location (from hardware such as GPS), time (from the device's clock), and details of the camera (from the operating system).
- We will not discuss video. Discussions of many details of video (such as codecs) require specialized domain knowledge that is outside the scope of a general system design interview.

12.2 Non-functional requirements

Here are some questions we may discuss on non-functional requirements:

- How many users and downloads via API do we expect?
  - Our system must be scalable. It should serve one billion users distributed across the world. We expect heavy traffic. Assume 1% of our users (10 million)

upload 10 high-resolution (10 MB) images daily. This works out to 1 PB of uploads daily, or 3.65 EB over 10 years. The average traffic is over 1 GB/second, but we should expect traffic spikes, so we should plan for 10 GB/second.

- Do the photos have to be available immediately after upload? Does deletion need to be immediate? Must privacy setting changes take immediate effect?
  - Photos can take a few minutes to be available to our entire user base. We can trade off certain non-functional characteristics for lower cost, such as consistency or latency, and likewise for comments. Eventual consistency is acceptable.
  - Privacy settings must be effective sooner. A deleted photo does not have to be erased from all our storage within a few minutes; a few hours is permissible. However, it should be inaccessible to all users within a few minutes.
- High-resolution photos require high network speeds, which may be expensive. How may we control costs?
  - After some discussion, we have decided that a user should only be able to download one high-resolution photo at a time, but multiple low-resolution thumbnails can be downloaded simultaneously. When a user is uploading files, we can upload them one at a time.

Other non-functional requirements are

- High availability, such as five 9s availability. There should be no outages that prevent users from downloading or uploading photos.
- High performance and low latency of 1-second P99 for thumbnails downloads; this is not needed for high-resolution photos.
- High performance is not needed for uploads.

A note regarding thumbnails is that we can use the CSS `img` tag with either the `width` (https://developer.mozilla.org/en-US/docs/Web/HTML/Element/img#attr-width) or `height` attributes to display thumbnails from full-resolution images. Mobile apps have similar markup tags. This approach has high network costs and is not scalable. To display a grid of thumbnails on the client, every image needs to be downloaded in its full resolution. We can suggest to the interviewer to implement this in our MVP (minimum viable product). When we scale up our service to serve heavy traffic, we can consider two possible approaches to generate thumbnails.

The first approach is for the server to generate a thumbnail from the full-resolution image each time a client requests a thumbnail. This will be scalable if it was computationally inexpensive to generate a thumbnail. However, a full-resolution image file is tens of MB in size. A viewer will usually request a grid of >10 thumbnails in a single request. Assuming a full-resolution image is 10 MB (it can be much bigger), this means the server will need to process >100 MB of data in much less than one second to fulfill a 1-second P99. Moreover, the viewer may make many such requests within a few seconds as they scroll through thumbnails. This may be computationally feasible if the storage and processing are done on the same machine, and that machine uses SSD hard disks and not spinning hard disks. But this approach will be prohibitively expensive. Moreover, we will not be able to do functional partitioning of processing and storage into separate services. The network latency of transferring many GBs between the processing and storage services every second will not allow 1-second P99. So, this approach is not feasible overall.

The only scalable approach is to generate and store a thumbnail just after the file is uploaded and serve these thumbnails when a viewer requests them. Each thumbnail will only be a few KBs in size, so storage costs are low. We can also cache both thumbnails and full-resolution image files on the client, to be discussed in section 12.7. We discuss this approach in this chapter.

12.3 *High-level architecture*

Figure 12.1 shows our initial high-level architecture. Both sharers and viewers make requests through a backend to upload or download image files. The backend communicates with an SQL service.

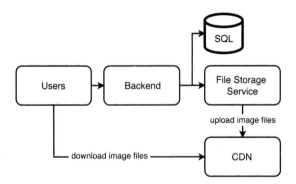

Figure 12.1   Our initial high-level architecture of our image-sharing service. Our users can download image files directly from a CDN. Uploads to the CDN can be buffered via a separate distributed file storage service. We can store other data such as user information or image file access permissions in SQL.

The first is a CDN for image files and image metadata (each image metadata is a formatted JSON or YAML string). This is most likely a third-party service.

Due to reasons including the following, we may also need a separate distributed file storage service for sharers to upload their image files, and this service handles interactions with the CDN. We can refer to this as our file storage service.

- Depending on our SLA contract with our CDN provider, our CDN may take up to a few hours to replicate images to its various data centers. During that time, it may be slow for our viewers to download this image, especially if there is a high rate of download requests because many viewers wish to download it.
- The latency of uploading an image file to the CDN may be unacceptably slow to a sharer. Our CDN may not be able to support many sharers simultaneously

uploading images. We can scale our file storage service as required to handle high upload/write traffic.

- We can either delete files from the file storage service after they are uploaded to the CDN, or we may wish to retain them as a backup. A possible reason to choose the latter may be that we don't want to completely trust the CDN's SLA and may wish to use our file storage service as a backup for our CDN should the latter experience outages. A CDN may also have a retention period of a few weeks or months, after which it deletes the file and downloads it again if required from a designated origin/source. Other possible situations may include the sudden requirement to disconnect our CDN because we suddenly discover that it has security problems.

12.4   SQL schema

We use an SQL database for dynamic data that is shown on the client apps, such as which photos are associated to which user. We can define the following SQL table schema in listing 12.1. The Image table contains image metadata. We can assign each sharer its own CDN directory, which we track using the ImageDir table. The schema descriptions are included in the CREATE statement.

Listing 12.1   SQL CREATE statements for the Image and ImageDir tables

```
CREATE TABLE Image (
cdn_path VARCHAR(255) PRIMARY KEY COMMENT="Image file path on the
➥ CDN.",
cdn_photo_key VARCHAR(255) NOT NULL UNIQUE COMMENT="ID assigned by the
➥ CDN.",
file_key VARCHAR(255) NOT NULL UNIQUE COMMENT="ID assigned by our File
➥ Storage Service. We may not need this column if we delete the image from
➥ our File Storage Service after it is uploaded to the CDN.",
resolution ENUM('thumbnail', 'hd') COMMENT="Indicates the image is a
➥ thumbnail or high resolution",
owner_id VARCHAR(255) NOT NULL COMMENT="ID of the user who owns the
➥ image.",
is_public BOOLEAN NOT NULL DEFAULT 1 COMMENT="Indicates if the image is
➥ public or private.",
INDEX thumbnail (Resolution, UserId) COMMENT="Composite index on the
➥ resolution and user ID so we can quickly find thumbnail or high
➥ resolution images that belong to a particular user."
) COMMENT="Image metadata.";

CREATE TABLE ImageDir (
cdn_dir VARCHAR(255) PRIMARY KEY COMMENT="CDN directory assigned to the
➥ user.",
user_id INTEGER NOT NULL COMMENT="User ID."
) COMMENT="Record the CDN directory assigned to each sharer.";
```

As fetching photos by user ID and resolution is a common query, we index our tables by these fields. We can follow the approaches discussed in chapter 4 to scale SQL reads.

We can define the following schema to allow a sharer to grant a viewer permission to view the former's photos and a viewer to favorite photos. An alternative to using two tables is to define an `is_favorite` Boolean column in the Share table, but the tradeoff is that it will be a sparse column that uses unnecessary storage:

```
CREATE TABLE Share (
  id            INT PRIMARY KEY
  cdn_photo_key VARCHAR(255),
  user_id       VARCHAR(255)
);

CREATE TABLE Favorite (
  id INT PRIMARY KEY
  cdn_photo_key VARCHAR(255) NOT NULL UNIQUE,
  user_id VARCHAR(255) NOT NULL UNIQUE
);
```

12.5 *Organizing directories and files on the CDN*

Let's discuss one way to organize CDN directories. A directory hierarchy can be user > album > resolution > file. We can also consider date because a user may be more interested in recent files.

Each user has their own CDN directory. We may allow a user to create albums, where each album has 0 or more photos. Mapping of albums to photos is one-to-many; that is, each photo can only belong to one album. On our CDN, we can place photos not in albums in an album called "default." So, a user directory may have one or more album directories.

An album directory can store the several files of the image in various resolutions, each in its own directory, and a JSON image metadata file. For example, a directory "original" may contain an originally-uploaded file "swans.png," and a directory "thumbnail" may contain the generated thumbnail "swans_thumbnail.png."

A CdnPath value template is <album_name>/<resolution>/<image_name.extension>. The user ID or name is not required because it is contained in the UserId field.

For example, a user with username "alice" may create an album named "nature," inside which they place an image called "swans.png." The CdnPath value is "nature/original/swans.png." The corresponding thumbnail has CdnPath "nature/thumbnail/swans_thumbnail.png." The tree command on our CDN will show the following. "bob" is another user:

```
$ tree ~ | head -n 8
.
├── alice
│   └── nature
│       ├── original
│       │   └── swans.png
│       └── thumbnail
│           └── swans_thumbnail.png
├── bob
```

In the rest of this discussion, we use the terms "image" and "file" interchangeably.

12.6   *Uploading a photo*

Should thumbnails be generated on the client or server? As stated in the preface, we should expect to discuss various approaches and evaluate their tradeoffs.

12.6.1   *Generate thumbnails on the client*

Generating thumbnails on the client saves computational resources on our backend, and the thumbnail is small, so it contributes little to network traffic. A 100 px thumbnail is about 40 KB, a negligible addition to a high-resolution photo, which may be a few MB to 10s of MB in size.

Before the upload process, the client may check if the thumbnail has already been uploaded to the CDN. During the upload process, the following steps occur, illustrated in figure 12.2:

1   Generate the thumbnail.
2   Place both files into a folder and then compress it with an encoding like Gzip or Brotli. Compression of a few MB to 10s of MB saves significant network traffic, but our backend will expend CPU and memory resources to uncompress the directory.
3   Use a POST request to upload the compressed file to our CDN directory. The request body is a JSON string that describes the number and resolution of images being uploaded.
4   On the CDN, create directories as necessary, unzip the compressed file, and write the files to disk. Replicate it to the other data centers (refer to the next question).

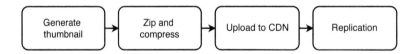

Figure 12.2   Process for a client to upload a photo to our image-sharing service

NOTE   As alluded to in the preface, in the interview, we are not expected to know the details of compression algorithms, cryptographically secure hashing algorithms, authentication algorithms, pixel-to-MB conversion, or the term "thumbnail." We are expected to reason intelligently and communicate clearly. The interviewer expects us to be able to reason that thumbnails are smaller than high-resolution images, that compression will help in transferring large files over a network and that authentication and authorization are needed for files and users. If we don't know the term "thumbnail," we can use clear terms like "a grid of small preview photos" or "small grid photos" and clarify that "small" refers to a small number of pixels, which means small file size.

DISADVANTAGES OF CLIENT-SIDE GENERATION

However, the disadvantages of client-side processing are non-trivial. We do not have control of the client device or detailed knowledge of its environment, making bugs difficult to reproduce. Our code will also need to anticipate many more failure scenarios that can occur on clients compared to servers. For example, image processing may fail because the client ran out of hard disk space because the client was consuming too much CPU or memory on other applications, or because the network connection suddenly failed.

We have no control over many of these situations that may occur on a client. We may overlook failure scenarios during implementation and testing, and debugging is more difficult because it is harder to replicate the situation that occurred on a client's device than on a server that we own and have admin access to.

Many possible factors such as the following may affect the application, making it difficult to determine what to log:

- Generating on the client requires implementing and maintaining the thumbnail generation in each client type (i.e., browser, Android, and iOS). Each uses a different language, unless we use cross-platform frameworks like Flutter and React Native, which come with their own tradeoffs.

- Hardware factors, such as a CPU that is too slow or insufficient memory, may cause thumbnail generation to be unacceptably slow.

- The specific OS version of the operating system running on the client may have bugs or security problems that make it risky to process images on it or cause problems that are very difficult to anticipate or troubleshoot. For example, if the OS suddenly crashes while uploading images, it may upload corrupt files, and this will affect viewers.

- Other software running on the client may consume too much CPU or memory, and cause thumbnail generation to fail or be unacceptably slow. Clients may also be running malicious software, such as viruses that interfere with our application. It is impractical for us to check if clients contain such malicious software, and we cannot ensure that clients are following security best practices.

- Related to the previous point, we can follow security best practices on our own systems to guard against malicious activity, but have little influence over our clients in ensuring they do the same. For this reason, we may wish to minimize data storage and processing in our clients and store and process data only on the server.

- Our clients' network configurations may interfere with file uploads, such as blocked ports, hosts, or possibly VPNs.

- Some of our clients may have unreliable network connectivity. We may need logic to handle sudden network disconnects. For example, the client should save a generated thumbnail to device storage before uploading it to our server. Should the upload fail, the client will not need to generate the thumbnail again before retrying the upload.

- Related to the previous point, there may be insufficient device storage to save the thumbnail. In our client implementation, we need to remember to check that there is sufficient device storage before generating the thumbnail, or our sharers may experience a poor user experience of waiting for the thumbnail to be generated and then experience an error due to lack of storage.

- Also related to the same point, client-side thumbnail generation may cause our app to require more permissions, such as the permission to write to local storage. Some users may be uncomfortable with granting our app write access to their devices' storage. Even if we do not abuse this permission, external or internal parties may compromise our system, and hackers may then go through our system to perform malicious activities on our users' devices.

A practical problem is that each individual problem may affect only a small number of users, and we may decide that it is not worth to invest our resources to fix this problem that affects these few users, but cumulatively all these problems may affect a non-trivial fraction of our potential user base.

A MORE TEDIOUS AND LENGTHY SOFTWARE RELEASE LIFECYCLE

Because client-side processing has higher probability of bugs and higher cost of remediation, we will need to spend considerable resources and time to test each software iteration before deployment, which will slow down development. We cannot take advantage of CI/CD (continuous integration/continuous deployment) like we can in developing services. We will need to adopt a software release lifecycle like that shown in figure 12.3. Each new version is manually tested by internal users and then gradually released to progressively larger fractions of our user base. We cannot quickly release and roll back small changes. Since releases are slow and tedious, each release will contain many code changes.

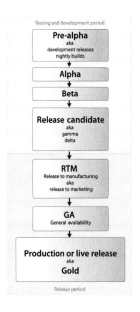

Figure 12.3   An example software release lifecycle. A new version is manually tested by internal users during the alpha phase and then it is released to progressively larger fractions of our users in each subsequent phase. The software release lifecycles of some companies have more stages than illustrated here. By Heyinsun (https://commons.wikimedia.org/w/index.php?curid=6818861), CC BY 3.0 (https://creativecommons.org/licenses/by/3.0/deed.en).

In a situation where releasing/deploying code changes (either to clients or servers) is slow, another possible approach to preventing bugs in a new release is to include the new code without removing the old code in the following manner, illustrated in figure 12.4. This example assumes we are releasing a new function, but this approach can generalize to new code in general:

1 Add the new function. Run the new function on the same input as the old function, but continue to use the output of the old function instead of the new function. Surround the usages of the new function in try-catch statements, so an exception will not crash the application. In the catch statement, log the exception and send the log to our logging service, so we can troubleshoot and debug it.

2 Debug the function and release new versions until no more bugs are observed.

3 Switch the code from using the old function to the new function. Surround the code in try catch blocks, where the catch statement will log the exception and use our old function as a backup. Release this version and observe for problems. If problems are observed, switch the code back to using the old function (i.e., go back to the previous step).

4 When we are confident that the new function is sufficiently mature (we can never be sure it is bug-free), remove the old function from our code. This cleanup is for code readability and maintainability.

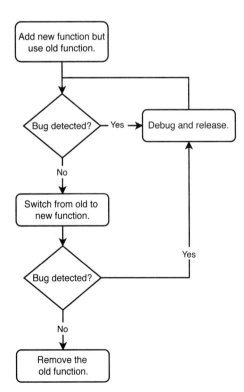

**Figure 12.4
Flowchart of a
software release
process that
releases new code
in stages, only
gradually removing
the old code**

A limitation of this approach is that it is difficult to introduce non-backward-compatible code. Another disadvantage is that the code base is bigger and less maintainable. Moreover, our developer team needs the discipline to follow this process all the way through, rather than be tempted to skip steps or disregard the last step.

The approach also consumes more computational resources and energy on the client, which may be a significant problem for mobile devices.

Finally, this extra code increases the client app's size. This effect is trivial for a few functions, but can add up if much logic requires such safeguards.

12.6.2 *Generate thumbnails on the backend*

We just discussed the tradeoffs of generating thumbnails on the client. Generating on a server requires more hardware resources, as well as engineering effort to create and maintain this backend service, but the service can be created with the same language and tools as other services. We may decide that the costs of the former outweigh the latter.

This section discusses the process of generating thumbnails on the backend. There are three main steps:

1 Before uploading the file, check if the file has been uploaded before. This prevents costly and unnecessary duplicate uploads.
2 Upload the file to the file storage service and CDN.
3 Generate the thumbnail and upload it to the file storage service and CDN.

When the file is uploaded to the backend, the backend will write the file to our file storage service and CDN and then trigger a streaming job to generate the thumbnail.

The main purpose of our file storage service is as a buffer for uploading to CDN, so we can implement replication between hosts within our data center but not on other data centers. In the event of a significant data center outage with data loss, we can also use the files from the CDN for recovery operations. We can use the file storage service and CDN as backups for each other.

For scalable image file uploads, some of the image file upload steps can be asynchronous, so we can use a saga approach. Refer to section 5.6 for an introduction to saga.

CHOREOGRAPHY SAGA APPROACH

Figure 12.5 illustrates the various services and Kafka topics in this choreography saga. The detailed steps are as follows. The step numbers are labeled on both figures:

1 The user first hashes the image and then makes a GET request to the backend check if the image has already been uploaded. This may happen because the user successfully uploaded the image in a previous request, but the connection failed while the file storage service or backend was returning success, so the user may be retrying the upload.

2 Our backend forwards the request to the file storage service.

3 Our file storage service returns a response that indicates if the file had already been successfully uploaded.

4 Our backend returns this response to the user.

5 This step depends on whether the file has already been successfully uploaded.

    a If this file has not been successfully uploaded before, the user uploads this file to our file storage service via the backend. (The user may compress the file before uploading it.)

    b Alternatively, if the file has already been successfully uploaded, our backend can produce a thumbnail generation event to our Kafka topic. We can skip to step 8.

6 Our file storage service writes the file to the object storage service.

7 After successfully writing the file, our file storage service produces an event to our CDN Kafka topic and then returns a success response to the user via the backend.

8 Our file storage service consumes the event from step 6, which contains the image hash.

9 Similar to step 1, our file storage service makes a request to the CDN with the image hash to determine whether the image had already been uploaded to the CDN. This could have happened if a file storage service host had uploaded the image file to the CDN before, but then failed before it wrote the relevant checkpoint to the CDN topic.

10 Our file storage service uploads the file to the CDN. This is done asynchronously and independently of the upload to our file storage service, so our user experience is unaffected if upload to the CDN is slow.

11 Our file storage service produces a thumbnail generation event that contains the file ID to our thumbnail generation Kafka topic and receives a success response from our Kafka service.

12 Our backend returns a success response to the user that the latter's image file is successfully uploaded. It returns this response only after producing the thumbnail generation event to ensure that this event is produced, which is necessary to ensure that the thumbnail generation will occur. If producing the event to Kafka fails, the user will receive a 504 Timeout response. The user can restart this process from step 1. What if we produce the event multiple times to Kafka? Kafka's exactly once guarantee ensures that this will not be a problem.

13 Our thumbnail generation service consumes the event from Kafka to begin thumbnail generation.

14 The thumbnail generation service fetches the file from the file storage service, generates the thumbnails, and writes the output thumbnails to the object storage service via the file storage service.

Why doesn't the thumbnail generation service write directly to the CDN?

- The thumbnail generation service should be a self-contained service that accepts a request to generate a thumbnail, pulls the file from the file storage service, generates the thumbnail, and writes the result thumbnail back to the file storage service. Writing directly to other destinations such as the CDN introduces additional complexity, e.g., if the CDN is currently experiencing heavy load, the thumbnail generation service will have to periodically check if the CDN is ready to accept the file, while also ensuring that the former itself does not run out of storage in the meanwhile. It is simpler and more maintainable if writes to the CDN are handled by the file storage service.

- Each service or host that is allowed to write to the CDN is an additional security maintenance overhead. We reduce the attack surface by not allowing the thumbnail generation service to access the CDN.

15 The thumbnail generation service writes a ThumbnailCdnRequest to the CDN topic to request the file storage service to write the thumbnails to the CDN.

16 The file storage service consumes this event from the CDN topic and fetches the thumbnail from the object storage service.

17 The file storage service writes the thumbnail to the CDN. The CDN returns the file's key.

18 The file storage service inserts this key to the SQL table (if the key does not already exist) that holds the mapping of user ID to keys. Note that steps 16–18 are blocking. If the file storage service host experiences an outage during this insert step, its replacement host will rerun from step 16. The thumbnail size is only a few KB, so the computational resources and network overhead of this retry are trivial.

19 Depending on how soon our CDN can serve these (high-resolution and thumbnail) image files, we can delete these files from our file storage service immediately, or we can implement a periodic batch ETL job to delete files that were created an hour ago. Such a job may also query the CDN to ensure the files have been replicated to various data centers, before deleting them from our file storage service, but that may be overengineering. Our file storage service may retain the file hashes, so it can respond to requests to check if the file had been uploaded before. We may implement a batch ETL job to delete hashes that were created more than one hour ago.

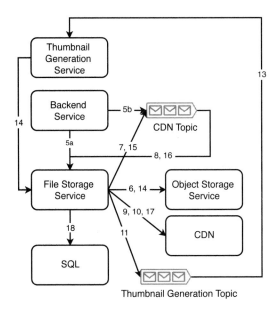

Figure 12.5 **Choreography of thumbnail generation, starting from step 5a. The arrows indicate the step numbers described in the main text. For clarity, we didn't illustrate the user. Some of the events that the file storage service produces and consumes to the Kafka topics are to signal it to transfer image files between the object storage service and the CDN. There are also events to trigger thumbnail generation, and to write CDN metadata to the SQL service.**

Identify the transaction types

Which are the compensable transactions, pivot transaction, and retriable transactions? The steps before step 11 are the compensable transactions because we have not sent the user a confirmation response that the upload has succeeded. Step 11 is the pivot transaction because we will then confirm with the user that the upload has succeeded, and retry is unnecessary. Steps 12–16 are retriable transactions. We have the required (image file) data to keep retrying these (thumbnail generation) transactions, so they are guaranteed to succeed.

If instead of just a thumbnail and the original resolution, we wish to generate multiple images, each with a different resolution and then the tradeoffs of both approaches become more pronounced.

What if we use FTP instead of HTTP POST or RPC to upload photos? FTP writes to disk, so any further processing will incur the latency and CPU resources to read it from disk to memory. If we are uploading compressed files, to uncompress a file, we first need to load it from disk to memory. This is an unnecessary step that does not occur if we used a POST request or RPC.

The upload speed of the file storage service limits the rate of thumbnail generation requests. If the file storage service uploads files faster than the thumbnail generation service can generate and upload thumbnails, the Kafka topic prevents the thumbnail generation service from being overloaded with requests.

ORCHESTRATION SAGA APPROACH

We can also implement the file upload and thumbnail generation process as an orchestration saga. Our backend service is the orchestrator. Referring to figure 12.6, the steps in the orchestration saga of thumbnail generation are as follows:

1 The first step is the same as in the choreography approach. The client makes a GET request to the backend to check if the image has already been uploaded.

2 Our backend service uploads the file to the object store service (not shown on figure 12.6) via the file storage service. Our file storage service produces an event to our file storage response topic to indicate that the upload succeeded.

3 Our backend service consumes the event from our file storage response topic.

4 Our backend service produces an event to our CDN topic to request the file to be uploaded to the CDN.

5 (a) Our file storage service consumes from our CDN topic and (b) uploads the file to the CDN. This is done as a separate step from uploading to our object store service, so if the upload to the CDN fails, repeating this step does not involve a duplicate upload to our object store service. An approach that is more consistent with orchestration is for our backend service to download the file from the file storage service and then upload it to the CDN. We can choose to stick with the orchestration approach throughout or deviate from it here so the file does not have to move between three services. Keep in mind that if we do choose this deviation, we will need to configure the file storage service to make requests to the CDN.

6 Our file storage service produces an event to our CDN response topic to indicate that the file was successfully uploaded to the CDN.

7 Our backend service consumes from our CDN response topic.

8 Our backend service produces to our thumbnail generation topic to request that our thumbnail generation service generate thumbnails from the uploaded image.

9 Our thumbnail generation service consumes from our thumbnail generation topic.

10 Our thumbnail generation service fetches the file from our file storage service, generates the thumbnails, and writes them to our file storage service.

11 Our thumbnail generation service produces an event to our file storage topic to indicate that thumbnail generation was successful.

12 Our file storage service consumes the event from our file storage topic and uploads the thumbnails to the CDN. The same discussion in step 4, about orchestration versus network traffic, also applies here.

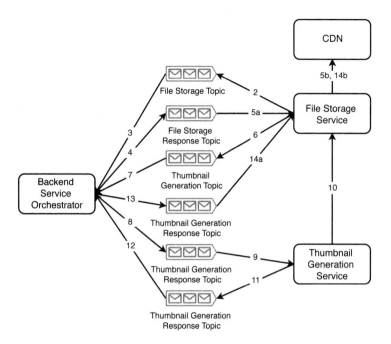

Figure 12.6   Orchestration of thumbnail generation, starting from step 2. Figure 12.5 illustrated the object storage service, which we omit on this diagram for brevity. For clarity, we also don't illustrate the user.

12.6.3   *Implementing both server-side and client-side generation*

We can implement both server-side and client-side thumbnail generation. We can first implement server-side generation, so we can generate thumbnails for any client. Next, we can implement client-side generation for each client type, so we realize the benefits of client-side generation. Our client can first try to generate the thumbnail. If it fails, our server can generate it. With this approach, our initial implementations of client-side generation do not have to consider all possible failure scenarios, and we can choose to iteratively improve our client-side generation.

This approach is more complex and costly than just server-side generation, but may be cheaper and easier than even just client-side generation because the client-side generation has the server-side generation to act as a failover, so client-side bugs and crashes will be less costly. We can attach version codes to clients, and clients will include these version codes in their requests. If we become aware of bugs in a particular version, we can configure our server-side generation to occur for all requests sent by these clients. We can correct the bugs and provide a new client version, and notify affected users to update their clients. Even if some users do not perform the update, this is not a serious problem because we can do these operations server-side, and these client devices will age and eventually stop being used.

12.7   *Downloading images and data*

The images and thumbnails have been uploaded to the CDN, so they are ready for viewers. A request from a viewer for a sharer's thumbnails is processed as follows:

1   Query the Share table for the list of sharers who allow the viewer to view the former's images.

2   Query the Image table to obtain all CdnPath values of thumbnail resolutions images of the user. Return the CdnPath values and a temporary OAuth2 token to read from the CDN.

3   The client can then download the thumbnails from the CDN. To ensure that the client is authorized to download the requested files, our CDN can use the token authorization mechanism that we will introduce in detail in section 13.3.

Dynamic content may be updated or deleted, so we store them on SQL rather than on the CDN. This includes photo comments, user profile information, and user settings. We can use a Redis cache for popular thumbnails and popular full-resolution images. When a viewer favorites an image, we can take advantage of the immutable nature of the images to cache both the thumbnails and the full-resolution image on the client if it has sufficient storage space. Then a viewer's request to view their grid of favorite images will not consume any server resources and will also be instantaneous.

For the purpose of the interview, if we were not allowed to use an available CDN and then the interview question becomes how to design a CDN, which is discussed in the next chapter.

12.7.1   *Downloading pages of thumbnails*

Consider the use case where a user views one page of thumbnails at a time, and each page is maybe 10 thumbnails. Page 1 will have thumbnails 1–10, page 2 will have thumbnails 11–20, and so on. If a new thumbnail (let's call it thumbnail 0) is ready when the user is on page 1, and the user goes to page 2, how can we ensure that the user's request to download page 2 returns a response that contains thumbnails 11–20 instead of 10–19?

One technique is to version the pagination like `GET thumbnails?page=<page>&page_version=<page_version>`. If `page_version` is omitted, the backend can substitute the latest version by default. The response to this request should contain `page_version`, so the user can continue using the same `page_version` value for subsequent requests as appropriate. This way, a user can smoothly flip through pages. When the user returns to page 1, they can omit `page_version` and the latest page 1 of thumbnails will be displayed.

However, this technique only works if thumbnails are added to or deleted from the beginning of the list. If thumbnails are added to or deleted from other positions in the list while the user is flipping through pages, the user will not see the new thumbnails or continue to see the deleted thumbnails. A better technique is for the client to pass the current first item or last item to the backend. If the user is flipping forward, use GET thumbnails?previous_last=<last_item>. If the user is flipping backward, use GET thumbnails?previous_first=<first_item>. Why this is so is left as a simple exercise to the reader.

12.8 Monitoring and alerting

Besides what was discussed in section 2.5, we should monitor and alert on both file uploads and downloads, and requests to our SQL database.

12.9 Some other services

There are many other services we may discuss in no particular order of priority, including monetization such as ads and premium features, payments, censorship, personalization, etc.

12.9.1 Premium features

Our image-sharing service can offer a free tier, with all the functionalities we have discussed so far. We can offer sharers premium features such as the following.

Sharers can state that their photos are copyrighted and that viewers must pay to download their full-resolution photos and use them elsewhere. We can design a system for sharers to sell their photos to other users. We will need to record the sales and keep track of photo ownership. We may provide sellers with sales metrics, dashboards, and analytics features for them to make better business decisions. We may provide recommender systems to recommend sellers what type of photos to sell and how to price them. All these features may be free or paid.

We can offer a free tier of 1,000 photos for free accounts and larger allowances for various subscription plans. We will also need to design usage and billing services for these premium features.

12.9.2 Payments and taxes service

Premium features require a payments service and a tax service to manage transactions and payments from and to users. As discussed in section 15.1, payments are very complex topics and generally not asked in a system design interview. The interviewer may ask them as a challenge topic. The same concerns apply to taxes. There are many possible types of taxes, such as sales, income, and corporate taxes. Each type can have many components, such as country, state, county, and city taxes. There can be tax-exemption rules regarding income level or a specific product or industry. Tax rates may be progressive. We may need to provide relevant business and income tax forms for the locations where the photos were bought and sold.

12.9.3 Censorship/content moderation

Censorship, also commonly called content moderation, is important in any application where users share data with each other. It is our ethical (and in many cases also legal) responsibility to police our application and remove inappropriate or offensive content, regardless of whether the content is public or only shared with select viewers.

We will need to design a system for content moderation. Content moderation can be done both manually and automatically. Manual methods include mechanisms for viewers to report inappropriate content and for operations staff to view and delete this content. We may also wish to implement heuristics or machine-learning approaches for content moderation. Our system must also provide administrative features such as warning or banning sharers and make it easy for operations staff to cooperate with local law enforcement authorities.

12.9.4 Advertising

Our clients can display ads to users. A common way is to add a third-party ads SDK to our client. Such an SDK is provided by an ad network (e.g., Google Ads). The ad network provides the advertiser (i.e., us) with a console to select categories of ads that we prefer or do not desire. For example, we may not wish to show mature ads or ads from competitor companies.

Another possibility is to design a system to display ads for our sharers internally within our client. Our sharers may wish to display ads within our client to boost their photo sales. One use case of our app is for viewers to search for photos to purchase to use for their own purposes. When a viewer loads our app's homepage, it can display suggested photos, and sharers may pay for their photos to appear on the homepage. We may also display "sponsored" search results when a viewer searches for photos.

We may also provide users with paid subscription packages in exchange for an ad-free experience.

12.9.5 Personalization

As our service scales to a large number of users, we will want to provide personalized experiences to cater to a wide audience and increase revenue. Based on the user's activity both within the app and from user data acquired from other sources, a user can be provided with personalized ads, search, and content recommendations.

Data science and machine-learning algorithms are usually outside the scope of a system design interview, and the discussion will be focused on designing experimentation platforms to divide users into experiment groups, serve each group from a different machine-learning model, collect and analyze results, and expand successful models to a wider audience.

12.10 Other possible discussion topics

Other possible discussion topics include the following:

- We can create an Elasticsearch index on photo metadata, such as title, description, and tags. When a user submits a search query, the search can do fuzzy matching on tags as well as titles and descriptions. Refer to section 2.6.3 for a discussion on creating an Elasticsearch cluster.

- We discussed how sharers can grant view access to their images to viewers. We can discuss more fine-grained access control to images, such as access control on individual images, permissions to download images in various resolutions, or permission for viewers to share images to a limited number of other viewers. We can also discuss access control to user profiles. A user can either allow anyone to view their profile or grant access to each individual. Private profiles should be excluded from search results.

- We can discuss more ways to organize photos. For example, sharers may add photos to groups. A group may have photos from multiple sharers. A user may need to be a group member to view and/or share photos to it. A group may have admin users, who can add and remove users from the group. We can discuss various ways to package and sell collections of photos and the related system design.

- We can discuss a system for copyright management and watermarking. A user may assign a specific copyright license to each photo. Our system may attach an invisible watermark to the photo and may also attach additional watermarks during transactions between users. These watermarks can be used to track ownership and copyright infringement.

- The user data (image files) on this system is sensitive and valuable. We may discuss possible data loss, prevention, and mitigation. This includes security breaches and data theft.

- We can discuss strategies to control storage costs. For example, we can use different storage systems for old versus new files or for popular images versus other images.

- We can create batch pipelines for analytics. An example is a pipeline to compute the most popular photos, or uploaded photo count by hour, day, and month. Such pipelines are discussed in chapter 17.

- A user can follow another user and be notified of new photos and/or comments.

- We can extend our system to support audio and video streaming. Discussing video streaming requires domain-specific expertise that is not required in a general system design interview, so this topic may be asked in interviews for specific roles where said expertise is required, or it may be asked as an exploratory or challenge question.

Summary

- Scalability, availability, and high download performance are required for a file- or image-sharing service. High upload performance and consistency are not required.

- Which services are allowed to write to our CDN? Use a CDN for static data, but secure and limit write access to sensitive services like a CDN.

- Which processing operations should be put in the client vs. the server? One consideration is that processing on a client can save our company hardware resources and cost, but may be considerably more complex and incur more costs from this complexity.

- Client-side and server-side have their tradeoffs. Server-side is generally preferred where possible for ease of development/upgrades. Doing both allows the low computational cost of client-side and the reliability of server-side.

- Which processes can be asynchronous? Use techniques like sagas for those processes to improve scalability and reduce hardware costs.

Design a Content
Distribution Network

13

This chapter covers
- Discussing the pros, cons, and unexpected situations
- Satisfying user requests with frontend metadata storage architecture
- Designing a basic distributed storage system

A CDN (Content Distribution Network) is a cost-effective and geographically distributed file storage service that is designed to replicate files across its multiple data centers to serve static content to a large number of geographically distributed users quickly, serving each user from the data center that can serve them fastest. There are secondary benefits, such as fault-tolerance, allowing users to be served from other data centers if any particular data center is unavailable. Let's discuss a design for a CDN, which we name CDNService.

13.1   *Advantages and disadvantages of a CDN*

Before we discuss the requirements and system design for our CDN, we can first discuss the advantages and disadvantages of using a CDN, which may help us understand our requirements.

13.1.1   *Advantages of using a CDN*

If our company hosts services on multiple data centers, we likely have a shared object store that is replicated across these data centers for redundancy and availability. This shared object store provides many of the benefits of a CDN. We use a CDN if our geographically distributed userbase can benefit from the extensive network of data centers that a CDN provides.

The reasons to consider using a CDN were discussed in section 1.4.4, and some are repeated here:

- *Lower latency*—A user is served from a nearby data center, so latency is lower. Without a third-party CDN, we will need to deploy our service to multiple data centers, which carries considerable complexity, such as monitoring to ensure availability. Lower latency may also carry other benefits, such as improving SEO (search engine optimization). Search engines tend to penalize slow web pages both directly and indirectly. An example of an indirect penalty is that users may leave a website if it loads slowly; such a website can be described as having a high bounce rate, and search engines penalize websites with high bounce rates.
- *Scalability*—With a third-party provider, we do not need to scale our system ourselves. The third party takes care of scalability.
- *Lower unit costs*—A third-party CDN usually provides bulk discount, so we will have lower unit costs as we serve more users and higher loads. It can provide lower costs as it has economies of scale from serving traffic for many companies and spread the costs of hardware and appropriately skilled technical personnel over this larger volume. The fluctuating hardware and network requirements of multiple companies can normalize each other and result in more stable demand versus serving just a single company.
- *Higher throughput*—A CDN provides additional hosts to our service, which allows us to serve a larger number of simultaneous users and higher traffic.
- *Higher availability*—The additional hosts can serve as a fallback should our service's hosts fail, especially if the CDN is able to keep to its SLA. Being geographically distributed across multiple data centers is also beneficial for availability, as a disaster that causes an outage on a single data center will not affect other data centers located far away. Moreover, unexpected traffic spikes to a single data center can be redirected and balanced across the other data centers.

13.1.2 *Disadvantages of using a CDN*

Many sources discuss the advantages of a CDN, but few also discuss the disadvantages. An interview signal of an engineer's maturity is their ability to discuss and evaluate tradeoffs in any technical decision and anticipate challenges by other engineers. The interviewer will almost always challenge your design decisions and probe if you have considered various non-functional requirements. Some disadvantages of using a CDN include the following:

- The additional complexities of including another service in our system. Examples of such complexities include:
  - An additional DNS lookup
  - An additional point of failure
- A CDN may have high unit costs for low traffic. There may also be hidden costs, like costs per GB of data transfer because CDNs may use third-party networks.
- Migrating to a different CDN may take months and be costly. Reasons to migrate to another CDN include:
  - A particular CDN may not have hosts located near our users. If we acquire a significant user base in a region not covered by your CDN, we may need to migrate to a more suitable CDN.
  - A CDN company may go out of business.
  - A CDN company may provide poor service, such as not fulfilling its SLA, which affects our own users; provide poor customer support; or experience incidents like data loss or security breaches.
- Some countries or organizations may block the IP addresses of certain CDNs.
- There may be security and privacy concerns in storing your data on a third party. We can implement encryption at rest so the CDN cannot view our data, which will incur additional cost and latency (from encrypting and decrypting data). The design and implementation must be implemented or reviewed by qualified security engineers, which adds additional costs and communication overhead to our team.
- Another possible security concern is that it's possible to insert malicious code into JavaScript libraries, and we cannot personally ensure the security and integrity of these remotely hosted libraries.
- The flip side of allowing a third-party to ensure high availability is that if technical problems occur with the CDN occur, we do not know how long it will take for the CDN company to fix them. Any service degradation may affect our customers, and the communication overhead of communicating with an external company may be greater than communication within our company. The CDN company may provide an SLA, but we cannot be sure that it will be honored, and migrating to another CDN is costly, as we just discussed. Moreover, our SLA becomes dependent on a third party.

- The configuration management of a CDN or any third-party tool/service in general may be insufficiently customizable for certain of our use cases, leading to unexpected problems. The next section discusses an example.

13.1.3 *Example of an unexpected problem from using a CDN to serve images*

This section discusses an example of an unexpected problem that can occur from using a CDN or third-party tools or services in general.

A CDN may read a GET request's User-Agent (https://developer.mozilla.org/en-US/docs/Web/HTTP/Headers/User-Agent) header to determine if the request is from a web browser, and if so, return images in WebP (https://developers.google.com/speed/webp) format instead of the format it was uploaded in (such as PNG or JPEG). In some services, this may be ideal, but other browser applications that want images to be returned in their original formats have three choices:

1 Override the User-Agent header in our web application.
2 Configure the CDN to serve WebP images for certain services and images in the original formats for other services.
3 Route the request through a backend service.

Regarding solution 1, as of publication of this book, Chrome web browser does not allow applications to override the User-Agent header, while Firefox does (Refer to https://bugs.chromium.org/p/chromium/issues/detail?id=571722, https://bugzilla.mozilla.org/show_bug.cgi?id=1188932, and https://stackoverflow.com/a/42815264.) Solution 1 will limit our users to specific web browsers, which may be infeasible.

Regarding solution 2, the CDN may not provide the ability to customize this setting for individual services. It may only allow the setting to serve images in WebP format to be broadly turned on or off across all our services. Even if it does provide such individualized configuration, the relevant infrastructure team in our company that manages CDN configurations may be unable or unwilling to set this configuration for individual services in our company. This problem may be more prevalent in large companies.

Solution 3 requires developers to expose an API endpoint just to fetch the original image from the CDN. This solution should be best avoided because it negates most of all the benefits of a CDN. It adds additional latency and complexity (including documentation and maintenance overhead). The backend host may be geographically far from the user, so the user loses the benefit from the CDN of being served from a nearby data center. This backend service will need to scale with demand for the images; if the request rate for the images is high, both the CDN and the backend service need be scaled up. Rather than adopting this solution, it makes more sense to store the files in a cheaper object store whose hosts are in the same data center as our backend service. Unfortunately, I have personally seen this "solution" used in big companies because the application and the CDN were owned by different teams, and management was uninterested in fostering cooperation between them.

13.2 Requirements

Functional requirements are simple. Authorized users should be able to create directories, upload files with 10 GB file size limit, and download files.

NOTE We will not discuss content moderation. Content moderation is essential in any application where users see content created by others. We assume that it is the responsibility of the organizations that use our CDN, not the responsibility of the company that provides the CDN.

Most of the non-functional requirements are the advantages of a CDN:

- *Scalable*—The CDN may scale to support petabytes of storage and download volumes of terabytes per day.
- *High availability*—Four or five 9s uptime required.
- *High performance*—A file should be downloaded from the data center that can serve it fastest to the requestor. However, synchronization may take time, so upload performance is less important, as long as the file is available on at least one data center before synchronization is complete.
- *Durable*—A file must not be corrupted.
- *Security and privacy*—The CDN serves requests and sends files to destinations outside the data center. Files should only be downloaded and uploaded by authorized users.

13.3 CDN authentication and authorization

As discussed in appendix B, the purpose of authentication is to verify a user's identity, while the purpose of authorization is to ensure that a user accessing a resource (such as a file in our CDN) has permission to do so. These measures prevent *hotlinking*, in which a site or service accesses CDN assets without permission. Our CDN incurs the costs of serving these users without getting paid for it, and unauthorized file or data access may be a copyright violation.

TIP Refer to appendix B for an introduction to authentication and authorization.

CDN authentication and authorization can be done with either cookie-based authentication or token-based authentication. As discussed in section B.4, token-based authentication uses less memory, can use third-party services with more security expertise, and allow fine-grained access control. Besides these benefits, token authentication for our CDN also allows requestors to be restricted to allowed IP addresses or specific user accounts.

In this section, we discuss a typical implementation for CDN authentication and authorization. The following sections discuss a possible CDN system design that we may discuss during an interview, including how this authentication and authorization process can be done in our design.

13.3.1 *Steps in CDN authentication and authorization*

In this discussion, we refer to a CDN customer as a site or service that uploads assets to a CDN and then directs its users/clients to the CDN. We refer to a CDN user as a client that downloads assets from a CDN.

The CDN issues each customer a secret key and provides an SDK or library to generate access tokens from the following information. Referring to figure 13.1, the access token generation process is as follows:

1 The user sends an authentication request to the customer app. The customer app may perform the authentication using an authentication service. (The details of the authentication mechanism are irrelevant for the CDN access token generation process. Refer to appendix B for an introduction to various authentication protocols like Simple Login and OpenID Connect.)

2 The customer app generates an access token using the SDK, with the following inputs:

   a *Secret key*—The customer's secret key.

   b *CDN URL*—The CDN URL that the generated access token is valid for.

   c *Expiry*—The access token's expiry timestamp, after which the user needs a new access token. When a user makes a request to the CDN with an expired token, the CDN can return a 302 response to redirect the user to the customer. The customer generates a new access token and then returns this access token to the user with a 302 response to retry the request on the CDN.

   d *Referrer*—This is a Referrer HTTP request header.

Referrer header and security

When a client/user makes an HTTP request to a CDN, it should include the customer's URL as its `Referrer` HTTP header. The CDN only allows authorized referrers, so this prevents unauthorized referrers from using the CDN.

However, this is not a legitimate security mechanism. Clients can easily spoof `Referrer` headers by simply using a different URL as the `Referrer` header. A site/service can spoof a referrer header by impersonating an authorized site/service and fool clients to believe that the latter are communicating with the authorized site/service.

---

   e *Allowed IPs*—This may be a list of IP address ranges that are authorized to download CDN assets.

   f *Allowed countries or regions*—We may include a blacklist or whitelist of countries/regions. This "Allowed IPs" field already indicates which countries/regions are allowed, but we can still include this field for convenience.

3 The customer app stores the token and then returns this token to the user. For additional security, the token can be stored in an encrypted form.

4 Whenever a customer app gives a user a CDN URL, and the user makes a GET request for this CDN asset, the GET request should be signed with the access token. This is called URL signing. An example of a signed URL is http://12345.r.cdnsun.net/photo.jpeg?secure=DMF1ucDxtHCxwYQ (from https://cdnsun.com/knowledgebase/cdn-static/setting-a-url-signing-protect -your-cdn-content). "secure=DMF1ucDxtHCxwYQ" is a query parameter to send the access token to the CDN. The CDN performs authorization. It verifies that the user's token is valid and that the asset can be downloaded with that token, as well as with the user's IP or country/region. Finally, the CDN returns the asset to the user.

5 When a user logs out, the customer app destroys the user's token. The user will need to generate another token when logging in.

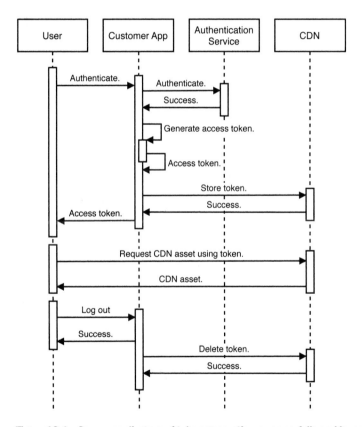

Figure 13.1 Sequence diagram of token generation process, followed by using the token to request CDN assets, and destroying the token upon user logout. The process of destroying the token can be asynchronous as illustrated here, or it can be synchronous because logouts are not frequent events.

Deleting the token can be asynchronous as illustrated in figure 13.1, or it can be synchronous because logouts are not frequent events. If token deletion is asynchronous, there is a risk that tokens will not be deleted if the customer app host handling this deletion suddenly fails. One solution is to simply ignore this problem and allow some tokens to not be destroyed. Another solution is to use an event-driven approach. The customer app host can produce a token deletion event to a Kafka queue, and a consumer cluster can consume these events and delete the tokens on the CDN. A third solution is to implement token deletion as synchronous/blocking. If token deletion fails because the customer app host suddenly fails, the user/client will receive a 500 error, and the client can retry the logout request. This approach will result in higher latency for the logout request, but this may be acceptable.

Refer to sources like https://docs.microsoft.com/en-us/azure/cdn/cdn-token-auth, https://cloud.ibm.com/docs/CDN?topic=CDN-working-with-token-authentication, https://blog.cdnsun.com/protecting-cdn-content-with-token-authentication-and-url -signing for more information on CDN token authentication and authorization.

13.3.2 *Key rotation*

A customer's key may be periodically changed, just in case a hacker manages to steal the key, the damage can be limited as it will only be useful to him until the key is changed.

The key is rotated rather than suddenly changed. *Key rotation* is a key renewal process, which contains a period where both the old and new keys are valid. It will take time for a new key to be disseminated to all the customer's systems, so the customer may continue using both the old and new key in the meantime. At a set expiry time, the old key will expire, and users cannot access CDN assets with expired keys.

It is also useful to establish this procedure for cases where we know that a hacker has stolen the key. The CDN can rotate the key and set a short time to expiration for the old key. The customer can switch to the new key as soon as possible.

13.4 *High-level architecture*

Figure 13.2 shows high-level architecture of our CDN. We adopt a typical API gateway-metadata-storage/database architecture. A user request is handled by an API gateway, which is a layer/service that makes requests to various other services. (Refer to section 1.4.6 for an overview of API gateway.) These include SSL termination, authentication and authorization, rate limiting (refer to chapter 8), and logging to a shared logging service for purposes such as analytics and billing. We can configure the API gateway to look up the metadata service to determine which storage service host to read or write to for any user. If the CDN asset is encrypted at rest, the metadata service can also record this, and we can use a secrets management service to manage the encryption keys.

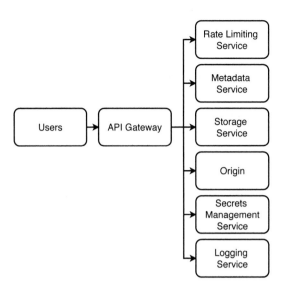

Figure 13.2 High-level architecture of our CDN. User requests are routed through an API gateway, which makes requests to the appropriate services, including rate limiting and logging. Assets are stored on a storage service, and the metadata service keeps track of the storage service hosts and file directories that store each asset. If the assets are encrypted, we use a secrets management service to manage the encryption keys. If the requested asset is missing, the API gateway retrieves it from the origin (i.e., our service; this is configured in the metadata service), adds it to the storage service, and updates the metadata service.

We can generalize the operations into reads (download) vs. writes (directory creation, upload, and file deletion). For simplicity of the initial design, every file can be replicated to every data center. Otherwise, our system will have to handle complexities such as:

- The metadata service will track which data centers contain which files.
- A file distribution system that periodically uses user query metadata to determine the optimal file distribution across the data centers. This includes the number and locations of replicas.

13.5 *Storage service*

The storage service is a cluster of hosts/nodes which contain the files. As discussed in section 4.2, we should not use a database to store large files. We should store files in the hosts' filesystems. Files should be replicated for availability and durability, with each file assigned to multiple (e.g., three) hosts. We need availability monitoring and a failover process that updates the metadata service and provisions replacement nodes. The host manager can be in-cluster or out-cluster. An in-cluster manager directly manages nodes, while an out-cluster manager manages small independent clusters of nodes, and each small cluster manages itself.

13.5.1 *In-cluster*

We can use a distributed file system like HDFS, which includes ZooKeeper as the in-cluster manager. ZooKeeper manages leader election and maintains a mapping between files, leaders, and followers. An in-cluster manager is a highly sophisticated component that also requires reliability, scalability, and high performance. An alternative that avoids such a component is an out-cluster manager.

13.5.2 *Out-cluster*

Each cluster managed by an out-cluster manager consists of three or more nodes distributed across several data centers. To read or write a file, the metadata service identifies the cluster it is or should be stored in and then reads or writes the file from a randomly selected node in the cluster. This node is responsible for replication to other nodes in the cluster. Leader election is not required, but mapping files to clusters is required. The out-cluster manager maintains a mapping of files to clusters.

13.5.3 *Evaluation*

In practice, out-cluster manager is not really simpler than in-cluster manager. Table 13.1 compares these two approaches.

Table 13.1   Comparison of in-cluster manager and out-cluster manager

In-cluster manager	Out-cluster manager
Metadata service does not make requests to the in-cluster manager.	Metadata service makes requests to the out-cluster manager.
Manages file assignment within individual roles in the cluster.	Manages file assignment to a cluster, but not to individual nodes.
Needs to know about every node in the cluster.	May not know about each individual node, but needs to know about each cluster.
Monitors heartbeats from nodes.	Monitors health of each independent cluster.
Deals with host failures. Nodes may die, and new nodes may be added to the cluster.	Tracks each cluster's utilization and deals with overheated clusters. New files may no longer be assigned to clusters that reach their capacity limits.

13.6 *Common operations*

When the client makes a request with our CDN service's domain (e.g., cdnservice.flickr
.com) rather than an IP address, GeoDNS (refer to sections 1.4.2 and 7.9) assigns the
IP address of the closest host, where a load balancer directs it an API gateway host. As
described in section 6.2, the API gateway performs a number of operations, including
caching. The frontend service and its associated caching service can assist with caching
frequently accessed files.

13.6.1 *Reads: Downloads*

For a download, the next step is to select a storage host to serve this request. The metadata service aids in this selection by maintaining and providing the following metadata. It can use Redis and/or SQL:

- The storage service hosts which contain the files. Some or all the hosts may be on
  other data centers, so that information must be stored, too. Files take time to be
  replicated across hosts.
- The metadata service of each data center keeps track of the current load of its
  hosts. A host's load can be approximated by the sum of the sizes of the files it is
  currently serving.
- For purposes such as estimating how much time a file takes to download from a
  host or to distinguish between files with the same name (but this is usually done
  with MD5 or SHA hash).
- File ownership and access control.
- Health status of hosts.

DOWNLOAD PROCESS

Figure 13.3 is a sequence diagram of the steps taken by the API gateway to download a
file, assuming the CDN does contain this asset. We omit some steps such as SSL termination, authentication and authorization, and logging.

1 Query the rate limiting service to check if the request exceeds the client's rate
  limit. We assume that rate limiter allows the request through.
2 Query the metadata service to get the storage service hosts that contain this asset.
3 Select a storage host and stream the asset to the client.
4 Update the metadata service with the load increase of the storage host. If the
  metadata service records the asset's size, this step can be done in parallel with
  step 3. Otherwise, the API gateway will need to measure the asset's size, to update
  the metadata service with the correct load increase.

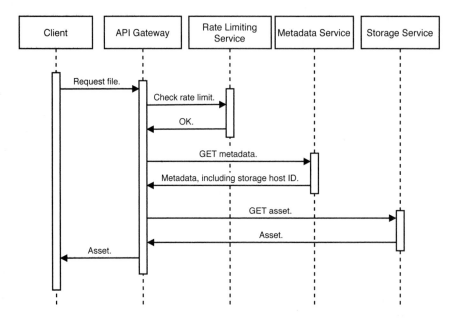

Figure 13.3   Sequence diagram of a client making a CDN download. We assume rate limiter allows the request through. The sequence is straightforward if the asset is present.

An alert reader may note that the last step of the API gateway updating the load to the metadata service can be done asynchronously. If the API gateway host experiences an outage during this update, the metadata service may not receive it. We can choose to ignore this error and allow the user to use the CDN more than the former is allowed to. Alternatively, the API gateway host can produce this event to a Kafka topic. Either the metadata service can consume from this topic, or we can use a dedicated consumer cluster to consume from the topic and then update the metadata service.

The CDN may not contain this asset. It may have deleted it for reasons including the following:

- There may be a set retention period for assets, such as a few months or years, and this period had passed for that asset. The retention period may also be based on when the asset was last accessed.
- A less likely reason is that the asset was never uploaded because the CDN ran out of storage space (or had other errors), but the customer believed that the asset was successfully uploaded.
- Other errors in the CDN.

Referring to figure 13.4, if the CDN does not have the asset, it will need to download it from the origin, which is a backup location provided by the customer. This will increase latency. It will then need to store it by uploading it to the storage service and updating the metadata service. To minimize latency, the storage process can be done in parallel with returning the asset to the client.

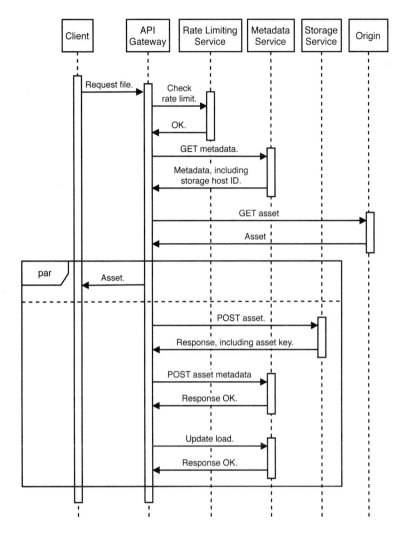

Figure 13.4 Sequence diagram of a CDN download process if the CDN does not contain the requested asset. The CDN will need to download the asset from the origin (a backup location provided by the customer), and return it to the user, as well as store the asset for future requests. POST asset metadata and upload load can be done as a single request, but we can keep them as separate requests for simplicity.

DOWNLOAD PROCESS WITH ENCRYPTION AT REST

What if we needed to store assets in encrypted form? Referring to figure 13.5, we can store the encryption keys in a secrets management service (which requires authentication). When an API gateway host is initialized, it can authenticate with the secrets management service, which will pass the former a token for future requests. Referring to figure 13.5, when an authorized user requests an asset, the host can first obtain the asset's encryption key from the secrets management service, fetch the encrypted asset from the storage service, decrypt the asset, and return it to the user. If the asset is large, it may be stored in multiple blocks in the storage service, and each block will need to be separately fetched and decrypted.

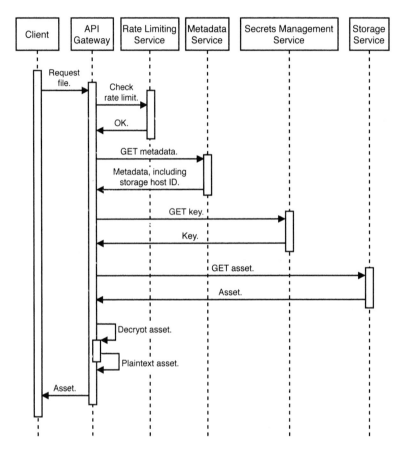

Figure 13.5   Sequence diagram of downloading an asset that is encrypted at rest, assuming the asset is present in the CDN. If the asset is large, it may be stored in multiple blocks in the storage service, and each block will need to be separately fetched and decrypted.

Figure 13.6 illustrates the process that occurs if a request is made to fetch an encrypted asset that the CDN does not possess. Similar to figure 13.5, the API gateway will need to fetch the asset from the origin. Next, the API gateway can parallelly return the asset to the user while storing it in the storage service. The API gateway can generate a random encryption key, encrypt the asset, write the asset to the storage service, and write the key to the secrets management service.

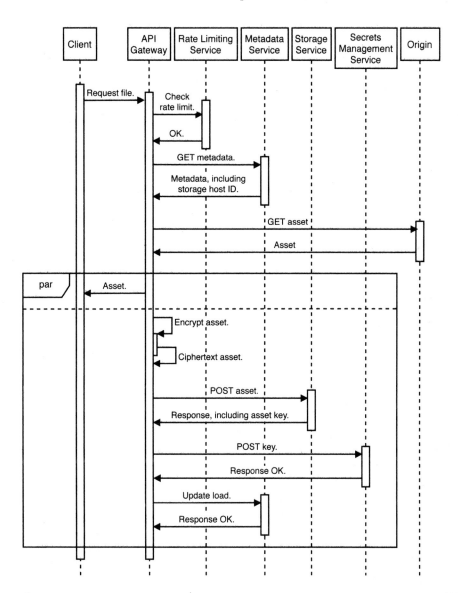

Figure 13.6   Sequence diagram of the steps to download an encrypted file. POST asset and POST key can also be done in parallel.

13.6.2   *Writes: Directory creation, file upload, and file deletion*

A file is identified by its ID, not its content. (We cannot use file names as identifiers because different users can give different files the same name. Even an individual user may give the same name to different files.) We consider files with different IDs but the same contents to be different files. Should identical files with different owners be stored separately, or should we attempt to save storage by keeping only one copy of a file? To save storage in this manner, we will have to build an additional layer of complexity to manage groups of owners, so that any owner may see that a file is accessible by other owners that they recognize, rather than owners that belong to other groups. We assume that the number of identical files is a small fraction of all the files, so this may be over-engineering. Our initial design should store such files separately, but we must remember that there are no absolute truths in system design (thus system design is an art, not a science). We can discuss with our interviewer that as the total amount of storage our CDN uses becomes large, the cost savings of saving storage by deduplicating the files may be worth the additional complexity and cost.

A file can be GB or TB in size. What if file upload or download fails before it is complete? It will be wasteful to upload or download the file from the beginning. We should develop a process similar to checkpointing or bulkhead to divide a file into chunks, so a client only needs to repeat the upload or download operations on the chunks that have not completed. Such an upload process is known as *multipart upload*, and we can also apply the same principles to downloads, too.

We can design a protocol for multipart uploads. In such a protocol, uploading a chunk can be equivalent to uploading an independent file. For simplicity, chunks can be of fixed size, such as 128 MB. When a client begins a chunk upload, it can send an initial message that contains the usual metadata such as the user ID, the filename, and size. It can also include the number of the chunk about to be uploaded. In multipart upload, the storage host will now need to allocate a suitable address range on the disk to store the file and record this information. When it starts receiving a chunk upload, it should write the chunk to the appropriate addresses. The metadata service can track which chunk uploads have completed. When the client completes uploading the final chunk, the metadata service marks the file as ready for replication and download. If a chunk upload fails, the client can reupload just this chunk instead of the entire file.

If the client stops uploading the file before all chunks are successfully uploaded, these chunks will uselessly occupy space in our storage host. We can implement a simple cron job or a batch ETL job that periodically deletes these chunks of incompletely uploaded files. Other possible discussion topics include:

- Allowing the client to choose the chunk size.
- Replicating the file as it is being uploaded, so the file can be ready for download sooner across the CDN. This introduces additional complexity and is unlikely to be required, but we can discuss such a system should such high performance be required.
- A client can start playing a media file as soon as it downloads the first chunk. We will briefly discuss this in section 13.9.

NOTE   The multipart upload with checkpointing that we discussed here is unrelated to multipart/form-data HTML encoding. The latter is for uploading form data that contains files. Refer to sources such as https://swagger.io/docs/specification/describing-request-body/multipart-requests/ and https://developer.mozilla.org/en-US/docs/Web/HTTP/Methods/POST for more details.

Another question is how to handle adding, updating (the contents), and deleting files on this distributed system. Section 4.3 discussed replication of update and delete operations, their complications, and some solutions. We can discuss some possible solutions adopted from that section:

- A single-leader approach that designates a particular data center to perform these operations and propagate the changes to the other data centers. This approach may be adequate for our requirements, especially if we do not require the changes to be rapidly available on all data centers.
- The multi-leader approaches discussed, including tuples. (Refer to Martin Kleppmann's book *Designing Data-Intensive Systems* for a discussion on tuples.)
- The client acquires a lock on this file in every data center, performs this operation on every data center, and then releases the locks.

In each of these approaches, the frontend updates the metadata service with the file's availability on the data centers.

DO NOT KEEP FILE COPIES ON ALL DATA CENTERS

Certain files may be used mostly by particular regions (e.g., audio or text files in human languages predominantly used in a particular region), so not all data centers need to contain a copy of the files. We can set replication criteria to determine when a file should be copied to a particular data center (e.g., number of requests or users for this file within the last month). However, this means that the file needs to be replicated within a data center for fault-tolerance.

Certain contents are separated into multiple files because of application requirements to serve certain file combinations to certain users. For example, a video file may be served to all users, and it has an accompanying audio file in a particular language. This logic can be handled at the application level rather than by the CDN.

REBALANCING THE BATCH ETL JOB

We have a periodic (hourly or daily) batch job to distribute files across the various data centers and replicate files to the appropriate number of hosts to meet demand. This batch job obtains the file download logs of the previous period from the logging service, determines the request counts of the files, and uses these numbers to adjust the numbers of storage hosts for each file. Next, it creates a map of which files should be added to or deleted from each node and then uses this map to make the corresponding shuffling.

For real-time syncing, we can develop the metadata service further to constantly analyze file locations and access and redistribute files.

Cross data center replication is a complex topic, and you are unlikely to discuss this in deep detail during a system design interview, unless you are interviewing for roles that request such expertise. In this section, we discuss a possible design to update the file mappings in the metadata service and the files in the storage service.

NOTE Refer to sources like https://serverfault.com/questions/831790/how-to
-manage-failover-in-zookeeper-across-datacenters-using-observers, https://
zookeeper.apache.org/doc/r3.5.9/zookeeperObservers.html, and https://
stackoverflow.com/questions/41737770/how-to-deploy-zookeeper-across
-multiple-data-centers-and-failover for more information on how to configure
cross data center replication on ZooKeeper. Refer to https://solr.apache.org/
guide/8_11/cross-data-center-replication-cdcr.html for a guide on how cross
data center replication can be configured in Solr, a search platform that uses
ZooKeeper to manage its nodes.

Let's discuss an approach to write new file metadata to the metadata service and shuffle the files accordingly between the data centers (in the in-cluster approach) or hosts (in the out-cluster approach) of the storage service. Our approach will need to make requests to the storage service to transfer files between its hosts across various data centers. To prevent inconsistency between the metadata service and storage service in case of failed write requests, the metadata service should only update its file location metadata when it receives a success response from the storage service, indicating that the files are successfully written to their new locations. The storage service relies on its manager (in-cluster or out-cluster) to ensure consistency within its own nodes/hosts. This ensures the metadata service does not return file locations before the files have been successfully written to those locations.

Moreover, files should be deleted from their previous nodes only after they are successfully written to their new locations, so if file writes to the new locations fail, the files continue to exist at their old locations, and the metadata service can continue to return these old file locations when it receives requests for those files.

We can use a saga approach (refer to section 5.6). Figure 13.7 illustrates a choreography approach, while figure 13.8 illustrates an orchestration approach where the metadata service is the orchestrator.

The steps in figure 13.7 are as follows:

1 The shuffling job produces an event to the shuffling topic, which corresponds to moving a file from certain locations to others. This event may also contain information such as the recommended replication factor of this file, corresponding to the number of leader nodes that should contain this file.

2 The storage service consumes this event and writes the file to their new locations.

3 The storage service produces an event to the metadata topic to request the metadata service to update its file location metadata.

4 The metadata service consumes from the metadata topic and updates the file location metadata.

5 The metadata service produces an event to the file deletion topic to request the storage service to delete the files from their old locations.

6 The storage service consumes this event and deletes the file from its old locations.

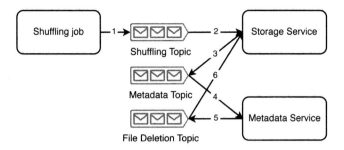

Figure 13.7 A choreography saga to update the metadata service and storage service

Identify the transaction types

Which are the compensable transactions, pivot transaction, and retriable transactions?

All transactions before step 6 can be compensated. Step 6 is the pivot transaction because the file deletion is irreversible. It is the final step, so there are no retriable transactions.

That being said, we can implement file deletion as *soft delete* (mark data as deleted, but not actually delete it). We can periodically *hard delete* (delete data from our storage hardware with no intention to use or recover it again) data from our database. In this case, all the transactions are compensable, and there will be no pivot transaction.

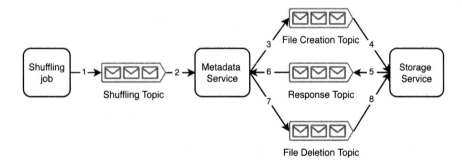

Figure 13.8 An orchestration saga to update the metadata service and storage service

The steps in figure 13.8 are as follows:

1. This is the same step as step 1 of the choreography approach previously discussed.
2. The metadata service consumes this event.
3. The metadata service produces an event to the file creation topic to request the storage service to create the file at the new locations.
4. The storage service consumes this event and writes the files to their new locations.

5 The storage service produces an event to the response topic to inform the metadata service that the file writes were successfully completed.

6 The metadata service consumes this event.

7 The metadata service produces an event to the file deletion topic to request the storage service to delete the file from its old locations.

8 The storage service consumes this event and deletes the file from its old locations.

13.7 Cache invalidation

As a CDN is for static files, cache invalidation is much less of a concern. We can fingerprint the files as discussed in section 4.11.1. We discussed various caching strategies (section 4.8) and designing a system to monitor the cache for stale files. This system will have to anticipate high traffic.

13.8 Logging, monitoring, and alerting

In section 2.5, we discussed key concepts of logging, monitoring, and alerting that one must mention in an interview. Besides what was discussed in section 2.5, we should monitor and send alerts for the following:

- Uploaders should be able to track the state of their files, whether the upload is in progress, completed, or failed.
- Log CDN misses and then monitors and triggers low-urgency alerts for them.
- The frontend service can log the request rate for files. This can be done on a shared logging service.
- Monitor for unusual or malicious activity.

13.9 Other possible discussions on downloading media files

We may wish media files to be playable before they are fully downloaded. A solution is to divide the media file into smaller files, which can be downloaded in sequence and assembled into a media file that is a partial version of the original. Such a system requires a client-side media player that can do such assembly while playing the partial version. The details may be beyond the scope of a system design interview. It involves piercing together the files' byte strings.

As the sequence is important, we need metadata that indicates which files to download first. Our system splits a file into smaller files and assigns each small file with a sequence number. We also generate a metadata file that contains information on the order of the files and their total number. How can the files be efficiently downloaded in a particular sequence? We can also discuss other possible video streaming optimization strategies.

Summary

- A CDN is a scalable and resilient distributed file storage service, which is a utility that is required by almost any web service that serves a large or geographically distributed user base.

- A CDN is geographically distributed file storage service that allows each user to access a file from the data center that can serve them the fastest.

- A CDN's advantages include lower latency, scalability, lower unit costs, higher throughput, and higher availability.

- A CDN's disadvantages include additional complexity, high unit costs for low traffic and hidden costs, expensive migration, possible network restrictions, security and privacy concerns, and insufficient customization capabilities.

- A storage service can be separate from a metadata service that keeps track of which storage service hosts store particular files. The storage service's implementation can focus on host provisioning and health.

- We can log file accesses and use this data to redistribute or replicate files across data centers to optimize latency and storage.

- CDNs can use third-party token-based authentication and authorization with key rotation for secure, reliable, and fine-grained access control.

- A possible CDN high-level architecture can be a typical API gateway-metadata-storage/database architecture. We customize and scale each component to suit our specific functional and non-functional requirements.

- Our distributed file storage service can be managed in-cluster or out-cluster. Each has its tradeoffs.

- Frequently accessed files can be cached on the API gateway for faster reads.

- For encryption at rest, a CDN can use a secrets management service to manage encryption keys.

- Large files should be uploaded with a multipart upload process that divides the file into chunks and manages the upload of each chunk separately.

- To maintain low latency of downloads while managing costs, a periodic batch job can redistribute files across data centers and replicate them to the appropriate number of hosts.

14

Design a text messaging app

This chapter covers

- Designing an app for billions of clients to send short messages
- Considering approaches that trade off latency vs. cost
- Designing for fault-tolerance

Let's design a text messaging app, a system for 100K users to send messages to each other within seconds. Do not consider video or audio chat. Users send messages at an unpredictable rate, so our system should be able to handle these traffic surges. This is the first example system in this book that considers exactly-once delivery. Messages should not be lost, nor should they be sent more than once.

14.1 Requirements

After some discussion, we determined the following functional requirements:

- Real-time or eventually-consistent? Consider either case.
- How many users may a chatroom have? A chatroom can contain between two to 1,000 users.
- Is there a character limit for a message? Let's make it 1000 UTF-8 characters. At up to 32 bits/character, a message is up to 4 KB in size.
- Notification is a platform-specific detail that we need not consider. Android, iOS, Chrome, and Windows apps each have their platform-specific notification library.
- Delivery confirmation and read receipt.
- Log the messages. Users can view and search up to 10 MB of their past messages. With one billion users, this works out to 10 PB of storage.
- Message body is private. We can discuss with the interviewer if we can view any message information, including information like knowing that a message was send from one user to another. However, error events such as failure to send a message should trigger an error that is visible to us. Such error logging and monitoring should preserve user privacy. End-to-end encryption will be ideal.
- No need to consider user onboarding (i.e., the process of new users signing on to our messaging app).
- No need to consider multiple chatrooms/channels for the same group of users.
- Some chat apps have template messages that users can select to quickly create and send, such as "Good morning!" or "Can't talk now, will reply later." This can be a client-side feature that we do not consider here.
- Some messaging apps allow users to see if their connections are online. We do not consider this.
- We consider sending text only, not media like voice messages, photos, or videos.

Non-functional requirements:

- *Scalability:* 100K simultaneous users. Assume each user sends a 4 KB message every minute, which is a write rate of 400 MB/min. A user can have up to 1,000 connections, and a message can be sent to up to 1,000 recipients, each of whom may have up to five devices.
- *High availability:* Four nines availability.
- *High performance:* 10-second P99 message delivery time.
- *Security and privacy:* Require user authentication. Messages should be private.
- *Consistency:* Strict ordering of messages is not necessary. If multiple users send messages to each other more or less simultaneously, these messages can appear in different orders to different users.

14.2   Initial thoughts

At first glance, this seems to be similar to the notification/alerting service we discussed in chapter 9. Looking closer, we see some differences, listed in table 14.1. We cannot naively reuse our notification/alerting service's design, but we can use it as a starting point. We identify similar requirements and their corresponding design components and use the differences to increase or reduce our design's complexity as appropriate.

Table 14.1   Differences between our messaging app and our notification/alerting service

Messaging app	Notification/alerting service
All messages are equal priority and have a 10-second P99 delivery time.	Events can have different priority levels.
Messages are delivered from one client to others, all within a single channel on a single service. No need to consider other channels or services.	Multiple channels, such as email, SMS, automated phone calls, push notifications, or notifications within apps.
Only a manual trigger condition.	An event can be manually, programmatically, or periodically triggered.
No message templates. (Except perhaps message suggestions.)	Users can create and manage notification templates.
Due to end-to-end encryption, we cannot see the user's messages, so there is less freedom to identify and deduplicate common elements into functions to reduce computational resource consumption.	No end-to-end encryption. We have more freedom to create abstractions, such as a template service.
Users may request for old messages.	Most notifications only need to be sent once.
Delivery confirmation and read receipt are part of the app.	We may not have access to most notification channels, such as email, texting, push notifications, etc., so delivery and read confirmations may not be possible.

14.3   Initial high-level design

A user first selects the recipient (by name) of their message from a list of recipients. Next, they compose a message on a mobile, desktop, or browser app and then hit a Send button. The app first encrypts the message with the recipient's public key and then makes a request to our messaging service to deliver the message. Our messaging service sends the message to the recipient. The recipient sends delivery confirmation and read receipt messages to the sender. This design has the following implications:

- Our app needs to store each recipient's metadata, including names and public keys.
- Our messaging service needs to maintain an open WebSocket connection to each recipient.

- If there is more than one recipient, the sender needs to encrypt the message with each recipient's public key.
- Our messaging service needs to handle unpredictable traffic surges from many senders suddenly deciding to send messages within a short period.

Referring to figure 14.1, we create separate services to serve different functional requirements and optimize for their different nonfunctional requirements.

- *Sender service:* Receives messages from senders and immediately delivers them to recipients. It also records these messages in the message service, described next.
- *Message service:* Senders can make requests to this service for their sent messages, while recipients can make requests to this service for both their received and unreceived messages.
- *Connection service:* For storage and retrieval of users' active and blocked connections, add other users to one's contact list, block other users from sending messages. The connection service also stores connection metadata, such as names, avatars, and public keys.

Figure 14.1 illustrates our high-level architecture with the relationships between our services. Users make requests to our services via an API gateway. Our sender service makes requests to our message service to record messages, including messages that failed to be delivered to recipients. It also makes requests to our connection service to check if a recipient has blocked the message sender. We discuss more details in subsequent sections.

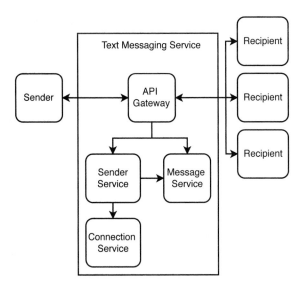

Figure 14.1 High-level architecture with the relationships between our services. A recipient can make requests to send delivery confirmations and read receipts, which are sent to the sender. Any user (sender or receiver) can request the message service for old or undelivered messages.

14.4 Connection service

The connection service should provide the following endpoints:

- *GET /connection/user/{userId}:* GET all of a user's connections and their metadata, including both active and blocked connections and active connections' public keys. We may also add additional path or query parameters for filtering by connection groups or other categories.
- *POST /connection/user/{userId}/recipient/{recipientId}:* New connection request from a user with userId to another user with recipientId.
- *PUT /connection/user/{userId}/recipient/{recipientId}/request/{accept}:* Accept is a Boolean variable to accept or reject a connection request.
- *PUT /connection/user/{userId}/recipient/{recipientId}/block/{block}:* Block is a Boolean variable to block or unblock a connection.
- *DELETE /connection/user/{userId}/recipient/{recipientId}:* Delete a connection.

14.4.1 Making connections

Users' connections (including both active and blocked connections) should be stored on users' devices (i.e., in their desktop or mobile apps) or in browser cookies or localStorage, so the connection service is a backup for this data in case a user changes devices or to synchronize this data across a user's multiple devices. We do not expect heavy write traffic or a large amount of data, so we can implement it as a simple stateless backend service that stores data in a shared SQL service.

14.4.2 Sender blocking

We refer to a blocked connection as a blocked sender connection if a user has blocked this sender and a blocked recipient connection if a user is blocked by this recipient. In this section, we discuss an approach to blocking senders to maximize our messaging app's performance and offline functionality. Referring to figure 14.2, we should implement blocking at every layer—that is, on the client (both the sender's and recipient's devices) and on the server. The rest of this section discusses some relevant considerations of this approach.

Figure 14.2   Blocking should be implemented at every layer. When a blocked sender attempts to send a message, his device should block it. If this blocking fails and the message went to the server, the server should block it. If the server failed to block the message and it reached the recipient's device, the recipient's device should block it.

REDUCE TRAFFIC

To reduce traffic to the server, blocked recipient connections should be stored on a user's device, so the device can prevent the user from interacting with this recipient, and the server does not have to block such undesired interactions. Whether we wish to inform a user that another user has blocked them is a UX design decision that is up to us.

ALLOW IMMEDIATE BLOCKING/UNBLOCKING

When a user submits a request on the client to block a sender, the client should also send the relevant PUT request to block the sender. However, in case this particular endpoint is unavailable, the client can also record that it had blocked the sender, so it can hide any messages from the blocked sender and not display new message notifications. The client performs the analogous operations for unblocking a sender. These requests can be sent to a dead letter queue on the device and then sent to the server when that endpoint is available again. This is an example of graceful degradation. Limited functionality is maintained even when part of a system fails.

This may mean that a user's other devices may continue to receive messages from the intended blocked sender or may block messages from the intended unblocked sender.

Our connection service can keep track of which devices have synchronized their connections with our service. If a synchronized device sends a message to a recipient that has blocked the sender, this indicates a possible bug or malicious activity, and our connection service should trigger an alert to the developers. We discuss this further in section 14.6.

HACKING THE APP

There is no practical way to prevent a sender from attempting to hack into the app to delete data about recipients that have blocked them. If we encrypt the blocked recipients on the sender's device, the only secure way to store the key is on the server, which means that the sender's device needs to query the server to view blocked recipients, and this defeats the purpose of storing this data on the sender's device. This security concern is another reason to implement blocking at every layer. A detailed discussion of security and hacking is outside the scope of this book.

POSSIBLE CONSISTENCY PROBLEM

A user may send the same blocking or unblocking requests from multiple devices. At first, it seemed that this would not cause any problems because the PUT request is idempotent. However, inconsistency may result. Our graceful degradation mechanism had made this feature more complex. Referring to figure 14.3, if a user makes a blocking request and then an unblocking request on one device and also makes a blocking request on another device, it is unclear if the final state is to block or unblock the sender. As stated in other places in this book, attaching a device's timestamp to the request to determine the requests' order is not a solution because the devices' clocks cannot be perfectly synchronized.

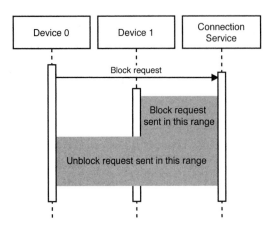

Figure 14.3   If multiple
devices can send requests
to the connection service,
inconsistency may result. If
device 0 makes a blocking
request followed by an
unblocking request, while
device 1 makes a blocking
request after device 0, it is
unclear if the user's intention
is to block or unblock.

Allowing only one device to be connected at a time does not solve this problem because we allow these requests to be queued on a user's device if the request to the server could not be made. Referring to figure 14.4, a user may connect to one device and make some requests that are queued, then connect to another device and make other requests that are successful, and then the first device may successfully make the requests to the server.

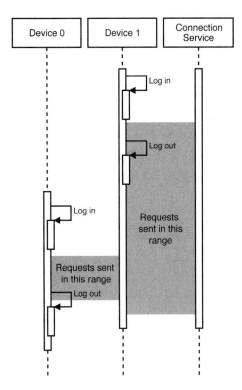

Figure 14.4   Inconsistency
may occur even if a device
needs to be logged in for a
request to be made because
a request may be queued on
a device, then sent to the
connection service after the
user logged out.

This general consistency problem is present when an app offers offline functionality that involves write operations.

One solution is to ask the user to confirm the final state of each device. (This is the approach followed by this app written by the author: https://play.google.com/store/apps/details?id=com.zhiyong.tingxie.) The steps may be as follows:

1 A user does such a write operation on one device, which then updates the server.

2 Another device synchronizes with the server and finds that its state is different from the server.

3 The device presents a UI to the user that asks the user to confirm the final state.

Another possible solution is to place limits on the write operations (and offline functionality) in a way to prevent inconsistency. In this case, when a device sends a block request, it should not be allowed to unblock until all other devices have synchronized with the server, and vice versa for unblock requests.

A disadvantage of both approaches is that the UX is not as smooth. There is a tradeoff between usability and consistency. The UX will be better if a device can send arbitrary write operations regardless of its network connectivity, which is impossible to keep consistent.

PUBLIC KEYS

When a device installs (or reinstalls) our app and starts our app for the first time, it generates a public-private key pair. It should store its public key in the connection service. The connection service should immediately update the user's connections with the new public key via their WebSocket connections.

As a user may have up to 1,000 connections, each with five devices, a key change may require up to 5,000 requests, and some of these requests may fail because the recipients may be unavailable. Key changes will likely be rare events, so this should not cause unpredicted traffic surges, and the connection service should not need to use message brokering or Kafka. A connection who didn't receive the update can receive it in a later GET request.

If a sender encrypts their message with an outdated public key, it will appear as gibberish after the recipient decrypts it. To prevent the recipient device from displaying such errors to the recipient user, the sender can hash the message with a cryptographic hash function such as SHA-2 and include this hash as part of the message. The recipient device can hash the decrypted message and display the decrypted message to the recipient user only if the hashes match. The sender service (discussed in detail in the next section) can provide a special message endpoint for a recipient to request the sender to resend the message. The recipient can include its public key, so the sender will not repeat this error and can also replace its outdated public key with the new one.

One way to prevent such errors is that a public key change should not be effective immediately. The request to change a public key can include a grace period (such as seven days) during which both keys are valid. If a recipient receives a message encrypted with the old key, it can send a special message request to the Sender Service containing the new key, and the sender service requests the sender to update the latter's key.

14.5   *Sender service*

The sender service is optimized for scalability, availability, and performance of a single function, which is to receive messages from senders and deliver them to recipients in near real time. It should be made as simple as possible to optimize debuggability and maintainability of this critical function. If there are unpredicted traffic surges, it should be able to buffer these messages in a temporary storage, so it can process and deliver them when it has sufficient resources.

Figure 14.5 is the high-level architecture of our sender service. It consists of two services with a Kafka topic between them. We name them the new message service and the message-sending service. This approach is similar to our notification service backend in section 9.3. However, we don't use a metadata service here because the content is encrypted, so we cannot parse it to replace common components with IDs.

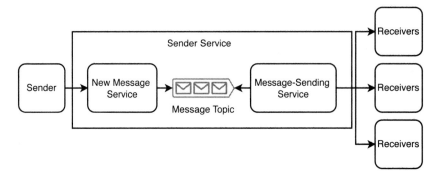

Figure 14.5   High-level architecture of our sender service. A sender sends its message to the sender service via an API gateway (not illustrated).

A message has the fields sender ID, a list of up to 1,000 recipient IDs, body string, and message sent status enum (the possible statuses are "message sent," "message delivered," and "message read").

14.5.1   *Sending a message*

Sending a message occurs as follows. On the client, a user composes a message with a sender ID, recipient IDs, and a body string. Delivery confirmation and read receipt are initialized to false. The client encrypts the body and then sends the message to the sender service.

The new message service receives a message request, produces it to the new message Kafka topic, then returns 200 success to the sender. A message request from one sender may contain up to 5,000 recipients, so it should be processed asynchronously this way. The new message service may also perform simple validations, such as whether the request was properly formatted, and return 400 error to invalid requests (as well as trigger the appropriate alerts to developers).

Figure 14.6 illustrates the high-level architecture of our message-sending service. The message generator consumes from the new message Kafka topic and generates a separate message for each recipient. The host may fork a thread or maintain a thread pool to generate a message. The host produces the message to a Kafka topic, which we call the recipient topic. The host may also write a checkpoint to a distributed in-memory database such as Redis. If the host fails while generating messages, its replacement can look up this checkpoint, so it doesn't generate duplicate messages.

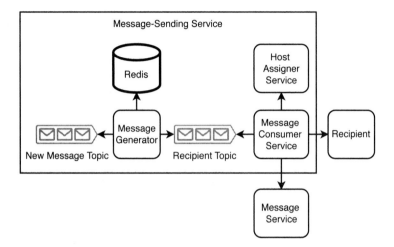

Figure 14.6   High-level architecture of our message-sending service. The message consumer service may go through other services to send the message to the recipient, instead of directly sending it to the recipient as illustrated here.

The message consumer service consumes from the recipient topic and then does the following steps.

1 Check if the sender should have been blocked. The message-sending service should store this data, instead of having to make a request to the connection service for every message. If a message has a blocked sender, it indicates that the client-side blocking mechanism has failed, possibly due to bugs or malicious activity. In this case, we should trigger an alert to developers.

2 Each message-sending service host has WebSocket connections with a number of recipients. We can experiment with this number to determine a good balance. Using a Kafka topic allows each host to serve a larger number of recipients, since it can consume from the Kafka topic only when it is ready to deliver a message. The service can use a distributed configuration service like ZooKeeper to assign hosts to devices. This ZooKeeper service can be behind another service that provides the appropriate API endpoints for returning the host that serves a particular recipient. We can call this the host assigner service.

   a The message-sending service host that is handling the current message can query the host assigner service for the appropriate host and then request that host to deliver the message to the recipient. Refer to section 14.6.3 for more details.

b In parallel, the message-sending service should also log the message to the message service, which is discussed further in the next section. Section 14.6 has a more detailed discussion of the message-sending service.

3 The sender service sends the message to the recipient client. If the message cannot be delivered to the recipient client (most likely because the recipient device is off or doesn't have internet connectivity), we can simply drop the message because it has already been recorded in the message service and can be retrieved by the device later.

4 The receiver can ensure that the message isn't a duplicate and then display it to the user. The receiver app can also trigger a notification on the user's device.

5 When the user reads the message, the app can send a read receipt message to the sender, which can be delivered in a similar manner.

Steps 1–4 are illustrated in our sequence diagram in figure 14.7.

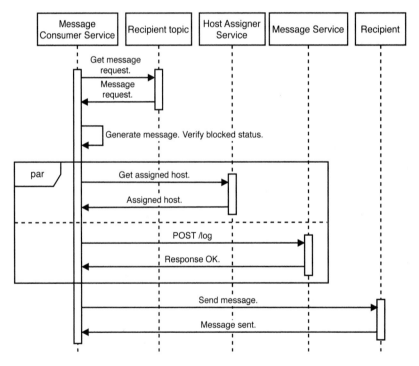

Figure 14.7 Sequence diagram of consuming a message from the recipient Kafka topic and then sending it to our recipient

EXERCISE How can these steps be performed with choreography saga or orchestration saga? Draw the relevant choreography and orchestration saga diagrams.

How can a device only retrieve its unreceived messages? One possibility we may think of is for the message service to record which of the user's devices hasn't received that message and use this to provide an endpoint for each device to retrieve only its unreceived messages. This approach assumes that the message service never needs to deliver the same message more than once to each device. Messages may be delivered but then lost. A user may delete their messages, but then wish to read them again. Our messaging app may have bugs, or the device may have problems, which cause the user to lose their messages. For such a use case, the Message Service API may expose a path or query parameter for devices to query for messages newer than their latest message. A device may receive duplicate messages, so it should check for duplicate messages.

As mentioned earlier, the message service can have a retention period of a few weeks, after which it deletes the message.

When a recipient device comes online, it can query the messaging service for new messages. This request will be directed to its host, which can query the metadata service for the new messages and return them to the recipient device.

The message-sending service also provides an endpoint to update blocked/unblocked senders. The connection service makes requests to the message-sending service to update blocked/unblocked senders. The connection service and message-sending service are separate to allow independent scaling; we expect more traffic on the latter than the former.

14.5.2 *Other discussions*

We may go through the following questions:

- What happens if a user sends a backend host a message, but the backend host dies before it responds to the user that it has received it?

If a backend host dies, the client will receive a 5xx error. We can implement the usual techniques for failed requests, such as exponential retry and backoff and a dead letter queue. The client can retry until a producer host successfully enqueues the message and returns a 200 response to the backend host which can likewise return a 200 response to the sender.

If a consumer host dies, we can implement an automatic or manual failover process such that another consumer host can consume the message from that Kafka partition and then update that partition's offset:

- What approach should be taken to solve message ordering?

We can use consistent hashing, so that messages to a particular receiver are produced to a particular Kafka partition. This ensures that messages to a particular receiver are consumed and received in order.

If a consistent hashing approach causes certain partitions to be overloaded with messages, we can increase the number of partitions and alter the consistent hashing algorithm to evenly spread the messages across the larger number of partitions. Another way is to use an in-memory database like Redis to store a receiver to partition mapping, and adjust this mapping as needed to prevent any particular partition from becoming overburdened.

Finally, the client can also ensure that messages arrive in order. If messages arrive out of order, it can trigger low-urgency alerts for further investigation. The client can also deduplicate messages:

- What if messages were n:n/many:many instead of 1:1?

We can limit the number of people in a chatroom.

The architecture is scalable. It can scale up or down cost-efficiently. It employs shared services such as an API gateway and a shared Kafka service. Using Kafka allows it to handle traffic spikes without outages.

Its main disadvantage is latency, particularly during traffic spikes. Using pull mechanisms such as queues allows eventual consistency, but they are unsuitable for real-time messaging. If we require real-time messaging, we cannot use a Kafka queue, but must instead decrease the ratio of hosts to devices and maintain a large cluster of hosts.

14.6 *Message service*

Our message service serves as a log of messages. Users may make requests to it for the following purposes:

- If a user just logged in to a new device or the device's app storage was cleared, the device will need to download its past messages (both its sent and received messages).
- A message may be undeliverable. Possible reasons include being powered off, being disabled by the OS, or no network connectivity to our service. When the client is turned on, it can request the message service for messages that were sent to it while it was unavailable.

For privacy and security, our system should use end-to-end encryption, so messages that pass through our system are encrypted. An additional advantage of end-to-end encryption is that messages are automatically encrypted both in transit and at rest.

End-to-end encryption

We can understand end-to-end encryption in three simple steps:

1 A receiver generates a public-private key pair.
2 A sender encrypts a message with the receiver's public key and then sends the receiver the message.
3 A receiver decrypts a message with their private key.

After the client successfully receives the messages, the message service can have a retention period of a few weeks, after which it deletes the messages to save storage and for better privacy and security. This deletion prevents hackers from exploiting possible security flaws in our service to obtain message contents. It limits the amount of data that hackers can steal and decrypt from our system should they manage to steal private keys from users' devices.

However, a user may have multiple devices running this messaging app. What if we want the message to be delivered to all devices?

One way is to retain the messages in the undelivered message service and perhaps have a periodic batch job to delete data from the dead letter queue older than a set age.

Another way is to allow a user to log in to only one phone at any time and provide a desktop app that can send and receive messages through the user's phone. If the user logs in through another phone, they will not see their old messages from their previous phone. We can provide a feature that lets users backup their data to a cloud storage service (such as Google Drive or Microsoft OneDrive) so they can download it to another phone.

Our message service expects high write traffic and low read traffic, which is an ideal use case for Cassandra. The architecture of our message service can be a stateless backend service and a shared Cassandra service.

14.7 Message-sending service

Section 14.5 discussed the sender service, which contains a new message service to filter out invalid messages and then buffer the messages in a Kafka topic. The bulk of the processing and the message delivery is carried out by the message-sending service, which we discuss in detail in this section.

14.7.1 Introduction

The sender service cannot simply send messages to the receiver without the latter first initiating a session with the former because the receiver devices are not servers. It is generally infeasible for user's devices to be servers for reasons including the following:

- *Security:* Nefarious parties can send malicious programs to devices, such as hijacking them for DDoS attacks.
- *Increased network traffic to devices:* Devices will be able to receive network traffic from others without first initiating a connection. This may cause their owners to incur excessive fees for this increased traffic.
- *Power consumption:* If every app required the device to be a server, the increased power consumption will considerably reduce battery life.

We can use a P2P protocol like BitTorrent, but it comes with the tradeoffs discussed earlier. We will not discuss this further.

The requirement for devices to initiate connections means that our messaging service must constantly maintain a large number of connections, one for each client. We require a large cluster of hosts, which defeats the purpose of using a message queue.

Using WebSocket will also not help us because open WebSocket connections also consume host memory.

The consumer cluster may have thousands of hosts to serve up to 100K simultaneous receivers/users. This means that each backend host must maintain open WebSocket connections with a number of users, as shown in figure 14.1. This statefulness is inevitable. We will need a distributed coordination service such as ZooKeeper to assign hosts to users. If a host goes down, ZooKeeper should detect this and provision a replacement host.

Let's consider a failover procedure when a message-sending service host dies. A host should emit heartbeats to its devices. If the host dies, its devices can request our message-sending service for new WebSocket connections. Our container orchestration system (such as Kubernetes) should provision a new host, use ZooKeeper to determine its devices, and open WebSocket connections with these devices.

Before the old host died, it may have successfully delivered the message to some but not all the recipients. How can the new host avoid redelivering the same message and cause duplicates?

One way is to do checkpointing after each message. We can use an in-memory database such as Redis and partition the Redis cluster for strong consistency. The host can write to Redis each time after a message is successfully delivered to a recipient. The host also reads from Redis before delivering a message, so the host will not deliver duplicate messages.

Another way is to simply resend the messages to all recipients and rely on the recipient's devices to deduplicate the message.

A third way is for the sender to resend the message if it does not receive an acknowledgment after a few minutes. This message may be processed and delivered by another consumer host. If this problem persists, it can trigger an alert to a shared monitoring and alerting service to alert developers of this problem.

14.7.2 High-level architecture

Figure 14.8 shows the high-level architecture of the message-sending service. The main components are:

1 The messaging cluster. This is a large cluster of hosts, each of which is assigned to a number of devices. Each individual device can be assigned an ID.

2 The host assigner service. This is a backend service that uses a ZooKeeper service to maintain a mapping of device IDs to hosts. Our cluster management system such as Kubernetes may also use the ZooKeeper service. During failover, Kubernetes updates the ZooKeeper service to remove the record of the old host and add records concerning any newly-provisioned hosts.

3 The connection service, discussed earlier in this chapter.

4 The message service, which was illustrated in figure 14.6. Every message that is received or sent to a device is also logged in the message service.

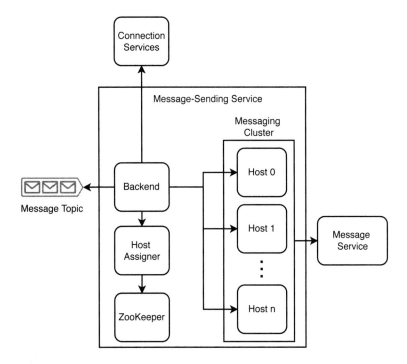

Figure 14.8 **High-level architecture of the message-sending service that assigns clients to dedicated hosts. Message backup is not illustrated.**

Every client is connected to our sender service via WebSocket, so hosts can send messages to client with near real-time latency. This means that we need a sizable number of hosts in the messaging cluster. Certain engineering teams have managed to establish millions of concurrent connections on a single host (https://migratorydata .com/2013/10/10/scaling-to-12-million-concurrent-connections-how-migratorydata -did-it/). Every host will also need to store its connections' public keys. Our messaging service needs an endpoint for its connections to send their hosts' the formers' new public keys as necessary.

However, this does not mean that a single host can simultaneously process messages to and from millions of clients. Tradeoffs must be made. Messages that can be delivered in a few seconds have to be small, limited to a few hundred characters of text. We can create a separate messaging service with its own host cluster for handling files such as photos and videos and scale this service independently of the messaging service that handles text. During traffic spikes, users can continue to send messages to each other with a few seconds of latency, but sending a file may take minutes.

Each host may store messages up to a few days old, periodically deleting old messages from memory. Referring to figure 14.9, when a host receives a message, it may store the message in its memory, while forking a thread to produce the message to a Kafka queue. A consumer cluster can consume from the queue and write the message to a shared Redis service. (Redis has fast writes, but we can still use Kafka to buffer writes for higher fault-tolerance.) When a client requests old messages, this request is passed through the backend to its host, and the host reads these old messages from the shared Redis service. This overall approach prioritizes reads over writes, so read requests can have low latency. Moreover, since write traffic will be much greater than read traffic, using a Kafka queue ensures that traffic spikes do not overwhelm the Redis service.

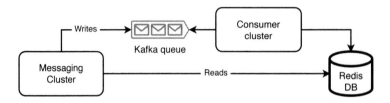

Figure 14.9 **Interaction between the messaging cluster and Redis database. We can use a Kafka queue to buffer reads for higher fault-tolerance.**

The host assigner service can contain the mapping of client/chatroom IDs to hosts, keeping this mapping in a Redis cache. We can use consistent hashing, round robin, or weighted round robin to assign IDs to hosts, but this may quickly lead to a hot shard problem (certain hosts process a disproportionate load). The metadata service can contain information on the traffic of each host, so the host assigner service can use this information to decide which host to assign a client or chatroom to, to avoid the hot shard problem (certain hosts process a disproportionate load). We can balance the hosts such that each host can serve the same proportion of clients that have heavy traffic and clients with light traffic.

The metadata service can also contain information on each user's devices.

A host can log its request activity (i.e., messaging processing activity) to a logging service, which may store it in HDFS. We can run a periodic batch job to rebalance hosts by reassigning clients and hosts and updating the metadata service. To improve the load rebalancing further, we can consider using more sophisticated statistical approaches such as machine learning.

14.7.3 Steps in sending a message

We can now discuss step 3a in section 14.5.1 in more detail. When the backend service sends a message to another individual device or to a chatroom, the following steps can occur separately for the text and file contents of that message:

1 The backend host makes a request to the host assigner service, which does a lookup to ZooKeeper to determine which host serves the recipient individual client or chatroom. If there is no host assigned yet, ZooKeeper can assign a host.

2 The backend host sends the message to those hosts, which we refer to as recipient hosts.

14.7.4 *Some questions*

We may expect questions from the interviewer about statefulness. This design breaks the tenets of cloud native, which extols eventual consistency. We can discuss that this is unsuitable for this use case of a text messaging app, particularly for group chats. Cloud native makes certain tradeoffs, like higher write latency and eventual consistency for low read latency, higher availability, etc., which may not be fully applicable to our requirements of low write latency and strong consistency. Some other questions that may be discussed are as follows:

- *What happens if a server dies before it delivers the message to the receiver or the "sent" notification to a sender?* We have discussed how to handle the situation where any of a receiver's devices are offline. How do we ensure that "sent" notifications are delivered to a sender? One approach is for the client and recipient hosts to store recent "message sent" events. We can use Cassandra for its fast writes. If a sender did not receive a response after some time, it can query our messaging service to determine if the message was sent. The client or recipient host can return a successful response to the sender. Another approach is to treat a "sent" notification as a separate message. A recipient host can send a "sent" notification to the sender device.

- *What approach should be taken to solve message ordering?* Each message has a timestamp from the sender client. It may be possible that later messages may be successfully processed and delivered before earlier messages. If a recipient device displays messages in order, and a user is viewing their device, earlier messages can suddenly appear before later ones, which may confuse the user. A solution is for an earlier message to be discarded if a later message has already been delivered to a recipient's device. When a recipient client receives a message, it can determine if there are any messages with later timestamps, and if so, return a 422 error with a suitable error message. The error can propagate to the sender's device. The user who sent the message can decide to send the message again with the knowledge that it will appear after a later message that was successfully delivered.

- *What if messages were n:n/many:many instead of 1:1?* We will limit the number of people in a chatroom.

14.7.5 *Improving availability*

In the high-level architecture in figure 14.8, each client is assigned to a single host. Even if there is a monitoring service that receives heartbeats from hosts, it will take at least tens of seconds to recover from a host failure. The host assigner needs to execute a complicated algorithm to redistribute clients across hosts.

We can improve availability by having a pool of hosts on standby that do not usually serve clients, but only send heartbeats. When a host fails, the host assigner can immediately assign all its clients to a standby host. This will reduce the downtime to seconds, which we can discuss with the interviewer whether this is acceptable.

A design that minimizes downtime is to create mini clusters. Assign one or two secondary hosts to each host. We can call the latter the primary host. This primary host will constantly forward all its requests to its secondary hosts, ensuring that the secondary hosts are up to date with the primary host and are always ready to take over as primary host. When a primary host fails, failover to a secondary host can happen immediately. We can use Terraform to define this infrastructure. Define a Kubernetes cluster of 3 pods. Each pod has one node. Overall, this approach may be too costly and complex.

14.8   Search

Each user can only search on their own messages. We may implement search-to-search directly in text messages, and not build a reverse index on each client, avoiding the costs of design, implementation, and maintenance of a reverse index. The storage size of an average client's messages will probably be far less than 1 GB (excluding media files). It is straightforward to load these messages into memory and search them.

We may search on media file names, but not on the content of the files themselves. Search on byte strings is outside the scope of this book.

14.9   Logging, monitoring, and alerting

In section 2.5, we discussed key concepts of logging, monitoring, and alerting that one must mention in an interview. Besides what was discussed in section 2.5, we should log the following:

- Log requests between services, such as the API gateway to the backend service.
- Log message sent events. To preserve user privacy, we can log certain details but not others.
- For user privacy, never log the contents of a message, including all its fields (i.e., sender, receiver, body, delivery confirmation, and read receipt).
- Log if a message was sent within a data center or from one data center to another.
- Log error events, such as errors in sending messages, delivery confirmation events, and read receipt events.

Besides what was discussed in section 2.5, we should monitor and send alerts for the following:

- As usual, we monitor errors and timeouts. We monitor utilization of various services for scaling decisions. We monitor the storage consumption of the Undelivered Message Service.
- A combination of no errors on the backend service and a consistently small storage utilization in the undelivered message service indicates that we may investigate decreasing the sender service cluster size.
- We also monitor for fraud and anomalous situations, such as a client sending a high rate of messages. Programmatic sending is not allowed. Consider placing a rate limiter in front of the API gateway or backend service. Block such clients completely from sending or receiving messages while we investigate the problem.

14.10 *Other possible discussion topics*

Here are some other possible discussion topics for this system:

- For one user to send messages to another, the former must first request the latter for permission. The latter may accept or block. The latter may change their mind and grant permission after blocking.

- A user can block another user at any time. The latter cannot select the former to send messages to. These users cannot be in the same chatroom. Blocking a user will remove oneself from any chatroom containing that user.

- What about logging in from a different device? We should only allow one device to log in at a time.

- Our system does not ensure that messages are received in the order they were sent. Moreover, if a chatroom has multiple participants who send messages close in time, the other participants may not receive the messages in order. The messages may arrive in different orders for various participants. How do we design a system that ensures that messages are displayed in order? What assumptions do we make? If participant A sends a message while their device is not connected to the internet, and other participants connected to the internet send messages shortly after, what order should the messages be displayed on others' devices, and what order should they appear on participant A's device?

- How may we expand our system to support file attachments or audio and video chat? We can briefly discuss the new components and services.

- We did not discuss message deletion. A typical messaging app may provide users the ability to delete messages, after which it should not receive them again. We should allow a user to delete messages even when their device is offline, and these deletes should be synchronized with the server. This synchronization mechanism can be a point for further discussion.

- We can further discuss the mechanism to block or unblock users in greater detail.

- What are the possible security and privacy risks with our current design and possible solutions?

- How can our system support synchronization across a user's multiple devices?

- What are the possible race conditions when users add or remove other users to a chat? What if silent errors occur? How can our service detect and resolve inconsistencies?

- We did not discuss messaging systems based on peer-to-peer (P2P) protocols like Skype or BitTorrent. Since a client has a dynamic rather than static IP address (static IP address is a paid service to the client's internet service provider), the client can run a daemon that updates our service whenever its IP address changes. What are some possible complications?

- To reduce computational resources and costs, a sender can compress its message before encrypting and sending it. The recipients can uncompress the message after they receive and decrypt it.

- Discuss a system design for user onboarding. How can a new user join our messaging app? How may a new user add or invite contacts? A user can manually type in contacts or add contacts using Bluetooth or QR codes. Or our mobile app can access the phone's contact list, which will require the corresponding Android or iOS permissions. Users may invite new users by sending them a URL to download or sign on to our app.

- Our architecture is a centralized approach. Every message needs to go through our backend. We can discuss decentralized approaches, such as P2P architecture, where every device is a server and can receive requests from other devices.

Summary

- The main discussion of a simple text messaging app system design is about how to route large numbers of messages between a large number of clients.

- A chat system is similar to a notification/alerting service. Both services send messages to large numbers of recipients.

- A scalable and cost-efficient technique to handle traffic spikes is to use a message queue. However, latency will suffer during traffic spikes.

- We can decrease latency by assigning fewer users to a host, with the tradeoff of higher costs.

- Either solution must handle host failures and reassign a host's users to other hosts.

- A recipient's device may be unavailable, so provide a GET endpoint to retrieve messages.

- We should log requests between services and the details of message sent events and error events.

- We can monitor usage metrics to adjust cluster size and monitor for fraud.

Design Airbnb

The question is to design a service for landlords to rent rooms for short-term stays to travelers. This may be both a coding and system design question. A coding discussion will be in the form of coding and object-oriented programming (OOP) solution of multiple classes. In this chapter, we assume this question can be applied to reservation systems in general, such as

- Movie tickets
- Air tickets
- Parking lots
- Taxis or ridesharing, though this has different non-functional requirements and different system design.

15.1 Requirements

Before we discuss requirements, we can discuss the kind of system that we are designing. Airbnb is:

1 A reservation app, so there is a type of user who makes reservations on finite items. Airbnb calls them "guests." There is also a type of user who creates listings of these items. Airbnb calls them "hosts."

2 A marketplace app. It matches people who sell products and services to people who buy them. Airbnb matches hosts and guests.

3 It also handles payments and collects commissions. This means there are internal users who do customer support and operations (commonly abbreviated as "ops"), to mediate disputes and monitor and react to fraud. This distinguishes Airbnb from simpler apps like Craigslist. The majority of employees in companies like Airbnb are customer support and operations.

At this point, we may clarify with the interviewer whether the scope of the interview is limited to hosts and guests or includes the other types of users. In this chapter, we discuss hosts, guests, operations, and analytics.

A host's use cases include the following. This list can be very long, so we will limit our discussion to the following use cases.

- Onboarding and updates to add, update, and delete listings. Updates may include small tasks like changing listing photos. There may be much intricate business logic. For example, a listing may have a minimum and/or maximum booking duration, and pricing may vary by day of week or other criteria. The app may display pricing recommendations. Listings may be subject to local regulations. For example, San Francisco's short-term rental law limits rentals where the host is not present in the unit to a maximum of 90 days per year. Certain listing changes may also require approval from operations staff before they are published.

- Handle bookings—for example accept or reject booking requests:
  - A host may be able to view a guest's ratings and reviews by other hosts, before accepting or rejecting the guest's booking request.
  - Airbnb may provide additional options such as automated acceptances under certain host-specified criteria, such as guests with a high average rating.
  - Cancel a booking after accepting it. This may trigger monetary penalties or suspension listing privileges. The exact rules may be complicated.

- Communicate with guests, such as via in-app messaging.

- Post a rating and review of a guest and view the guest's rating and review.

- Receive payment from the guest (minus Airbnb's commission).

- Receive tax filing documents.

- Analytics, such as viewing earnings, ratings, and review contents over time.

- Communicate with operations staff, including requests for mediation (such as requesting guests to pay for damages) or reporting fraud.

A guest's use cases include the following:

- Search and view listings.
- Submit a booking request and payment and check the statuses of booking requests.
- Communicate with hosts.
- Post a rating and review of a listing and view the host's rating and review.
- Communicate with operations staff, analogous to hosts.

Ops' use cases include

- Reviewing listing requests and removing inappropriate listings.
- Communicating with customers for purposes such as dispute mediation, offering alternative listings, and sending refunds.

We will not discuss payments in detail because payments are complex. A payment solution must consider numerous currencies and regulations (including taxes) that differ by country, state, city, and other levels of government and are different for various products and services. We may impose different transaction fees by payment type (e.g., a maximum transaction amount for checks or a discount for payments made via gift cards to encourage the purchase of gift cards). The mechanisms and regulations on refunds differ by payment type, product, country, customer, and numerous other factors. There are hundreds or thousands of ways to accept payments, such as

- Cash.
- Various debit and credit card processors like MasterCard, Visa, and many others. Each has their own API.
- Online payment processors like PayPal or Alipay.
- Check/cheque.
- Store credit.
- Payment cards or gift cards that may be specific to certain combinations of companies and countries.
- Cryptocurrency.

Going back to our discussion on requirements, after approximately 5–10 minutes of rapid discussion and scribbling, we clarify the following functional requirements:

- A host may list a room. Assume a room is for one person. Room properties are city and price. The host may provide up to 10 photos and a 25 MB video for a room.
- A guest may filter rooms by city, check-in, and check-out date.

- A guest may book a room with a check-in and check-out date. Host approval for booking is not required.

- A host or guest may cancel a booking at any time before it begins.

- A host or guest may view their list of bookings.

- A guest can have only one room booked for any particular date.

- Rooms cannot be double-booked.

- For simplicity, unlike the actual Airbnb, we exclude the following features:
  - Let a host manually accept or reject booking requests.
  - Cancel a booking (by the guest or host) after it is made is out of scope.
  - We can briefly discuss notifications (such as push or email) to guests and hosts but will not go into depth.
  - Messaging between users, such as between guests and hosts and between ops and guests/hosts.

The following are outside the scope of this interview. It is good to mention these possible functional requirements to demonstrate your critical thinking and attention to detail.

- Other fine details of a place, such as:
  - Exact address. Only a city string is necessary. Ignore other location details like state and country.
  - We assume every listing only permits one guest.
  - Whole place vs. private room vs. shared room.
  - Details of amenities, such as private versus shared bathrooms or kitchen details.
  - Child-friendly.
  - Pet-friendly.
- Analytics.
- Airbnb may provide hosts with pricing recommendations. A listing may set a minimum and maximum price/night, and Airbnb may vary the price within this range.
- Additional pricing options and properties, such as cleaning fees and other fees, different prices on peak dates (e.g., weekends and holidays) or taxes.
- Payments or refunds, including cancellation penalties.
- Customer support, including dispute mediation. A good clarifying question is whether we need to discuss how ops reviews listing requests. We can also ask if the customer support that is out of scope refers to just the booking process or also includes customer support during the listing process. We can clarify that the term "customer" refers to both hosts and guests. In this interview, we assume that the interviewer may request to briefly discuss listing reviews by ops.

- Insurance.
- Chat or other communication between any parties, such as host and guest. This is out of scope because it is a messaging service or notifications service (which we discussed in other chapters) and not a reservation service.
- Signup and login.
- Compensation of hosts and guests for outages.
- User reviews, such as a guest reviewing their stay or a host reviewing their guest's behavior.

If we need to discuss API endpoints for listing and booking rooms, they can be as follows:

- `findRooms(cityId, checkInDate, checkOutDate)`
- `bookRoom(userId, roomId, checkInDate, checkOutDate)`
- `cancelBooking(bookingId)`
- `viewBookings(hostId)`
- `viewBookings(guestId)`

Our non-functional requirements are as follows:

- Scalable to 1 billion rooms or 100 million daily bookings. Past booking data can be deleted. No programmatically generated user data.
- Strong consistency for bookings, or more precisely listing availability, so there will be no double bookings or bookings on unavailable dates in general. Eventual consistency for other listing information such as description or photos may be acceptable.
- High availability because there are monetary consequences of lost bookings. However, as we explain later in section 15.2.5, we cannot completely prevent lost bookings if we wish to prevent double bookings.
- High performance is unnecessary. P99 of a few seconds is acceptable.
- Typical security and privacy requirements. Authentication required. User data is private. Authorization is not a requirement for the functionalities in this interview's scope.

15.2 Design decisions

As we discuss the design for listing and booking rooms, we soon come across a couple of questions.

1 Should we replicate rooms to multiple data centers?
2 How should the data model represent room availability?

15.2.1   Replication

Our Airbnb system is similar to Craigslist in that the products are localized. A search can be only done on one city at a time. We can take advantage of this to allocate a data center host to a city with many listings or to multiple cities that have fewer listings. Because write performance is not critical, we can use single-leader replication. To minimize read latency, the secondary leader and the followers can be geographically spread out across data centers. We can use a metadata service to contain a mapping of city to leader and follower host IP addresses, for our service to look up the geographically closest follower host to fetch the rooms of any particular city or to write to the leader host corresponding to that city. This mapping will be tiny in size and only modified by admins infrequently, so we can simply replicate it on all data centers, and admins can manually ensure data consistency when updating the mapping.

We can use a CDN to store the room photos and videos, and as usual other static content like JavaScript and CSS.

Contrary to usual practice, we may choose not to use an in-memory cache. In search results, we only display available rooms. If a room is highly desirable, it will soon be reserved and no longer displayed in searches. If a room keeps being displayed in searches, it is likely to be undesirable, and we may choose not to incur the costs and additional complexity of providing a cache. Another way of stating this is that cache freshness is difficult to maintain, and the cached data quickly becomes stale.

As always, these decisions are debatable, and we should be able to discuss their tradeoffs.

15.2.2   Data models for room availability

We should quickly brainstorm various ways to represent room availability in our data model and discuss their tradeoffs. In an interview, one must display the ability to evaluate multiple approaches and not just propose one approach:

- *(room_id, date, guest_id) table*—This is conceptually simple, with the tradeoff of containing multiple rows that differ only by date. For example, if room 1 is booked by guest 1 for the whole of January, there will be 31 rows.
- *(room_id, guest_id, check_in, check_out) table*—This is more compact. When a guest submits a search with a check-in and check-out date, we require an algorithm to determine if there are overlapping dates. Should we code this algorithm in the database query or in the backend? The former will be more difficult to maintain and test. But if backend hosts have to fetch this room availability data from the database, this incurs I/O costs. The code for both approaches can be asked in coding interviews.

There are many possible database schemas.

15.2.3 *Handling overlapping bookings*

If multiple users attempt to book the same room with overlapping dates, the first user's booking should be granted, and our UI should inform the other users that this room is no longer available for the dates they selected and guide them through finding another available room. This may be a negative UX experience, so we may want to briefly brainstorm a couple of alternative approaches. You may suggest other possibilities.

15.2.4 *Randomize search results*

We can randomize the order of the search results to reduce such occurrences, though that may interfere with personalization (such as recommender systems.)

15.2.5 *Lock rooms during booking flow*

When a user clicks on a search result to view the details of a room and possibly submit a booking request, we can lock these dates for the room for a few minutes. During this time, searches by other users with overlapping dates will not return this room in the result list. If this room is locked after other users have already received their search results, clicking on the room's details should present a notification of the lock and possibly its remaining duration if those users wish to try again, just in case that user did not book that room.

This means that we will lose some bookings. We may decide that preventing double bookings is worth the tradeoff of losing bookings. This is a difference between Airbnb and hotels. A hotel can allow overbooking of its cheaper rooms because it can expect a few cancellations to occur. If the cheaper rooms are overbooked on a particular date, the hotel can upgrade the excess guests to more expensive rooms. Airbnb hosts cannot do this, so we cannot allow double bookings.

Section 2.4.2 describes a mechanism to prevent concurrent update conflicts from multiple users from simultaneously updating a shared configuration.

15.3 *High-level architecture*

From the previous section's requirements discussion, we draw our high-level architecture, shown in figure 15.1. Each service serves a group of related functional requirements. This allows us to develop and scale the services separately:

- *Booking service*—For guests to make bookings. This service is our direct revenue source and has the most stringent non-functional requirements for availability and latency. Higher latency directly translates to lower revenue. Downtime on this service has the most serious effect on revenue and reputation. However, strong consistency may be less important, and we can trade off consistency for availability and latency.
- *Listing service*—For hosts to create and manage listings. It is important but less critical than the booking and listing services. It is a separate service because it has different functional and non-functional requirements than the booking and availability services, so it should not share resources with them.

- *Availability service*—The availability service keeps track of listing availability and is used by both the booking and listing services. The availability and latency requirements are as stringent as the booking service. Reads must be scalable, but writes are less frequent and may not require scalability. We discuss this further in section 15.8.

- *Approval service*—Certain operations like adding new listings or updating certain listing information may require ops approval prior to publishing. We can design an approval service for these use cases. We name the service the "approval service" rather than the more ambiguous-sounding "review service."

- *Recommender service*—Provides personalized listing recommendations to guests. We can see it as an internal ads service. A detailed discussion is out of scope in the interview, but we can include it in the diagram and discuss it just for a short moment.

- *Regulations service*—As discussed earlier, the listing service and booking service need to consider local regulations. The regulations service can provide an API to the listing service, so the latter can provide hosts with the appropriate UX for creating listings that comply with local regulations. The listing service and regulation service can be developed by separate teams, so each team member can concentrate on gaining domain expertise relevant to their respective service. Dealing with regulations may be initially outside the scope of an interview, but the interviewer may be interested to see how we handle it.

- *Other services:* Collective label for certain services for internal uses like analytics, which are mostly outside the scope of this interview.

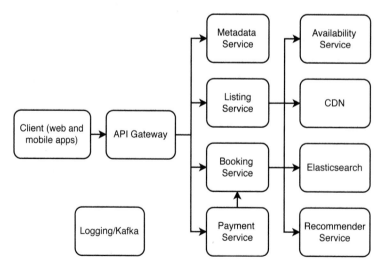

Figure 15.1   High-level architecture. As usual, instead of an API gateway, we can use a service mesh in our listing and booking services.

15.4 Functional partitioning

We can employ functional partitioning by geographical region, similar to the approach discussed with Craigslist in section 7.9. Listings can be placed in a data center. We deploy our application into multiple data centers and route each user to the data center that serves their city.

15.5 Create or update a listing

Creating a listing can be divided into two tasks. The first task is for the host to obtain their appropriate listing regulations. The second task is for the host to submit a listing request. In this chapter, we refer to both creating and updating listings as listing requests.

Figure 15.2 is a sequence diagram of obtaining the appropriate regulations. The sequence is as follows:

1. The host is currently on the client (a webpage mobile app component) that provides a button to create a new listing. When the host clicks on the button, the app sends a request to the listing service that contains the user's location. (The host's location can be obtained by asking the host to manually provide it or by asking the host to grant permission to access their location.)

2. The listing service forwards their location to the regulation service (refer to section 15.10.1). The regulation service responds with the appropriate regulations.

3. The listing service returns the regulations to the client. The client may adjust the UX to accommodate the regulations. For example, if there is a rule that a booking must last at least 14 days, the client will immediately display an error to the host if they enter a minimum booking period of less than 14 days.

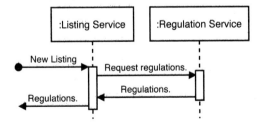

Figure 15.2 Sequence diagram of obtaining the appropriate listing regulations

Figure 15.3 is a sequence diagram of a simplified listing request. The host enters their listing information and submits it. This is sent as a POST request to the listing service. The listing service does the following:

1   Validates the request body.

2   Writes to a SQL table for listings, which we can name the Listing table. New listings and certain updates need manual approval by the Ops staff. The Listing SQL table can contain a Boolean column named "Approved" that indicates if a listing has been approved by ops.

3   If Ops approval is required, it sends a POST request to the Approval service to notify Ops to review the listing.

4   Sends the client a 200 response.

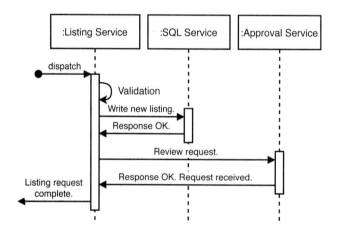

Figure 15.3   Sequence diagram of a simplified request to create or update a listing

Referring to figure 15.4, steps 2 and 3 can be done in parallel using CDC. All steps are *idempotent*. We can use INSERT IGNORE on SQL tables to prevent duplicate writes (https://stackoverflow.com/a/1361368/1045085). We can also use transaction log tailing, discussed in section 5.3.

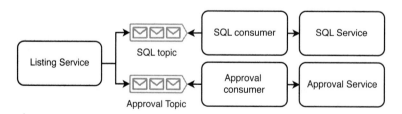

Figure 15.4   Using CDC for a distributed transaction to the SQL service and approval service

This is a simplified design. In a real implementation, the listing process may consist of multiple requests to the listing service. The form to create a listing may be divided into multiple parts, and a host may fill and submit each part separately, and each submission is a separate request. For example, adding photos to a listing may be done one at a time. A host may fill in a listing's title, type, and description and submit it as one request and then fill in pricing details and submit it as another request, and so on.

Another point to note is to allow a host to make additional updates to their listing request while it is pending review. Each update should UPDATE the corresponding listing table row.

We will not discuss notifications in detail because the exact business logic for notifications may be intricate and often change. Notifications can be implemented as a batch ETL job that makes requests to the listing service and then requests a shared notifications service to send notifications. The batch job can query for incomplete listings then

- Notify hosts to remind them that they have not completed the listing process.
- Notify ops of incomplete listings, so ops staff can contact hosts to encourage and guide them to complete the listing process.

15.6 Approval service

The interviewer may be more interested in the booking process, so this discussion on the approval service may be brief.

The approval service is an internal application with low traffic and can have a simple architecture. Referring to figure 15.5, the design consists of a client web application and a backend service, which makes requests to the listings service and a shared SQL service. We assume that manual approval is required for all requests; for example, we cannot automate any approvals or rejections.

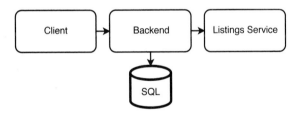

Figure 15.5   High-level architecture of the approval service, for Ops personnel to review certain operations, such as adding or updating listings

The approval service provides a POST endpoint for the listing service to submit listing requests that require review. We can write these requests to a SQL table we call "listing_request," which contains the following columns:

- *id*—An ID. The primary key.
- *listing_id*—The listing ID in the Listing table in the listing service. If both tables were in the same service, this would be a foreign key.
- *created_at*—Timestamp that this listing request was created or updated.

- *listing_hash*—We may include this column as part of an additional mechanism to ensure that an Ops staff member does not submit an approval or rejection of a listing request that changed while they were reviewing it.

- *status*—An enum of the listing request, which can be one of the values "none," "assigned," and "reviewed."

- *last_accessed*—Timestamp that this listing request was last fetched and returned to an Ops staff member.

- *review_code*—An enum. May be simply "APPROVED" for approved listing requests. There may be multiple enums that correspond to categories of reasons to reject a listing request. Examples include VIOLATE_LOCAL_REGULATIONS, BANNED_HOST, ILLEGAL_CONTENT, SUSPICIOUS, FAIL_QUALITY_STANDARDS, etc.

- *reviewer_id*—The ID of the operations staff member who was assigned this listing request.

- *review_submitted_at*—Timestamp that the Ops staff member submitted their approval or rejection.

- *review_notes*—An Ops staff member may author some notes on why this listing request was approved or rejected.

Assuming we have 10,000 Operations staff, and each staff member reviews up to 5000 new or updated listings weekly, Ops will write 50 million rows weekly to the SQL table. If each row occupies 1 KB, the approval table will grow by 1 KB * 50M * 30 days = 1.5 TB monthly. We can keep 1–2 months of data in the SQL table and run a periodic batch job to archive old data into object storage.

We can also design endpoints and an SQL table for each ops staff to obtain and perform their assigned work/reviews. An Ops staff member can first make a GET request containing their ID to fetch a listing request from the listing_request table. To prevent multiple staff from being assigned the same listing request, the backend can run an SQL transaction with the following steps:

1 If a staff member has already been assigned a listing request, return this assigned request. SELECT a row with status "assigned" and with the staff member's ID as the reviewer_id.

2 If there is no assigned listing request, SELECT the row with the minimum created_at timestamp that has status "none". This will be the assigned listing request.

3 UPDATE the status to "assigned," and the reviewer_id to the ops staff member's ID.

The backend returns this listing request to the Ops staff, who will review it and approve or reject it. Figure 15.6 is a sequence diagram of a synchronous approval process. Approval or rejection is a POST request to the Approval, which triggers the following steps:

1 UPDATE the row into the listing_request table. UPDATE the columns status, review_code, review_submitted_at, and review_notes.

There is a possible race condition where a host may update their listing request while an Ops staff member is reviewing it, so the POST request should contain the listing hash that the approval service had earlier returned to the Ops staff member, and the backend should ensure this hash is identical to the present hash. If the hashes are different, return the updated listing request to the Ops staff member, who will need to repeat the review.

We may try to identify this race condition by checking if listing_request.last_accessed timestamp is more recent than listing_request.review_submitted_at. However, this technique is unreliable because the clocks of the various hosts that timestamp columns are not perfectly synchronized. Also, the time may have been changed for any multitude of reasons such as daylight savings, server restarts, the server clock may be periodically synchronized with a reference server, etc. In distributed systems, it is not possible to rely on clocks to ensure consistency (Martin Kleppmann, *Designing Data-Intensive Applications* (O'Reilly, 2017)).

Lamport clock and vector clock

Lamport clock (https://martinfowler.com/articles/patterns-of-distributed-systems/lamport-clock.html) is a technique for ordering events in a distributed system. Vector clock is a more sophisticated technique. For more details, refer to chapter 11 of the book by George Coulouris, Jean Dollimore, Tim Kindberg, and Gordon Blair, *Distributed Systems: Concepts and Design,* Pearson, 2011.

2 Send a PUT request to the Listing Service, which will UPDATE the listing_request.status and listing_request.reviewed_at columns. Again, first SELECT the hash and verify that it is identical to the submitted hash. Wrap both SQL queries in a transaction.

3 Send a POST request to the Booking Service, so the booking service may begin showing this listing to guests. An alternative approach is described in figure 15.7.

4 The backend also requests a shared notification service (chapter 9) to notify the host of the approval or rejection.

5 Finally, the backend sends a 200 response to the client. These steps should be written in an idempotent manner, so any or all steps can be repeated if a host fails during any step.

Discuss how this POST request can be idempotent in case it fails before all steps are completed and we must retry the same request. For example:

- The backend can query the notification service to check if a particular notification request has already been made, before making the notification request.
- To prevent duplicate rows in the approval table, the SQL row insertion can use a "IF NOT EXISTS" operator.

As we can see, this synchronous request involves requests to multiple services and may have long latency. A failed request to any service will introduce inconsistency.

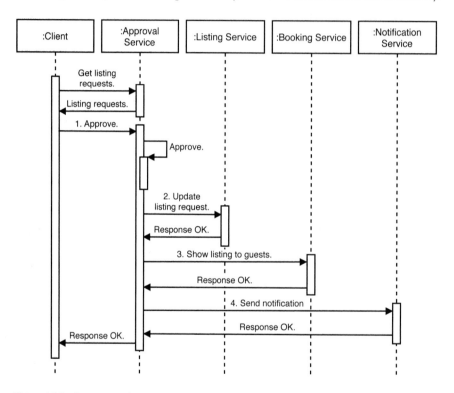

Figure 15.6   Sequence diagram of fetching listing requests followed by a synchronous approval of a listing request. The approval service can be a saga orchestrator.

Should we use change data capture (CDC) instead? Figure 15.7 illustrates this asynchronous approach. In an approval request, the approval service produces to a Kafka queue and returns 200. A consumer consumes from the Kafka queue and makes the requests to all these other services. The rate of approvals is low, so the consumer can employ exponential backoff and retry to avoid rapidly polling the Kafka queue when the latter is empty, and poll only once per minute when the queue is empty.

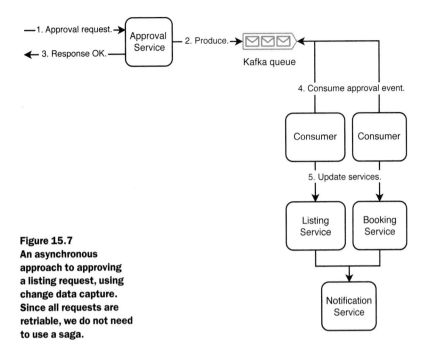

Figure 15.7
An asynchronous
approach to approving
a listing request, using
change data capture.
Since all requests are
retriable, we do not need
to use a saga.

The notification service should notify the host only after the listing and booking services are updated, so it consumes from two Kafka topics, one corresponding to each service. When the notification service consumes an event from one topic corresponding to a particular listing approval event, it must wait for the event from the other service that corresponds to the same listing approval event, and then it can send the notification. So, the notification service needs a database to record these events. This database is not shown in figure 15.7.

As an additional safeguard against silent errors that may cause inconsistency between the services, we can implement a batch ETL job to audit the three services. This job can trigger an alert to developers if it finds inconsistency.

We use CDC rather than saga for this process because we do not expect any of the services to reject the request, so there will not be any required compensating transactions. The listing service and booking service have no reason to prevent the listing from going live, and the notification service has no reason not to send the user a notification.

But what if a user cancels their account just before their listing is approved? We will need a CDC process to either deactivate or delete their listings and make requests to other services as appropriate. If the various services involved in the approval process of figure 15.6 receive the user deletion request just before the approval request, they can either record that the listing is invalid or delete the listing. Then the approval request will not cause the listing to become active. We should discuss with our interviewer on the tradeoffs of various approaches and other relevant concerns that come to mind. They will appreciate this attention to detail.

There may be other requested features. For example, a listing review may involve more than one Ops staff member. We can bring up these points and discuss them if the interviewer is interested.

An Ops staff may specialize in reviewing listing requests of certain jurisdictions, so how may we assign their appropriate listing requests? Our application is already functionally partitioned by geographical region, so if a staff member can review listing requests of listings in a particular data center, nothing else is required in our design. Otherwise, we can discuss some possibilities:

- A JOIN query between the listing_request table and the listing table to fetch listing requests with a particular country or city. Our listing_request table and listing table are in different services, so we will need a different solution:
  - Redesign our system. Combine the listing and approval services, so both tables are in the same service.
  - Handle the join logic in the application layer, which carries disadvantages such as I/O cost of data transfer between services.
  - Denormalize or duplicate the listing data, by adding a location column to listing_request table or duplicating the listing table in the approvals service. A listing's physical location does not change, so there is low risk of inconsistency due to denormalization or duplication, though inconsistency can happen, such as from bugs or if the initially entered location was wrong then corrected.
- A listing ID can contain a city ID, so one can determine the listing's city by the listing ID. Our company can maintain a list of (ID, city), which can be accessed by any service. This list should be append-only so we will not need to do expensive and error-prone data migrations.

As stated here, approved listings will be copied to the booking service. Because the booking service may have high traffic, this step may have the highest failure rate. As per our usual approaches, we can implement exponential backoff and retry or a dead letter queue. The traffic from our approval service to the booking service is negligible compared to traffic from guests, so we will not try to reduce the probability of booking service downtime by reducing traffic from the approval service.

Last, we can also discuss automation of some approvals or rejections. We can define rules in a SQL table "Rules," and a function can fetch these rules and apply them on the listing contents. We can also use machine learning; we can train machine-learning models in a machine-learning service, and place selected model IDs into the Rules table, so the function can send the listing contents along with the model IDs to the machine learning service, which will return approval, rejection, or inconclusive (i.e., requires manual review). The listing_request.reviewer_id can be a value like "AUTOMATED," while the listing_request.review_code value of an inconclusive review can be "INCONCLUSIVE."

15.7 Booking service

The steps of a simplified booking/reservation process are as follows:

1. A guest submits a search query for the listing that matches the following and receives a list of available listings. Each listing in the result list may contain a thumbnail and some brief information. As discussed in the requirements section, other details are out of scope.
   - City
   - Check-in date
   - Check-out date

2. The guest may filter the results by price and other listing details.

3. The guest clicks on a listing to view more details, including high-resolution photos and videos if any. From here, the guest may go back to the result list.

4. The guest has decided on which listing to book. They submit a booking request and receive a confirmation or error.

5. If the guest receives a confirmation, they are then directed to make payment.

6. A guest may change their mind and submit a cancellation request.

Similar to the listing service discussed earlier, we may choose to send notifications such as

- Notify guests and hosts after a booking is successfully completed or canceled.

- If a guest filled in the details of a booking request but didn't complete the booking request, remind them after some hours or days to complete the booking request.

- Recommend listings to guests based on various factors like their past bookings, listings they have viewed, their other online activity, their demographic, etc. The listings can be selected by a recommender system.

- Notifications regarding payments. Regarding payment, we may choose to escrow payments before the host accepts or request payment only after the host accepts. The notification logic will vary accordingly.

Let's quickly discuss scalability requirements. As discussed earlier, we can functionally partition listings by city. We can assume that we have up to one million listings in a particular city. We can make a generous overestimate of up to 10 million daily requests for search, filtering, and listing details. Even assuming that these 10 million requests are concentrated in a single hour of the day, this works out to less than 3,000 queries per second, which can be handled by a single or small number of hosts. Nonetheless, the architecture discussed in this section will be capable of handling much larger traffic.

Figure 15.8 is a high-level architecture of the booking service. All queries are processed by a backend service, which queries either the shared Elasticsearch or SQL services as appropriate.

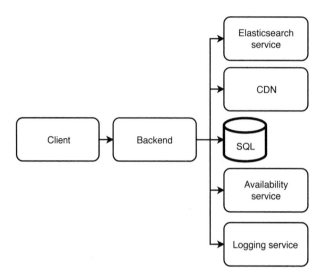

Figure 15.8   High-level architecture of the booking service

Search and filter requests are processed on the Elasticsearch service. The Elasticsearch service may also handle pagination (https://www.elastic.co/guide/en/elasticsearch/reference/current/paginate-search-results.html), so it can save memory and CPU usage by returning only a small number of results at a time. Elasticsearch supports fuzzy search, which is useful to guests who misspell locations and addresses.

A request to CRUD details of a listing is formatted into a SQL query using an ORM and made against the SQL service. Photos and videos are downloaded from the CDN. A booking request is forwarded to the availability service, which is discussed in detail in the next section. Write operations to the booking service's SQL database are by

1   Booking requests.
2   The approval service as described in the previous section. The approval service makes infrequent updates to listing details.
3   Requests to cancel bookings and make the listings available again. This occurs if payments fail.

Our SQL service used by this booking service can use the leader-follower architecture discussed in section 4.3.2. The infrequent writes are made to the leader host, which will replicate them to the follower hosts. The SQL service may contain a Booking table with the following columns:

- *id*—A primary key ID assigned to a booking.
- *listing_id*—The listing's ID assigned by the Listing service. If this table was in the listing service, this column would be a foreign key.
- *guest_id*—The ID of the guest who made the booking.
- *check_in*—Check-in date.
- *check_out*—Check-out date.
- *timestamp*—The time this row was inserted or updated. This column can be just for record-keeping.

The other write operations in this process are to the availability service:

1 The booking or cancellation request will alter a listing's availability on the relevant dates.

2 We may consider locking the listing for five minutes at step 3 in the booking process (request more of a listing's details) because the guest may make a booking request. This means that the listing will not be shown to other guests who made search queries with dates that overlap the current guest's. Conversely, we may unlock the listing early (before the five minutes are up) if the guest makes a search or filtering request, which indicates that they are unlikely to book this listing.

The Elasticsearch index needs to be updated when a listing's availability or details change. Adding or updating a listing requires write requests to both the SQL service and Elasticsearch service. As discussed in chapter 5, this can be handled as a distributed transaction to prevent inconsistency should failures occur during writes to either service. A booking request requires writes to the SQL services in both the booking service and availability service (discussed in the next section) and should also be handled as a distributed transaction.

If the booking causes the listing to become ineligible for further listings, the booking service must update its own database to prevent further bookings and also update the Elasticsearch service so this listing stops appearing in searches.

The Elasticsearch result may sort listings by decreasing guest ratings. The results may also be sorted by a machine learning experiment service. These considerations are out of scope.

Figure 15.9 is a sequence diagram of our simplified booking process.

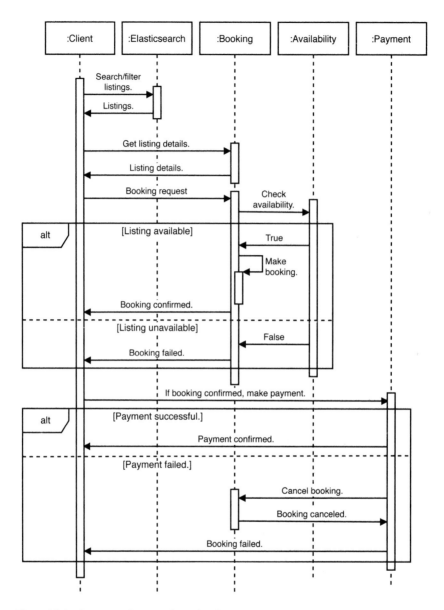

Figure 15.9   Sequence diagram of our simplified booking process. Many details are glossed over. Examples: Getting the listing details may involve a CDN. We don't give hosts the option to manually accept or reject booking requests. Making payment will involve a large number of requests to multiple services. We did not illustrate requests to our notification service.

Last, we may consider that many guests may search for listings and view the details of many listings before making a booking request, so we can consider splitting the search and view functions vs. the booking function into separate services, so they can scale separately. The service to search and view listings will receive more traffic and be allocated more resources than the service to make booking requests.

15.8   Availability service

The availability service needs to avoid situations like the following:

- Double bookings.
- A guest's booking may not be visible to the host.
- A host may mark certain dates as unavailable, but a guest may book those dates.
- Our customer support department will be burdened by guest and host complaints from these poor experiences.

The availability service provides the following endpoints:

- Given a location ID, listing type ID, check-in date, and check-out date, GET available listings.
- Lock a listing from a particular check-in date to check-out date for a few (e.g., five) minutes.
- CRUD a reservation, from a particular check-in date to check-out date.

Figure 15.10 is the high-level architecture of the availability service. It consists of a backend service, which makes requests to a shared SQL service. The shared SQL service has a leader-follower architecture, illustrated in figures 4.1 and 4.2.

Figure 15.10   High-level architecture of the availability service

The SQL service can contain an availability table, which can have the following columns. There is no primary key:

- *listing_id*—The listing's ID assigned by the listing service.
- *date*—The availability date.
- *booking_id*—The booking/reservation ID assigned by the booking service when a booking is made.
- *available*—A string field that functions as an enum. It indicates if the listing is available, locked, or booked. We may save space by deleting the row if this (listing_id, date) combination is not locked or booked. However, we aim to achieve high occupancy, so this space saving will be insignificant. Another disadvantage is that our SQL service should provision sufficient storage for all possible rows, so if we save space by not inserting rows unless required, we may not realize that we have insufficient storage provisioned until we have a high occupancy rate across our listings.
- *timestamp*—The time this row was inserted or updated.

We discussed a listing lock process in the previous section. We can display a six-minute timer on the client (web or mobile app). The timer on the client should have a slightly longer duration than the timer on the backend because the clocks on the client and the backend host cannot be perfectly synchronized.

This lock listing mechanism can reduce, but not completely prevent, multiple guests from making overlapping booking requests. We can use SQL row locking to prevent overlapping bookings. (Refer to https://dev.mysql.com/doc/refman/8.0/en/glossary .html#glos_exclusive_lock and https://www.postgresql.org/docs/current/explicit -locking.html#LOCKING-ROWS.) The backend service must use an SQL transaction on the leader host. First, make a SELECT query to check if the listing is available on the requested dates. Second, make an INSERT or UPDATE query to mark the listing accordingly.

A consistency tradeoff of the leader-follower SQL architecture is that a search result may contain unavailable listings. If a guest attempts to book an unavailable listing, the booking service can return a 409 response. We do not expect the effect on user experience to be too severe because a user can expect that a listing may be booked while they are viewing it. However, we should add a metric to our monitoring service to monitor such occurrences, so we will be alerted and can react as necessary if this occurs excessively.

Earlier in this chapter, we discussed why we will not cache popular (listing, date) pairs. If we do choose to do so, we can implement a caching strategy suited for read-heavy loads; this is discussed in section 4.8.1.

How much storage is needed? If each column occupies 64 bits, a row will occupy 40 bytes. One million listings will occupy 7.2 GB for 180 days of data, which can easily fit on a single host. We can manually delete old data as required to free up space.

An alternative SQL table schema can be similar to the Booking table discussed in the previous section, except that it may also contain a column named "status" or "availability" that indicates if the listing is locked or booked. The algorithm to find if a listing is available between a certain check-in and check-out date can be a coding interview question. You may be asked to code a solution in a coding interview, but not in a system design interview.

15.9   Logging, monitoring, and alerting

Besides what was discussed in section 2.5, such as CPU, memory, disk usage of Redis, and disk usage of Elasticsearch, we should monitor and send alerts for the following.

We should have anomaly detection for an unusual rate of bookings, listings, or cancellations. Other examples include an unusually high rate of listings being manually or programmatically flagged for irregularities.

Define end-to-end user stories, such as the steps that a host takes to create a listing or the steps a guest takes to make a booking. Monitor the rate of completed vs. non-completed user stories/flows, and create alerts for unusually high occurrences of situations where users do not go through an entire story/flow. Such a situation is also known as a low funnel conversion rate.

We can define and monitor the rate of undesirable user stories, such as booking requests either not being made or being canceled after communication between guests and hosts.

15.10 *Other possible discussion topics*

The various services and business logic discussed in this chapter read like a smattering of topics and a gross oversimplification of a complex business. In an interview, we may continue designing more services and discussing their requirements, users, and inter-service communication. We may also consider more details of the various user stories and the corresponding intricacies in their system design:

- A user may be interested in listings that do not exactly match their search criteria. For example, the available check-in date and/or check-out date may be slightly different, or listings in nearby cities may also be acceptable. How may we design a search service that returns such results? May we modify the search query before submitting it to Elasticsearch, or how may we design an Elasticsearch index that considers such results as relevant?

- What other features may we design for hosts, guests, Ops, and other users? For example, can we design a system for guests to report inappropriate listings? Can we design a system that monitors host and guest behavior to recommend possible punitive actions such as restrictions on using the service or account deactivation?

- Functional requirements defined earlier as outside the scope of the interview. Their architecture details, such as whether the requirements are satisfied in our current services or should be separate services.

- We did not discuss search. We may consider letting guests search for listings by keywords. We will need to index our listings. We may use Elasticsearch or design our own search service.

- Expand the product range, such as offering listings suited to business travelers.

- Allow double-booking, similar to hotels. Upgrade guests if rooms are unavailable, since more expensive rooms tend to have high vacancy.

- Chapter 17 discusses an example analytics system.

- Show users some statistics (e.g., how popular a listing is).

- Personalization, such as a recommender system for rooms. For example, a recommender service can recommend new listings so they will quickly have guests, which will be encouraging to new hosts.

- A frontend engineer or UX designer interview may include discussion of UX flows.

- Fraud protection and mitigation.

15.10.1 *Handling regulations*

We can consider designing and implementing a dedicated regulation service to provide a standard API for communicating regulations. All other services must be designed to interact with this API, so they are flexible to changing regulations or at least be more easily redesigned in response to unforeseen regulations.

In the author's experience, designing services to be flexible to changing regulations is a blind spot in many companies, and considerable resources are spent on re-architecture, implementation, and migration each time regulations change.

> **Exercise**
>
> A possible exercise is to discuss differences in regulations requirements between Airbnb and Craigslist.

Data privacy laws are a relevant concern to many companies. Examples include COPPA (https://www.ftc.gov/enforcement/rules/rulemaking-regulatory-reform-proceedings/childrens-online-privacy-protection-rule), GDPR (https://gdpr-info.eu/), and CCPA (https://oag.ca.gov/privacy/ccpa). Some governments may require companies to share data on activities that occur in their jurisdictions or that data on their citizens cannot leave the country.

Regulations may affect the core business of the company. In the case of Airbnb, there are regulations directly on hosts and guests. Examples of such regulations may include

- A listing may only be hosted for a maximum number of days in a year.
- Only properties constructed before or after a certain year can be listed.
- Bookings cannot be made on certain dates, such as certain public holidays.
- Bookings may have a minimum or maximum duration in a specific city.
- Listings may be disallowed altogether in certain cities or addresses.
- Listing may require safety equipment such as carbon monoxide detectors, fire detectors, and fire escapes.
- There may be other livability and safety regulations.

Within a country, certain regulations may be specific to listings that meet certain conditions, and the specifics may differ by each specific country, state, city, or even address (e.g., certain apartment complexes may impose their own rules).

Summary

- Airbnb is a reservation app, a marketplace app, and a customer support and operations app. Hosts, guests, and Ops are the main user groups.
- Airbnb's products are localized, so listings can be grouped in data centers by geography.
- The sheer number of services involved in listing and booking is impossible to comprehensively discuss in a system design interview. We can list a handful of main services and briefly discuss their functionalities.
- Creating a listing may involve multiple requests from the Airbnb host to ensure the listing complies with local regulations.
- After an Airbnb host submits a listing request, it may need to be manually approved by an Ops/admin member. After approval, it can be found and booked by guests.
- Interactions between these various services should be asynchronous if low latency is unnecessary. We employ distributed transactions techniques to allow asynchronous interactions.
- Caching is not always a suitable strategy to reduce latency, especially if the cache quickly becomes stale.
- Architecture diagrams and sequence diagrams are invaluable in designing a complex transaction.

Design a news feed

This chapter covers

- Designing a personalized scalable system
- Filtering out news feed items
- Designing a news feed to serve images and text

Design a news feed that provides a user with a list of news items, sorted by approximate reverse chronological order that belong to the topics selected by the user. A news item can be categorized into 1–3 topics. A user may select up to three topics of interest at any time.

This is a common system design interview question. In this chapter, we use the terms "news item" and "post" interchangeably. In social media apps like Facebook or Twitter, a user's news feed is usually populated by posts from friends/connections. However, in this news feed, users get posts written by other people in general, rather than by their connections.

16.1 Requirements

These are the functional requirements of our news feed system, which as usual we can discuss/uncover via an approximately five-minute Q&A with the interviewer.

- A user can select topics of interest. There are up to 100 tags. (We will use the term "tag" in place of "news topic" to prevent ambiguity with the term "Kafka topic.")
- A user can fetch a list of English-language news items 10 at a time, up to 1,000 items.
- Although a user need only fetch up to 1,000 items, our system should archive all items.
- Let's first allow users to get the same items regardless of their geographical location and then consider personalization, based on factors like location and language.
- Latest news first; that is, news items should be arranged in reverse chronological order, but this can be an approximation.
- Components of a news item:
  - A new item will usually contain several text fields, such as a title with perhaps a 150-character limit and a body with perhaps a 10,000-character limit. For simplicity, we can consider just one text field with a 10,000-character limit.
  - UNIX timestamp that indicates when the item was created.
  - We initially do not consider audio, images, or video. If we have time, we can consider 0–10 image files of up to 1 MB each.

TIP The initial functional requirements exclude images because images add considerable complexity to the system design. We can first design a system that handles only text and then consider how we can expand it to handle images and other media.

- We can consider that we may not want to serve certain items because they contain inappropriate content.

The following are mostly or completely out of scope of the functional requirements:

- Versioning is not considered because an article can have multiple versions. An author may add additional text or media to an article or edit the article to correct errors.
- We initially do not need to consider analytics on user data (such as their topics of interest, articles displayed to them, and articles they chose to read) or sophisticated recommender systems.
- We do not need any other personalization or social media features like sharing or commenting.
- We need not consider the sources of the news items. Just provide a POST API endpoint to add news items.

- We initially do not need to consider search. We can consider search after we satisfy our other requirements.

- We do not consider monetization such as user login, payments, or subscriptions. We can assume all articles are free. We do not consider serving ads along with articles.

The non-functional requirements of our news feed system can be as follows:

- Scalable to support 100K daily active users each making an average of 10 requests daily, and one million news items/day.

- High performance of one-second P99 is required for reads.

- User data is private.

- Eventual consistency of up to a few hours is acceptable. Users need not be able to view or access an article immediately after it is uploaded, but a few seconds is desirable. Some news apps have a requirement that an item can be designated as "breaking news," which must be delivered immediately with high priority, but our news feed need not support this feature.

- High availability is required for writes. High availability for reads is a bonus but not required, as users can cache old news on their devices.

16.2 *High-level architecture*

We first sketch a very high-level architecture of our news feed system, shown in figure 16.1. The sources of the news items submit news items to an ingestion service in our backend, and then they are written to a database. Users query our news feed service, which gets the news items from our database and returns them to our users.

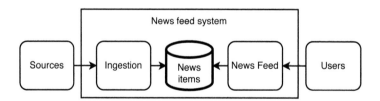

Figure 16.1 Initial very high-level architecture of our news feed. News sources submit news items to an ingestion service, which processes them and persists them to a database. On the other side, users query our news feed service, which gets news items from our database.

A few observations we can make from this architecture:

- The ingestion service must be highly available and handle heavy and unpredictable traffic. We should consider using an event streaming platform like Kafka.

- The database needs to archive all items but only provide up to 1,000 items to a user. This suggests that we can use one database to archive all items and others to serve the required items. We can choose a database technology best suited for each use case. A news item has 10,000 characters, which equals 10 KB. If they are UTF-8 characters, the size of the text will be 40 KB:

- For serving 1,000 items and 100 tags, the total size of all news items is 1 GB, which can easily fit in a Redis cache.
- For archival, we can use a distributed sharded file system like HDFS.

- If eventual consistency of up to a few hours is acceptable, a user's device may not need to update its news items more frequently than hourly, reducing the load on our News feed service.

Figure 16.2 shows our high-level architecture. The queue and HDFS database are an example of CDC (Change Data Capture, refer to section 5.3), while the ETL job that reads from HDFS and writes to Redis is an example of CQRS (Command Query Responsibility Segregation, refer to section 1.4.6).

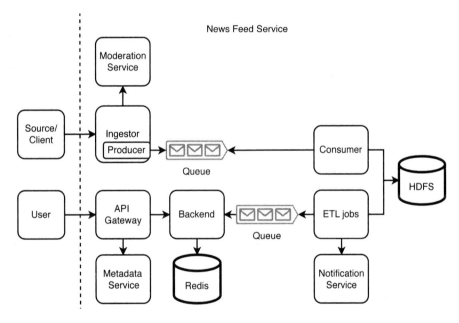

Figure 16.2 High-level architecture of our news feed service. A client submits a post to our news feed service. Our ingestor receives the post and performs some simple validations. If the validations pass, our ingestor produces it to a Kafka queue. Our consumer cluster consumes the post and writes it to HDFS. Our batch ETL jobs process the posts and produce them to another Kafka queue. They may also trigger notifications via a notification service. User requests for posts go through our API gateway, which may retrieve users' tags from our metadata service and then retrieve posts from our Redis table via our backend service. When backend hosts are idle, they consume from the queue and update the Redis table.

Our news feed service's sources push new posts to the ingestor. The ingestor performs validation tasks that can be done on the news item alone; it does not perform validations that depend on other news items or other data in general. Examples of such validation tasks:

- Sanitize the values to avoid SQL injection.
- Filtering and censorship tasks, such as detecting inappropriate language. There can be two sets of criteria: one for immediate rejection, where items that satisfy these criteria are immediately rejected, and another criteria where items that satisfy these criteria are flagged for manual review. This flag can be appended to the item before it is produced to the queue. We discuss this further in the next section.
- A post is not from a blocked source/user. The ingestor obtains the list of blocked users from a moderation service. These blocked users are added to the moderation service either manually by our operations staff or automatically, after certain events.
- Required fields have non-zero length.
- A field that has a maximum length does not contain a value that exceeds that length.
- A field that cannot contain certain characters (such as punctuation) does not have a value containing such characters.

These validation tasks can also be done on our app in the source's client before it submits a post to the ingestor. However, in case any validation tasks are skipped due to any bugs or malicious activity on the client, the ingestor can repeat these validations. If any validation fails in the ingestor, it should trigger an alert to the developers to investigate why the client and ingestor return different validation results.

Requests from certain sources may need to pass through an authentication and authorization service before they reach the ingestor. This is not shown in figure 16.2. Refer to appendix B for a discussion of OAuth authentication and OpenID authorization.

We use a Kafka queue to handle this unpredictable traffic. If the ingestor validations pass, the ingestor produces the post to the Kafka queue and returns 200 Success to the source. If any validation fails, the ingestor returns 400 Bad Request to the source and may also include an explanation of the validations that failed.

The consumer just polls from the queue and writes to HDFS. We need at least two HDFS tables: one for raw news items submitted by the consumer and one for news items that are ready to be served to users. We may also need a separate table for items that require manual review before they are served to users. A detailed discussion of a manual review system is likely outside the scope of the interview. These HDFS tables are partitioned by tag and hour.

Users make GET /post requests to our API gateway, which queries our metadata service for the user's tags and then queries the appropriate news items from a Redis cache via our backend service. The Redis cache key can be a (tag, hour) tuple, and a value can be the corresponding list of news items. We can represent this data structure as {(tag, hour), [post]}, where tag is a string, hour is an integer, and post is an object that contains a post ID string and a body/content string.

The API gateway also has its usual responsibilities as described in section 6.1, such as handling authentication and authorization, and rate limiting. If the number of hosts increases to a large number, and the usual responsibilities of the frontend have different hardware resources compared to querying the metadata service and Redis service, we can split the latter two functionalities away into a separate backend service, so we can scale these capabilities independently.

Regarding the eventual consistency requirement and our observation that a user's device may not need to update its news items more frequently than hourly, if a user requests an update within an hour of their previous request, we can reduce our service load in at least either of these two approaches:

1 Their device can ignore the request.

2 Their device can make the request, but do not retry if the response is a 504 timeout.

The ETL jobs write to another Kafka queue. When backend hosts are not serving user requests for posts, they can consume from the Kafka queue and update the Redis table. The ETL jobs fulfill the following functions:

Before the raw news items are served to users, we may first need to run validation or moderation/censorship tasks that depend on other news items or other data in general. For simplicity, we will collectively refer to all such tasks as "validation tasks." Referring to figure 16.3, these can be parallel ETL tasks. We may need an additional HDFS table for each task. Each table contains the item IDs that passed the validations. Examples are as follows:

- Finding duplicate items.
- If there is a limit on the number of news items on a particular tag/subject that can be submitted within the last hour, there can be a validation task for this.
- Determine the intersection of the item IDs from the intermediate HDFS tables. This is the set of IDs that passed all validations. Write this set to a final HDFS table. Read the IDs from the final HDFS table and then copy the corresponding news items to overwrite the Redis cache.

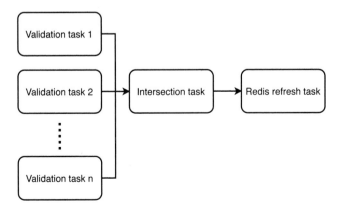

Figure 16.3   ETL job DAG. The validation tasks run in parallel. Each validation task outputs a set of valid post IDs. When the tasks are done, the intersection task determines the intersection of all these sets, which are the IDs of posts that users can be served.

We may also have ETL jobs to trigger notifications via a notification service. Notification channels may include our mobile and browser apps, email, texting, and social media. Refer to chapter 9 for a detailed discussion on a notification service. We will not discuss this in detail in this chapter.

Notice the key role of moderation in our news feed service, as illustrated in figure 16.2 and discussed in the context of our ETL jobs. We may also need to moderate the posts for each specific user, e.g., as discussed earlier, blocked users should not be allowed to make requests. Referring to figure 16.4, we can consider unifying all this moderation into a single moderation service. We discussed this further in section 16.4.

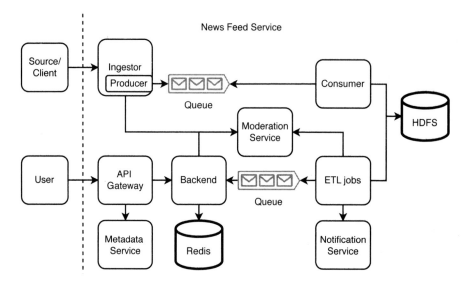

Figure 16.4   High-level architecture of our news feed system with all content moderation centralized in a moderation service. Developers can define all content moderation logic in this service.

16.3   *Prepare feed in advance*

In our design in figure 16.2, each user will need one Redis query per (tag, hour) pair. Each user may need to make many queries to obtain their relevant or desired items, causing high read traffic and possibly high latency on our news feed service.

We can trade off higher storage for lower latency and traffic by preparing a user's feed in advance. We can prepare two hash maps, {user ID, post ID} and {post ID, post}. Assuming 100 tags with 1K 10K-character items each, the latter hash map occupies slightly over 1 GB. For the former hash map, we will need to store one billion user IDs and up to 100*1000 possible post IDs. An ID is 64 bits. Total storage requirement is up to 800 TB, which may be beyond the capacity of a Redis cluster. One possible solution is to partition the users by region and store just two to three regions per data center, so there are up to 20M users per data center, which works out to 16 TB. Another possible solution is to limit the storage requirement to 1 TB by limiting it to a few dozen post IDs, but this does not fulfill our 1,000-item requirement.

Another possible solution is to use a sharded SQL implementation for the {user ID, post ID} pair, as discussed in section 4.3. We can shard this table by hashed user ID, so user IDs are randomly distributed among the nodes, and the more intensive users are randomly distributed too. This will prevent hot shard problems. When our backend receives request for a user ID's posts, it can hash the user ID and then make a request to the appropriate SQL node. (We will discuss momentarily how it finds an appropriate SQL node.) The table that contains the {post ID, post} pairs can be replicated across every node, so we can do JOIN queries between these two tables. (This table may also contain other dimension columns for timestamp, tag, etc.) Figure 16.5 illustrates our sharding and replication strategy.

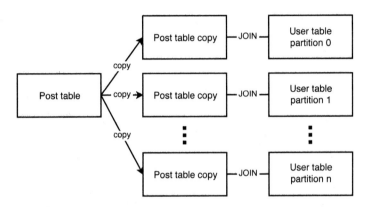

Figure 16.5   Illustration of our sharding and replication strategy. The table with {hashed user ID, post ID} is sharded and distributed across multiple leader hosts and replicated to follower hosts. The table with {post ID, post} is replicated to every host. We can JOIN on post ID.

Referring to figure 16.6, we can divide the 64-bit address space of hashed user IDs among our clusters. Cluster 0 can contain any hashed user IDs in $[0, (2^{64} - 1)/4)$, cluster 1 can contain any hashed user IDs in $[(2^{64} - 1)/4, (2^{64} - 1)/2)$, cluster 2 can contain any hashed user IDs in $[(2^{64} - 1)/2, 3 * (2^{64} - 1)/4)$, and cluster 3 can contain any hashed user IDs in $[3 * (2^{64} - 1)/4, 2^{64} - 1)$. We can start with this even division. As traffic will be uneven between clusters, we can balance the traffic by adjusting the number and sizes of the divisions.

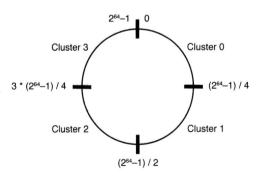

Figure 16.6   Consistent hashing of hashed user IDs to cluster names. We can divide clusters across the 64-bit address space. In this illustration, we assume we have four clusters, so each cluster takes one-quarter of the address space. We can start with even divisions and then adjust the number and sizes of divisions to balance the traffic between them.

How does our backend find an appropriate SQL node? We need a mapping of hashed user IDs to cluster names. Each cluster can have multiple A records, one for each follower, so a backend host is randomly assigned to a follower node in the appropriate cluster.

We need to monitor traffic volume to the clusters to detect hot shards and rebalance the traffic by resizing clusters appropriately. We can adjust the host's hard disk capacity to save costs. If we are using a cloud vendor, we can adjust the VM (virtual machine) size that we use.

Figure 16.7 illustrates the high-level architecture of our news feed service with this design. When a user makes a request, the backend hashes the user ID as just discussed. The backend then does a lookup to ZooKeeper to obtain the appropriate cluster name and sends the SQL query to the cluster. The query is sent to a random follower node, executed there, and then the result list of posts is returned to the user.

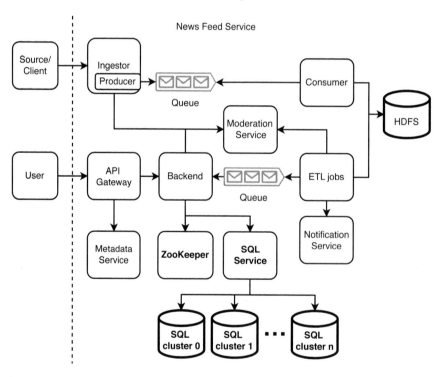

Figure 16.7   High-level architecture of our news feed service with user feeds prepared in advance. Differences from figure 16.4 are bolded. When a user request arrives at our backend, our backend first obtains the appropriate SQL cluster name and then queries the appropriate SQL cluster for the posts. Our backend can direct user requests to a follower node that contains the requested user ID. Alternatively, as illustrated here, we can separate the routing of SQL requests into an SQL service.

If our only client is a mobile app (i.e., no web app), we can save storage by storing posts on the client. We can then assume that a user only needs to fetch their posts once and delete their rows after they are fetched. If a user logs in to a different mobile device, they will not see the posts that they had fetched on their previous device. This occurrence may be sufficiently uncommon, and so it is acceptable to us, especially because news quickly becomes outdated, and a user will have little interest in a post a few days after it is published.

Another way is to add a timestamp column and have an ETL job that periodically deletes rows that are older than 24 hours.

We may decide to avoid sharded SQL by combining both approaches. When a user opens the mobile app, we can use a prepared feed to serve only their first request for their posts and only store the number of post IDs that can fit into a single node. If the user scrolls down, the app may make more requests for more posts, and these requests can be served from Redis. Figure 16.8 illustrates the high-level architecture of this approach with Redis. This approach has tradeoffs of higher complexity and maintenance overhead for lower latency and cost.

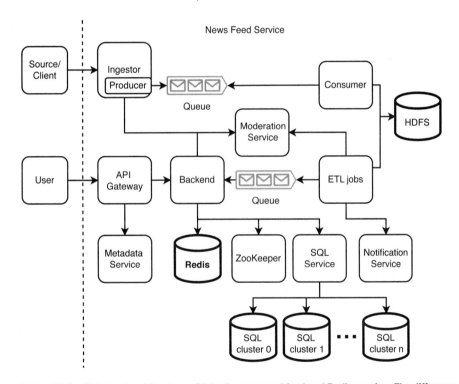

Figure 16.8 High-level architecture with both a prepared feed and Redis service. The difference from figure 16.7 is the added Redis service, which is bolded.

Let's discuss a couple of ways a client can avoid fetching the same posts from Redis more than once:

1 A client can include the post IDs that it currently has in its GET /post request, so our backend can return posts that the client hasn't fetched.

2 Our Redis table labels posts by hour. A client can request its posts of a certain hour. If there are too many posts to be returned, we can label posts by smaller

time increments (such as blocks of 10 minutes per hour). Another possible way is to provide an API endpoint that returns all post IDs of a certain hour and a request body on the GET /post endpoint that allows users to specify the post IDs that it wishes to fetch.

16.4 Validation and content moderation

In this section, we discuss concerns about validation and possible solutions. Validation may not catch all problems, and posts may be erroneously delivered to users. Content filtering rules may differ by user demographic.

Refer to section 15.6 for a discussion of an approval service for Airbnb, which is another approach to validation and content moderation. We will briefly discuss this here. Figure 16.9 illustrates our high-level architecture with an approval service. Certain ETL jobs may flag certain posts for manual review. We can send such posts to our approval service for manual review. If a reviewer approves a post, it will be sent to our Kafka queue to be consumed by our backend and served to users. If a reviewer rejects a post, our approval service can notify the source/client via a messaging service.

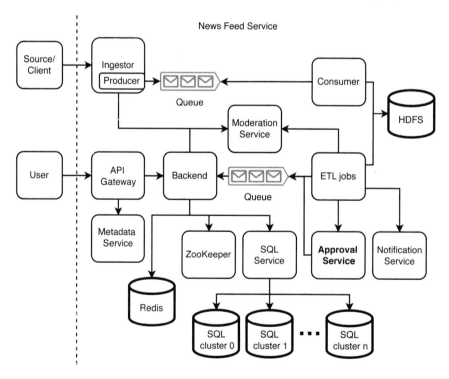

Figure 16.9   **ETL jobs can flag certain posts for manual approval. These posts can be sent to our approval service (in bold; this service is added to figure 16.8) for manual review, instead of being produced by a Kafka queue. (If we have a high rate of posts flagged for review, our approval service itself may need to contain a Kafka queue.) If a reviewer approves a post, it will be sent back to our Kafka queue via an ETL job to be consumed by our backend (or it can send the post directly to our backend). If a reviewer rejects a post, our approval service can notify the source/client via a messaging service, not illustrated in this figure.**

16.4.1 *Changing posts on users' devices*

Certain validations are difficult to automate. For example, a post may be truncated. For simplicity, consider a post with just one sentence: "This is a post." A truncated post can be: "This is a." A post with spelling mistakes is easy to detect, but this post has no spelling mistakes but is clearly invalid. Such problems are difficult for automated validation.

Certain inappropriate content, like inappropriate words is easy to detect, but much inappropriate content like age-inappropriate content, bomb threats, or fake news is extremely difficult to automatically screen for.

In any system design, we should not try to prevent all errors and failures. We should assume that mistakes and failures are inevitable, and we should develop mechanisms to make it easy to detect, troubleshoot, and fix them. Certain posts that should not be delivered may be accidentally delivered to users. We need a mechanism to delete such posts on our news feed service or overwrite them with corrected posts. If users' devices cache posts, they should be deleted or overwritten with the corrected versions.

To do this, we can modify our GET /posts endpoint. Each time a user fetches posts, the response should contain a list of corrected posts and a list of posts to be deleted. The client mobile app should display the corrected posts and delete the appropriate posts.

One possible way is to add an "event" enum to a post, with possible values REPLACE and DELETE. If we want to replace or delete an old post on a client, we should create a new post object that has the same post ID as the old post. The post object should have an event with the value REPLACE for replacement or DELETE for deletion.

For our news feed service to know which posts on a client need to be modified, the former needs to know which posts the client has. Our news feed service can log the IDs of posts that clients downloaded, but the storage requirement may be too big and costly. If we set a retention period on clients (such as 24 hours or 7 days) so they automatically delete old posts, we can likewise delete these old logs, but storage may still be costly.

Another solution is for clients to include their current post IDs in GET /post requests, our backend can process these post IDs to determine which new posts to send (as we discussed earlier) and also determine which posts need to be changed or deleted.

In section 16.4.3, we discuss a moderation service where one of the key functions is that admins can view currently available posts on the news feed service and make moderation decisions where posts are changed or deleted.

16.4.2 *Tagging posts*

We can assume an approval or rejection is applied to an entire post. That is, if any part of a post fails validation or moderation, we simply reject the entire post instead of attempting to serve part of it. What should we do with posts that fail validation? We may simply drop them, notify their sources, or manually review them. The first choice may cause poor user experience, while the third choice may be too expensive if done at scale. We can choose the second option.

We can expand the intersection task of figure 16.3 to also message the responsible source/user if any validation fails. The intersection task can aggregate all failed validations and send them to the source/user in a single message. It may use a shared messaging service to send messages. Each validation task can have an ID and a short description of the validation. A message can contain the IDs and descriptions of failed validations for the user to reference if it wishes to contact our company to discuss any necessary changes to their post or to dispute the rejection decision.

Another requirement we may need to discuss is whether we need to distinguish rules that apply globally versus region-specific rules. Certain rules may apply only to specific countries because of local cultural sensitivities or government laws and regulations. Generalizing this, a user should not be shown certain posts depending on their stated preferences and their demographic, such as age or region. Furthermore, we cannot reject such posts in the ingestor because doing so will apply these validation tasks to all users, not just specific users. We must instead tag the posts with certain metadata that will be used to filter out specific posts for each user. To prevent ambiguity with tags for user interests, we can refer to such tags as filter tags, or "filters" for short. A post can have both tags and filters. A key difference between tags and filters is that users configure their preferred tags, while filters are completely controlled by us. As discussed in the next subsection, this difference means that filters will be configured in the moderation service, but tags are not.

We assume that when a new tag/filter is added or a current tag/filter is deleted, this change will only apply to future posts, and we do not need to relabel past posts.

A single Redis lookup is no longer sufficient for a user to fetch their posts. We'll need three Redis hash tables, with the following key-value pairs:

- *{post ID, post}:* For fetching posts by ID
- *{tag, [post ID]}:* For filtering post IDs by tag
- *{post ID, [filter]}:* For filtering out posts by filter

Multiple key-value lookups are needed. The steps are as follows:

1 A client makes a GET /post request to our news feed service.
2 Our API gateway queries our metadata service for a client's tags and filters. Our client can also store its own tags and filters and provide them in a GET /post request, and then we can skip this lookup.
3 Our API gateway queries Redis to obtain the post IDs with the user's tags and filters.
4 It queries Redis for the filter of each post ID and excludes this post ID from the user if it contains any of the user's filters.
5 It queries Redis for the post of each post ID and then returns these posts to the client.

Note that the logic to filter out post IDs by tags must be done at the application level. An alternative is to use SQL tables instead of Redis tables. We can create a post table with (post_id, post) columns, a tag table with (tag, post_id) columns, and a filter table with (filter, post_id) columns, and do a single SQL JOIN query to obtain a client's posts:

```
SELECT post
FROM post p JOIN tag t ON p.post_id = t.post_id
LEFT JOIN filter f ON p.post_id = f.post_id
WHERE p.post_id IS NULL
```

Section 16.3 discussed preparing users' feeds in advance by preparing the Redis table with {user_id, post_id}. Even with the post filtering requirements discussed in this section, we can have an ETL job that prepares this Redis table.

Last, we note that with a region-specific news feed, we may need to partition the Redis cache by region or introduce an additional "region" column in the Redis key. We can also do this if we need to support multiple languages.

16.4.3 *Moderation service*

Our system does validation at four places: the client, ingestor, ETL jobs, and in the backend during GET /post requests. We implement the same validations in the various browser and mobile apps and in the ingestor, even though this means duplicate development and maintenance and higher risk of bugs. The validations add CPU processing overhead but reduce traffic to our news feed service, which means a smaller cluster size and lower costs. This approach is also more secure. If hackers bypass client-side validations by making API requests directly to our news feed service, our server-side validations will catch these invalid requests.

Regarding the server-side validations, the ingestor, ETL jobs, and backend have different validations. However, referring to figure 16.4, we can consider consolidating and abstracting them into a single service that we can call the moderation service.

As alluded to in the previous subsection about tags vs. filters, the general purpose of the moderation service is for us (not users) to control whether users will see submitted posts. Based on our discussion so far, the moderation service will provide the following features for admins:

1 Configure validation tasks and filters.
2 Execute moderation decisions to change or delete posts.

Consolidating moderation into a single service ensures that teams working on various services within our news feed service do not accidentally implement duplicate validations and allows non-technical staff in content moderation teams to perform all moderation tasks without having to request engineering assistance. The moderation service also logs these decisions for reviews, audits, or rollback (reverse a moderation decision).

> **Using tools to communicate**
>
> In general, communicating with engineering teams and getting engineering work prioritized is difficult, particularly in large organizations, and any tools that allow one to perform their work without this communication are generally good investments.

This moderation request can be processed in the same manner as other write requests to our news feed service. Similar to the ETL jobs, the moderation service produces to the news feed topic, and our news feed service consumes this event and writes the relevant data to Redis.

16.5 *Logging, monitoring, and alerting*

In section 2.5, we discussed key concepts of logging, monitoring, and alerting that one must mention in an interview. Besides what was discussed in section 2.5, we should monitor and send alerts for the following:

- Unusually large or small rate of traffic from any particular source.
- An unusually large rate of items that fail validation, across all items and within each individual source.
- Negative user reactions, such as users flagging articles for abuse or errors.
- Unusually long processing of an item across the pipeline. This can be monitored by comparing the item's timestamp when it was uploaded to the current time when the item reaches the Redis database. Unusually long processing may indicate that certain pipeline components need to be scaled up, or there may be inefficient pipeline operations that we should reexamine.

16.5.1 *Serving images as well as text*

Let's allow a news item to have 0–10 images of up to 1 MB each. We will consider a post's images to be part of a post object, and a tag or filter applies to the entire post object, not to individual properties like a post's body or any image.

This considerably increases the overhead of GET /post requests. Image files are considerably different from post body strings:

- Image files are much larger than bodies, and we can consider different storage technologies for them.
- Image files may be reused across posts.
- Validation algorithms for image files will likely use image processing libraries, which are considerably different from validation of post body strings.

16.5.2 *High-level architecture*

We first observe that the 40 KB storage requirement of an article's text is negligible compared to the 10 MB requirement for its images. This means that uploading or processing operations on an article's text is fast, but uploading or processing images takes more time and computational resources.

Figure 16.10 shows our high-level architecture with a media service. Media upload must be synchronous because the source needs to be informed if the upload succeeded or failed. This means that the ingestor service's cluster will be much bigger than before we added media to articles. The media service can store the media on a shared object service, which is replicated across multiple data centers, so a user can access the media from the data center closest to them.

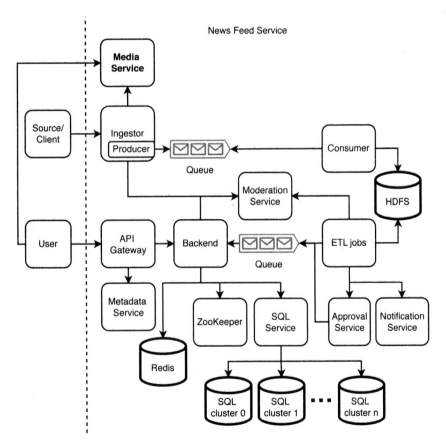

Figure 16.10 Adding a media service (in bold; this service is added to figure 16.9), which allows our news items to contain audio, images and videos. A separate media service also makes it easier to manage and analyze media separately of its news items.

Figure 16.11 is a sequence diagram of a source uploading an article. Because media uploads require more data transfer than metadata or text, the media uploads should complete before producing the article's metadata and text onto the Kafka queue. If the media uploads succeed but producing to the queue fails, we can return a 500 error to the source. During a file upload process to the media service, the ingestor can first hash the file and send this hash to the media service to check if the file has already been uploaded. If so, the media service can return a 304 response to the ingestor, and a costly network transfer can be avoided. We note that in this design, the consumer cluster can be much smaller than the Media service cluster.

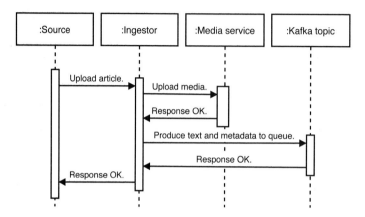

Figure 16.11   Sequence diagram of a source uploading an article. Media is almost always larger than text, so our ingestor first uploads media to our Media Service. After our ingestor successfully uploads the media, it produces the text and metadata to our Kafka topic, to be consumed and written to HDFS as discussed in this chapter.

What if the ingestor host fails after the media was successfully uploaded but before it can produce to the Kafka topic? It makes sense to keep the media upload rather than delete it because the media upload process is resource-intensive. The source will receive an error response and can try the upload again. This time, the media service can return a 304 as discussed in the previous paragraph, and then the ingestor can produce the corresponding event. The source may not retry. In that case, we can periodically run an audit job to find media that do not have accompanying metadata and text in HDFS and delete this media.

If our users are widely geographically distributed, or user traffic is too heavy for our media service, we can use a CDN. Refer to chapter 13 for a discussion on a CDN system design. The authorization tokens to download images from the CDN can be granted by the API gateway, using a service mesh architecture. Figure 16.12 shows our high-level architecture with a CDN. A new item will contain text fields for content such as title, body, and media URLs. Referring to figure 16.12, a source can upload images to our image service and text content to our news feed service. A client can

- Download article text and media URLs from Redis.
- Download media from the CDN.

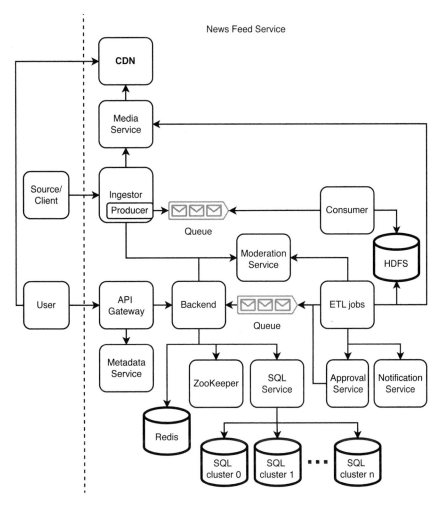

Figure 16.12 Using a CDN (in bold; this service is added to figure 16.10) to host media. Users will download images directly from our CDN, gaining the benefits of a CDN such as lower latency and higher availability.

The main differences with figure 16.10 are the following:

- The media service writes media to the CDN, and users download media from the CDN.
- ETL jobs and the approval service make requests to the media service.

We use both a media service and a CDN because some articles will not be served to users, so some images don't need to be stored on the CDN, which will reduce costs. Certain ETL jobs may be automatic approvals of articles, so these jobs need to inform the media service that the article is approved, and the media service should upload the article's media to the CDN to be served to users. The approval service makes similar requests to the media service.

We may discuss the tradeoffs of handling and storing text and media in separate services vs. a single service. We can refer to chapter 13 to discuss more details of hosting images on a CDN, such as the tradeoffs of hosting media on a CDN.

Taking this a step further, we can also host complete articles on our CDN, including all text and media. The Redis values can be reduced to article IDs. Although an article's text is usually much smaller than its media, there can still be performance improvements from placing it on a CDN, particularly for frequent requests of popular articles. Redis is horizontally scalable but inter data center replication is complex.

In the approval service, should the images and text of an article be reviewed separately or together? For simplicity, reviewing an article can consist of reviewing both its text and accompanying media as a single article.

How can we review media more efficiently? Hiring review staff is expensive, and a staff will need to listen to an audio clip or watch a video completely before making a review decision. We can consider transcribing audio, so a reviewer can read rather than listen to audio files. This will allow us to hire hearing-impaired staff, improving the company's inclusivity culture. A staff can play a video file at 2x or 3x speed when they review it and read the transcribed audio separately from viewing the video file. We can also consider machine learning solutions to review articles.

16.6 *Other possible discussion topics*

Here are other possible discussion topics that may come up as the interview progresses, which may be suggested by either the interviewer or candidate:

- Create hashtags, which are dynamic, rather than a fixed set of topics.
- Users may wish to share news items with other users or groups.
- Have a more detailed discussion on sending notifications to creators and readers.
- Real-time dissemination of articles. ETL jobs must be streaming, not batch.
- Boosting to prioritize certain articles over others.

We can consider the items that were out-of-scope in the functional requirements discussion:

- Analytics.
- Personalization. Instead of serving the same 1,000 news items to all users, serve each user a personalized set of 100 news items. This design will be substantially more complex.
- Serving articles in languages other than English. Potential complications, such as handling UTF or language transations.
- Monetizing the news feed. Topics include:
  - Design a subscription system.
  - Reserve certain posts for subscribers.
  - An article limit for non-subscribers.
  - Ads and promoted posts.

Summary

- When drawing the initial high-level architecture of the news feed system, consider the main data of interest and draw the components that read and write this data to the database.

- Consider the non-functional requirements of reading and writing the data and then select the appropriate database types and consider the accompanying services, if any. These include the Kafka service and Redis service.

- Consider which operations don't require low latency and place them in batch and streaming jobs for scalability.

- Determine any processing operations that must be performed before and after writes and reads and wrap them in services. Prior operations may include compression, content moderation, and lookups to other services to get relevant IDs or data. Post operations may include notifications and indexing. Examples of such services in our news feed system include the ingestor service, consumer service, ETL jobs, and backend service.

- Logging, monitoring, and alerting should be done on failures and unusual events that we may be interested in.

17

Design a dashboard of top 10 products on Amazon by sales volume

This chapter covers

- Scaling an aggregation operation on a large data stream
- Using a Lambda architecture for fast approximate results and slow accurate results
- Using Kappa architecture as an alternative to Lambda architecture
- Approximating an aggregation operation for faster speed

Analytics is a common discussion topic in a system design interview. We will always log certain network requests and user interactions, and we will perform analytics based on the data we collect.

The *Top K Problem (Heavy Hitters)* is a common type of dashboard. Based on the popularity or lack thereof of certain products, we can make decisions to promote or discontinue them. Such decisions may not be straightforward. For example, if a product is unpopular, we may decide to either discontinue it to save the costs of selling it, or we may decide to spend more resources to promote it to increase its sales.

The Top K Problem is a common topic we can discuss in an interview when discussing analytics, or it may be its own standalone interview question. It can take on endless forms. Some examples of the Top K Problem include

- Top-selling or worst-selling products on an ecommerce app by volume (this question) or revenue.
- The most-viewed or least-viewed products on an ecommerce app.
- Most downloaded apps on an apps store.
- Most watched videos on a video app like YouTube.
- Most popular (listened to) or least popular songs on a music app like Spotify.
- Most traded stocks on an exchange like Robinhood or E*TRADE.
- Most forwarded posts on a social media app, such as the most retweeted Twitter tweets or most shared Instagram post.

17.1 Requirements

Let's ask some questions to determine the functional and non-functional requirements. We assume that we have access to the data centers of Amazon or whichever ecommerce app we are concerned with

- How do we break ties?

High accuracy may not be important, so we can choose any item in a tie:

- Which time intervals are we concerned with?

Our system should be able to aggregate by certain specified intervals such as hour, day, week, or year:

- The use cases will influence the desired accuracy (and other requirements like scalability). What are the use cases of this information? What is the desired accuracy and desired consistency/latency?

That's a good question. What do you have in mind?

It will be resource-intensive to compute accurate volumes and ranking in real time. Perhaps we can have a Lambda architecture, so we have an eventually consistent solution that offers approximate sales volumes and rankings within the last few hours and accurate numbers for time periods older than a few hours.

We can also consider trading off accuracy for higher scalability, lower cost, lower complexity, and better maintainability. We expect to compute a particular Top K list within a particular period at least hours after that period has passed, so consistency is not a concern.

Low latency is not a concern. We can expect that generating a list will require many minutes:

- Do we need just the Top K or top 10, or the volumes and ranking of an arbitrary number of products?

Similar to the previous question, we can accept a solution that provides the approximate volumes and ranking of the top 10 products within the last few hours, and volumes and ranking of any arbitrary number of products for time periods older than a few hours, potentially up to years. It's also fine if our solution can display more than 10 products:

- Do we need to show the sale counts on the Top K list or just the product sales rankings?

We will show both the rankings and counts. This seems like a superfluous question, but there might be possible design simplifications if we don't need to display certain data:

- Do we need to consider events that occur after a sale? A customer may request a refund, an exchange for the same or different product(s), or a product may be recalled.

This is a good question that demonstrates one's industry experience and attention to detail. Let's assume we can consider only the initial sales events and disregard subsequent events like disputes or product recalls:

- Let's discuss scalability requirements. What is the sales transaction rate? What is the request rate for our Heavy Hitters dashboard? How many products do we have?

Assume 10 billion sales events per day (i.e., heavy sales transaction traffic). At 1 KB/event, the write rate is 10 TB/day. The Heavy Hitters dashboard will only be viewed by employees, so it will have low request rate. Assume we have ~1M products.

We do not have other non-functional requirements. High availability or low latency (and the corresponding complexities they will bring to our system design) are not required.

17.2 *Initial thoughts*

Our first thought may be to log the events to a distributed storage solution, like HDFS or Elasticsearch, and run a MapReduce, Spark, or Elasticsearch query when we need to compute a list of Top K products within a particular period. However, this approach is computationally intensive and may take too long. It may take hours or days to compute a list of Top K products within a particular month or year.

If we don't have use cases for storing our sales event logs other than generating this list, it will be wasteful to store these logs for months or years just for this purpose. If we log millions of requests per second, it can add up to PBs/year. We may wish to store a few months or years of raw events for various purposes, including serving customer disputes and refunds, for troubleshooting or regulatory compliance purposes. However, this retention period may be too short for generating our desired Top K list.

We need to preprocess our data prior to computing these Top K lists. We should periodically perform aggregation and count the sales of our products, bucketing by hour, day, week, month, and year. Then we can perform these steps when we need a Top K list:

1 If needed, sum the counts of the appropriate buckets, depending on the desired period. For example, if we need the Top K list of a period of one month, we simply use that month's bucket. If we need a particular three-month period, we sum the counts of the one-month buckets of that period. This way, we can save storage by deleting events after we sum the counts.

2 Sort these sums to obtain the Top K list.

We need to save the buckets because the sales can be very uneven. In an extreme situation, a product "A" may have 1M sales within a particular hour during a particular year, and 0 sales at all other times during that year, while sales of all other products may sum to far less than 1M total sales in that year. Product A will be in the Top K list of any period that includes that hour.

The rest of this chapter is about performing these operations at scale in a distributed manner.

17.3 Initial high-level architecture

We first consider Lambda architecture. *Lambda architecture* is an approach to handling massive quantities of data by using both batch and streaming methods (Refer to https://www.databricks.com/glossary/lambda-architecture or https://www.snowflake.com/guides/lambda-architecture.) Referring to figure 17.1, our lambda architecture consists of two parallel data processing pipelines and a serving layer that combines the results of these two pipelines:

1 A streaming layer/pipeline that ingests events in real time from all data centers where sales transactions occur and uses an approximation algorithm to compute the sales volumes and rankings of the most popular products.

2 A batch layer, or batch pipelines that run periodically (hourly, daily, weekly, and yearly) to compute accurate sales volumes and rankings. For our users to see the accurate numbers as they become available, our batch pipeline ETL job can contain a task to overwrite the results of the streaming pipeline with the batch pipeline's whenever the latter are ready.

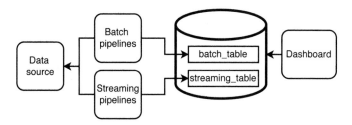

Figure 17.1 A high-level sketch of our Lambda architecture. Arrows indicate the direction of requests. Data flows through our parallel streaming and batch pipelines. Each pipeline writes its final output to a table in a database. The streaming pipeline writes to the speed_table while the batch pipeline writes to the batch_table. Our dashboard combines data from the speed_table and batch_table to generate the Top K lists.

Following an EDA (Event Driven Architecture) approach, the sales backend service sends events to a Kafka topic, which can be used for all downstream analytics such as our Top K dashboard.

17.4   Aggregation service

An initial optimization we can make to our Lambda architecture is to do some aggregation on our sales events and pass these aggregated sales events to both our streaming and batch pipelines. Aggregation can reduce the cluster sizes of both our streaming and batch pipelines. We sketch a more detailed initial architecture in figure 17.2. Our streaming and batch pipelines both write to an RDBMS (SQL), which our dashboard can query with low latency. We can also use Redis if all we need is simple key-value lookups, but we will likely desire filter and aggregation operations for our dashboard and other future services.

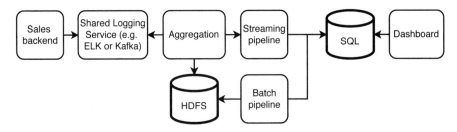

Figure 17.2   Our Lambda architecture, consisting of an initial aggregation service and streaming and batch pipelines. Arrows indicate the direction of requests. The sales backend logs events (including sales events) to a shared logging service, which is the data source for our dashboard. Our aggregation service consumes sales events from our shared logging service, aggregates them, and flushes these aggregated events to our streaming pipeline and to HDFS. Our batch pipeline computes the counts from our HDFS data and writes it to the SQL batch_table. Our streaming pipeline computes the counts faster and less accurately than our batch pipeline and writes it to the SQL speed_table. Our dashboard uses a combination of data from batch_table and speed_table to generate the Top K lists.

NOTE   Event Driven Architecture (EDA) uses events to trigger and communicate between decoupled services (https://aws.amazon.com/event-driven -architecture/). Refer to other sources for more information, such as section 5.1 or page 295 of *Web Scalability for Startup Engineers* (2015) by Artur Ejsmont for an introduction to event-driven architecture.

We discussed aggregation and its benefits and tradeoffs in section 4.5. Our aggregation service consists of a cluster of hosts that subscribe to the Kafka topic that logs sales events, aggregates the events, and flushes/writes the aggregated events to HDFS (via Kafka) and to our streaming pipeline.

17.4.1 Aggregating by product ID

For example, a raw sales event may contain fields like (timestamp, product ID) while an aggregated event may be of the form (product_id, start_time, end_time, count, aggregation_host_id). We can aggregate the events since their exact timestamps are unimportant. If certain time intervals are important (e.g., hourly), we can ensure that (start_time, end_time) pairs are always within the same hour. For example, (0100, 0110) is ok, but (0155, 0205) is not.

17.4.2 Matching host IDs and product IDs

Our aggregation service can partition by product ID, so each host is responsible for aggregating a certain set of IDs. For simplicity, we can manually maintain a map of (host ID, product ID). There are various implementation options for this configuration, including

1 A configuration file included in the service's source code. Each time we change the file, we must restart the entire cluster.
2 A configuration file in a shared object store. Each host of the service reads this file on startup and stores in memory the product IDs that it is responsible for. The service also needs an endpoint to update its product IDs. When we change the file, we can call this endpoint on the hosts that will consume different product IDs.
3 Storing the map as a database table in SQL or Redis.
4 Sidecar pattern, in which a host makes a fetch request to the sidecar. The sidecar fetches an event of the appropriate product IDs and returns it to the host.

We will usually choose option 2 or 4 so we will not need to restart the entire cluster for each configuration change. We choose a file over a database for the following reasons:

- It is easy to parse a configuration file format such as YAML and JSON directly into a hash map data structure. More code is required to achieve the same effect with a database table. We will need to code with an ORM framework, code the database query and the data access object, and match the data access object with the hash map.
- The number of hosts will likely not exceed a few hundred or a few thousand, so the configuration file will be tiny. Each host can fetch the entire file. We do not need a solution with the low latency read performance of a database.
- The configuration does not change frequently enough to justify the overhead of a database like SQL or Redis.

17.4.3 Storing timestamps

If we need the exact timestamps to be stored somewhere, this storage should be handled by the sales service and not by an analytics or Heavy Hitters service. We should maintain separation of responsibility. There will be numerous analytics pipelines being defined on the sales events besides Heavy Hitters. We should have full freedom to develop and decommission these pipelines without regard to other services. In other words, we should be careful in deciding if other services should be dependencies of these analytics services.

17.4.4 Aggregation process on a host

An aggregation host contains a hash table with key of product ID and value of count. It also does checkpointing on the Kafka topic that it consumes, writing checkpoints to Redis. The checkpoints consist of the IDs of the aggregated events. The aggregation service can have more hosts than the number of partitions in the Kafka topic, though this is unlikely to be necessary since aggregation is a simple and fast operation. Each host repeatedly does the following:

1 Consume an event from the topic.
2 Update its hash table.

An aggregation host may flush its hash table with a set periodicity or when its memory is running out, whichever is sooner. A possible implementation of the flush process is as follows:

1 Produce the aggregated events to a Kafka topic that we can name "Flush." If the aggregated data is small (e.g., a few MB), we can write it as a single event, consisting of a list of product ID aggregation tuples with the fields ("product ID," "earliest timestamp," "latest timestamp," "number of sales"), such as, for example, [(123, 1620540831, 1620545831, 20), (152, 1620540731, 1620545831, 18), . . .].
2 Using change data capture (CDC, refer to section 5.3), each destination has a consumer that consumes the event and writes to it:
   a Write the aggregated events to HDFS.
   b Write a tuple checkpoint to Redis with the status "complete" (e.g., {"hdfs": "1620540831, complete"}).
   c Repeat steps 2a–c for the streaming pipeline.

If we did not have this "Flush" Kafka topic, and a consumer host fails while writing an aggregated event to a particular destination, the aggregation service will need to reaggregate those events.

Why do we need to write two checkpoints? This is just one of various possible algorithms to maintain consistency.

If a host fails during step 1, another host can consume the flush event and perform the writes. If the host fails during step 2a, the write to HDFS may have succeeded or failed, and another host can read from HDFS to check if the write succeeded or if it needs to be retried. Reading from HDFS is an expensive operation. As a host failure is a rare event, this expensive operation will also be rare. If we are concerned with this expensive failure recovery mechanism, we can implement the failure recovery mechanism as a periodic operation to read all "processing" checkpoints between a minute and a few minutes old.

The failure recovery mechanism should itself be idempotent in case it fails while in progress and has to be repeated.

We should consider fault-tolerance. Any write operation may fail. Any host in the aggregation service, Redis service, HDFS cluster, or streaming pipeline can fail at any time. There may be network problems that interrupt write requests to any host on a service. A write event response code may be 200 but a silent error actually occurred. Such events will cause the three services to be in an inconsistent state. Therefore, we write a separate checkpoint for HDFS and our streaming pipeline. The write event should have an ID, so the destination services may perform deduplication if needed.

In such situations where we need to write an event to multiple services, what are the possible ways to prevent such inconsistency?

1 Checkpoint after each write to each service, which we just discussed.

2 We can do nothing if our requirements state that inconsistency is acceptable. For example, we may tolerate some inaccuracy in the streaming pipeline, but the batch pipeline must be accurate.

3 Periodic auditing (also called supervisor). If the numbers do not line up, discard the inconsistent results and reprocess the relevant data.

4 Use distributed transaction techniques such as 2PC, Saga, Change Data Capture, or Transaction Supervisor. These were discussed in chapter 4 and appendix D.

As discussed in section 4.5, the flip side of aggregation is that real-time results are delayed by the time required for aggregation and flushing. Aggregation may be unsuitable for if our dashboard requires low-latency updates.

17.5 *Batch pipeline*

Our batch pipeline is conceptually more straightforward than the streaming pipeline, so we can discuss it first.

Figure 17.3 shows a simplified flow diagram of our batch pipeline. Our batch pipeline consists of a series of aggregation/rollup tasks by increasing intervals. We roll up by hour, then day, then week, and then month and year. If we have 1M product IDs:

1 Rollup by hour will result in 24M rows/day or 168M rows/week.

2 Rollup by month will result in 28–31M rows/month or 336–372M rows/year.

3 Rollup by day will result in 7M rows/week or 364M rows/year.

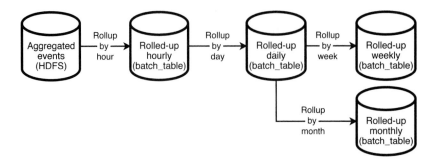

Figure 17.3   Simplified flow diagram of the rollup tasks in our batch pipeline. We have a rollup job that progressively rolls up by increasing time intervals to reduce the number of rows processed in each stage.

Let's estimate the storage requirements. 400M rows each with 10 64-bit columns occupy 32 GB. This can easily fit into a single host. The hourly rollup job may need to process billions of sales events, so it can use a Hive query to read from HDFS and then write the resulting counts to the SQL batch_table. The rollups for other intervals use the vast reduction of the number of rows from the hourly rollup, and they only need to read and write to this SQL batch_table.

In each of these rollups, we can order the counts by descending order, and write the Top K (or perhaps K*2 for flexibility) rows to our SQL database to be displayed on our dashboard.

Figure 17.4 is a simple illustration of our ETL DAG for one stage in our batch pipeline (i.e., one rollup job). We will have one DAG for each rollup (i.e., four DAG in total). An ETL DAG has the following four tasks. The third and fourth are siblings. We use Airflow terminology for DAG, task, and run:

1   For any rollup greater than hourly, we need a task to verify that the dependent rollup runs have successfully completed. Alternatively, the task can verify that the required HDFS or SQL data is available, but this will involve costly database queries.

2   Run a Hive or SQL query to sum the counts in descending order and write the result counts to the batch_table.

3   Delete the corresponding rows on the speed_table. This task is separate from task 2 because the former can be rerun without having to rerun the latter. Should task 3 fail while it is attempting to delete the rows, we should rerun the deletion without having to rerun the expensive Hive or SQL query of step 2.

4   Generate or regenerate the appropriate Top K lists using these new batch_table rows. As discussed later in section 17.5, these Top K lists most likely have already been generated using both our accurate batch_table data and inaccurate speed_table table, so we will be regenerating these lists with only our batch_table. This task is not costly, but it can also be rerun independently if it fails, so we implement it as its own task.

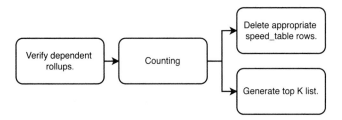

Figure 17.4 An ETL DAG for one rollup job. The constituent tasks are to verify that dependent rollups have completed, perform the rollup/counting and persist the counts to SQL, and then delete the appropriate speed_table rows because they are no longer needed.

Regarding task 1, the daily rollup can only happen if all its dependent hourly rollups have been written to HDFS, and likewise for the weekly and monthly rollups. One daily rollup run is dependent on 24 hourly rollup runs, one weekly rollup run is dependent on seven daily rollup runs, and one monthly rollup run is dependent on 28–30 daily rollup runs depending on the month. If we use Airflow, we can use `ExternalTaskSensor` (https://airflow.apache.org/docs/apache-airflow/stable/howto/operator/external _task_sensor.html#externaltasksensor) instances with the appropriate `execution _date` parameter values in our daily, weekly, and monthly DAGs to verify that the dependent runs have successfully completed.

17.6 *Streaming pipeline*

A batch job may take many hours to complete, which will affect the rollups for all intervals. For example, the Hive query for the latest hourly rollup job may take 30 minutes to complete, so the following rollups and by extension their Top K lists will be unavailable:

- The Top K list for that hour.
- The Top K list for the day that contains that hour will be unavailable.
- The Top K lists for the week and month that contains that day will be unavailable.

The purpose of our streaming pipeline is to provide the counts (and Top K lists) that the batch pipeline has not yet provided. The streaming pipeline must compute these counts much faster than the batch pipeline and may use approximation techniques.

After our initial aggregation, the next steps are to compute the final counts and sort them in descending order, and then we will have our Top K lists. In this section, we approach this problem by first considering an approach for a single host and then find how to make it horizontally scalable.

17.6.1 *Hash table and max-heap with a single host*

Our first attempt is to use a hash table and sort by frequency counts using a max-heap of size K. Listing 17.1 is a sample top K Golang function with this approach.

Listing 17.1 Sample Golang function to compute Top K list

```go
type HeavyHitter struct {
  identifier string
  frequency int
}

func topK(events []String, int k) (HeavyHitter) {
  frequencyTable := make(map[string]int)
  for _, event := range events {
    value := frequencyTable[event]
    if value == 0 {
      frequencyTable[event] = 1
    } else {
      frequencyTable[event] = value + 1
    }
  }

  pq = make(PriorityQueue, k)
  i := 0
  for key, element := range frequencyTable {
    pq[i++] = &HeavyHitter{
      identifier: key,
      frequency: element
    }
    if pq.Len() > k {
      pq.Pop(&pq).(*HeavyHitter)
    }
  }

  /*
   * Write the heap contents to your destination.
   * Here we just return them in an array.
   */
  var result [k]HeavyHitter
  i := 0
  for pq.Len() > 0 {
    result[i++] = pq.Pop(&pq).(*HeavyHitter)
  }
  return result
}
```

In our system, we can run multiple instances of the function in parallel for our various time buckets (i.e., hour, day, week, month, and year). At the end of each period, we can store the contents of the max-heap, reset the counts to 0, and start counting for the new period.

17.6.2 *Horizontal scaling to multiple hosts and multi-tier aggregation*

Figure 17.5 illustrates horizontal scaling to multiple hosts and multi-tier aggregation. The two hosts in the middle column sum the (product, hour) counts from their upstream hosts in the left column, while the max-heaps in the right column aggregate the (product, hour) counts from their upstream hosts in the middle column.

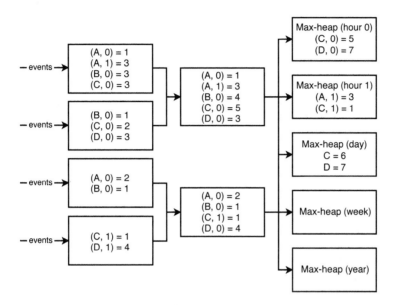

Figure 17.5 **If the traffic to the final hash table host is too high, we can use a multi-tier approach for our streaming pipeline. For brevity, we display a key in the format (product, hour). For example, "(A, 0)" refers to product A at hour 0. Our final layer of hosts can contain max heaps, one for each rollup interval. This design is very similar to a multi-tier aggregation service discussed in section 4.5.2. Each host has an associated Kafka topic, which we don't illustrate here.**

In this approach, we insert more tiers between the first layer of hosts and the final hash table host, so no host gets more traffic than it can process. This is simply shifting the complexity of implementing a multi-tier aggregation service from our aggregation service to our streaming pipeline. The solution will introduce latency, as also described in section 4.5.2. We also do partitioning, following the approach described in section 4.5.3 and illustrated in figure 4.6. Note the discussion points in that section about addressing hot partitions. We partition by product ID. We may also partition by sales event timestamp.

> ### Aggregation
> Notice that we aggregate by the combination of product ID and timestamp. Before reading on, think about why.

Why do we aggregate by the combination of product ID and timestamp? This is because a Top K list has a period, with a start time and an end time. We need to ensure that each sales event is aggregated in its correct time ranges. For example, a sales event that occurred at 2023-01-01 10:08 UTC should be aggregated in

1 The hour range of [2023-01-01 10:08 UTC, 2023-01-01 11:00 UTC).
2 The day range of [2023-01-01, 2023-01-02).
3 The week range of [2022-12-28 00:00 UTC, 2023-01-05 00:00 UTC). 2022-12-28 and 2023-01-05 are both Mondays.
4 The month range of [2023-01-01, 2013-02-01).
5 The year range of [2023, 2024).

Our approach is to aggregate by the smallest period (i.e., hour). We expect any event to take only a few seconds to go through all the layers in our cluster, so it is unlikely for any key in our cluster that is more than an hour old. Each product ID has its own key. With the hour range appended to each key, it is unlikely that the number of keys will be greater than the number of product IDs times two.

One minute after the end of a period—for example, at 2023-01-01 11:01 UTC for [2023-01-01 10:08 UTC, 2023-01-01 11:00 UTC) or 2023-01-02 00:01 UTC for [2023-01-01, 2023-01-02)—the respective host in the final layer (whom we can refer to as *final hosts*) can write its heap to our SQL speed_table, and then our dashboard is ready to display the corresponding Top K list for this period. Occasionally, an event may take more than a minute to go through all the layers, and then the final hosts can simply write their updated heaps to our speed_table. We can set a retention period of a few hours or days for our final hosts to retain old aggregation keys, after which they can delete them.

An alternative to waiting one minute is to implement a system to keep track of the events as they pass through the hosts and trigger the final hosts to write their heaps to the speed_table only after all the relevant events have reached the final hosts. However, this may be overly complex and also prevents our dashboard from displaying approximations before all events have been fully processed.

17.7   *Approximation*

To achieve lower latency, we may need to limit the number of layers in our aggregation service. Figure 17.6 is an example of such a design. We have layers that consist of just max-heaps. This approach trades off accuracy for faster updates and lower cost. We can rely on the batch pipeline for slower and highly accurate aggregation.

Why are max-heaps in separate hosts? This is to simplify provisioning new hosts when scaling up our cluster. As mentioned in section 3.1, a system is considered scalable if it can be scaled up and down with ease. We can have separate Docker images for hash table hosts and the max-heap host, since the number of hash table hosts may change frequently while there is never more than one active max-heap host (and its replicas).

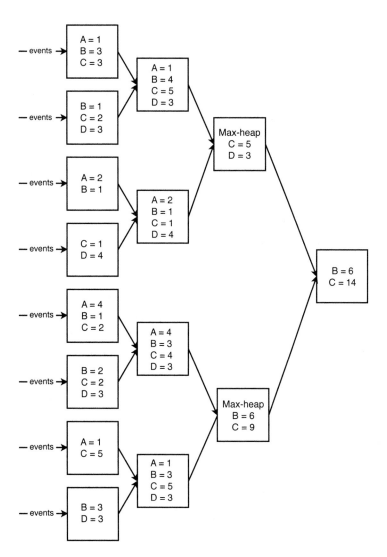

Figure 17.6 Multi-tier with max-heaps. The aggregation will be faster but less accurate. For brevity, we don't display time buckets in this figure.

However, the Top K list produced by this design may be inaccurate. We cannot have a max-heap in each host and simply merge the max-heaps because if we do so, the final max-heap may not actually contain the Top K products. For example, if host one had a hash table {A: 7, B: 6, C: 5}, and host B had a hash table {A: 2, B: 4, C: 5}, and our max-heap is of size 2, host 1's max-heap will contain {A: 7, B: 6} and host 2's max-heap will contain {B: 4, C: 5}. The final combined max-heap will be {A: 7, B: 10}, which erroneously leaves C out of the top two list. The correct final max-heap should be {B: 10, C: 11}.

17.7.1 Count-min sketch

The previous example approaches require a large amount of memory on each host for a hash table of the same size as the number of products (in our case ~1M). We can consider trading off accuracy for lower memory consumption by using approximations.

Count-min sketch is a suitable approximation algorithm. We can think of it as a two-dimensional (2D) table with a width and a height. The width is usually a few thousand while the height is small and represents a number of hash functions (e.g., 5). The output of each hash function is bounded to the width. When a new item arrives, we apply each hash function to the item and increment the corresponding cell.

Let's walk through an example of using count-min sketch with a simple sequence "A C B C C." C is the most common letter and occurs three times. Tables 17.1–17.5 illustrate a count-min sketch table. We bold the hashed value in each step to highlight it.

   1 Hash the first letter "A" with each of the five hash functions. Table 17.1 illustrates that each hash function hashes "A" to a different value.

Table 17.1 Sample count-min sketch table after adding a single letter "A"

1					
	1				
				1	
	1				
	1				

   2 Hash the second letter "C." Table 17.2 illustrates that the first four hash functions hash "C" to a different value than "A." The fifth hash function has a collision. The hashed values of "A" and "C" are identical, so that value is incremented.

Table 17.2 Sample count-min sketch table after adding "A C"

1				**1**	
	1		**1**		
1				1	
	1		**1**		
	2 (collision)				

   3 Hash the third letter "B." Table 17.3 illustrates that the fourth and fifth hash functions have collisions.

Table 17.3 Sample count-min sketch table after adding "A C B"

1		**1**		1	
	1		1		**1**
1	**1**			1	
	2 (collision)		1		
	3 (collision)				

4 Hash the fourth letter "C." Table 17.4 illustrates that only the fifth hash function has a collision.

Table 17.4 Sample count-min sketch table after adding "A C B C"

1		1		**2**	
	1		**2**		1
2	1			1	
	2		**2**		
	4 (collision)				

5 Hash the fifth letter "C." The operation is identical to the previous step. Table 17.5 is the count-min sketch table after a sequence "A C B C C."

Table 17.5 Sample count-min sketch table after a sequence "A C B C C"

1		1		**3**	
	1		**3**		1
3	1			1	
	2		**3**		
	5 (collision)				

To find the item with the highest number of occurrences, we first take the maximum of each row {3, 3, 3, 3, 5} and then the minimum of these maximums "3." To find the item with the second highest number of occurrences, we first take the second highest number in each row {1, 1, 1, 2, 5} and then the minimum of these numbers "1." And so on. By taking the minimum, we decrease the chance of overestimation.

There are formulas that help to calculate the width and height based on our desired accuracy and the probability we achieve that accuracy. This is outside the scope of this book.

The count-min sketch 2D array replaces the hash table in our previous approaches. We will still need a heap to store a list of heavy hitters, but we replace a potentially big hash table with a count-min sketch 2D array of predefined size that remains fixed regardless of the data set size.

17.8   Dashboard with Lambda architecture

Referring to figure 17.7, our dashboard may be a browser app that makes a GET request to a backend service, which in turn runs a SQL query. The discussion so far has been about a batch pipeline that writes to batch_table and a streaming pipeline that writes to speed_table, and the dashboard should construct the Top K list from both tables.

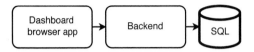

Figure 17.7   Our dashboard has a simple architecture, consisting of a browser app that makes GET requests to a backend service, which in turn makes SQL requests. The functional requirements of our browser app may grow over time, from simply displaying the top 10 lists of a particular period (e.g., the previous month), to include larger lists, more periods, filtering, or aggregation (like percentile, mean, mode, max, min).

However, SQL tables do not guarantee order, and filtering and sorting the batch_table and speed_table may take seconds. To achieve P99 of <1 second, the SQL query should be a simple SELECT query against a single view that contains the list of rankings and counts, which we refer to as the `top_1000` view. This view can be constructed by selecting the top 1,000 products from the speed_table and batch_table in each period. It can also contain an additional column that indicates whether each row is from the speed_table or batch_table. When a user requests a Top K dashboard for a particular interval, our backend can query this view to obtain as much data from the batch table as possible and fill in the blanks with the speed table. Referring to section 4.10, our browser app and backend service can also cache the query responses.

> **Exercise**
> As an exercise, define the SQL query for the top_1000 view.

17.9   Kappa architecture approach

Kappa architecture is a software architecture pattern for processing streaming data, performing both batch and streaming processing with a single technology stack (https://hazelcast.com/glossary/kappa-architecture). It uses an append-only immutable log like Kafka to store incoming data, followed by stream processing and storage in a database for users to query.

In this section, we compare Lambda and Kappa architecture and discuss a Kappa architecture for our dashboard.

17.9.1 *Lambda vs. Kappa architecture*

Lambda architecture is complex because the batch layer and streaming layer each require their own code base and cluster, along with associated operational overhead and the complexity and costs of development, maintenance, logging, monitoring, and alerting.

Kappa architecture is a simplification of Lambda architecture, where there is only a streaming layer and no batch layer. This is akin to performing both streaming and batch processing on a single technology stack. The serving layer serves the data computed from the streaming layer. All data is read and transformed immediately after it is inserted into the messaging engine and processed by streaming techniques. This makes it suitable for low-latency and near real-time data processing like real-time dashboards or monitoring. As discussed earlier regarding the Lambda architecture streaming layer, we may choose to trade off accuracy for performance. But we may also choose not to make this tradeoff and compute highly accurate data.

Kappa architecture originated from the argument that batch jobs are never needed, and streaming can handle all data processing operations and requirements. Refer to https://www.oreilly.com/radar/questioning-the-lambda-architecture/ and https://www.kai-waehner.de/blog/2021/09/23/real-time-kappa-architecture -mainstream-replacing-batch-lambda/, which discuss the disadvantages of batch and how streaming does not have them.

In addition to the points discussed in these reference links, another disadvantage of batch jobs compared to streaming jobs is the former's much higher development and operational overheads because a batch job that uses a distributed file system like HDFS tends to take at least minutes to complete even when running on a small amount of data. This is due to HDFS's large block size (64 or 128 MB compared to 4 KB for UNIX file systems) to trade off low latency for high throughput. On the other hand, a streaming job processing a small amount of data may only take seconds to complete.

Batch job failures are practically inevitable during the entire software development lifecycle from development to testing to production, and when a batch job fails, it must be rerun. One common technique to reduce the amount of time to wait for a batch job is to divide it into stages. Each stage outputs data to intermediate storage, to be used as input for the next stage. This is the philosophy behind Airflow DAGs. As developers, we can design our batch jobs to not take more than 30 minutes or one hour each, but developers and operations staff will still need to wait 30 minutes or one hour to see if a job succeeded or failed. Good test coverage reduces but does not eliminate production problems.

Overall, errors in batch jobs are more costly than in streaming jobs. In batch jobs, a single bug crashes an entire batch job. In streaming, a single bug only affects processing of that specific event.

Another advantage of Kappa vs. Lambda architecture is that the relative simplicity of the former, which uses a single processing framework while the latter may require different frameworks for its batch and streaming pipelines. We may use frameworks like Redis, Kafka, and Flink for streaming.

One consideration of Kappa architecture is that storing a large volume of data in an event-streaming platform like Kafka is costly and not scalable beyond a few PBs, unlike HDFS, which is designed for large volumes. Kafka provides infinite retention with *log compaction* (https://kafka.apache.org/documentation/#compaction), so a Kafka topic saves storage by only storing the latest value for each message key and delete all earlier values for that key. Another approach is to use object storage like S3 for long-term storage of data that is seldom accessed. Table 17.6 compares Lambda and Kappa architecture.

Table 17.6   Comparison between Lambda and Kappa architecture

Lambda	Kappa
Separate batch and streaming pipelines. Separate clusters, code bases, and processing frameworks. Each needs its own infrastructure, monitoring, logs, and support.	Single pipeline, cluster, code base, and processing framework.
Batch pipelines allow faster performance with processing large amounts of data.	Processing large amounts of data is slower and more expensive than Lambda architecture. However, data is processed as soon as it is ingested, in contrast to batch jobs which run on a schedule, so the latter may provide data sooner.
An error in a batch job may require all the data to be reprocessed from scratch.	An error in a streaming job only requires reprocessing of its affected data point.

17.9.2   *Kappa architecture for our dashboard*

A Kappa architecture for our Top K dashboard can use the approach in section 17.3.2, where each sales event is aggregated by its product ID and time range. We do not store the sales event in HDFS and then perform a batch job. A count of 1M products can easily fit in a single host, but a single host cannot ingest 1B events/day; we need multi-tier aggregation.

A serious bug may affect many events, so we need to log and monitor errors and monitor the rate of errors. It will be difficult to troubleshoot such a bug and difficult to rerun our streaming pipeline on a large number of events, so we can define a critical error rate and stop the pipeline (stop the Kafka consumers from consuming and processing events) if the error rate exceeded this defined critical error rate.

Figure 17.8 illustrates our high-level architecture with Kappa architecture. It is simply our Lambda architecture illustrated in figure 17.2 without the batch pipeline and aggregation service.

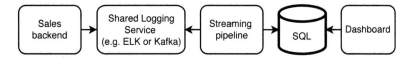

Figure 17.8 Our high-level architecture that uses Kappa architecture. It is simply our Lambda architecture in figure 17.2 without the batch pipeline and aggregation service.

17.10 *Logging, monitoring, and alerting*

Besides what was discussed in section 2.5, we should monitor and send alerts for the following.

Our shared batch ETL platform should already be integrated with our logging, monitoring, and alerting systems. We will be alerted to unusually long run time or failures of any of the tasks within our rollup job.

The rollup tasks write to HDFS tables. We can use the data quality monitoring tools described in chapter 10 to detect invalid datapoints and raise alerts.

17.11 *Other possible discussion topics*

Partition these lists by other characteristics, such as country or city. What design changes will we need to return the Top K products by revenue instead of sales volume? How can we track the Top K products by change in sales volume and/or revenue?

It may be useful to look up rankings and statistics of certain products with names or descriptions that match patterns. We can design a search system for such use cases.

We may discuss programmatic users of the Top K lists, such as machine learning and experimentation services. We had assumed a low request rate and that high availability and low latency were not required. These assumptions will no longer hold as programmatic users introduce new non-functional requirements.

Can our dashboard display approximations for the Top K lists before the events are fully counted, or perhaps even before the events occur?

A considerable complication with counting sales is disputes, such as customer requests for refunds or exchanges. Should sale numbers include disputes in progress? Do we need to correct the past data to consider refunds, returns, or exchanges? How do we recount sales events if refunds are granted or rejected or if there are exchanges for the same product or other product(s)?

We may offer a warranty of several years, so a dispute may occur years after the sale. Database queries may need to search for sales events that occurred years before. Such jobs may run out of memory. This is a challenging problem that is still faced by many engineers to this day.

There may be drastic events, such as a product recall. For example, we may need to recall a toy because it was suddenly found to be unsafe to children. We may discuss whether the counts of sales events should be adjusted if such problems occur.

Besides regenerating the Top K lists for the previous reasons, we may generalize this to regenerating the Top K lists from any data change.

Our browser app only displays the Top K list. We can extend our functional requirements, such as displaying sales trends or predicting future sales of current or new products.

17.12 References

This chapter used material from the Top K Problem (Heavy Hitters) (https://youtu.be/kx-XDoPjoHw) presentation in the System Design Interview YouTube channel by Mikhail Smarshchok.

Summary

- When accurate large-scale aggregation operations take too long, we can run a parallel streaming pipeline that uses approximation techniques to trade off accuracy for speed. Running a fast, inaccurate and a slow, accurate pipeline in parallel is called Lambda architecture.
- One step in large-scale aggregation is to partition by a key that we will later aggregate over.
- Data that is not directly related to aggregation should be stored in a different service, so it can be easily used by other services.
- Checkpointing is one possible technique for distributed transactions that involve both destinations with cheap read operations (e.g., Redis) and expensive read operations (e.g., HDFS).
- We can use a combination of heaps and multi-tier horizontal scaling for approximate large-scale aggregation operations.
- Count-min sketch is an approximation technique for counting.
- We can consider either Kappa or Lambda architecture for processing a large data stream.

Monoliths
vs. microservices

This appendix evaluates monoliths vs. microservices. The author's personal experience is that it seems many sources describe the advantages of microservice over monolith architecture but do not discuss the tradeoffs, so we will discuss them here. We use the terms "service" and "microservice" interchangeably.

Microservice architecture is about building a software system as a collection of loosely-coupled and independently developed, deployed, and scaled services. *Monoliths* are designed, developed, and deployed as a single unit.

A.1 Advantages of monoliths

Table A.1 discusses the advantages of monoliths over services.

Table A.1   Advantages of monoliths over services

Monolith	Service
Faster and easier to develop at first because it is a single application.	Developers need to handle serialization and deserialization in every service, and handle requests and responses between the services.
	Before we begin development, we first need to decide where the boundaries between the services should be, and our chosen boundaries may turn out to be wrong. Redeveloping services to change their boundaries is usually impractical.
A single database means it uses less storage, but this comes with tradeoffs.	Each service should have its own database, so there may be duplication of data and overall greater storage requirements.
With a single database and fewer data storage locations in general, it may be easier to comply with data privacy regulations.	Data is scattered in many locations, which makes it more difficult to ensure that data privacy regulations are complied with throughout the organization.
Debugging may be easier. A developer can use breakpoints to view the function call stack at any line of code and understand all logic that is happening at that line.	Distributed tracing tools like Jaegar or Zipkin are used to understand request fan-out, but they do not provide many details, such as the function call stack of the services involved in the request. Debugging across services is generally harder than in a monolith or individual service.
Related to the previous point, being able to easily view all the code in a single location and trace function calls may make the application/system as a whole generally easier to understand than in a service architecture.	A service's API is presented as a black box. While not having to understand an API's details may make it easier to use, it may become difficult to understand many of the fine details of the system.
Cheaper to operate and better performance. All processing occurs within the memory of a single host, so there are no data transfers between hosts, which are much slower and more expensive.	A system of services that transfer large amounts of data between each other can incur very high costs from the data transfers between hosts and data centers. Refer to https://www.primevideotech.com/video-streaming/scaling-up-the-prime-video-audio-video-monitoring-service-and-reducing-costs-by-90 for a discussion on how an Amazon Prime Video reduced the infrastructure costs of a system by 90% by merging most (but not all) of their services in a distributed microservices architecture into a monolith.

A.2   *Disadvantages of monoliths*

Monoliths have the following disadvantages compared to microservices:

- Most capabilities cannot have their own lifecycles, so it is hard to practice Agile methodologies.
- Need to redeploy the entire application to apply any changes.
- Large bundle size. High resource requirements. Long startup time.
- Must be scaled as a single application.
- A bug or instability in any part of a monolith can cause failures in production.

- Must be developed with a single language, so it cannot take advantage of the capabilities offered by other languages and their frameworks in addressing requirements of various use cases.

A.3   Advantages of services

The advantages of services over monoliths include the following:

1 Agile and rapid development and scaling of product requirements/business functionalities.
2 Modularity and replaceability.
3 Failure isolation and fault-tolerance.
4 More well-defined ownership and organizational structure.

A.3.1   Agile and rapid development and scaling of product requirements and business functionalities

Designing, implementing, and deploying software to satisfy product requirements is slower with a monolith than a service because the monolith has a much bigger code-base and more tightly coupled dependencies.

When we develop a service, we can focus on a small set of related functionalities and the service's interface to its users. Services communicate via network calls through the service interfaces. In other words, services communicate via their defined APIs over industry-standard protocols such as HTTP, gRPC, and GraphQL. Services have obvious boundaries in the form of their APIs, while monoliths do not. In a monolith, it is far more common for any particular piece of code to have numerous dependencies scattered throughout the codebase, and we may have to consider the entire system when developing in a monolith.

With cloud-based container native-infrastructure, a service can be developed and deployed much quicker than comparable features in a monolith. A service that provides a well-defined and related set of capabilities may be CPU-intensive or memory-intensive, and we can select the optimal hardware for it, cost-efficiently scaling it up or down as required. A monolith that provides many capabilities cannot be scaled in a manner to optimize for any individual capability.

Changes to individual services are deployed independently of other services. Compared to a monolith, a service has a smaller bundle size, lower resource requirements, and faster startup time.

A.3.2   Modularity and replaceability

The independent nature of services makes them modular and easier to replace. We can implement another service with the same interface and swap out the existing service with the new one. In a monolith, other developers may be changing code and interfaces at the same time as us, and it is more difficult to coordinate such development vs. in a service.

We can choose technologies that best suit the service's requirements (e.g., a specific programming language for a frontend, backend, mobile, or analytics service).

A.3.3   *Failure isolation and fault-tolerance*

Unlike a monolith, a microservices architecture does not have a single point of failure. Each service can be separately monitored, so any failure can be immediately narrowed down to a specific service. In a monolith, a single runtime error may crash the host, affecting all other functionalities. A service that adopts good practices for fault-tolerance can adapt to high latency and unavailability of the other services that it is dependent on. Such best practices are discussed in section 3.3, including caching other services' responses or exponential backoff and retry. The service may also return a sensible error response instead of crashing.

Certain services are more important than others. For example, they may have a more direct effect on revenue or are more visible to users. Having separate services allows us to categorize them by importance and allocate development and operations resources accordingly.

A.3.4   *Ownership and organizational structure*

With their well-defined boundaries, mapping the ownership of services to teams is straightforward compared to monoliths. This allows concentration of expertise and domain knowledge; that is, a team that owns a particular service can develop a strong understanding of it and expertise in developing it. The flip side is that developers are less likely to understand other services and possess less understanding and ownership of the overall system, while a monolith may force developers to understand more of the system beyond the specific components that they are responsible to develop and maintain. For example, if a developer requires some changes in another service, they may request the relevant team to implement those changes rather than doing so themselves, so development time and communication overhead are higher. Having those changes done by developers familiar with the service may take less time and have a lower risk of bugs or technical debt.

The nature of services with their well-defined boundaries also allows various service architectural styles to provide API definition techniques, including OpenAPI for REST, protocol buffers for gRPC, and Schema Definition Language (SDL) for GraphQL.

A.4   *Disadvantages of services*

The disadvantages of services compared to monoliths include duplicate components and the development and maintenance costs of additional components.

A.4.1   *Duplicate components*

Each service must implement inter-service communication and security, which is mostly duplicate effort across services. A system is as strong as its weakest point, and the large number of services exposes a large surface area that must be secured, compared to a monolith.

Developers in different teams who are developing duplicate components may also duplicate mistakes and the efforts needed to discover and fix these mistakes, which is development and maintenance waste. This duplication of effort and waste of time also extends to users and operations staff of the duplicate services who run into the bugs caused by these mistakes, and expend duplicate effort into troubleshooting and communicating with developers.

Services should not share databases, or they will no longer be independent. For example, a change to a database schema to suit one service will break other services. Not sharing databases may cause duplicate data and lead to an overall higher amount and cost of storage in the system. This may also make it more complex and costly to comply with data privacy regulations.

A.4.2 Development and maintenance costs of additional components

To navigate and understand the large variety of services in our organization, we will need a service registry and possibly additional services for service discovery.

A monolithic application has a single deployment lifecycle. A microservice application has numerous deployments to manage, so CI/CD is a necessity. This includes infrastructure like containers (Docker), container registry, container orchestration (Kubernetes, Docker Swarm, Mesos), CI tools such as Jenkins, and CD tools, which may support deployment patterns like blue/green deployment, canary, and A/B testing.

When a service receives a request, it may make requests to downstream services in the process of handling this request, which in turn may make requests to further downstream services. This is illustrated in figure A.1. A single request to Netflix's homepage causes a request to fan out to numerous downstream services. Each such request adds networking latency. A service's endpoint may have a one-second P99 SLA, but if multiple endpoints are dependencies of each other (e.g., service A calls service B, which calls service C, and so on), the original requester may experience high latency.

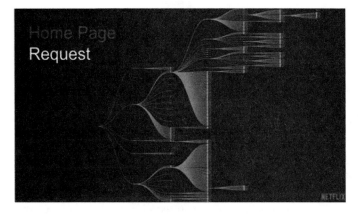

Figure A.1 Illustration of request fan-out to downstream services that occurs on a request to get Netflix's homepage. Image from https://www.oreilly.com/content/application-caching-at-netflix-the -hidden-microservice/.

Caching is one way to mitigate this, but it introduces complexity, such as having to consider cache expiry and cache refresh policies to avoid stale data, and the overhead of developing and maintaining a distributed cache service.

A service may need the additional complexity and development and maintenance costs of implementing exponential backoff and retry (discussed in section 3.3.4) to handle outages of other services that it makes requests to.

Another complex additional component required by microservices architecture is distributed tracing, which is used for monitoring and troubleshooting microservices-based distributed systems. Jaeger and Zipkin are popular distributed tracing solutions.

Installing/updating a library on a monolith involves updating a single instance of that library on the monolith. With services, installing/updating a library that is used in multiple services will involve installing/updating it across all these services. If an update has breaking changes, each service's developers manually update their libraries and update broken code or configurations caused by backward incompatibility. Next, they must deploy these updates using their CI/CD (continuous integration/continuous deployment) tools, possibly to several environments one at a time before finally deploying to the production environment. They must monitor these deployments. Along the way in development and deployment, they must troubleshoot any unforeseen problems. This may come down to copying and pasting error messages to search for solutions on Google or the company's internal chat application like Slack or Microsoft Teams. If a deployment fails, the developer must troubleshoot and then retry the deployment and wait for it again to succeed or fail. Developers must handle complex scenarios (e.g., persistent failures on a particular host) All of this is considerable developer overhead. Moreover, this duplication of logic and libraries may also add up to a non-trivial amount of additional storage.

A.4.3   *Distributed transactions*

Services have separate databases, so we may need distributed transactions for consistency across these databases, unlike a monolith with a single relational database that can make transactions against that database. Having to implement distributed transactions is yet another source of cost, complexity, latency, and possible errors and failures. Chapter 5 discussed distributed transactions.

A.4.4   *Referential integrity*

Referential integrity refers to the accuracy and consistency of data within a relationship. If a value of one attribute in a relation references a value of another attribute and then the referenced value must exist.

Referential integrity in a monolith's single database can be easily implemented using foreign keys. Values in a foreign key column must either be present in the primary key that is referenced by the foreign key, or they must be null (https://www.interfacett.com/blogs/referential-integrity-options-cascade-set-null-and-set-default). Referential integrity is more complicated if the databases are distributed across services. For referential integrity in a distributed system, a write request that involves multiple services must succeed in every service or fail/abort/rollback in every service. The write process must include steps such as retries or rollbacks/compensating transactions. Refer to chapter 5 for more discussion of distributed transactions. We may also need a periodic audit across the services to verify referential integrity.

A.4.5 *Coordinating feature development and deployments that span multiple services*

If a new feature spans multiple services, development and deployment need to be coordinated between them. For example, one API service may be dependent on others. In another example, the developer team of a Rust Rocket (https://rocket.rs/) RESTful API service may need to develop new API endpoints to be used by a React UI service, which is developed by a separate team of UI developers. Let's discuss the latter example.

In theory, feature development can proceed in parallel on both services. The API team need only provide the specification of the new API endpoints. The UI team can develop the new React components and associated node.js or Express server code. Since the API team has not yet provided a test environment that returns actual data, the server code or mock or stub responses from the new API endpoints and use them for development. This approach is also useful for authoring unit tests in the UI code, including spy tests (refer to https://jestjs.io/docs/mock-function-api for more information).

Teams can also use feature flags to selectively expose incomplete features to development and staging environments, while hiding them from the production environment. This allows other developers and stakeholders who rely on these new features to view and discuss the work in progress.

In practice, the situation can be much more complicated. It can be difficult to understand the intricacies of a new set of API endpoints, even by developers and UX designers with considerable experience in working with that API. Subtle problems can be discovered by both the API developers and UI developers during the development of their respective services, the API may need to change, and both teams must discuss a solution and possibly waste some work that was already done:

- The data model may be unsuitable for the UX. For example, if we develop a version control feature for templates of a notifications system (refer to section 9.5), the UX designer may design the version control UX to consider individual templates. However, a template may actually consist of subcomponents that are versioned separately. This confusion may not be discovered until both UI and API development are in progress.
- During development, the API team may discover that the new API endpoints require inefficient database queries, such as overly large SELECT queries or JOIN operations between large tables.
- For REST or RPC APIs (i.e., not GraphQL), users may need to make multiple API requests and then do complex post-processing operations on the responses before the data can be returned to the requester or displayed on the UI. Or the

provided API may fetch much more data than required by the UI, which causes unnecessary latency. For APIs that are developed internally, the UI team may wish to request some API redesign and rework for less complex and more efficient API requests.

A.4.6   *Interfaces*

Services can be written in different languages and communicate with each other via a text or binary protocol. In the case of text protocols like JSON or XML, these strings need to be translated to and from objects. There is additional code required for validation and error and exception handling for missing fields. To allow graceful degradation, our service may need to process objects with missing fields. To handle the case of our dependent services returning such data, we may need to implement backup steps such as caching data from dependent services and returning this old data, or perhaps also return data with missing fields ourselves. This may cause implementation to differ from documentation.

A.5   References

This appendix uses material from the book *Microservices for the Enterprise: Designing, Developing, and Deploying* by Kasun Indrasiri and Prabath Siriwardena (2018, Apress).

OAuth 2.0 authorization and OpenID Connect authentication[1]

B.1 Authorization vs. authentication

Authorization is the process of giving a user (a person or system) permission to access a specific resource or function. *Authentication* is identity verification of a user. *OAuth 2.0* is a common authorization algorithm. (The OAuth 1.0 protocol was published in April 2010, while OAuth 2.0 was published in October 2012.) *OpenID Connect* is an extension to OAuth 2.0 for authentication. Authentication and authorization/access control are typical security requirements of a service. OAuth 2.0 and OpenID Connect may be briefly discussed in an interview regarding authorization and authentication.

A common misconception online is the idea of "login with OAuth2." Such online resources mix up the distinct concepts of authorization and authentication. This section is an introduction to authorization with OAuth2 and authentication with OpenID Connect and makes their authorization versus authentication distinction clear.

---

[1] This section uses material from the video "OAuth 2.0 and OpenID Connect (in plain English)," http://oauthacademy.com/talk, an excellent introductory lecture by Nate Barbettini, and https://auth0.com/docs. Also refer to https://oauth.net/2/ for more information.

B.2   Prelude: Simple login, cookie-based authentication

The most basic type of authentication is commonly referred to as *simple login, basic authentication,* or *forms authentication.* In simple login, a user enters an (identifier, password) pair. Common examples are (username, password) and (email, password). When a user submits their username and password, the backend will verify that the password is correct for the associated username. Passwords should be salted and hashed for security. After verification, the backend creates a session for this user. The backend creates a cookie that will be stored in both the server's memory and in the user's browser. The UI will set a cookie in the user's browser, such as Set-Cookie: sessionid=f00b4r; Max-Age: 86400;. This cookie contains a session ID. Further requests from the browser will use this session ID for authentication, so the user does not have to enter their username and password again. Each time the browser makes a request to the backend, the browser will send the session ID to the backend, and the backend will compare this sent session ID to its own copy to verify the user's identity.

This process is called *cookie-based authentication.* A session has a finite duration, after which it expires/times out and the user must reenter their username and password. Session expiration has two types of timeouts: absolute and inactivity. *Absolute timeout* terminates the session after a specified period has elapsed. *Inactivity timeout* terminates the solution after a specified period during which a user has not interacted with the application.

B.3   Single sign-on

Single sign-on (SSO) allows one to log in to multiple systems with a single master account, such as an Active Directory account. SSO is typically done with a protocol called Security Assertion Markup Language (SAML). The introduction of mobile apps in the late 2000s necessitated the following:

- Cookies are unsuitable for devices, so a new mechanism was needed for long-lived sessions, where a user remains logged into a mobile app even after they close the app.
- A new use case called *delegated authorization.* The owner of a set of resources can delegate access to some but not all of these resources to a designated client. For example, one may grant a certain app permission to see certain kinds of their Facebook user information, such as their public profile and birthday, but not post on your wall.

B.4   Disadvantages of simple login

The disadvantages of simple login include complexity, lack of maintainability, and no partial authorization.

B.4.1 Complexity and lack of maintainability

Much of a simple login (or session-based authentication in general) is implemented by the application developer, including the following:

- The login endpoint and logic, including the salting and hashing operations
- The database table of usernames and salted+hashed passwords
- Password creation and reset, including 2FA operations such as password reset emails

This means that the application developer is responsible for observing security best practices. In OAuth 2.0 and OpenID Connect, passwords are handled by a separate service. (This is true of all token-based protocols. OAuth 2.0 and OpenID Connect are token-based protocols.) The application developer can use a third-party service that has good security practices, so there is less risk of passwords being hacked.

Cookies require a server to maintain state. Each logged-in user requires the server to create a session for it. If there are millions of sessions, the memory overhead may be too expensive. Token-based protocols have no memory overhead.

The developer is also responsible for maintaining the application to stay in compliance with relevant user privacy regulations such as the General Data Protection Regulation (GDPR), California Consumer Privacy Act (CCPA), and the Health Insurance Portability and Accountability Act (HIPAA).

B.4.2 No partial authorization

Simple login does not have the concept of partial access control permissions. One may wish to grant another party partial access to the former's account for specific purposes. Granting complete access is a security risk. For example, one may wish to grant a budgeting app like Mint permission to see their bank account balance, but not other permissions like transferring money. This is impossible if the bank app only has simple login. The user must pass their bank app account's username and password to Mint, giving Mint complete access to their bank account, just for Mint to view their bank balance.

Another example was Yelp before the development of OAuth. As illustrated in figure B.1, at the end of one's Yelp user registration, Yelp will request the user for their Gmail login, so it can send a referral link or invite link to their contact list. The user has to grant Yelp complete access to their Gmail account just to send a single referral email to each of their contacts.

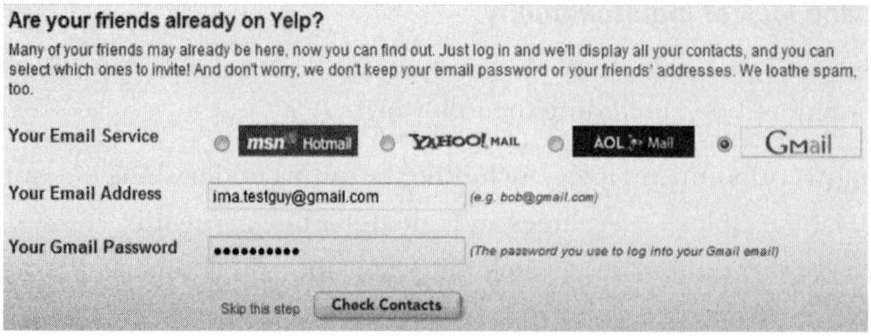

Are your friends already on Yelp?

Many of your friends may already be here, now you can find out. Just log in and we'll display all your contacts, and you can select which ones to invite! And don't worry, we don't keep your email password or your friends' addresses. We loathe spam, too.

Your Email Service   ○ **msn** Hotmail   ○ **YAHOO!** MAIL   ○ **AOL** Mail   ● Gmail

Your Email Address   ima.testguy@gmail.com   *(e.g. bob@gmail.com)*

Your Gmail Password   ●●●●●●●●●●   *(The password you use to log into your Gmail email)*

Skip this step   **Check Contacts**

Figure B.1   Screenshot of Yelp's browser app referral feature prior to OAuth, reflecting a shortcoming of no partial authorization in simple login. The user is requested to enter their email address and password, granting Yelp full permissions to their email account even though Yelp only wishes to send a single email to each of their contacts. Image from http://oauthacademy.com/talk.

OAuth 2.0 adoption is now widespread, so most apps do not use such practices anymore. A significant exception is the banking industry. As of 2022, most banks have not adopted OAuth.

B.5   OAuth 2.0 flow

This section describes an OAuth 2.0 flow, how an app like Google can use OAuth 2.0 for users to authorize apps like Yelp to access resources belonging to a Google user, such as send emails to a user's Google contacts.

Figure B.2 illustrates the steps in an OAuth 2.0 flow between Yelp and Google. We closely follow figure B.2 in this chapter.

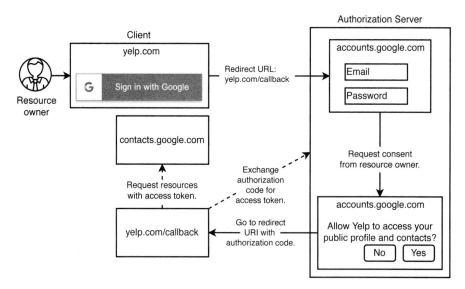

Figure B.2   Illustration of OAuth2 flow, discussed in detail through this section. Front-channel communications are represented by solid lines. Back-channel communications are represented by dashed lines.

B.5.1   OAuth 2.0 terminology

- *Resource owner*—The user who owns the data or controls certain operations that the application is requesting for. For example, if you have contacts in your Google account, you are the resource owner of that data. You can grant permission to an application to access that data. In this section, we refer to a resource owner as a user for brevity.
- *Client*—The application that is requesting the resources.
- *Authorization server*—The system the user uses to authorize the permission, such as accounts.google.com.
- *Resource server*—API of the system that holds the data the client wants, such as the Google Contacts API. Depending on the system, the authorization server and resource server may be the same or separate systems.
- *Authorization grant*—The proof of the user's consent to the permission necessary to access the resources.
- *Redirect URI, also called callback*—The URI or destination when the authorization server redirects back to the client.
- *Access token*—The key that the client uses to get the authorized resource.
- *Scope*—The authorization server has a list of scopes that it understands (e.g., read a user's Google contacts list, read emails, or delete emails). A client may request a certain set of scopes, depending on its required resources.

B.5.2   Initial client setup

An app (like Mint or Yelp) has to do a one-time setup with the authorization server (like Google) to become a client and enable users to use OAuth. When Mint requests Google to create a client Google provides:

- Client ID, which is typically a long, unique string identifier. This is passed with the initial request on the front channel.
- Client secret, which is used during token exchange.

1. GET AUTHORIZATION FROM THE USER

The flow begins with the (Google) resource owner on the client app (Yelp). Yelp displays a button for a user to grant access to certain data on their Google account. Clicking that button puts the user through an OAuth flow, a set of steps that results in the application having authorization and being able to access only the requested information.

When the user clicks on the button, the browser is redirected to the authorization server (e.g., a Google domain, which may be accounts.google.com, or a Facebook or Okta authorization server). Here, the user is prompted to log in (i.e., enter their email and password and click Login). They can see in their browser's navigation bar that they is in a Google domain. This is a security improvement, as they provide their email and password to Google, rather than another app like Mint or Yelp.

In this redirect, the client passes configuration information to the authorization server via a query with a URL like "https://accounts.google.com/o/oauth2/v2/auth?client_id=yelp&redirect_uri=https%3A%2F%2Foidcdebugger.com%2Fdebug&scope=openid&response_type=code&response_mode=query&state=foobar&nonce=u-wtukpm946m". The query parameters are:

- *client_id*—Identifies the client to the authorization server; for example, tells Google that Yelp is the client.
- *redirect_uri (also called callback URI)*—The redirect URI.
- *scope*—The list of requested scopes.
- *response_type*—The type of authorization grant the client wants. There are a few different types, to be described shortly. For now, we assume the most common type, called an authorization code grant. This is a request to the authorization server for a code.
- *state*—The state is passed from the client to the callback. As discussed in step 4 below, this prevents cross-site request forgery (CSRF) attacks.
- *nonce*—Stands for "number used once." A server-provided random value used to uniquely label a request to prevent replay attacks (outside the scope of this book).

2. USER CONSENTS TO CLIENT'S SCOPE

After they log in, the authorization server prompts the user to consent to the client's requested list of scopes. In our example, Google will present them with a prompt that states the list of resources that the other app is requesting (such as their public profile and contact list) and a request for confirmation that they consent to granting these resources to that app. This ensures they are not tricked into granting access to any resource that they did not intend to grant.

Regardless of whether they click "no" or "yes," the browser is redirected back to the app's callback URI with different query parameters depending on the user's decision. If they click "no," the app is not granted access. The redirect URI may be something like "https://yelp.com/callback?error=access_denied&error_description=The user did not consent." If they click "yes," the app can request the user's granted resources from a Google API such as the Google Contacts API. The authorization server redirects to the redirect URI with the authorization code. The redirect URI may be something like https://yelp.com/callback?code=3mPDQbnIOyseerTTKPV&state=foobar, where the query parameter "code" is the authorization code.

3. REQUEST ACCESS TOKEN

The client sends a POST request to the authorization server to exchange the authorization code for an access token, which includes the client's secret key (that only the client and authorization server know). Example:

```
POST www.googleapis.com/oauth2/v4/token
Content-Type: application/x-www-form-urlencoded

code=3mPDQbnIOyseerTTKPV&client_id=yelp&client_secret=secret123&grant_
type=authorization_code
```

The authorization server validates the code and then responds with the access token, and the state that it received from the client.

4. REQUEST RESOURCES

To prevent CSRF attacks, the client verifies that the state it sent to the server is identical to the state in the response. Next, the client uses the access token to request the authorized resources from the resource server. The access token allows the client to access only the requested scope (e.g., read-only access to the user's Google contacts). Requests for other resources outside the scope or in other scopes will be denied (e.g., deleting contacts or accessing the user's location history):

```
ET api.google.com/some/endpoint
Authorization: Bearer h9pyFgK62w1QZDox0d0WZg
```

B.5.3 *Back channel and front channel*

Why do we get an authorization code and then exchange it for the access token? Why don't we just use the authorization code, or just get the access token immediately?

We introduce the concepts of a back channel and a front channel, which are network security terminology.

Front-channel communication is communication between two or more parties that are observable within the protocol. *Back-channel communication* is communication that is not observable to at least one of the parties within the protocol. This makes back channel more secure than front channel.

An example of a back channel or highly secure channel is a SSL-encrypted HTTP request from the client's server to a Google API server. An example of a front channel is a user's browser. A browser is secure but has some loopholes or places where data may leak from the browser. If you have a secret password or key in your web application and put it in the HTML or JavaScript of a web app, this secret is visible to someone who views the page source. The hacker can also open the network console or Chrome Developer Tools and see and modify the JavaScript. A browser is considered to be a front channel because we do not have complete trust in it, but we have complete trust in the code that is running on our backend servers.

Consider a situation where the client is going over to the authorization server. This is happening in the front channel. The full-page redirects, outgoing requests, redirect to the authorization server, and content of the request to the authorization server are all being passed through the browser. The authorization code is also transmitted through the browser (i.e., the front channel). If this authorization code was intercepted, for example, by a malicious toolbar or a mechanism that can log the browser requests, the hacker cannot obtain the access code because the token exchange happens on the back channel.

The token exchange happens between the backend and the authorization channel, not the browser. The backend also includes its secret key in the token exchange, which the hacker does not know. If the transmission of this secret key is via the browser, the hacker can steal it, so the transmission happens via the back channel.

The OAuth 2.0 flow is designed to take advantage of the best characteristics of the front channel and back channel to ensure it is highly secure. The front channel is used to interact with the user. The browser presents the user the login screen and consent screen because it is meant to interact directly with the user and present these screens. We cannot completely trust the browser with secret keys, so the last step of the flow (i.e., the exchange, happens on the back channel, which is a system we trust).

The authorization server may also issue a refresh token to allow a client to obtain a new access token if the access token is expired, without interacting with the user. This is outside the scope of this book.

B.6   *Other OAuth 2.0 flows*

We described the authorization code flow, which involves both back channel and front channel. The other flows are the implicit flow (front channel only), resource owner password credentials (back channel only), and client credentials (back channel only).

An implicit flow is the only way to use OAuth 2.0 if our app does not have a backend. Figure B.3 illustrates an example of implicit flow. All communications are front channel only. The authorization server returns the access code directly, with no authorization code and no exchange step.

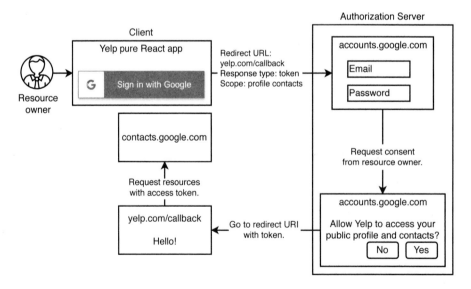

Figure B.3   Illustration of an OAuth2 implicit flow. All communications are front channel. Note that the request to the authorization server has response type "token" instead of "code."

Implicit flow carries a security tradeoff because the access token is exposed to the browser.

The resource owner password flow or resource owner password credentials flow is used for older applications and is not recommended for new applications. The back-end server uses its credentials to request the authorization server for an access token. The client credentials flow is sometimes used when you're doing a machine-to-machine or service communications.

B.7 OpenID Connect authentication

The Login with Facebook button was introduced in 2009, followed by the Login with Google button and similar buttons by many other companies like Twitter, Microsoft, and LinkedIn. One could login to a site with your existing credentials with Facebook, Google, or other social media. These buttons became ubiquitous across the web. The buttons served the login use cases well and were built with OAuth 2.0 even though OAuth 2.0 was not designed to be used for authentication. Essentially, OAuth 2.0 was being used for its purpose beyond delegated authorization.

However, using OAuth for authentication is bad practice because there is no way of getting user information in OAuth. If you log in to an app with OAuth 2.0, there is no way for that app to know who just logged in or other information like your email address and name. OAuth 2.0 is designed for permissions scopes. All it does is verify that your access token is scoped to a particular resource set. It doesn't verify who you are.

When the various companies built their social login buttons, using OAuth under the hood, they all had to add custom hacks on top of OAuth to allow clients to get the user's information. If you read about these various implementations, keep in mind that they are different and not interoperable.

To address this lack of standardization, OpenID Connect was created as a standard for adopting OAuth 2.0 for authentication. OpenID Connect is a thin layer on top of OAuth 2.0 that allows it to be used for authentication. OpenID Connect adds the following to OAuth 2.0:

- *ID token*—The ID token represents the user's ID and has some user information. This token is returned by the authorization server during token exchange.
- *User info endpoint*—If the client wants more information than contained in the ID token returned by the authorization server, the client can request more user information from the user info endpoint.
- *Standard set of scopes.*

So, the only technical difference between OAuth 2.0 and OpenID Connect is that OpenID Connect returns both an access code and ID token, and OpenID Connect provides a user info endpoint. A client can request the authorization server for an OpenID scope in addition to its desired OAuth 2.0 scopes and obtain both an access code and ID token.

Table B.1 summarizes the use cases of OAuth 2.0 (authorization) vs. OpenID Connect (authentication).

Table B.1   Use cases of OAuth 2.0 (authorization) vs. OpenID Connect (authentication)

OAuth2 (authorization)	OpenID Connect (authentication)
Grant access to your API.	User login
Get access to user data in other systems.	Make your accounts available in other systems.

An ID token consists of three parts:

- *Header*—Contains several fields, such as the algorithm used to encode the signature.
- *Claims*—The ID token body/payload. The client decodes the claims to obtain the user information.
- *Signature*—The client can use the signature to verify that the ID token has not been changed. That is, the signature can be independently verified by the client application without having to contact the authorization server.

The client can also use the access token to request the authorization server's user info endpoint for more information about the user, such as the user's profile picture. Table B.2 describes which grant type to use for your use case.

Table B.2   Which grant type to use for your use case

Web application with server backend	Authorization code flow
Native mobile app	Authorization code flow with PKCE (Proof Key for Code Exchange) (outside the scope of this book)
JavaScript Single-Page App (SPA) with API backend	Implicit flow
Microservices and APIs	Client credentials flow

C4 Model

The C4 model (https://c4model.com/) is a system architecture diagram technique created by Simon Brown to decompose a system into various levels of abstraction. This section is a brief introduction to the C4 model. The website has good introductions and in-depth coverage of the C4 model, so we will only briefly go over the C4 model here; readers should refer to the website for more details. The C4 model defines four levels of abstraction.

A *context diagram* represents the system as a single box, surrounded by its users and other systems that it interacts with. Figure C.1 is an example context diagram of a new internet banking system that we wish to design on top of our existing mainframe banking system. Its users will be our personal banking customers, who will use our internet banking system via UI apps we develop for them. Our internet banking system will also use our existing email system. In figure C.1, we draw our users and systems as boxes and connect them with arrows to represent the requests between them.

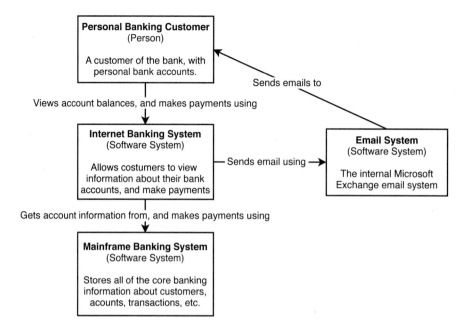

Figure C.1   A context diagram. Image from https://c4model.com/, licensed under https:// creativecommons.org/licenses/by/4.0/. In this case, we want to design an internet banking system. Its users are our personal banking customers, who are people using our internet banking system via the latter's UI apps. Our internet banking system makes requests to our legacy mainframe banking system. It also uses our existing email system to email our users. Many of the other shared services it may use are not available yet, and may be discussed as part of this design.

A *container diagram* is defined on c4model.com as "a separately runnable/deployable unit that executes code or stores data." We can also understand containers as the services that make up our system. Figure C.2 is an example container diagram. We break up our internet banking system that we represented as a single box in figure C.1.

A web/browser user can download our single-page (browser) app from our web application service and then make further requests through this single-page app. A mobile user can download our mobile app from an app store and make all requests through this app.

Our browser and mobile apps make requests to our (backend) API application/service. Our backend service makes requests to its Oracle SQL database, mainframe banking system, and our email system.

A *component diagram* is a collection of classes behind an interface to implement a functionality. Components are not separately deployable units. Figure 6.3 is an example component diagram of our (backend) API application/service from figure 6.2, illustrating its interfaces and classes, and their requests with other services.

Our browser and mobile apps make requests to our backend, which are routed to the appropriate interfaces:

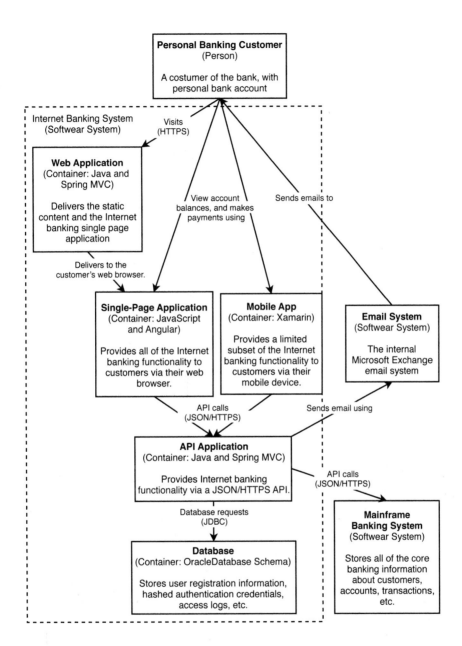

Figure C.2 A container diagram. Adapted from https://c4model.com/, licensed under https://creativecommons.org/licenses/by/4.0/.

Our sign-in controller receives sign in requests. Our reset password controller receives password reset requests. Our security component has functions to process these security-related functionalities from the sign-in controller and reset password controller. It persists data to an Oracle SQL database.

Our email component is a client that makes requests to our email system. Our reset password controller uses our email component to send password reset emails to our users.

Our account summary controller provides users with their bank account balance summaries. To obtain this information, it calls functions in our mainframe banking system façade, which in turn makes requests to our mainframe banking system. There may also be other components in our backend service, not illustrated in figure C.3, which use our mainframe banking system façade to make requests to our mainframe banking system.

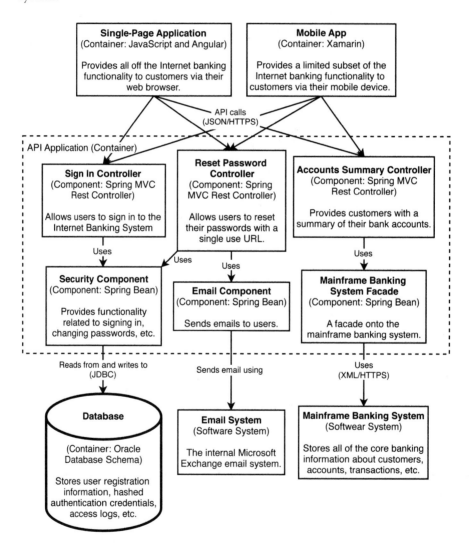

Figure C.3   A component diagram. Image adapted from https://c4model.com/, licensed under https://creativecommons.org/licenses/by/4.0/.

A *code diagram* is a UML class diagram. (Refer to other sources such as https://www.uml
.org/ if you are unfamiliar with UML.) You may use object-oriented programming
(OOP) design patterns in designing an interface.

Figure C.4 is an example code diagram of our mainframe banking system façade
from figure C.3. Employing the façade pattern, our `MainframeBankingSystem`
`Facade` interface is implemented in our `MainframeBankingSystemFacadeImpl` class.
We employ the factory pattern, where a `MainframeBankingSystemFacadeImpl` object
creates a `GetBalanceRequest` object. We may use the template method pattern to define
an `AbstractRequest` interface and `GetBalanceRequest` class, define an `Internet`
`BankingSystemException` interface and a `MainframeBankingSystemException`
class, and define an `AbstractResponse` interface and `GetBalanceResponse` class. A
`MainframeBankingSystemFacadeImpl` object may use a `BankingSystemConnection`
connection pool to connect and make requests to our mainframe banking system *and*
throw a `MainframeBankingSystemException` object when it encounters an error. (We
didn't illustrate dependency injection in figure C.4.)

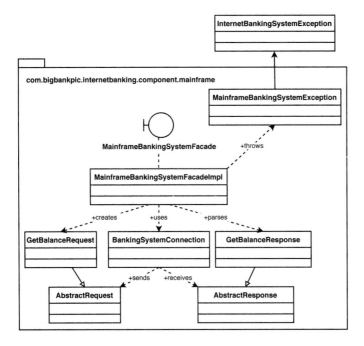

**Figure C.4   A code (UML class) diagram. Image adapted from https://c4model.com/, licensed under
https://creativecommons.org/licenses/by/4.0/.**

Diagrams drawn during an interview or in a system's documentation tend not to contain only components of a specific level, but rather usually mix components of levels
1–3.

The value of the C4 model is not about following this framework to the letter, but
rather about recognizing its levels of abstraction and fluently zooming in and out of a
system design.

Two-phase commit (2PC)

We discuss two-phase commit (2PC) here as a possible distributed transactions technique, but emphasize that it is unsuitable for distributed services. If we discuss distributed transactions during an interview, we can briefly discuss 2PC as a possibility and also discuss why it should not be used for services. This section will cover this material.

Figure D.1 illustrates a successful 2PC execution. 2PC consists of two phases (hence its name), the prepare phase and the commit phase. The coordinator first sends a prepare request to every database. (We refer to the recipients as databases, but they may also be services or other types of systems.) If every database responds successfully, the coordinator then sends a commit request to every database. If any database does not respond or responds with an error, the coordinator sends an abort request to every database.

418

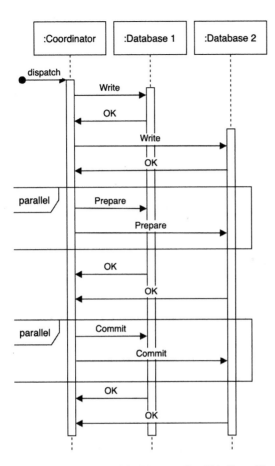

Figure D.1 A successful 2PC execution. This figure illustrates two databases, but the same phases apply to any number of databases. Figure adapted from *Designing Data-Intensive Applications* by Martin Kleppmann, 2017, O'Reilly Media.

2PC achieves consistency with a performance tradeoff from the blocking requirements. A weakness of 2PC is that the coordinator must be available throughout the process, or inconsistency may result. Figure D.2 illustrates that a coordinator crash during the commit phase may cause inconsistency, as certain databases will commit, but the rest will abort. Moreover, coordinator unavailability completely prevents any database writes from occurring.

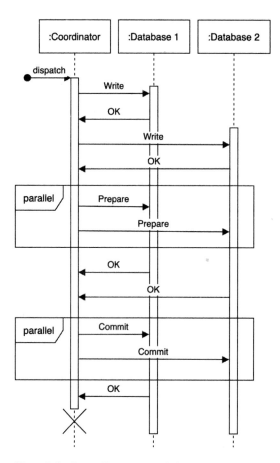

Figure D.2   A coordinator crash during the commit phase will cause inconsistency. Figure adapted from *Designing Data-Intensive Applications* **by Martin Kleppmann, O'Reilly Media, 2017.**

Inconsistency can be avoided by participating databases neither committing nor aborting transactions until their outcome is explicitly decided. This has the downside that those transactions may hold locks and block other transactions for a long time until the coordinator comes back.

2PC requires all databases to implement a common API to interact with the coordinator. The standard is called X/Open XA (eXtended Architecture), which is a C API that has bindings in other languages too.

2PC is generally unsuitable for services, for reasons including the following:

- The coordinator must log all transactions, so during a crash recovery it can compare its log to the databases to decide on synchronization. This imposes additional storage requirements.
- Moreover, this is unsuitable for stateless services, which may interact via HTTP, which is a stateless protocol.

- All databases must respond for a commit to occur (i.e., the commit does not occur if any database is unavailable). There is no graceful degradation. Overall, there is lower scalability, performance, and fault-tolerance.

- Crash recovery and synchronization must be done manually because the write is committed to certain databases but not others.

- The cost of development and maintenance of 2PC in every service/database involved. The protocol details, development, configuration, and deployment must be coordinated across all the teams involved in this effort.

- Many modern technologies do not support 2PC. Examples include NoSQL databases, like Cassandra and MongoDB, and message brokers, like Kafka and RabbitMQ.

- 2PC reduces availability, as all participating services must be available for commits. Other distributed transaction techniques, such as Saga, do not have this requirement.

Table D.1 briefly compares 2PC with Saga. We should avoid 2PC and prefer other techniques like Saga, Transaction Supervisor, Change Data Capture, or checkpointing for distributed transactions involving services.

Table D.1 2PC vs. Saga

2PC	Saga
XA is an open standard, but an implementation may be tied to a particular platform/vendor, which may cause lock-in.	Universal. Typically implemented by producing and consuming messages to Kafka topics. (Refer to chapter 5.)
Typically for immediate transactions.	Typically for long-running transactions.
Requires a transaction to be committed in a single process.	A transaction can be split into multiple steps.

index